The Politics of Education Policy in an Era of Inequality

In a context of increased politicization led by state and federal policymakers, corporate reformers, and for-profit educational organizations, *The Politics of Education Policy in an Era of Inequality* explores a new vision for leading schools grounded in culturally relevant advocacy and social justice theories. This timely volume tackles the origins and implications of growing accountability for educational leaders and reconsiders the role that educational leaders should and can play in education policy and political processes. This book provides a critical perspective and analysis of today's education policy landscape and leadership practice; explores the challenges and opportunities associated with teaching in and leading schools; and examines the structural, political, and cultural interactions among school principals, district leaders, and state and federal policy actors. An important resource for practicing and aspiring leaders, *The Politics of Education Policy in an Era of Inequality* shares a theoretical framework and strategies for building bridges between education researchers, practitioners, and policymakers.

Sonya Douglass Horsford is Associate Professor of Education Leadership at Teachers College, Columbia University, USA.

Janelle T. Scott is the Robert C. and Mary Catherine Birgeneau Distinguished Chair in Educational Disparities and Associate Professor of Education Policy, Politics, and Leadership at the University of California, Berkeley, USA.

Gary L. Anderson is Professor of Educational Leadership at New York University, USA.

EDUCATIONAL LEADERSHIP FOR EQUITY AND DIVERSITY

Series Editor: Colleen A. Capper

Leadership for Increasingly Diverse Schools
George Theoharis and Martin Scanlan

Organizational Theory for Equity and Diversity
Leading Integrated, Socially Just Education
Colleen A. Capper

The Politics of Education Policy in an Era of Inequality
Possibilities for Democratic Schooling
Sonya Douglass Horsford, Janelle T. Scott, and Gary L. Anderson

For more information about this series, please visit: https://www.routledge.com/ Educational-Leadership-for-Equity-and-Diversity/book-series/ELED

The Politics of Education Policy in an Era of Inequality

Possibilities for Democratic Schooling

Sonya Douglass Horsford,
Janelle T. Scott, and
Gary L. Anderson

NEW YORK AND LONDON

First published 2019
by Routledge
52 Vanderbilt Avenue, New York, NY 10017

and by Routledge
2 Park Square, Milton Park, Abingdon, Oxon, OX14 4RN

Routledge is an imprint of the Taylor & Francis Group, an informa business

© 2019 Taylor & Francis

The right of Sonya Douglass Horsford, Janelle T. Scott, and Gary L. Anderson to be identified as authors of this work has been asserted by them in accordance with sections 77 and 78 of the Copyright, Designs and Patents Act 1988.

Library of Congress Cataloging-in-Publication Data
A catalog record for this title has been requested

ISBN: 978-1-138-93018-6 (hbk)
ISBN: 978-1-138-93019-3 (pbk)
ISBN: 978-1-315-68068-2 (ebk)

Typeset in Aldine 401 and Helvetice Neue
by codeMantra

Contents

List of Figures, Tables, and Boxes

Figures

Tables

Boxes

Series Editor Introduction

The *Educational Leadership for Equity and Diversity* book series aims to publish the primary text for each pre-K to 12 educational leadership preparation course while allowing educators in schools and districts to rely on the same books for leadership development. I cannot imagine a more timely and brilliantly written book for current and prospective educational leaders as this text, *The Politics of Education Policy in an Era of Inequality.*

Conceptually framed by critical policy analysis, this book presents an alternative to traditional education policy and politics texts by focusing on issues of power, voice, democratic participation, and the reproduction of inequality in the policymaking process. As importantly, through the narrative, discussion questions, and real-life case examples, the text lays out how educational leaders can disrupt this policy inequality at multiple levels.

Perhaps for many educational leaders, federal, state, local, and school policies may seem elusive, and often, in the context of a myriad of competing responsibilities, educational leaders reactively respond to policy mandates at all levels. Instead, Horsford, Scott, and Anderson advocate for a critical policy analysis perspective as the lens for addressing and creating educational policy and doing so in three ways.

First, critical policy analysis requires a critical, social justice interpretation and application of existing policies. Authors Horsford, Scott, and Anderson challenge leaders to lead beyond policy compliance. They remind us that how we view and then enact policy at all levels depends on our own belief system. For example, some educational leaders interpret federal and state special education policy in ways that maintain segregated environments within schools. Educational leaders leading for equity can leverage the same policies to eliminate segregation and in ways to advance the proportional representation of students labeled with disabilities across all settings. Both interpretations of the policy are compliant, but only one interpretation advances equity.

Second, critical policy analysis asks leaders to join their communities to challenge policies that perpetuate inequities (and this text shows them how through case examples). Third, critical policy analysis asks educational leaders and their communities to move beyond critique and to create and advance policies that advance equity for all. Importantly, this book does not stop at critique of the policy field status quo. The book draws across the literature on social justice leadership, community organizing, and student empowerment literature to consider the role of educational leaders and teachers in democratic education.

As Horsford, Scott, and Anderson mention in Chapter 1, the field of educational leadership for social justice has, in some cases, advanced without full recognition of the history of social justice across communities that has preceded the educational equity leaders. Throughout the text, the authors bring this history forward as a context to help leaders understand the origination of public school choice, markets, and competition, and the various forms it takes in their local communities. The book examines the multiple levels of federal and state education policy and reform and in local school district governance. The authors address an emerging field of research related to philanthropy, donors, and private influence over public education, and the new public management. Thus, the book helps prospective and practicing leaders to position themselves as part of a much larger and historical social justice, civil rights movement.

As Series Editor, I am thrilled that this book found its way to the Series to fulfill its vision of providing the core text for each leadership preparation program course/experience and to provide critical guidance for practicing school leaders. I am grateful that the leadership candidates in our program and all education preparation programs will have access to this text for their leadership and policy courses to further develop leaders for equity who truly make a difference.

Preface

We live in precarious times. "Alternative facts" and ideologically motivated think tanks and advocacy groups seem to have more influence on policymaking and public opinion than science and serious scholarship (Rich, 2013). Our democracy and our media are threatened by unlimited corporate money (Mayer, 2016). Long-standing American principles and commitments to broadening equality, such as the separation of church and state and the Voting Rights Act, are being rolled back. Our society has become more economically unequal and racially segregated, and globally, religious fundamentalism, nationalism, racism, patriarchy, and classism are all making a comeback. And if none of that is cause for concern, human life on our planet may not survive another century (Klein, 2015).

Before you burrow under the covers and toss this book out the window, we want to be clear that we don't see everything as gloom and doom. We are witnessing broad-based mobilizations around the world to defend democratic principles. As of this writing, in the U.S., teachers in West Virginia, Oklahoma, Kentucky, Arizona, and Colorado are striking and walking out to protest austerity policies and disinvestment in public education, and progressive caucuses of the national teachers unions are pushing those organizations to connect their missions to grassroots education justice groups. Students too are marching in support of their teachers as well as to protest gun violence and the abuse of refugees seeking asylum at our borders. We see a new kind of public sector professional emerging, one that is prepared to defend a democratic public sector that is under attack. This book is mainly about the emergence of this new democratic professional, but they will need a deep understanding of the educational and social policies that surround them. We didn't get here by accident, and only leaders steeped in an understanding of policy and reform can promote public schools that work for all children. In subsequent chapters, we will meticulously document how austerity policies and the attack on the public sector have been led by a bipartisan group of reformers who promote New Public Management (NPM) schemes to use markets and other business principles to privatize public schools under the banner of "modernization" (Anderson & Cohen, 2018).

More recently, these reformers have been joined by an education industry that sees the public sector as an emerging profit center. One of the characteristics of late capitalism is what Harvey (2005) calls capital "accumulation by dispossession." This means that corporations have exhausted their private sector opportunities for capital accumulation and have now turned to the exploitation of our public assets. Our military, our prisons, our schools, our health-care system, our social security, and our pensions have all become profit centers for entrepreneurs.

To some, these claims about reformers will seem exaggerated or even wrong-headed, but none of them are based on "alternative facts." They are all carefully documented, and within the community of scholars, there is wide agreement that the privatization of the public sphere is well underway, though some may differ as to why it is happening or whether it should happen. But scholarly evidence is too often drowned out in a sea of corporate-owned media, think tanks, 24/7 cable news, and a justifiably angry citizenry deprived of real information. Much ink has been spilled for decades, trying to explain why academic scholarship has so little influence on public and educational policies (Weiss, 1977). But in these times, we feel that it is important to take a stand on the importance of scholarship and evidence in fighting back against forces of misinformation and corporate interests (Anderson, 2007). Such a stand is especially necessary, given the equally strong evidence that the privatization of public institutions perpetuates and deepens economic and racial inequalities (Apple, 2013; Horsford, 2011).

Our goal in writing this book is to get the facts straight and provide a defense of our public sphere, if not exactly of our public schools as they have existed so far. We also attempt to provide an alternative perspective. What if we look at schooling from the perspective of those who have not been well served: the poor and working class, nonwhites, women, LGBTQ people, the disabled, immigrants, and freethinkers. We hope to provide a kind of people's account of American public schooling that acknowledges its vast limitations without buying into the myths promoted by those who would destroy the public institutional infrastructure of our democracy.

In a world in which everything seems to be about branding, advocacy, and indignant anger, some might prefer a more evenhanded academic approach to making our case. Some prefer a policy pragmatism that is agnostic about the role of public and private institutions in delivering education. The problem is that presenting "both sides" too often results in a false equivalency. For instance, the fossil fuel and pharmaceutical industries produce their own research, which creates alternative facts that support their industries. Advocacy think tanks, mostly from the political right, produce reports that are largely not vetted or peer-evaluated, and few of these advocacy think tanks employ serious researchers (Haas, 2007). The scholarship that we cite in this book is mostly taken from peer-reviewed journal articles and books published with university or other academic presses. Yet we also attempt to use this scholarship to sound the alarm that our public schools and our democracy are being impoverished.

David Wallace-Wells (2017) writes in *New York magazine* that given the dire predictions concerning climate change, the average American is nowhere near as alarmed as they should be.

> But no matter how well-informed you are, you are surely not alarmed enough. Over the past decades, our culture has gone apocalyptic with zombie movies and *Mad Max* dystopias, perhaps the collective result of displaced climate anxiety, and yet when it comes to contemplating real-world warming dangers, we suffer from an incredible failure of imagination. The reasons for that are many: the timid language of scientific probabilities, which the climatologist James Hansen once called "scientific reticence" in a paper chastising scientists for editing their own observations so conscientiously that they failed to communicate how dire the threat really was; the fact that the country is dominated by a group of technocrats who believe any problem can be solved and an opposing culture that doesn't even see warming as a problem worth addressing; the way that climate denialism has made scientists even more cautious in offering speculative warnings; the simple speed of change and, also, its slowness, such that we are only seeing effects now of warming from decades past.
>
> (par. 3)

Though perhaps not quite as dire as the extinction of our species, we believe that the slow demise of our public sector and with it our democracy are concern for a similar level of alarm and that educators and educational researchers have a moral obligation to lead the way on sounding that alarm.

This book can be read in many ways and by many audiences, but we conceive of it as a text primarily for those who want to be educational leaders. Here, we use "leader" broadly to include teachers, principals, superintendents, and others who lead organizations outside schools. Therefore, we have interspersed chapters with descriptions of leaders that we consider to be exemplary of the kind of democratic professional that we envision. We also follow each chapter with discussion questions that can help readers to reflect on the chapters and that will hopefully stimulate some critical discussions of chapter content and assumptions.

Because we conceive of this book as a text for education practitioners and policy leaders, we walk a thin line between the impulse to be reassuring and provide a pep talk, and taking a "chicken little" approach in which we warn that the sky is falling. There is a viewpoint out there that professors shouldn't demoralize students who want to lead schools. We believe that being informed is always empowering, even when the news isn't good. The book doesn't shy away from critique, but it is also critically optimistic and hopeful. We reject the notion that to call attention to out-of-school factors that contribute to school failure is to "make excuses" (Berliner, 2009, 2013). We believe that changing the odds for underserved children requires changes both inside and outside of schools (Green & Gooden, 2014). Anything less not only allows the status quo to continue but fails to confront the forces that have already marketized and privatized huge swaths of our public schools.

This is a difficult time to be an educator if you view your job as keeping your head down and allowing reformers who are mostly non-educators to define you professionally. But if you are committed to your students and their families and communities, and are willing to struggle to change policies and practices inside schools and join with those trying to make changes outside of schools, then these are exciting times to be an educator. This book is for those advocates for social justice who want to better understand who the puppet masters are behind school reform and how we might wrestle some power away to create equitably financed, democratic, public schools in which children can have their intellectual, emotional, affective, aesthetic, and physical needs met. Those schools already exist for the privileged. Our struggle for social justice consists in making them a reality for all children within a society that places people ahead of profit.

Overview of the Book

Chapter 1, The Politics of Education Policy in an Era of Inequality, examines the politics of education policy in an era of deepening inequality and provides a critical perspective and analysis of today's education policy landscape. More specifically, we (1) explore the challenges and opportunities associated with teaching in and leading schools in an era of widening race and class inequality, (2) present a critical perspective and analysis of the politics of education policy and leadership practice, and (3) present leadership for justice grounded in policy advocacy as part of a larger social justice project to protect and rethink one of our democracy's most valued institutions—its public schools.

In Chapter 2, Critical Policy Analysis: Interrogating Process, Politics, and Power, we introduce and provide an overview of *critical policy analysis* as an alternative to traditional approaches that present policymaking as a rational, objective, and scientific process. The critical lens applied throughout the book reveals the ways in which traditional policy perspectives have and continue to advantage policy elites and well-resourced special interests while ignoring or excluding altogether the voices, perspectives, and participation of those who have the most to gain or lose from proposed policies (i.e. students, parents, teachers, and school leaders). We consider the politics of ideology with a focus on how liberalism, namely classical liberalism, neoliberalism, and social democracy, shape and are shaped by social, political, and economic forces. These ideologies inform commitments to distinctly different goals of schooling, which are central to education policy and its desired outcomes.

Chapter 3, Public Schools or Private Goods? The Politics of Choice, Markets, and Competition, explores the impact of neoliberalism and "disruptive innovation" on education policy through its focus on markets, privatization, and the politics of choice and competition. It focuses on how the expansion of charters and vouchers, and dismantling the government's role in education limits the democratic possibilities of schooling and its subsequent impact on students, educators, and American education as a public good.

Chapter 4, National or Special Interests? Federal and State Education Policy and Reform, presents the changing landscape of education policy and politics at the state and federal levels. It focuses on the perennial tension between each state's constitutional obligation to provide a common education and the federal government's interest in workforce development and international competition, creating a unique leadership challenge for teachers and administrators in their implementation of policy as they navigate competing aims. It describes this post-Civil Rights Era shift from the *Brown v. Board of Education* decision's declaration of separate schools as inherently unequal to the period of massive resistance and White flight that ensued. It also highlights the move from educational equality to educational excellence, as instigated by the 1983 Nation at Risk report, and concludes with a discussion of new non-state policy actors and networks operating at the state and federal levels.

Chapter 5, School District Governance and Education Leadership: A Shifting Landscape, discusses current shifts in district governance from an administrative/professional regime to a market regime. At the school level, the chapter takes up the issue of school micro-politics and how schools might move from becoming school-centric to becoming more community-centric.

Chapter 6, Philanthropy, Donors, and Private Influence over Public Education, explores the increased role of private venture philanthropy in the education policy-making process. It begins with a history of traditional philanthropy in serving the public good and the recent shift to a more aggressive "new" philanthropy and its implications for educational inequality; opportunity; and reform at the local, state, and national levels.

Chapter 7, The New Professional: Teaching and Leading Under New Public Management, presents an overview of New Public Management and the emergence of the "new" professional, including the proliferation of entrepreneurial education reform projects fueling the politics of choice and competition that undermine the deliberation and collaboration essential to building public consensus and valuing education as a public good. This new governance holds important implications for not only public school and district leaders but the field broadly as we consider more expansive notions of school leadership, given the range of delivery models for education in the current policy era.

Chapter 8, In Pursuit of Democratic Education, considers democracy within the context of education and revisits Dewey's notions of democratic education in terms of school and district governance; inclusion in enjoying the benefits of society; and, in the case of public education, what it means for a school to truly be *public*. It also explores the sociological concept of social reproduction and the possibilities associated with leveraging the cultural production of minoritized and marginalized groups in ways that advance a new social movement that supports and invests in high-quality public schools.

Chapter 9, Building Power: Community Organizing, Student Empowerment, and Public Accountability, articulates a new vision for public education, along with strategies and suggestions to inform a new politics and paradigm of school leadership committed to social justice and democratic schooling. It considers the role educational leaders should play in the post-reform era and contributes a critical and timely analysis of the special interests driving education policy today. In addition to presenting a critical and forward-leaning vision for examining education policy and politics, it calls for new visions of school leadership that support policy transformation through practical strategies grounded in advocacy leadership, culturally responsive and relevant leadership, and applied critical leadership for justice.

Chapter 10, Reclaiming Democracy and the Transformative Power of Education: Possibilities for Democratic Schooling, concludes the book with the importance of education leaders' engaging in the policy process in ways that reclaim and restore the democratic ideal and power of education, highlighting its significance to how Americans think about and understand their role as citizens of the U.S. and the world. We revisit critical policy analysis and address implications for practice.

REFERENCES

Anderson, G. L. (2009). *Advocacy leadership: Toward a post-reform agenda in education.* New York, NY: Routledge.

Anyon, J. (2014). *Radical possibilities: Public policy, urban education, and a new social movement.* New York, NY: Routledge.

Bailey, M. J., & Dynarski, S. M. (2011). *Gains and gaps: Changing inequality in U.S. college entry and completion.* (Working Paper No.17633). National Bureau of Economic Research, Cambridge, MA.

Berliner, D. (2009). *Poverty and potential: Out-of-school factors and school success.* Boulder and Tempe: Education and the Public Interest Center & Education Policy Research Unit. Retrieved from http://epicpolicy.org/publication/poverty-and-potential

Berliner, D. (2013). Effects of inequality and poverty vs. teachers and schooling on America's youth. *Teachers College Record, 115*(1), 1–26.

Center for Research on Education Outcomes (CREDO). (2009). *Multiple choice: Charter school performance in 16 states.* Stanford, CA: CREDO.

Frattura, E. M., & Capper, C. (2007). *Leading for social justice: Transforming schools for all learners.* Thousand Oaks, CA: Corwin.

Green, T. L., & Gooden, M. A. (2014). Transforming out-of-school challenges into opportunities: Community schools reform in the urban Midwest. *Urban Education, 49*(8), 930–954.

Haas, E. (2007). False equivalency: Think Tank references on education in the news media. *Peabody Journal of Education, 82*(1), 63–102.

Harvey, D. (2005). *A brief history of neoliberalism.* Oxford, UK: Oxford University Press.

Horsford, S. D. (2017a). A race to the top from the bottom of the well? The paradox of race in U.S. education reform. *The Educational Forum, 81*(2), 136–147.

Horsford S. D. (2017b). Making America's schools great now: Reclaiming democracy and activist leadership under Trump. *Journal of Educational Administration and History, 50*(1), 3–11.

Lubienski, C., & Lubienski, S. (2014). *The public school advantage: Why public schools outperform private schools.* Chicago, IL: The University of Chicago Press.

Mayer, J. (2016). *Dark money: The hidden history of the billionaires behind the rise of the radical right.* New York, NY: Anchor.

Miron, G., Coryn, C., & Mackety, D. (2007). *Evaluating the impact of charter schools on student achievement: A longitudinal look at the Great Lakes States.* Boulder CO: National Education Policy Center (NEPC).

Osborne, D. (2016). *An educational revolution in Indianapolis.* Progressive Policy Institute. Retrieved from http://www.progressivepolicy.org/wp-content/uploads/2016/12/PPI_An-Educational-Revolution-in-Indianapolis-.pdf

Scott, J. (2018). The problem we all still live with: Neo-plessyism, charter school, and school choice policies in the Post-Obama Era. In I. Rotberg & J. Glazer (Eds.), *Parallel education systems: Charter schools and diversity.* New York, NY: Teachers College Press.

Scott, J., & Wells, A. S. (2013). A more perfect union: Reconciling school choice policies with equality of opportunity goals. In P. L. Carter & K. G. Welner (Eds.), *The opportunity gap: What we must do to give every child a chance* (pp. 123–142). Oxford, UK: Oxford University Press.

Theoharis, G. (2009). *The school leaders our children deserve: Seven keys to equity, social justice, and reform.* New York, NY: Teachers College Press.

Wallace-Wells, D. (2017, July 9). *The uninhabitable Earth: Famine, economic collapse, a sun that cooks us: What climate change could wreak—sooner than you think.* New York, NY. Retrieved from http://nymag.com/daily/intelligencer/2017/07/climate-change-earth-too-hot-for-humans.html

Weiss, C. (1977). Research for policy's sake: The enlightenment function of social research. *Policy Analysis, 3*(Fall), 531–545.

CHAPTER 1

The Politics of Education Policy in an Era of Inequality

The growing problem of racial and social inequalities in the U.S. has taken center stage in the policy arena, providing an important opportunity for researchers, policymakers, and advocates to remind the public about the important role that public institutions play. Despite this policy window, school district leaders and education advocates face significant structural, economic, and institutional barriers that make it increasingly difficult for schools to serve as sites of opportunity, especially for the nation's most disadvantaged students. Record levels of economic inequality and reduced social mobility amid widening and deepening class divides present tremendous challenges for school district leaders and education advocates committed to ensuring equality of educational opportunity for all students (Wilson & Horsford, 2013). In fact, the impact of rising economic inequality across the domains of health, social welfare, politics, and culture does not bode well for ending educational inequality, which continues to be fueled by resource and opportunity gaps (Carter & Welner, 2013; Darling-Hammond, 2010), and the troubling segregation of schools by race and class (Horsford, 2016; Reardon & Owens, 2014).

These trends and conditions have normalized race, gender, and class inequalities in ways that have likely convinced our children to believe such "social inequality and social divisions are the natural order of things" (Carter & Reardon, 2014, p. 2). There is a long-held belief in America that education has the potential to reduce inequality and expand opportunity in ways that advance the American Dream. But widening inequality in schools threatens not only America's opportunity narrative, which has relied heavily on education as the "great equalizer" (Mann, 1849), but also obstructs the pathway to its proverbial dream (Putnam, 2015).

For decades, demographers have anticipated the "browning of America" and declining White population that would make the U.S. a "majority-minority" country by 2020. Indeed, the school-aged population has already reached that designation. According to the National Center for Education Statistics, since 2014, America's schools have been majority nonwhite—49.5% White, 16% Black, 25% Latino, 5% Asian and Pacific Islander, and 1% indigenous, with the rest reporting two or more races—a significant change from the 1977–1978 school year, when 76% of public schoolchildren were White. While unsurprising for those educated in the U.S. within the last twenty years, a longer view of the history of American education reveals how markedly the racial composition of schools has changed and helps explain the movement to privatize and dismantle America's system of public schools.

WHO IS LEADING AMERICA'S SCHOOLS, AND TO WHAT END?

Throughout this book, we will call for greater bottom-up change, led by educators, students, parents, and communities, but currently, education reform is being led largely by non-educators, mostly corporate leaders, venture philanthropists, and politicians who know little about education research and policy. The increased support of top-down approaches to school improvement led by powerful non-educators has shown limited consideration of teacher, principal, and district leader perspectives. What is the role and responsibility of educators, given the current policy context and how it plays out in schools? Neither teacher or leader certification agencies have made social and education policies part of the training of educators. While leadership theories address the role of school and district leaders in the implementation of social and education policies, with notable exceptions (Anderson, 2009; Green, 2017; Ishimaru, 2014; Theoharis, 2007), they are silent on how leaders might push back on or influence these policies.

We might hope to seek some clarification in the Professional Standards for Educational Leaders (PSEL), which offers a broad articulation of what leaders must be able to do. PSEL views the role of education leaders as primarily being responsible for management of the school site (Murphy, 2016). Although PSEL, which is the 2015 revision of the previous leadership standards, focuses much more attention on instructional leadership and the ways in which leaders must engage in transformational practices to improve schools, it speaks very little, if at all, to the policy and political forces under which school leaders must lead. These forces have significant implications for each of the standards, which focus almost exclusively on management of the school site. In fact, one of the limitations of such standards is that they are grounded in "ideal theory" (Mills, 2017), assuming that equality, opportunity, and freedom are enjoyed by all when, in fact, the state of America's schools and society reflects a very different reality.

For example, transformational leadership has long been a hotly debated notion. George McGregor Burns contrasted it with transactional leadership and its more "give and take," don't "rock the boat" approach. Transformational leadership emphasized the leader's personality traits and ability to mobilize followers around a vision. But it begs the question of toward what end this transformation is directed. In this age of what business gurus call "disruptive innovation," are transformational leaders those who disrupt the public school "establishment," teacher unions, professional certification, and the welfare state? What are transformational leaders transforming, and why? Furthermore, how does a principal serve as a transformational leader in an education policy context where the proliferation of charter schools and privatization limit the growth potential of public education through limited resources and dwindling support from those politicians who seek to starve public schools in the interest of choice and competition? These factors contribute to a policy landscape where the influence of school and district leaders is diminished, despite how education policymaking might could benefit from their expertise, which again begs the question who is leading America's schools?

What is the role of education leaders amid historic levels of inequality and reduced social mobility? We agree that, on matters of educational equity and social justice, the standards "have historically fallen short of providing concrete guidance for school leaders on how to carry out these responsibilities through the lens of social justice" (Scanlan & Theoharis, 2015, p. 2). A limited focus on preparing school and district leaders for the politics of education and education policy not only undermines their ability to be effective administrators, but also to demonstrate the leadership capacity, political awareness, and advocacy central to leadership for social justice.

We see a similar trend in teacher certification. The National Council for Accreditation of Teacher Education (NCATE), under pressure from conservative organizations, agreed to take the word "social justice" out of Standard 4 of the 2008 standards. The previous language was that teacher candidates' dispositions should be "guided by beliefs and attitudes such as caring, fairness, honesty, responsibility and *social justice*." Right-wing organizations, such as the National Association of Scholars (NAS), the Foundation for Individual Rights in Education (FIRE), and the American Council of Trustees and Alumni (ACTA), had released statements which linked the language of social justice to the promotion of political ideology in the education of teachers. While this occurred during the conservative George W. Bush administration, Heybach (2009) argues that the slow demise of philosophers and scholars in the social foundations of education meant that no one was able to defend the concept. She cites Butin (2008), who states, "there was no one who could speak to the ancient origins of, societal consensus around, and empirical evidence for social justice as a cause for all individuals (and especially for future teachers) in a democratic and pluralistic society."

This book is an attempt to better understand how educators and school communities might take a more active role in education policy. While we take a standpoint that supports public schools, we do not defend wholesale public schools, which remain complicit in the reproduction of inequality. We will argue, however, that privatizing them and opening them up to profit seekers will only make things worse from democratic, quality, and equity perspectives.

Moreover, since 2008, public investment in education has plummeted, and the 2017 Tax Cuts and Jobs Act will only divert more funding away from public investment, promising to make the U.S. among the most unequal societies in the world. It locks in permanent and deep cuts to statutory corporate taxes (what corporations pay in reality, via loopholes, is half that amount), down from 52.8% in the 1960s to 32% during the last three decades to 21% in 2017. Meanwhile, rather than investing in research and development or the creation of new jobs, U.S. corporations are holding $2.1 trillion abroad to avoid paying taxes. The law also creates new exemptions in the estate tax and for pass-through corporations, which almost exclusively benefit the ultrarich, like the Trump family, which owns pass-through corporations. As a fig leaf, the bill temporarily reduces individual taxes for most, but by 2027, the richest 1% of Americans will see over 82% of its benefits. All told, this massive upward redistribution of wealth will add $1.5 trillion to the deficit, greasing the wheels for the cuts to Medicare and Social Security that Speaker Paul Ryan has already threatened (Kim, December 20, 2017, para 3).

Reformers have used a cynical discourse of "no excuses" to shame teachers and educational leaders into taking responsibility for the failure of the corporate sector and the state at all levels—local, state, and national—to provide an equitable society, especially in the last four decades. We will develop this argument in more detail later in the book, but it is evident that the public sector has become systematically vilified since the *Nation at Risk* report in 1983. In this book, we will highlight educators who have refused to be cowered by such language, and who are working to change conditions for children and families both within and outside of schools. We are also seeing the entry of for-profit and nonprofit organizations into the teacher and principal education fields. These alternatives, which include Kaplan, The University of Phoenix, and Laureate, to name only more reputable for-profits, and nonprofits like Relay Graduate School of Education and New Leaders for New Schools, have been actively supported by both Republican and Democratic administrations. Nor is this deregulation of teacher and principal certification a new phenomenon. According to Zeichner (2010),

> In 2001, $40 million dollar non-competitive grants from the U.S. Department of Education led to the founding of the American Board for the Certification of Teaching Excellence (ABCTE) which currently certifies teachers in 9 states based on two online examinations in content knowledge and professional knowledge. ABCTE does not require enrollment in a teacher education program or demonstration of teaching competence in a classroom for a teaching license.
>
> (p. 1545)

Smith and Pandolfo (2011) report that since 2007, the leading producers of teachers in Texas are two for-profit online programs, A+ Texas Teachers and iTeach Texas. The demise of professionalism across the public sector has been amply documented as teachers, nurses, doctors, social workers, and police officers are increasingly controlled from a distance by narrow outcomes measures (Evetts, 2011; Muller, 2018).

ARE MARKETS THE ANSWER TO PUBLIC SECTOR PROBLEMS?

The aims of education began to change as education was viewed solely as linked to U.S. competitiveness in the global economy (Labaree, 1997). While education has historically been viewed as both a cost and an investment in the country's future, the perception of its economic importance grew in the 1950s, when the Soviet Union put the first man into outer space and appeared to be surpassing us in math and science (Engel, 2000). Another jolt occurred in the 1980s as Japan and Germany appeared to be surpassing us in economic might. The rhetoric of *The Nation at Risk* report, commissioned by President Reagan in 1983, set off what we now think of as the current education reform movement that has transferred what many consider the failure of the corporate sector (Lock & Spender, 2011) onto public schools, replacing a public investment strategy with school choice and high-stakes testing (Adamson, Astrad, & Darling-Hammond, 2016; Mehta, 2013). In many ways, Milton Friedman's (1962) argument, first articulated from the White House by Ronald Reagan, that markets should replace or supplement government in nearly all sectors of society has gone from a fringe idea of the Libertarian right to mainstream thought in a mere four decades.

But it is important to understand why a market-based approach to school reform is fundamentally flawed. It fails to understand that if people are treated as customers instead of citizens, the skills of citizenship and political engagement will atrophy. But it also changes the ethos of public service as commitment to a common good, changing what it means to be an education professional (Anderson & Cohen, 2018; Cuban, 2004). Moreover, market-based approaches do not support state intervention in redressing racial, linguistic, and socioeconomic discrimination. In the following section, we provide an analysis of how a public service ethos of improving education for all children has been eroded in the last few decades and replaced by an entrepreneurial model that incentivizes school administrators to maximize their own schools' success (and their own careers) at the expense of others. We are not suggesting here that previous school administrators were not also career-oriented or, in too many cases, also constrained by biases of race, class, and gender. Rather, we want to highlight how leadership grounded in public service promoted a greater concern for the common good than a market approach does (Sullivan, 2004).

WHAT'S WRONG WITH ENTREPRENEURIAL LEADERSHIP IN EDUCATION?

We have critiqued the use of markets to discipline principals and teachers, and create entrepreneurial and competitive forms of leadership. Yet older, public servant approaches to leadership have also been heavily critiqued as failing to challenge the grammar of schooling and the inequalities that public schools have reproduced (Callahan, 1962). The premise of public school leadership has generally been to serve and be an advocate for *all* children, though this has seldom been equitably realized. One might, then, rightfully ask if a market-based approach might better serve all children and lead to greater achievement and equitable outcomes.

Before the age of market reforms, teachers who aspired to be principals were taught that their central task as an instructional leader was to help a teaching staff improve their instruction, even with a staff composed of teachers ranging from incompetent to outstanding. If the incompetent ones (usually only one or two) could not improve after working with them over time, then the task was to counsel them out of teaching or use documentation to move them out (Bridges, 1992). These aspiring principals were not taught to harass them or scapegoat unions, but rather, how to provide due process by helping struggling teachers improve while documenting their work in case they didn't (see Ayres, Laura, & Ayres, 2018).

They were also taught how to encourage professional renewal for burned-out or "plateaued" teachers, how to target professional development for the teachers with specific needs, and how to inspire the good teachers to become outstanding (Milstein, 1990). The dilemma for most principals back then was how to carry out both management and instructional leadership roles, given the constraints on their time (Rallis & Highsmith, 1986). Gradually, teacher leader positions, literacy coaches, and professional learning communities (PLCs) were added in many schools for additional support for teacher development and instructional mentoring.

Because most teachers saw teaching as a career and stayed in schools longer, there was time to do this kind of capacity building in the school, which also meant transferring this capacity building system-wide if these teachers moved to another school. All children benefited when teachers improved. This was seen as particularly important in low-income schools, where students needed skilled teachers and depended on teachers, counselors, and administrators for access to dominant social and cultural capital (Stanton-Salazar, 2011).

The new entrepreneurial principal, modeled after business CEOs, works in a different policy context and brings a different ethos and internal logic to the public sector (Ward, 2011). Particularly in urban school districts with school choice policies, there is a tendency for principals to recruit "low maintenance" students to their schools to improve test scores. "High maintenance" students, such as boys and those with learning disabilities, limited English, or behavior problems, require more effort, resources, and skilled teachers. Given the amount of time and effort some principals put into marketing their schools in these districts, there is often little time to mentor teachers, and sadly, these administrators anticipate that students with special needs or behavior problems may lower their overall test scores. While terms like "high and low maintenance" seem offensive—after all, these are children, not machines—we use them to show how market systems can commodify and dehumanize their clients.

In fact, schools that are skilled at serving these more resource-intensive students are penalized in a market system. They are likely to have lower test scores and may not attract families who view the school as serving children unlike their own. Under No Child Left Behind (NCLB), many of these good schools were closed or reconstituted for low test scores or underenrollment, even though they were responsive to their community and served their students well (Journey for Justice Alliance, 2014; Kemple, 2015). Charter schools, which are less regulated, are particularly geared for entrepreneurialism, and as a result, they tend to have far fewer homeless students, foster children, or children with behavior problems or special education or English language needs, leaving public schools to work with more of these students (Baker, 2012). But even public school principals in districts with school choice are pressured to engage in the same behavior (Lubienski & Lubienski, 2006). Some principals have figured out that if they recruit good teachers, their job is easier, their test scores improve, and their careers take off. Most principals would likely rather not play this cynical game, but if competition is the game, then they have to play.

Shipps and White (2009) interviewed principals in New York City. A typical response to the pressures of accountability was the following:

> We aggressively go after teachers…We spend a ton of money and effort on teacher recruitment, everything from having fancy materials that make our school look better than any other school, and banners…My hiring coordinator, you know, emails every [education] professor…at every major university around the country.
>
> (p. 368)

They found that principals also had strategies for recruiting students to make sure they got the "right kids." Here is one principal's strategy:

> I'm a competitive person by nature…so I think by nature you are always looking at where you stand in comparison to those in your community…I study the ones who don't come…[Ours] isn't always their first choice. There are two other choices they [tend to] make…So generally we go through all the applications…I get a thousand applicants for seventy-five seats. I'm never in a situation where I go begging for kids, I just need the right kids.
>
> (p. 368)

In a market system, resources that could be focused on instruction are diverted into marketing and recruiting. What is troubling about these quotes is that competition is changing not merely what professionals do but who they are. It is reconstructing their very identities, both personal and professional (Anderson & Cohen, 2018).

Competition is also common *within* schools. Students are often awarded with T-shirts or vouchers to buy snacks. Teachers, who are often evaluated by test scores, compete for the best scores, which means they mimic principals in trying not to have "more difficult" students assigned to their classes. Moreover, a principal who recruits great teachers to his or her school is not building capacity. Those teachers leave behind a classroom of equally deserving students at their former school. A promising candidate from a teacher education program merely gets recruited to one school instead of another. All this does is move resources around the district or between districts, with the goal of enhancing a particular school's (and, by extension, principal's) performance.

Closing, turning around, or reconstituting schools does the same thing. It just moves resources around the system on the pretext of getting rid of "bad teachers" without increasing achievement (Center for Research on Education Outcomes, 2017; Malen, Croninger, Muncey, & Redmond-Jones, 2002; Noguera, 2015; Sunderman, Coghlan, & Mintrop, 2017). The former notion of principals as instructional leaders, helping all teachers improve, increases system capacity and produces real value. The entrepreneurial model does not. Ironically, this approach mimics how markets have changed in the private sector as well. Whereas the goal used to be to produce value by making things, now, the focus is on financialization and increasing shareholder economic gain. Markets no longer produce much value. Instead, they move money (and, in the case of education markets, students) around (Piketty, 2014).

At least an entrepreneurial businessperson can argue that her self-interest in building a successful business allows her to support herself and her family, and create jobs for others. She wants to poach good employees from other companies because they are in competition for customers. This is the nature of a business start-up. But in public school systems, viewing a school as "my business" or "my start-up" produces pressures to recruit good teachers from other schools, to reject kids who might lower my test scores, and to market my school to far-flung parents. The nature of a public school is to work for the common good of all families and children, not just those in "my school." It is hard to imagine how this competitive business model can be viewed as serving or being an advocate for all children, and there is no evidence that it pays off significantly in higher overall achievement levels. In fact, there is evidence that it adds to an already highly stratified and segregated public school system.

There is also evidence that a focus on test scores as a metric for competition has caused school leaders to focus less on noncognitive skills, eliminating the affective, physical, civic, and socio-emotional dimensions of schooling (Lynch, Baker, & Lyons, 2009). As cited by Reardon, in discussing a growing social class achievement gap in testing and college attendance, indicates that

> A related trend during the last 20 years is the growing social-class gap in other important measures of adolescents' "soft skills" and behaviors related to civic engagement, such as participating in extracurricular activities, sports, and academic clubs; volunteering and participating in community life; and self-reports of social trust
>
> (Putnam, Frederick, & Snellman, 2012)

Of course, it is also true that public schools for poor families and children of color were not very good thirty years ago, before market logic entered education. But had districts continued to focus on an ethos of public service, PLCs, whole school reforms, authentic assessment, and ultimately more cultural responsive pedagogies, they might have made more progress by now than by using high-stakes tests and market logics to "incentivize" and punish teachers and principals (Payne, 2008).

We will never know how much progress we might have made. But we do know that we have lost many outstanding teachers and principals (and perhaps more than a few mediocre ones) because they no longer felt they could use their professional judgment to advocate for what they know is best for children. Entrepreneurialism can be a wonderful asset for someone starting a business, but it has too often been problematic in too many ways for our public education system. There may be some cases in which market choice may make sense. For instance, districts using "controlled choice" have intentionally used choice to desegregate schools (Alves & Willie, 1987;

Willie, Edwards, & Alves, 2002). In some cases, in which vouchers have been used for low-income families, parents express satisfaction with their choices, although there is no evidence of increased achievement (Carnoy, 2017). The argument that poor parents should have the same choices as middle- and upper-class parents is compelling, but when low-income parents "district hop" in an attempt to get a middle-class education for their children, they are criminalized (Faw & Jabbar, 2016). Unless we find the political will to change how we finance schools, allow students to cross district boundaries, and provide more equitable ways to distribute resources, those choices will continue to be illusory. In the next section, we will explore in more detail our seeming inability to achieve greater equity in our school system.

POSSIBILITIES FOR DEMOCRATIC SCHOOLING: COUNTERNARRATIVES TO PRIVATIZATION

As we consider the future of America's schools and the professional duty and responsibility of those who lead them, we are reminded of the tremendous responsibility school leaders possess, concerning not only the academic performance of students but also their cognitive development, social-emotional growth, and commitment to civic education. These areas of student development are critical to a thriving, sustainable democracy, not to mention their critical role in equipping America's students with the education and skills they will need to continue their education, enter the workforce, or start their own civic or entrepreneurial endeavors.

Fortunately, a robust body of research on social justice leadership has shaped the field in significant ways in just a short period of time (Anderson, 2009; Frattura & Capper, 2007; Theoharis, 2007; Tillman & Scheurich, 2013; Wilson & Horsford, 2015). We will highlight, throughout this book, many social justice leaders in schools and districts across the country (e.g. Jamaal Bowman, John Kuhn, Mike Matsuda, Betty Rosa, Glenda Ritz, and many more) who continue to carry on the tradition of leaders like Marcus Foster, Leonard Covello, Deborah Meier, and Barbara Sizemore. Meanwhile, community organizers, activists, unionists, and leaders (e.g. Reverend William Barber in North Carolina, Jitu Brown and Karen Lewis in Chicago, and Zakiyah Ansari in New York City) support their social justice work through advocacy beyond the schoolhouse doors. These coalitions among school practitioners, community activists, unionists, and educational researchers are crucial to opposing those with a privatization agenda who want to dismantle our public schools. These coalitions focus on building, strengthening, and sustaining public institutions rather than dismantling them.

What can education leaders contribute to the formation of education policy that is equitable and advances the needs of all students? For many leaders, trying to keep the peace and make everyone happy is a skill, an art, and even a goal to ensure fairness for all, but in the given moment, it is important to remember that there is a cost associated with silence. Perhaps more importantly, leaders should not get out ahead of their communities or make policy for their communities. Rather, they should be networked with authentic community leaders and move toward change *with* their communities.

School leaders are faced with a complex policy context that pulls them in multiple directions, and this varies from state to state and district to district. For instance, in some districts—especially urban districts—leaders are contending with gentrification, school choice, competition from charter schools, police in schools, colocation, and vendors trying to sell them services. In other districts—suburban and rural—these issues may be less of a factor, but dealing with social justice issues related to privilege, and what some are now calling "opportunity hoarding," may raise other kinds of policy issues (Lewis & Diamond, 2017; Reeves, 2017). However, issues of inequality and discrimination, whether by race, social class, gender, sexual orientation/gender identity, language, disability, or their intersections, are present in all districts, and school leaders must decide whether they will allow such inequalities to persist or whether they will take on the difficult task of working to change these conditions (Theoharis, 2007, 2009).

While there is plenty of bad news for those who support public schools with the ascendency of Betsy DeVos to Secretary of Education, there are also some promising developments due to a growing activism among educators and a growing body of critical educational research. The recent reauthorization of the Elementary and Secondary Education Act (ESEA) in 2015 helped to mitigate some of the worst excesses of high-stakes testing, in part due to a large "opt out" movement led by parents (Pizmony-Levy & Saraisky, 2016). Zero tolerance discipline policies in schools are also under attack as it has become apparent that Black and Latino students are being suspended at scandalous rates, contributing to a school-to-prison pipeline that reveals the tragic ways in which racially minoritized and disenfranchised students are prepared not for postsecondary education but rather for incarceration. More and more schools are experimenting with positive and restorative justice approaches to student discipline. Disproportionate referrals of Black males to special education are also under attack as well as the plight of New Language Learners, who languish in developmental English classes. More and more schools are implementing dual language programs.

But too often, there is a disconnect between those who make policy and those who enact it. In everyday practice, educators serve as policy implementers (Fowler, 2009), spending their waking hours learning, following, interpreting, carrying out, and having the quality of their work and effectiveness measured by the policies and regulations approved by policymakers. At the same time, policymakers (and their staffs) spend their time being informed and lobbied by representatives from advocacy groups, vocal constituencies, research organizations, and a range of special interest groups (Drutman, 2015; Spring, 2015), all vying for policies that benefit their own needs and people. Many educators are disconcerted and frustrated by the extent to which punitive and market-based policies depart from their professional judgment, research evidence, and practices that demonstrate what is effective in schools.

Why don't we implement the types of policies, funding decisions, and practices that have been found effective and that the best research and educators' accumulated experience tell us are effective? This is largely because there are so many other agendas and political forces at play in education that have little or nothing to do with teaching, learning, or improving educational experiences for children. As Giroux (1992) explained,

> Administrators and teachers in schools of education and leadership programs need. . . a language that is interdisciplinary, that moves skillfully among theory, practice, and politics. This is a language that makes issues of culture, power, and ethics primary to understanding how schools construct knowledge, identities, and ways of life that promote nurturing and empowering relations. We need a language in our leadership programs that defends schools as democratic public spheres.
>
> (p. 8)

Part of the work that education leaders must also engage in involves the earliest phases of the policy process, that is, framing and naming the problem (Horsford & D'Amico, 2015). One of the unfortunate limitations of education leadership research is its ahistorical nature (Horsford & D'Amico, 2015). While reformers, and corporate reformers, in particular, aim to present their efforts as "innovative" and "transformative," none of their approaches, efforts, initiatives, or models are new or even particularly innovative. In their classic text *Tinkering Toward Utopia: Toward a Century of Public School Reform*, Tyack and Cuban (1995), through their historical analysis of America's infatuation with corporate-led "education reform," debunk these claims. Mazzucato (2015), in *The Entrepreneurial State*, has documented how the public sector is in reality far more innovative than the more risk-averse private sector. Totally missing from this process is the counter-perspective of education leaders advancing social justice and equity, not to mention the parents, students, and community leaders whose lives are directly impacted by the decisions of others.

Schools are not immune to these larger contexts and forces of American society. In fact, we see these very trends and tensions magnified in schools. The problems of inadequate access to decent housing, quality health care, family-sustaining jobs, and affordable public transportation; mass incarceration; school suspensions; and displacement by gentrification and home foreclosures are just a few of the larger forces that impact the lives of students, their families, and their communities. These forces also affect the daily lives and practice of educators committed to providing students with high-quality amid a troubling era of widening inequality and reduced social mobility, whereby the American Dream is not only deferred but is, for a growing number of citizens, a nightmare.

FROM COMPETITION TO COLLECTIVE ACTION FOR CHANGE: AN EDUCATION MOVEMENT

While this is a book that attempts to provide a critical policy analysis of contemporary educational reform, it is also a book about taking collective action for change. The current forty-year experiment with market-based, metric-driven education reform has fallen far short of its initial hype (Mickelson, Giersch, Stearns, & Moller, 2013; Nichols & Berliner, 2007).

We believe that a post-reform era should be led from the bottom up by educators, students, parents, and communities. If such a coalition can be galvanized, the politicians will follow. It is notable that the 2018 wildcat strikes and walkouts by teachers occurred in "red states" not typically known for challenging austerity policies.

While we will be providing some social and political analyses that many educators and non-educators may find disheartening, we try to emphasize those grassroots movements and educational leaders who lead against the grain, and the ways that leadership often comes from below by organizing to build alliances to challenge those who have amassed inordinate levels of political and economic influence. In fact, historically, this is how significant change has usually occurred, and those who struggled from below in the past often faced far more daunting forces than those we enumerate in this book.

Those corporate-backed reformers who want to dismantle public education and the welfare state claim that those who want to address factors outside of schools that impact student success, especially low-income students of color, are making excuses for failing to teach poor children well. But anyone serious about social justice knows that change is needed both inside and outside of schools. The term social justice gets thrown around a lot, but while working for social justice is hard, most educators know that change has to happen both inside and outside schools if underserved or marginalized students are to have access to real opportunity.

We begin with what we can do inside schools. There are many ways to work for social justice within schools. Too many kids of color are being suspended and inappropriately referred to special education; too few English-language learners are in bilingual or dual language programs, and too many languish for years in English development classes in English-only programs; too many schools depend on zero tolerance discipline policies and a police presence in schools instead of restorative justice approaches that reduce suspensions. Too many schools fail to provide art, music, physical education, and a whole child approach to instruction. Too few schools have close relations with the local community and integrated services.

These are all important social justice issues, and they are within the immediate control of schools, but they will not address the larger structural issues that can lead to failure and are a result of broader social and education policies (Anyon, 2014; Berliner, 2009). History has taught us that the great social advancements, such as the eight-hour workday, collective bargaining, the Voting Rights Act, marriage equality, Social Security, the dismantling of Jim Crow laws, the Fair Housing Act, and even bilingual and special education, were only achieved through political advocacy and organizing.

We are beginning to see a social justice movement that operates both within and outside schools. Social justice work inside schools, such as that which we enumerated earlier, has received more scholarly attention, but there is a growing social movement, led by educators, that is challenging educational and social policies that hurt children, families, and communities. There is a proliferation of teacher, parent, student, union, and principal movements against high-stakes testing, school closings, gentrification and displacement, racism, deportations, fiscal inequities, large class sizes, zero tolerance discipline, Islamophobia, privatization, corporate influence, for-profit education, the militarization of schools, vouchers, charter co-location, and many more. The late Jean Anyon (2014) argued that several aspects of the machinery necessary to mobilize citizens around education are already in place:

1. Schools occupy both the physical and the psychological center of neighborhoods and communities.
2. The civil rights movement successfully made the claim that access to a quality public education is a civil right.
3. Parents face personal incentives to press for quality education for their children.
4. Teachers and administrators have access to community members that they can help organize.

The seeds of change are everywhere today, sometimes led by teachers, such as in the rolling 2018 strikes and walkouts of teachers in several states, and sometimes even led by the very students that are being impacted by education and social policies. In 2018, students across the country walked out in solidarity with the Parkland High School students in Florida, who, like previous students, had been the victims of gun violence. The Dreamers and anti-deportation movement has also been largely led by students. It was also high school students who led the movement for educational and social change in the U.S., Mexico, and France in 1968; in Beijing in 1989; and in Chile in 2011.

During the modern U.S. civil rights movement, it was African American high school and college students in Birmingham, Alabama, who raised the awareness of White Americans who watched them on the evening news being attacked by Bull Connor's dogs and fire hoses. And while this strategic exposure catapulted the civil rights movement from a regional to a national movement, there had been many prior civil rights battles fought since reconstruction against great odds by students, parents, and educators (Hale, 2016; Payne, 1995/2007, Siddle Walker, 1996).

Perhaps the most important example of the power of change from below is the history behind *Brown v. Board of Education*, a landmark ruling that made "separate" schooling for Black children illegal. In the fall of 1950, after many unsuccessful attempts to hold Topeka, Kansas, public schools accountable for denying its Black elementary school students admission to their neighborhood schools, the Topeka chapter of the NAACP (National Association for the Advancement of Colored People) organized its members and allies to challenge the doctrine of "separate-but-equal" in education. In Topeka, Black students were forced to travel outside their neighborhoods to attend Black segregated schools because their neighborhood schools, while closer in proximity and thus more convenient, refused to admit Black students.

But the alliance that the NAACP organized was built on the shoulders of the work of previous struggles against even greater odds. This 1950 struggle was the twelfth school desegregation case to be brought forth in Kansas since 1881.

Topeka's NAACP chapter president, McKinley Burnett; secretary, Lucinda Todd; and lawyers, Charles Scott, John Scott, and Charles Burnett, enlisted thirteen parents (representing twenty children) to join a class action lawsuit, arguing that Topeka's system of segregated schools violated their equal protection rights under the Fourteenth Amendment of the U.S. Constitution. To prove this, each parent would go to her neighborhood school to enroll her child, secure evidence of denied enrollment, and provide documentation to the NAACP legal team to serve as the basis for the lawsuit. Oliver L. Brown, the only male parent, was designated lead plaintiff in *Oliver L. Brown et al. v. The Board of Education of Topeka (KS)*, which was filed on February 28, 1951.

Although the U.S. District Court ruled in favor of the Topeka school board, this would not be the end of *Brown et al.* The plaintiffs appealed their case to the U.S. Supreme Court, and although *Brown v. Board of Education* (1954) is most often associated with Topeka, Kansas, it comprised five separate segregation cases including Delaware (*Belton v. Gebhart),* Washington, D.C. (*Bolling v. Sharp*), South Carolina (*Briggs v. Elliot*), Virginia (*Davis v. County School Board of Prince Edward County*), and Kansas (*Brown v. Board*). Each filed in 1951, these five lawsuits were either unsuccessful in their lower courts or won their local cases only to be confronted with White institutions and power structures that still refused to admit Black students, even if it meant breaking the law. Nonetheless, the collective of parents, student leaders, civil rights attorneys, and community organizers and activists representing Topeka, Kansas; Wilmington, Delaware; Washington, D.C.; Clarendon County, South Carolina; and Richmond, Virginia mobilized to resist racial discrimination and segregation in schools. They fought *not* for the right of Black children to attend schools with White children but rather for the right of Black children to attend well-resourced neighborhood schools just like White children did. Despite how it has been framed in mainstream education policy discourses, scholars have documented the extent to which the fight was less about *separate* and more about *equal* (Bell, 2004; Horsford, 2011, 2016; Shujaa, 1996; Walker, 2005).

While this book is about collective action and change, it is also about ideas. Like *Brown*, all of these social struggles represent the complex and competing ideas, values, and ideologies that are struggled for and negotiated in the public sphere. The works of political theorists and legal scholars like Deborah Stone (2002) and Martha Minow (2002) are especially useful in underscoring the significance of *ideas* as "the very stuff of politics" (Stone, p. 34). As Stone observed,

> People fight about ideas, fight for them, and fight against them. Political conflict is never simply over material conditions and choices, but over what is legitimate. The passion in politics comes from conflicting senses of fairness, justice, rightness, and goodness. Moreover, people fight *with* ideas as well as about them. The different sides in a conflict create different portrayals of the battle – who is affected, how they are affected, and what is at stake. Political fights are conducted with money, with rules, with votes, and with favors, to be sure, but they are conducted above all with words and *ideas*.
>
> (Stone, 2002, p. 34) [emphasis added]

These ideas, as informed by the values and ideologies of individuals, communities, and other policy actors, are key to understanding what animates their support and advocacy for certain policy proposals and political agendas over others. According to Stone (2002), the public interest exists within the *polis*—the place where political values are best deliberated and negotiated—but lacks value in the counterpart to the polis, the *market*. But even in the polis, the notion of public interest can conflict with private desires. For example, in the case of school desegregation discussed earlier, the unwillingness of White school administrators and school boards to enroll a Black child in her nearby neighborhood school reflects what Horsford (2016) described as "social justice for the advantaged," whereby the private desires of the dominant group hold greater value than the public good, undermining any meaningful efforts to address educational inequality in America's schools.

We also see a clash of perspectives and values when those who are relatively privileged but self-identify as politically liberal fail to understand why members of urban, low-income communities might choose a charter school over a public school or why they might support vouchers. Often, they may not be making these choices for ideological reasons but rather for reasons that have more to do with calculations based on a different social reality and a paucity of better options (see Pedroni, 2007). This suggests that coalitions for change should include or be led by low-income communities whose members live out the consequences of decisions made by those who influence education and social policy.

However, we are increasingly seeing what used to be considered urban issues occurring in rural areas: an increase of immigrant populations and English-language learners, a serious drug addiction problem, and increased poverty as good jobs are harder to find. There are even ways in which low-income rural children and youth are sometimes more disadvantaged. For instance, if students live in public housing in the Bronx, they can live at home and go to college. Youth on the Navajo reservation or in rural West Virginia often incur the additional cost of moving and paying for housing to attend college. Leaders in many rural areas negotiate between factions of a community that support a separation of church and state, and others that want prayer or Christian values, such as creationism, taught in schools. Empowering a local community may have different outcomes in urban areas where church and state separation is more likely to be taken-for-granted than in the so-called "Bible belt," where communities may expect schools to reflect their religious values.

Add to this the fact that, as the U.S. becomes more unequal and segregated by class, race, and political ideology, the middle class has become more economically anxious, and working-class Americans have seen the well-paid union jobs of their parents slowly disappear. This has resulted in less generosity toward others and a circling of the wagons against those perceived as outsiders or undeserving. Some of these anxious Americans have also formed social movements, such as the Tea Party, and since President Trump's election, there has been a revival of various hate groups (Thrush & Haberman, 2017). In this climate, we need, more than ever, strong social institutions and a public sphere in which informed deliberation can take place. We need public schools that prepare more than human capital for the economy. We also need them to prepare informed citizens capable of reenergizing a democracy diminished by corporate and moneyed interests, and civic indifference or cynicism.

This book brings the world of action and ideas together to redefine leadership and to develop it at all levels of education. We also hope to convince educators that in the current political climate, they need to add critical policy analysis, which we describe in Chapter 2, to their professional "toolkit." Framed by the critical policy analysis literature and written with students of educational leadership and policy and their faculty in mind, this book presents an alternative to traditional education policy and politics texts by focusing on issues of power, voice, democratic participation, reproduction of inequality in the policymaking process, and their implications for school leaders, teachers, and their students.

REFERENCES

Adamson, F., Astrad, B., & Darling-Hammond, L. (Eds.). (2016). *Global educational reform: How privatization and public investment influence education outcomes*. New York, NY: Routledge.

Alves, M., & Willie, C. (1987). Controlled choice assignments: A new and more effective approach to school desegregation. *Urban Review, 19*(2), 67–88.

Anderson, G. L. (2009). *Advocacy leadership: Toward a post-reform agenda in education*. New York, NY: Routledge.

Anderson, G. L., & Cohen, M. (2018). *The emerging democratic professional: Teachers and leaders resisting privatization & market-driven reforms*. New York, NY: Teachers College Press.

Anderson, G. L., & Montoro Donchik, L. (2016). The privatization of education and policymaking: The American Legislative Exchange Council (ALEC) and network governance in the United States. *Educational Policy, 30*(2), 322–364.

Anyon, J. (2014). *Radical possibilities: Public policy, urban education, and a new social movement*. New York: Routledge.

Ayres, W., Laura, C., & Ayres, R. (2018). *"You can't fire the bad ones": And 18 other myths about teachers, teachers' unions, and public education*. Boston, MA: Beacon Press.

Barton, P. E., & Coley, R. J. (2010). *The Black-White achievement gap: When progress stopped*. Policy Information Report. Educational Testing Service.

Bell, D. A. (2004). *Silent covenants:* Brown v. Board of Education *and the unfulfilled hopes for racial reform*. New York, NY: Oxford University Press.

Belton v. Gebhart 87 A.2d 862 (1952).

Berliner, D. (2009). *Poverty and potential: Out-of-school factors and school success*. Boulder and Tempe: Education and the Public Interest Center & Education Policy Research Unit. Retrieved from http://epicpolicy.org/publication/poverty-and-potential

Bolling v. Sharpe, 347 U.S. 497 (1954).

Bourdieu, P., & Passeron, J. C. (1977/1990). *Reproduction in education, society and culture*. Thousand Oaks, CA: Sage Publications.

Bridges, E. (1992). *The incompetent teacher: Managerial responses*. New York, NY: Routledge.

Briggs v. Elliott, 342 U.S. 350 (1952).

Brown v. Board of Education, 98 F. Supp. 797 (D. Kan. 1951).

Brown v. Board of Education, 347 U.S. 483 (1954).

Brown, E., & Makris, M. V. (2017). A different type of charter school: In prestige charters, a rise in cachet equals a decline in access. *Journal of Education Policy, 33*(1), 85.

Butin, D. (2006). Dark times indeed: NCATE, social justice, and the marginalization of multicultural foundations, *Journal of Educational Controversy 1*(1).

Callahan, R. (1962). *Education and the cult of efficiency.* Chicago, IL: The University of Chicago Press.

Carnoy, M. (2017). *School vouchers are not a proven strategy for improving student achievement.* Washington, DC: Economic Policy Institute.

Carter, P., & Reardon, S. (2014). *Inequality matters: Framing a strategic inequality research agenda.* Retrieved from https://ed.stanford.edu/news/inequality-matters-framing-strategic-inequality-research-agenda

Carter, P. L., & Welner, K. G. (Eds.). (2013). *Closing the opportunity gap: What America must do to give every child and even chance.* New York, NY: Oxford University Press.

Center for Research on Education Outcomes. (2017). *Lights off: Practice and impact of closing low-performing schools: Volume I and II.* Stanford, CA: Stanford University. Retrieved from http://credo.stanford.edu/closure-virtual-control-records

Coleman, J., Campbell, E., Hobson, C., & McPartland, J. (1966). *Equality of educational opportunity.* Washington, DC: U.S. Government Printing Office.

Crawford, J. (2007, June 6). A Diminished Vision of Civil Rights: No Child Left Behind and the growing divide in how educational equity is understood. *Education Week, 26*(39), 31, 40.

Cuban, L. (2004). *The blackboard and the bottom line: Why schools can't be businesses.* Cambridge: Harvard University Press.

Darling-Hammond, L. (2010). *The flat world and education: How America's commitment to equity will determine our future.* New York, NY: Teachers College Press.

Davis v. County School Board of Prince Edward County, 149 F. Supp. 431 (E.D. Va. 1957)

Drutman, L. (2015). *The business of America is lobbying: How corporations became politicized and politics became more corporate.* Oxford, UK: Oxford University Press.

Engel, M. (2000). *The struggle for control of public education. Market ideology vs. democratic values.* Philiadelphia: Temple University.

Evetts, J. (2011). A new professionalism? Challenges and opportunities. *Current Sociology, 59*(4), 406–422.

Faw, L., & Jabbar, H. (2016). Poor choices: The sociopolitical context of "Grand Theft Education." *Urban Education*, 1–35.

Foster, J. B. (2016). The opt out revolt: Democracy and Education. *Monthly Review, 67*(10) https://monthlyreview.org/2016/03/01/the-opt-out-revolt/

Fowler, F. C. (2009). *Policy studies for educational leaders: An introduction* (3rd ed.). Boston, MA: Pearson.

Frattura, E. M., & Capper, C. (2007). *Leading for social justice: Transforming schools for all learners.* Thousand Oaks, CA: Corwin.

Friedman, M. (1962). *Capitalism and freedom.* Chicago: University of Chicago Press.

Green, T. (2017). "We felt they took the heart out of the community": Examining a community-based response to urban school closure. *Education Policy Analysis Archives, 25*(21), 1–26.

Giroux, H. A. (1992). Educational leadership and the crisis of democratic government. *Educational Researcher, 21*(4), 4–11.

Hale, J. (2016). *The freedom schools: Student activists in the Mississippi civil rights.* New York, NY: Columbia University Press.

Hess, F. M., & West, M. R. (2005). A better bargain: Overhauling teacher collective bargaining for the 21st century. Cambridge, MA: Program on Education Policy & Governance.

Heybach, J. A. (2009). Rescuing social justice in education: A critique of the NCATE controversy. *Philosophical Studies in Education, 40*, 234–245.

Horsford, S. D. (2011). *Learning in a burning house: Educational inequality, ideology, and (dis)integration*. New York, NY: Teachers College Press.

Horsford, S. D. (2016). Social justice for the advantaged: Freedom from racial equality post-"Milliken." *Teachers College Record, 118*(3), 1–18.

Horsford, S. D., & D'Amico, D. (2015). The past as more than prologue: A call for historical research. *International Journal of Educational Management, 29*(7), 863–873.

Ishimaru, A. M. (2014). When new relationships meet old narratives: The journey towards improving parent-school relations in a district-community organizing collaboration. *Teachers College Record, 116*(2).

Journey for Justice Alliance. (2014). *Death by a thousand cuts: Racism, school closures, and public school sabotage: Voices from America's affected communities of color*. Retrieved from https://www.j4jalliance.com/wp-content/uploads/2014/02/J4JReport-final_05_12_14.pdf

Kemple, J. J. (2015). *High school closures in New York City: Impacts on students' academic outcomes, attendance, and mobility*. Research Alliance for New York City Schools. Retrieved from http://steinhardt.nyu.edu/research_alliance/publications/hs_closures_in_nyc

Labaree, D. (1997). *How to succeed in school without really learning: The credentials race in American education*. London, UK and New Haven, CT: Yale University Press.

Lakoff, G. (2008). *The political mind*. New York, NY: Penguin Books.

Lewis, A., & Diamond, J. (2017). *Despite the best intentions: How race inequality thrives in good schools*. Oxford, UK: Oxford University Press.

Lock, R., & Spender, J. C. (2011). *Confronting managerialism: How the business elite and their schools threw our lives out of balance*. New York, NY: Zed Books.

Lubienski, C., & Lubienski, S. T. (2006). *Charter, private, public schools and academic achievement: New evidence from NAEP mathematics data*. Retrieved February 1, 2006, from http://www.ncspe.org

Lynch, K., Baker, J., & Lyons, M. (2009). *Affective equality: Love, care, and injustice*. New York, NY: Palgrave Macmillan.

Malen, B., Croninger, R., Muncey, D., & Redmond-Jones, D. (2002). Reconstituting schools: "Testing" the "Theory of Action." *Educational Evaluation and Policy Analysis, 24*(2), 113–132.

Mann, H. (1849). *Twelfth annual report of the board of education, together with the twelfth annual report of the secretary of the board*. Boston, MA: Dutton and Wentworth, State Printers.

Mazzucato, M. (2015). *The entrepreneurial state: Debunking public vs. private sector myths*. New York: Perseus Books.

McDermott, K. A., & Nygreen, K. (2013). Educational new paternalism: Human capital, cultural capital, and the politics of equal opportunity. *Peabody Journal of Education, 88*(1), 84–97.

Mehta, J. (2013). *The allure of order: High hopes, dashed expectations, and the troubled quest to remake American schooling*. Oxford, UK: Oxford University Press.

Mickelson, R., Giersch, J., Stearns, E., & Moller, S. (2013). How (and Why) NCLB Failed to Close the Achievement Gap: Evidence from North Carolina, 1998–2004. *ECI Interdisciplinary Journal for Legal and Social Policy, 3*(1). http://ecipublications.org/ijlsp/vol3/iss1/1

Mills, C. (2017). *Black rights/white wrongs: The critique of racial liberalism*. New York, NY: Oxford University Press.

Milstein, M. (1990). Plateauing as an occupational phenomenon among teachers and administrators. *Journal of Personnel Evaluation in Education, 3*(4), 325–336.

Minow, M. (2002). *Partners, not rivals: Privatization and the public good*. Boston, MA: Beacon Press.

Muller, J. (2018). *The tyranny of metrics*. Princeton, NJ: Princeton University Press.

Murphy, J. F. (2016). *Professional standards for educational leaders: The empirical, moral, and experiential foundations*. Thousand Oaks, CA: Corwin Press.

Nichols, S. & Berliner, D. (2007). *Collateral damage: how high-stakes testing corrupts America's schools.* Cambridge, MA: Harvard University Press.

No Child Left Behind (NCLB) Act of 2001, 20 U.S.C.A. § 6301 *et seq.* (West 2003).

Noguera, P. A. (2015). Cities, schools, and social progress: The impact of school reform policies on low-income communities of color. In M. A. Pagano (Ed.), *The return of the neighborhood as an urban strategy* (pp. 107–132). Chicago: University of Illinois Press.

Payne, C. (1995/2007). *I've got the light of freedom: The organizing tradition and the Mississippi freedom struggle, with a new preface.* Berkeley: The University of California Press.

Payne, C. M. (2008). *So much reform, so little change: The persistence of failure in urban schools.* Cambridge, MA: Harvard Education Press.

Pedroni, T. (2007). *Market movements: African-American involvement in school voucher reform.* New York, NY: Routledge.

Piketty, T. (2014). *Capital in the twenty-first century.* Cambridge, MA: Belknap Press.

Pizmony-Levy, O., & Saraisky, N. G. (2016). *Who opts out and why? Results from a national survey on opting out of standardized tests.* New York, NY: Teachers College Press.

Putnam, R. D. (2015). *Our kids: The American dream in crisis.* New York, NY: Simon & Schuster.

Putnam, R. D., Frederick, C. B., & Snellman, K. (2012). *Growing class gaps in social connectedness among American youth.* Cambridge, MA: Harvard Kennedy School of Government. https://sites.hks.harvard.edu/saguaro/research/SaguaroReport_Diverging SocialConnectedness_20120808.pdf

Rallis, S. F., & Highsmith, M. C. (1986). The myth of the 'great principal': Questions of school management and instructional leadership. *The Phi Delta Kappan, 68*(4), 300–304.

Ravitch, D. (2010). *The death and life of the great American school system: How testing and choice are undermining education.* New York, NY: Basic Books.

Reardon, S. (2013). The widening income achievement gap. *Educational Leadership, 70*(8), 10–16.

Reardon, S., & Owens, A. (2014). 60 years after *Brown*: Trends and consequences of school segregation. *Annual Review of Sociology, 40,* 199–218.

Reeves, R. V. (2017). *Dream hoarders: How the American upper middle class is leaving everyone else in the dust, why that is a problem, and what do about it.* Washington, DC: Brookings Institute Press.

Scanlan, M., & Theoharis, G. (2015). Introduction: Intersectionality in educational leadership. In G. Theoharis & M. Scanlan (Eds.), *Leadership for increasingly diverse schools* (pp. 1–12). New York, NY: Routledge.

Scott, J. T. (2009). The politics of venture philanthropy in charter school policy and advocacy. *Educational Policy, 23*(1), 106–136.

Scott, J. (2012, Winter). Education movements, not market moments. *Dissent, 59*(1), 72–75.

Shipps, D., & White, M. (2009). A new politics of the principalship? Accountability-driven change in New York City. *Peabody Journal of Education, 84*(3), 350–373.

Shujaa, M. J. (1996). *Beyond desegregation: The politics of quality in African American schooling.* New York, NY: Sage Publications.

Siddle Walker, V. (1996). *Their highest potential: An African American school community in the segregated South.* Chapel Hill: University of North Carolina Press.

Smith, M., & Pandolfo, N. (2011, November 27). For-profit certification for teachers is booming. *New York Times.* 27th National Edition, p. A33A.

Spring, J. (2015). *American education* (17th ed.). New York, NY: Routledge.

Stanton-Salazar, R. D. (2011). A social capital framework for the study of institutional agents and their role in the empowerment of low-status students and youth. *Youth and Society, 43*(3), 1066–1109.

Stone, D. (2002). *Policy paradox: The art of political decision making.* New York, NY: W. W. Norton & Co.

Sullivan, W. (2004). *Work and integrity: The crisis and promise of professionalism in North America.* San Francisco: Jossey-Bass.

Sunderman, G. L., Coghlan, E., & Mintrop, R. (2017). *School closure as a strategy to remedy low performance.* Boulder, CO: National Education Policy Center. Retrieved from http://greatlakescenter.org/docs/Policy_Briefs/Sunderman-School-Closure.pdf

Theoharis, G. (2007). Social justice educational leaders and resistance: Toward a theory of social justice educational leadership. *Educational Administration Quarterly, 43*(2), 221–258.

Theoharis, G. (2009). *The school leaders our children deserve: Seven keys to equity, social justice, and reform.* New York, NY: Teachers College Press.

Thrush, G., & Haberman, M. (2017, August 15). Trump gives white supremacists an unequivocal boost. *New York Times.* https://www.nytimes.com/2017/08/15/us/politics/trump-charlottesville-white-nationalists.html

Tyack. D., & Cuban, L. (1995). *Tinkering Towards Utopia: A Century of Public School Reform.* Cambridge, MA: Harvard University Press.

Tillman, L. C., & Scheurich, J. J. (Eds.). (2013). *Handbook of research on educational leadership for equity and diversity.* New York, NY: Routledge.

Valenzuela, A. (1999). *Subtractive schooling: U.S.-Mexican youth and the politics of caring.* Albany, NY: SUNY Press.

Valenzuela, A. (Ed.). (2004). *Leaving children behind: How "Texas style" accountability fails Latino Youth.* Albany, NY: SUNY Press.

Walker, V. S. (2005). Organized resistance and Black educators' quest for school equality, 1878–1938. *Teachers College Record, 107*(3), 355–388.

Ward, S. (2011). The machinations of managerialism: New public management and the diminishing power of professionals. *Journal of Cultural Economy, 4*(2), 205–215.

Whitman, D. (2008). *Sweating the small stuff: Inner-city schools and the new paternalism.* Washington, DC: Thomas B. Fordham Institute.

Willie, C., Edwards, R., & Alves, M. (2002). *Student diversity, choice, and school improvement.* New York, NY: Praeger.

Wilson, C., & Horsford, S. D. (Eds.). (2013). *Advancing equity and achievement in America's diverse schools: Inclusive theories, policies, and practices* (pp. 9–24). New York, NY: Routledge.

Zeichner, K. (2010). Competition, economic rationalization, increased surveillance, and attacks on diversity: Neo-liberalism and the transformation of teacher education in the U.S. *Teaching and Teacher Education, 26*(8), 1544–1552.

CHAPTER 2

Critical Policy Analysis

Interrogating Process, Politics, and Power

For the last twenty years, critical scholars have worked to challenge and reshape what counts as education policy research (Anyon, 2005). Traditional policy analysis, while viewed to be an objective scientific process, has faced growing criticism. Its emphasis on a planned, linear, and incremental policy process of (1) issue or problem definition, (2) consultation and adoption, (3) implementation, and (4) monitoring and evaluation (Lasswell, 1936/1990) fails to account for unequal distributions of power, resources, and opportunity, and how they inform the extent to which policies work, for whom, and to what end. As part of this larger tradition, education policy research continues to reflect these taken-for-granted assumptions concerning rationality, positivism, and narrow conceptions of evidence that discount the ways in which process, politics, people, and power play important roles in how education policy is created, understood, and experienced.

In this chapter, we contrast traditional approaches to policy analysis with *critical policy analysis (CPA)*, the latter of which provides a realist perspective for analyzing policy in an era of widening inequality and political divisions across lines of race, class, gender, geography, and citizenship. But before we discuss CPA, there are two areas of conceptual confusion that need to be clarified. One is the confusing terminology that gets thrown around to describe what have become political "camps." This requires a discussion of liberalism as a political ideology and three branches of liberalism foundational to understanding contemporary U.S. education policy—*classical liberalism, neoliberalism,* and *social democracy.* The other is confusion or disagreements over the goals of schooling (both K-12 and postsecondary) in American society. These goals have drifted dangerously close to a view of schooling that is exclusively utilitarian.

We then present a guiding framework for CPA based on the following features: (1) *challenging traditional notions of power, politics, and governance*; (2) *examining policy as discourse and political spectacle*; (3) *centering the perspectives of the marginalized and oppressed*; (4) *interrogating the distribution of power and resources*; and (5) *holding those in power accountable for policy outcomes.* This chapter closes with a discussion of how these key features of CPA can be used to assess and perhaps recast current conceptions of schooling, education policy discourses, and school leadership practice and praxis in ways that reclaim and advance the democratic ideal in American education.

THE POWER OF IDEOLOGY: LIBERALISM, CAPITALISM, AND AMERICA'S SCHOOLS

A political ideology is "a certain set of ethical ideals, principles, doctrines, myths or symbols of a social movement, institution, class, or large group that explains how society should work, and offers some political and cultural blueprint for a certain social order." Its primary concern is the allocation of power and who benefits from how social goods are allocated. Since 1980, neoliberalism has been the prevailing ideology in American policy and politics, and the field of education has proven no exception. The expansion of school choice, privatization, venture philanthropy, education entrepreneurialism, and other market-based approaches to reform are just some examples of how neoliberal values and principles have permeated the landscape. A critical engagement and analysis of such policies requires an understanding of the political ideologies and assumptions that inform neoliberal education policy and reform.

Liberalism and U.S. Education Policy

> Liberalism is globally triumphant . . . whether in right- or left-wing versions, the dominant outlook of the modern age.
>
> (Mills, 2017, p. 28)

A political ideology emerging from Europe during the 17th and 18th centuries, liberalism is "predicated on the equal rights of morally equal individuals" (p. 5) and reflects a range of perspectives including everything from social democratic conceptions of liberalism to free market or "neoliberal" notions, which have gained significant traction over the last twenty years in the education policy arena. Political theorists such as John Locke, David Hume, Immanuel Kant, Adam Smith, and John Stuart Mill reflect the leading thinkers of liberal ideology, and their writings, perspectives, and epistemologies are visible in contemporary education policy—at least to the eye of the critical policy analyst or observer. Informed largely by "ideal theory" (Mills, 2017, p. 75; Rawls, 1971), liberalism focuses on concepts such as justice, equity, liberty, and freedom in ways that idealized society and its institutions, and was largely silent on issues of oppression and exclusion from these ideals.

One could argue that holding an ideal theory of society gives us something to work toward. Yet this ideal theory of liberalism has largely failed to acknowledge how different such idealized assumptions are from the everyday lived experiences of humans, their capacities, interaction, institutions, and society (Mills,

2017, p. 77). Although predicated on the equal rights of equal individuals, the liberalism on which American was founded has fallen far short of its espoused ideals and remains silent on questions of racism, sexism, discrimination, disenfranchisement, and oppression. As noted in the previous chapter, in education, agree that public schools should be "the great equalizer," those with more economic, social, and cultural capital manipulate our system of education for their own children's benefit. As political philosopher Charles Mills (2017) explained,

> The promise of liberalism was famously the granting of equal rights to all individuals, destroying the old social hierarchies and establishing a new social order where everybody, as an individual, could flourish, free of "estate" membership. But the reality turned out to be the preservation, albeit on a new theoretical foundation, of old hierarchies of gender and the establishment of new hierarchies of race. Thus, the struggle to realize the liberal ideal for everybody and not just a privileged minority still continues today, centuries later. If this struggle is ever to be successful, a prerequisite must be the acknowledgement of the extent to which dominant varieties of liberalism have developed so as to be complicit with rather than in opposition to social oppression.
>
> (p. xxi)

Thus, a mere critique of liberalism without an understanding of how they have been fed and sustained at the cultural level by racism, patriarchy, and classism is insufficient. Nor will we get very far with analyses of racism, patriarchy, and classism without a critique of its historical entanglements with the political economy of liberalism and neoliberalism. What is needed then is not an ideal theory of liberalism but rather a "non-ideal theory" that recognizes how capitalism intersects with patriarchy, White supremacy, and classism (Mills, 2017). In the following sections, we highlight three branches of liberalism: (a) classical liberalism, (b) neoliberalism, and (c) social democracy (liberalism/progressivism with social justice goals).

Classical Liberalism

While a full description of classical liberalism would fill the entire book, we will focus on two of its most important elements: individual liberty and economic liberty. Liberalism emerged as a reaction against monarchies and state religions that diminished the freedom of individuals. Notions of freedom of speech, freedom of the press, separation of church and state, and free markets were considered revolutionary ideas. In the late 18th century, American and French revolutions appropriated many liberal ideas as they formed republics. John Locke, credited as one of its founders, argued that men (but not necessarily women) had a natural right to life, liberty, and property.

These terms have been contested over time, with *libertarians* arguing for a narrower interpretation in terms of the role of the state, which they believe should be limited to police and military or the protection of life and property. Other liberals have viewed the role of state more broadly in ensuring greater equity and social welfare. The notion of economic liberty has been a mainstay of Liberalism, with Adam Smith viewing laissez-faire capitalism and markets as more moral than the corrupt systems they were replacing in the 18th century. Free-market ideas would reemerge in the 20th century, promoted by economists like Friedrich Hayak, Milton Freidman, and James Buchanan. This more extreme form of economic liberalism, which has taken hold as a key feature of education reform and policy, is referred to generally as *neoliberalism*, although neoliberals can be progressive on social and cultural issues.

From Social Democracy to Neoliberalism

Classical liberalism emphasized political freedom and individual rights (individual liberalism) and supported capitalist relations of production, private property, and unregulated markets (economic liberalism). But by the 1920s, unregulated capitalism had generated massive inequalities that resulted in the stock market crash of 1929 and a deep depression into the 1930s. A powerful labor movement pressured the Roosevelt administration to embrace what Polanyi (1944) and later Harvey (2005) called *embedded liberalism*. Others use terms like *social democracy* or in the case of Bernie Sanders, *democratic socialism,* that is, free trade and markets would be embedded in regulations determined by national governments. It also meant that the individual, who in the 1930s was unprotected from chronic unemployment, disability, support in old age, etc., would be embedded in a welfare state that would provide social supports. This Keynesian, mixed economy, economic theory and the notion of embedded liberalism was dominant well into the 1970s.

This terminology can be confusing since in the U.S. context, "liberals" were often viewed more colloquially as slightly left of center on the political spectrum, generally contrasted with conservatives. To the extent that they were embedded liberals, they were liberals who supported welfare state policies. They also tended to have progressive views on social policies regarding race, class, gender, and sexual orientation. This tended to describe the Democratic Party during the post-WWII years, but a split within the party in the 1980s further complicated the terminology. Within the U.S., "neoliberal" was first used in the mid-1980s to refer to a group of Democrats—including Bill Clinton—who helped to establish the Democratic Leadership Council, an organization within the Democratic Party that promoted free-trade policies (Rothenberg, 1984). They formed a think tank called the Progressive Policy Institute (PPI) that continues to promote their free-trade or "neoliberal" policies.

The reason they were referred to as neoliberals was that they wanted to disembed liberalism and return it to less regulated trade and markets. These Democrat neoliberals produced policies such as the North American Free Trade Act (NAFTA) and the repeal of the Banking Act of 1933 or the Glass-Steagall Act, which separated commercial and investment banking. Some have argued that the repeal of Glass-Steagall led ultimately to the 2008 bailout of the banks and the ensuing recession (Stiglitz, 2010). Both of these disembedding policies were accomplished during the Clinton administration. Although initiated by Ronald Reagan, neoliberal policies were generally supported by both Republican Bush administrations (father and son), the Democratic Clinton and Obama administrations, and the Trump administration.

However, while both Clinton and Obama followed a neoliberal ideology on economics (economic liberalism), they retained classical liberal notions of individual rights (individual liberalism), particularly regarding gender; race; and, eventually, sexual orientation. On economic issues, they were neoliberal, while on social and cultural issues, they were progressive. Today, there appears to be a realignment of both political parties that is still not well understood. Both parties were massively rejected in the 2016 election that brought Donald Trump to power with similar realignments occurring in England, France, and other countries. Until relatively recently, "neoliberalism" was more likely to be pronounced "neoliberalismo" since it referred to polices of *structural adjustment* that were demanded by international organizations like the World Bank and the International Monetary Fund in exchange for loans to developing nations. Structural adjustment was a euphemism for the creation of free markets and the privatization of national industries (Grugel & Riggirozzi, 2007).

While neoliberalism in its more global sense refers to the free-market economic models developed by Milton Freidman, Gary Becker, and other economists at the University of Chicago, its pervasiveness has extended to the political and cultural domains of society. In the political domain, new policy actors and networks and new forms of non-State governance have promoted neoliberal ideals that have changed the political landscape of the U.S. and the entire globe. At the cultural level, neoliberalism has changed how we teach, lead, and live our lives. In Chapter 7, we will describe in more detail how neoliberalism and the transfer of market and business principles into the public sector have changed what it means to be a professional.

Is Neoliberalism the Same as Capitalism?

For some, a critique of global neoliberalism is equivalent to a critique of capitalism. Such critics argue that neoliberalism is merely a later stage of capitalism and these critics use terms like "late capitalism" (a more predatory and culturally pervasive form) or "fast capitalism" (digitally enabled global capitalism). Marxist theorist, David Harvey, has argued that neoliberalism is grounded in class struggle, and that it represents a major global victory for the capitalist class (Harvey, 2005). Mark Fisher (2009) referred to "capitalist realism" in the sense that capitalism has become our reality, our common sense, and we can imagine nothing else. Fukuyama (1992) trumpeted the "end of history" after the fall of the Berlin Wall in 1989. Post-Communist Capitalism no longer had any competition for our hearts and minds. It was the new normal.

In 1848, Marx and Engels (1848), in *The Manifesto of the Communist Party*, observed a similar process of normalization during the earliest stage of Capitalism, as it replaced feudalism:

> Capital has drowned the most heavenly ecstasies of religious fervor, of chivalrous enthusiasm, of philistine sentimentalism, in the icy water of egotistical calculation. It has resolved personal worth into exchange value, and in place of the numberless indefeasible chartered freedoms, has set up that single, unconscionable freedom—Free Trade. In one word, for exploitation, veiled by religious and political illusions, it has substituted naked, shameless, direct, brutal exploitation.
>
> (pp. 15–16)

While under feudalism, "religious and political illusions" had previously "veiled" exploitation, today, some argue that exploitation—of both people and the planet—is veiled by the notion that there is no alternative to capitalism, even as its obsession with 3% annual growth threatens humans with extinction (Klein, 2015).

From 1917 to 1989, Communism, for a time, was viewed by some as an alternative to capitalism, though it is unlikely that Marx and Engels would have approved of what was done in their names. But by 1987, Margaret Thatcher famously said, "there is no such thing as society. There are individual men and women, and there are families." She was also known for saying that despite Capitalism's problems, "there is no alternative." This mantra became common sense, and was known as the TINA principle. Life after the end of history was life under unbridled and unopposed capitalism. You could either celebrate it or be resigned to it, but there was no room for dream and utopia.

Most Americans, however, were not anti-capitalist but preferred notions of good and bad capitalism. Neoliberals see good capitalism as unregulated markets in which the state has a marginal role (Baumol, Litan, & Schramm, 2007) and progressives or social democrats saw good capitalism as being embedded in a regulatory State and redistributive social policies (Stiglitz, 2010). Neoliberals believe unregulated capitalism was so successful in the private sector that it should be transferred to the public sector. They see the public sector, not as a collective public sphere promoting a common good but rather as a potential profit center and a market monopoly to be broken up. The notion that public schools are a "monopoly" only makes sense if one views the public sector as a marketplace.

The country with perhaps the longest history with neoliberalism is Chile. Neoliberal policies were imposed throughout the economy under the Pinochet dictatorship that was in power from 1973 to 1990. As a result of privatization under Pinochet, most public services, including social security, are privatized. A mere 37% of Chile's schools are public and serve the poorest families. And yet Chile has experienced the largest education-centered student movement in the world (Bellei, Cabalin, & Orellana, 2014). Even under extreme forms of neoliberalism, school leaders find ways to create humanizing forms of education. See Box 2.1 for an account of Tamara Contreras and the democratic public school she has fostered there.

BOX 2.1 TAMARA CONTRERAS, PRINCIPAL, LICEO CONFEDERACION SUIZA (SWISS CONFEDERATION HIGH SCHOOL), SANTIAGO, CHILE

Chile's education system is one of the most highly stratified in the world. The country became a laboratory for Milton Freidman's neoliberal policies during the Pinochet dictatorship (1973–1990) and these policies were written into the constitution, making them impossible to change without a constitutional convention. In Chile, about 8% of students attend elite, independent private schools. Another 55% attend private government-subsidized schools. These are somewhat like U.S. charter schools, except that they can charge tuition, though some do not. Only 37% of students attend public schools. Swiss confederation high school is a public school, although it is located in a working-class community with a large immigrant population as opposed to an area of extreme poverty (called "poblaciones" in Chile). The school receives those students who live nearby or whose parents cannot afford a private subsidized school. As in the U.S., principals are under tremendous pressure to raise scores on standardized tests, mainly the Sistema de Medición de la Calidad de la Educación (Education Quality Measurement System, SIMCE). Public schools are mandated to extend the academic day to 5:00 pm in hopes of raising test scores.

Tamara Contreras brings a radically participatory stance to her school. Schools are mandated to hold four school decision-making council meetings a year. These councils are supposed to include parents but are typically window dressing or controlled by the principal, as has traditionally occurred in many schools in the U.S. (Malen, 1994). Tamara not only holds these formal meetings ten times a year, but they are well attended and promote authentic and often tense dialogues about school priorities. In addition, she holds informal "assemblies" with students and teachers as a way to model democratic decision-making about everyday issues in the school.

One result of this participatory process was a collective decision by students and teachers to refuse to administer the SIMCE exam, which they have not administered for five years. Out from under the testing pressures, students, teachers, and parents decided to use the extended school day time for after-school programs that students were involved in selecting and organizing. These programs address the more affective, artistic, physical, activist, and creative sides of the students, and are an additional motivation for students to attend school.

After widespread consultation, they created a rich array of after-school programs on issues of interest to students and teachers. Their after-school programs fall into three categories: critical thinking/consciousness, health and sports, and the arts. So, the after-school curriculum includes rap/hip-hop (technique and composition); blues and jazz; debate; Mapuzungun language and culture; street art; community radio; yoga; martial arts; popular and self-education; critical theater; social movements; batucada; and more traditional classes, like basketball, dance, chess, and some precollege academic classes. The school's walls are covered with murals the students from the street art class have painted, many with political themes.

Tamara is constantly calculating how far she can push on the district policies. When one of us visited her school in Santiago, she confided that she wasn't sure how long her superiors would support her. Tamara is able to lead a school that teaches grassroots participation and critical consciousness, because she has built alliances with her students' parents and the larger community who defend her and their school. Here is a video (in Spanish) of Tamara and Liceo Confederacion Suiza: https://www.youtube.com/watch?v=uFm3Q_3eibM.

One result of the triumph of neoliberalism since the 1980s is that the goals of public schooling, which historically have changed as dominant ideologies have shifted, are now almost exclusively economic. In the following section, we will discuss how the goals of public schooling have shifted over time and how economic goals have crowded out the others.

NEOLIBERALISM, THE EDUCATION "CRISIS," AND THE GOALS OF SCHOOLING

The goals of our educational system have ranged from providing literacy for reading the Bible to "save our souls," to the formation of human capital to enhance our competitiveness in a global economy. Along the way, it has served, among other goals, to "Americanize" immigrants, provide homemaking and vocational skills, transmit a common set of values, and socialize the young into our democratic political system. Two decades ago, Labaree (1997) documented the shift in how Americans viewed the goals of schooling, as reflected in Table 2.1, from both an economic and humanistic perspective and with a focus on the individual and the social. These competing goals are important to understanding how neoliberalism has positioned itself effectively to address the "crisis" of American education—a narrative developed successfully from the mid-1980s to the present—kept alive until, as Friedman (1962) explained, "the politically impossible becomes politically inevitable" (p. ix).

Table 2.1 Goals of Schooling

	Economic	*Humanistic*
Individual	Individual self-interest	Personal fulfillment and enhancement
Social	Social efficiency	Democratic citizenship

Economic Goals of Schooling: Social Efficiency and Individual Self-Interest

The currently dominant goal of *social efficiency* and its link to human capital has been a rallying cry for school reform since the Soviet Union put Sputnik, the first satellite, into space. The link between schooling and the economy, again, came to the fore when the U.S. economy was perceived as falling behind that of Japan and Germany in the late 1970s (National Commission on Excellence in Education, 1983). A 2007 report of the Commission on the Skills of the American Workforce, *Tough Choices or Tough Times,* makes a similar argument, replacing competition from Japan and Germany with competition from India and China. Human capital theory and school-to-work programs continue to link schooling and economic growth, as well as argue that the "new" economy will produce a need for more highly skilled workers. What is becoming increasingly clearer is that the promise of an increase in demand for highly skilled workers in an information-age society has not material-ized, largely because of automation and outsourcing. According to economist James K. Galbraith (1998),

> What the existing economy needs is a fairly small number of first-rate technical talents combined with a small super class of managers and financiers, on top of a vast substructure of nominally literate and politically apathetic working people.
>
> (pp. 34–35)

So, while social efficiency goals may not increase national productivity, nor lead to better jobs, they have served as a way to make schools a scapegoat for national ills as well as a way for educators to argue for greater investment in education. In other words, regardless of who appropriates the human capital discourse, it has largely been used as a legitimating ritual for either supporting education fund-ing or scapegoating schools when the economy performs poorly. While human capital theory has been a useful tool for both liberals and conservatives, some have suggested replacing it with a discourse of human rights, which empha-sizes humans as ends in themselves rather than means to greater productivity (Hantzopoulos, 2016).

The individual version of the social efficiency goal of schooling is what Labaree called *individual self-interest,* which he argues has become the central motivating force of Americans. But individual self-interest cannot serve as a national ideal to inspire young people and, while it was always a force in American society, it was often tempered by larger ideals of democracy and equity. In a world in which students in elementary school are already building resumes for college, education has, according to Pope (2001), become "doing school, where they learn a hidden curriculum that includes manipulating the system, lying, sucking up, and doing whatever else it takes to keep a high grade-point average." (p. 4). As these students take their places as leaders, whether in the private or public sectors, they will find little incentive to change their behaviors.

Some socialist theorists see a more sinister set of goals that explain the vast restructuring of U.S. education advanced during the last three decades. These largely unstated goals, they argue, have been part of the Bush administration's *No Child Left Behind Act*, the Obama administration's Race to the Top, and proposals by the Trump Administration. Socialist scholar, John Bellamy Foster (2016), argues that dominant policy networks work for the vested interests of capital and seek to: (1) form a labor force of cheerful robots; (2) eliminate critical thinking from schools; (3) generate immense profits for the education industry and information firms; (4) end teacher tenure, seize control of classrooms from professional educators, and break teachers' unions; (5) privatize public education through charter schools and other means; (6) facilitate private profits and financial speculation through control of government education funding; (7) merge education for large sections of the poor and racial minorities with the military and penal systems; (8) decrease the role of democracy in education while increasing the corporate role; (9) create databases with detailed biometrics on almost everyone, to be exploited by corporations; and (10) manage the population in what is a potentially fractious society divided by race and class (para 2). While scholars may disagree on what motivates recent neoliberal shifts in the goals of schooling, the ripple effect of this shift is a pulling back from policies that benefit the common good, and toward policies that allow the middle and upper classes to cash in their relative advantage in economic, social, and cultural capital.

Humanistic Goals of Schooling: Personal Fulfillment and Democratic Citizenship

As a neoliberal economic model has become more dominant, humanistic goals for schools have receded in importance as neoliberalism has reduced the goals of public schooling to economic ones. For the individual, this means economic upward social mobility, and for the U.S., it means producing human capital that will make us more competitive in the global economy. There is very little evidence that K-12 schooling does either of those things (Levin, 1998). In fact, some have argued that schools serve to reproduce social class, gendered and racial hierarchies (Bourdieu & Passeron, 1990).

A notion of education for personal fulfillment and enhancement is currently viewed as elitist by many and appropriate only for affluent children. Education for *democratic citizenship*, or what we once called *civics*, has been diminished or replaced by the teaching of authoritarian forms of patriotism in many schools (Nguyen, 2016). In many cases, especially when the country is at war, teaching the skills of public debate on current issues is viewed as risky and controversial in many schools (Anderson, 2009; Westheimer, 2007). While one could argue that the humanistic goals of education were never dominant, the economic goals have undeniably become front and center in the wake of the ascendancy of neoliberalism with its emphasis on the individual as human capital and its promotion of a neoliberal State that has intensified competition among individuals.

The good news is that there is considerable pushback on schooling as focusing mainly on cognition and testing. Elsewhere, we have discussed the national "opt out of testing" movement led by parents and educators. There is also a growing awareness of a need for citizenship education, although the form it should take is still debated. Irish feminist scholar, Kathleen Lynch (2012), sums up the essential problem of limiting education to the economic and individual realms:

> Neoliberalism has deepened the disrespect for the relationally engaged, caring citizen that it has inherited from classical liberalism by devaluing not only the emotional work that has to be done to care, but by validating consumption and possessive individualism as defining features of human identity. Competitive individualism is no longer seen as an amoral necessity, but rather as a desirable and necessary attribute for a constantly reinventing entrepreneur. Neoliberal thinking in education has succeeded in doing what classical liberalism did not do; it subordinates and trivializes those aspects of education that have no (measurable) market value.
>
> (p. 83)

A GUIDING FRAMEWORK FOR CRITICAL POLICY ANALYSIS (CPA)

Most policy analysts use a framework that includes several phases of the policy process beginning with the definition of a problem and ending with the implementation and evaluation of a policy. While critical policy analysts tend to emphasize the powerful actors who define problems and solutions, and who influence the policy process (Domhoff, 1999), they would acknowledge that there are at least three broad phases, including (1) problem definition, (2) policy process, and (3) policy implementation. The first phase of *issue or problem definition* addresses how the policy issue or problem is defined. A critical approach also asks what "counts" as a problem or issue and who is defining it (Bacchi, 1999). The next phase is the *policy process* itself. Political systems theory argues that problems may get organized as demands on the political system and enter the system either as a court case or a bill that is introduced into a state or national legislature. It then exits as a new policy or case law (Easton, 1965). Not all policies go through state or national legislatures but are proposed at the local level though city councils, school boards, school districts, or schools. Even classrooms have policies that may either be imposed by the teacher or negotiated with students. At this stage of the policy process, CPA would highlight how legislative processes are influenced by powerful interests, as our discussion of the American Legislative Exchange Council illustrates in the following chapter.

The last stage is *policy implementation*, in which the policy or law becomes practice and is eventually institutionalized and periodically evaluated. A classic study of policy implementation was Weatherly and Lipsky's (1977) study of the implementation of the 1974 special education law in the state of Massachusetts (which the following year became federal policy as the Education for All Handicapped Children Act, EHA). A major finding of this study was the insight that ultimately practitioners are themselves policymakers to the extent that they decide at the street level which aspects of the policy they will implement. This led to theories of "mutual adaptation" which acknowledged that successful policies had to be adapted to the context of those implementing it (McLaughlin, 1976). Some analysts prefer the term "enactment" to implementation since it acknowledges the agency that teachers and leaders have in the policy process (Braun, Ball, Maguire, & Hoskins, 2011). However, as experimental research designs became the gold standard for education research, the notion of "fidelity" of implementation has become popular among neoliberal reformers.

As a research strategy and methodological approach, CPA interrogates processes, politics, and power. Unlike traditional policy analysis, which focuses on rationality, positivism, and narrow conceptions of "evidence," CPA is concerned with the subjectivity and complexity associated with all stages of the policy process, particularly the effect of its outcomes for disenfranchised people and communities (Diem, Young, Welton, Mansfield, & Lee, 2014). This is of particular concern when statistical studies of policy reduce complex social categories, like race, class, and gender, into one-dimensional variables. CPA is still a developing method and form of analysis, but here, we extend the work of scholars who have examined the emergence of CPA as an analytical approach, highlighting five key features of CPA that we believe are integral to this work: (1) challenging traditional notions of power, politics, and governance; (2) examining policy as discourse and political spectacle; (3) centering the perspectives of the marginalized and oppressed; (4) interrogating the distribution of power and resources; and (5) holding those in power accountable for policy outcomes. In Chapter 9, we introduce a critical policy praxis that is based on these tenets with a focus on reflection and action.

Challenging Traditional Notions of Power, Politics, and Governance

Critical policy analysts have often critiqued the traditional policy process for being too linear, rational, and wedded to narrow conceptions of evidence. In the 1980s, Kingdon (1984) drew on constructivist theories of organized anarchy in organizational theory, providing a theory of *multiple policy streams*, in which policy came about when windows of opportunity converged with political agendas and policy entrepreneurs, who have grown in number and influence. Post-structural policy analysis presents an even less rational view of the policy process, describing policy as a process of bricolage. Ball (1998) argues that policy is

> a matter of borrowing and copying bits and pieces of ideas from elsewhere …. cannibalizing theories, research, trends, and fashions and not infrequently flailing around for anything at all that looks as though it might work. Most policies are ramshackle, compromise, hit and miss, affairs, that are reworked, tinkered with, nuanced and inflected through complex processes of influence, text production, dissemination and, ultimately, re-creation in contexts of practice.
>
> (p. 126)

In this view, policy is produced, resisted, and reshaped in many different sites other than legislatures as well as through the production of texts and what Ball (2008) calls "little p-policies," policies that are often not formally codified but nevertheless become institutional practices. Gilborn (2014) argues that these big-p and little-p policies are always infused, often in ways difficult to discern through a traditional policy lens, with racism, patriarchy, and classism (see also Anyon, 2014; Fraser, 2013; Moses, 2002; Scott & Holme, 2017 for how policy is infused with racism, classism, and patriarchy).

What these more constructivist theories argue is that policies are always in play and that they can be influenced at all levels by strategic actions and advocacy. And yet, while the policy process is not linear, rational, or deterministic, there are major concentrations of power, and there are new, well-funded policy networks that work strategically to achieve their ideological projects (Ball & Junemann, 2012; Domhoff, 1999). Kingdon's (1984) notion of networks of policy entrepreneurs pushing policy agendas helps us understand how many policy actors outside the formal policy system have come to amass great power. CPA expands our attention from the old iron triangle of interest groups, executive agencies, and congressional representatives (Sabatier, 1999) to a plethora of intermediary organizations, both nonprofit and for-profit, to include actors such as think tanks, media, advocacy organizations, edu-businesses, charter management organizations, and venture philanthropists. The influence of these policy actors and the political strategies they use are referred to as "new governance" which includes the ways that *managerialist* or business models have entered the public sector (Locke & Spender, 2011; Smyth, 1999). In other words, at the macro-level, CPA is as focused on *new governance* and new policy networks as it is on traditional government and interest group interactions.

These new macro forms of governance have promoted managerialist and market ideologies that have cascaded down to the organizational or microlevel. School and district micropolitics are about understanding how power operates at the informal organizational level, and how this less visible level of struggle influences organizational outcomes in important ways. In the past, the analysis of micropolitics tended to draw on traditional "pluralist" notions of politics and power as exercised in public arenas and typically involving a clash among individuals and interest groups (Dahl, 1961). Newer views of power and politics employ theories that stress the various ways people's interests are shaped ideologically. This means that organizational politics involves both conflict over resources and over how is-sues are cognitively framed.

Following Gramsci (Forgacs, 2000), many contemporary theorists argue that the exercise of power includes not just conflict and negotiation in political arenas but also the social construction of our very "interests" and "needs." Thus, many in-stances of discrimination and inequality in schools are not challenged because they are taken for granted or viewed as "just the way things are." Their existence comes to be viewed as common sense and thus beyond question. This break with previous behaviorist and pluralist notions of power has shifted attention to more unobtrusive and cognitive modes of social control (Anderson & Grinberg, 1998; Lukes, 1974).

These more cognitive notions of power have helped to explain the outcomes of conflict and political struggle (or the lack thereof) in a postindustrial, information age in which the manipulation of public opinion has become a fine art (Kahne & Bowyer, 2017; Lukes, 2005). Conflict management may involve helping people negotiate immediate conflicts of interest, but it also includes the management of meaning and the legitimacy of the organization—what is increasingly referred to as "impression management." This means that leaders are essentially mediators, who mediate among people, among institutions, and among ideas. They are entrusted with managing the legitimacy of the school and of the social arrangements sur-rounding the school, including, for instance, racial and socioeconomic segregation (Anderson, 2009; Meyer & Rowan, 1977).

This new view of power, discourse, and ideology means that the micropoli-tics of schools involves a wider set of tactics and strategies than those described by traditional micropolitical literature. Thompson (2008), for instance, discusses the continuum of resistance and compliance among principals, which includes tactics such as simulation (as in simulating consent while resisting), emulation (taking actions to meet expectations), accommodation (e.g. complying in order to buy free-dom from further surveillance), and creative forms of mediation (of structures and policies). As our very subjectivities become privatized and we become normalized by accountability regimes, resistance becomes increasingly difficult. Under such conditions, the ask of teachers and leaders is to exercise a critical reflexivity with their school communities, problematizing a policy culture that has become taken-for-granted (Foucault, 1980).

We can see how the micropolitics of market regimes in education intersects with race and class as urban principals negotiate the gentrification of their neigh-borhoods and schools. In the context of gentrification in urban neighborhoods, principals often become gatekeepers who are expected to mediate between the ex-pectations of gentry parents and the concerns of local parents. This marketized context of school choice introduces a new logic of action for principals who now must become more entrepreneurial in how they think about the composition of their student bodies. In a market regime that commodifies parents and students, principals often encounter pressure to recruit these middle-class parents and the resources they bring, sometimes at the expense of low-income families of color who are displaced (Cucchiara, 2013; Posey-Maddox, 2014).

Examining Policy as Discourse and Political Spectacle

As described in the previous section, the policy process begins with problem definition and policy framing, which is critical to policy formation, implementation, and outcomes. Powerful networks of think tanks and media have deftly promoted narratives that lay deep in the American psyche. The viability and popularity of neoliberal market reforms have been prepared discursively and through mechanisms and processes that Murry Edelman described in his 1988 book *Constructing the Political Spectacle*. We provide a summary of the elements of political spectacle in Box 2.2.

More recently, Naomi Klein (2007) has described how political spectacle often follows natural disasters or military regimes. But it was Milton Friedman (1962) who captured it best in his book *Capitalism and Freedom* when he said,

> There is enormous inertia—a tyranny of the status quo—in private and especially government arrangements. Only a crisis—actual or perceived—produces real change. When that crisis occurs, the actions that are taken depend on the ideas that are lying around. That, I believe, is our basic function: To develop alternatives to existing policies, to keep them alive and available until the politically impossible becomes politically inevitable.
>
> (p. ix)

For the last three decades, we have seen manufactured crises, such as the *A Nation at Risk* report, as well as natural disasters, such as Hurricane Katrina. In each case, these crises were used to promote the neoliberal ideas that have been lying around and the policies (school choice, charter schools, vouchers, "education savings accounts," high-stakes testing, school closures, etc.) that they reflect. These ideas, which Freidman clearly articulated, aim at privatizing the public sector through the use of vouchers.

Drawing on Whitfield's (2001) study of the privatization process in Britain, Ball (2007) describes three stages through which the creative destruction of the public sector is accomplished. While this is not a coordinated, linear process, it has the following internal logic. The public sector is *destabilized* through discourses of derision and constant ridicule to undermine its credibility. This is accompanied by *disinvestment* from and shifting resources within the public sector. Finally, a process of *commodification* "reworks forms of service, social relations and public processes into forms that are measurable and thus contractible or marketable" (Ball, 2007, p. 24). In this way, new markets are created that attract private providers creating whole new arenas of commercial activity for "social entrepreneurs."

It is within the context of broader material and discursive change that the educational institutional terrain is prepared for NPM "reforms." As public institutions like schools and universities become more financially strapped, they need to seek funding from the private sector, in many cases from new philanthropic organizations with privatizing agendas. These patterns are evident in an example Ball (2007) offers from a school principal:

> You can't run on your ordinary budget, everyone knows that, so you have to get involved in various initiatives and cater for that, the initiative's priorities, and bend your curriculum and your priorities in order to get hold of that bit of money.
>
> (p. 23)

This principal articulates organizational barriers that are informed by broader discursive shifts. Reformist solutions, such as public-private partnerships that help to breach boundaries between the public and private (Verger, 2012), emerge as preferable only within these broader discursive and institutional contexts of public disinvestment. These shifting discourses create new material demands upon schools, which have increasingly become stabilized as a new normal that organizational leaders must adapt to. This creates a synergistic relationship between discourse and practice in which discourses shape practices and practices produce and reinforce discourses. Some use terms like "discursive practices" or "discourse-practices" to refer to this process of social construction (Cherryholmes, 1988).

Once ideological positions are no longer seen as ideology but rather as common sense, then notions like the rich are the "makers" and the poor are the "takers" are difficult to challenge. These myths, which have become accepted as common sense, are often widely shared. Wilson (2009) provides data comparing attitudes among Europeans and Americans that indicate that Americans overwhelmingly explain the existence of poverty as an individual shortcoming, whereas Europeans "focus much more on structural and social inequalities at large, not on individual behavior, to explain the causes of poverty and joblessness" (Wilson, 2009, pp. 45–46). In other words, Americans tend to use a frame that blames the poor for their situation in spite of the history of race, gender, and class-based discrimination that is copiously documented.

Linguist George Lakoff (2004, 2008) has demonstrated that our brains use the logic of frames, prototypes, and metaphors to make sense of the world, not the logic of rational argument. He has critiqued the Democrats for ignoring the power of framing political issues. He points out that when Democrats debate Republicans, they tend to think that it is a test of intellectual superiority and a firmer grasp of the facts. Yet Republicans like Ronald Reagan, George W. Bush, and Donald Trump are brilliant framers. Their frames of keeping Americans safe, "family values," the wealthy as job producers, and welfare creating dependency, and many others, have wide appeal in the U.S. In fact, as Lakoff points out, continual repetition of frames and discourses creates physiological, neural links to the brain. Between the creation of a new common sense and the physiological reinforcement of being constantly bombarded by talk radio and Fox News talking points, it is no wonder that knee-jerk American myths are so widely believed.

Although there are many approaches to viewing policy as discourse, Bacchi (2000) explained, "The premise behind a policy-as-discourse approach is that it is inappropriate to see governments as responding to 'problems' that exist 'out there' in the community. Rather 'problems' are 'created' or 'given shape' in the very policy proposals that are offered as 'responses'" (p. 48). Weaver-Hightower (2008), who argues that policy is a complex and fragile ecology, suggested that policy influences are nearly everywhere. He has found that popular discourses and texts can result in *de facto* policy.

> Key elements of policy ecologies might escape notice if analysts do not explore these notions of de facto policies and policies as texts and discourses. Documents that act in the capacity of policy create or uphold particular discourses or become de facto policy in the absence of mandates. Such quasi-policies are pivotal to the workings of many policy ecologies.
>
> (p. 158)

The importance of such texts as commissioned reports, such as *A Nation at Risk* (National Commission on Excellence in Education, 1983), and popular self-help and management theory books, such as *Good to Great* (Collins, 2001) are examples of de facto policy texts.

Examining policy as discourse also refers to the ways policies are constructed linguistically (Fairclough, 2013). Language and discourse do more than reflect reality: they also construct reality (Gee, 1999), and they form part of a larger arena in which power struggles over meaning take place. For instance, the language of business and economics creeps into education discourses with inadequate thought or critique (Mautner, 2010). As school principals and superintendents work to "leverage" change and "scale up" practices, some do so with little attention to the unexamined assumptions these engineering terms bring to learning organizations. An analysis of policy as discourse can deepen our understanding of the everyday social events that occur in schools and are influenced by the subtle ideologies embedded in language (Henze & Arriaza, 2006; Taylor, 1997). In fact, educational leaders are critical to this process given their location within the organizational hierarchy and the fact that they occupy pivotal discursive spaces through which policies and practices flow (Anderson, 2009).

BOX 2.2 UNDERSTANDING EDUCATION POLICY AS POLITICAL SPECTACLE

In *Constructing the Political Spectacle,* Edelman (1988) discusses the elements that make up the spectacle, which has proliferated with reality TV, social media, and think tanks. Edelman argues that an understanding of the following elements is crucial for an analysis of current social policy formation:

1. **The importance of language and discourse.** Perhaps more than any other political scientist, Edelman (1978) focused on the relationship

between language and politics and what he called "the linguistic structuring of social problems" (p. 26). He provides a methodology for studying policy based on the notion that "how the problem is named involves alternative scenarios, each with its own facts, value judgments, and emotions." (p. 29)

2. **The definition of events as crises.** "A crisis, like all new developments, is a creation of the language used to depict it; the appearance of a crisis is a political act, not a recognition of a fact or a rare situation." (p. 31) Berliner and Biddle (1995) describe how a "manufactured crisis" was needed to jump-start our current school reform policies that date back at least to *The Nation at Risk* report in 1983. Hurricane Katrina was a real crisis that was used to charterize and privatize the New Orleans school system (Saltman, 2007).

3. **A tendency to cover political interests with a discourse of rational policy analysis.** A crisis is often created through an appeal to scientific, rational, and neutral discourses. For example, political advantage on the Right has been gained not only through political rhetoric but also through privately funded, ideologically driven "think tanks" that sponsor and disseminate so-called "objective" research.

4. **The linguistic evocation of enemies and the displacement of targets.** Those with the power to manage meaning can cast tenured radicals, the welfare state, social promotion, progressive teaching methods, and teacher unions as the villains of educational reform. All displace attention from other possible actors and events. Perhaps the most notable displacement of a target is laying the blame on the education sector for poor economic performance instead of on the State and the corporate sector, which are largely unaccountable.

5. **The public as political spectators.** Democratic participation is limited to such reactive rituals as voting, being polled, or choosing schools in a marketplace. Meanwhile the skills of political democratic participation atrophy from misuse.

6. **The media as mediator of the political spectacle.** Edelman gave news reporting and other forms of media a central place in the construction of the political spectacle. Fake news and a constant repetition of disinformation through talk radio and Fox News, and a lack of in-depth analysis in mainstream media (CNN, MSNBC, etc.) seek to keep corporate sponsors happy and increase TV ratings. Social media is similarly balkanized and generally lacks in-depth analysis.

Centering the Perspectives of the Marginalized and Oppressed

Critical policy analysts study the taken-for-granted assumptions associated with dominant political ideologies and how they affect those at the margins. Unlike traditional policy analysis, CPA seeks to emphasize the voices, experiences, and desires of marginalized people in the policy process as it finds inherent value in what are often underrepresented or ignored worldviews. The standpoint, voice, and perspective of those most directly impacted by policy are of particular interest and value in CPA. As Ladson-Billings and Tate (1995) explained in their pioneering work on critical race theory (CRT) in education, "Without authentic voices of people of color (as teachers, parents, administrators, students, and community members) it is doubtful that we can say or know anything useful about education in their communities" (p. 58).

CRT began as a friendly critique of Critical Legal Studies scholars who were trying to bring attention to how the poor were unable to get justice within the criminal justice system. CRT scholars argued that the system didn't just discriminate based on income levels but rather had a strong racial bias. This early critique of the legal system has culminated in the recognition by many of a "new Jim Crow" in our criminal justice system (Alexander, 2010; Davis, 1981). CPA shares CRT's tenets in terms of the value it places on the voices of the racially minoritized through *counterstorytelling*. It makes sense that unless there is a methodological focus on narrative, these voices will not be heard. There are many other tenets of CRT but not space to discuss them in detail. For instance, by centering race in its analysis, CRT has moved beyond legal studies to emphasize the notions that Whiteness can be viewed as a form of property and that the only time the interests of people of color are achieved is when they coincide with those of the dominant group, and the observation that race (and racism) has become a permanent fixture in American life (Crenshaw, 1988; Guinier, 2004; Guinier & Torres, 2002; Horsford, 2010, 2011; López, 2003; Parker & Villalpondo, 2007). In a sense, CRT examined how race operated within American systems and institutions in ways that ensured the unequal distribution of resources based on a political and social construction of race designed to maintain a system of racial caste limiting upward mobility and undermining equal opportunity for all (Horsford, 2016).

Bensimon and Marshall (1997) also highlighted the need for policy analysts to "reveal the gender biases (as well as racial, sexual, and social class biases) inherent in commonly accepted theories, constructs, methodologies, and concepts" (p. 6). Indeed, this work was introduced largely based on the struggle of Black women, grounded in a Black feminist thought distinct from feminisms that largely ignored or undermined the experiences of women of color (Davis, 1981; hooks, 1984). While policy analysts in education seem to understand the importance of race, gender, class, sexual orientation, and disability, they have struggled with understanding and describing how these all intersect. As such, the idea of intersectionality is crucial in order to understand conceptually how various forms of oppression are linked in complex and interlocking ways (Collins & Bilge, 2016; Crenshaw, 1995;

Davis, 1981). Collins and Bilge (2016) argue that there is a wide gap between academic conversations about intersectionality and the struggles experienced by those who are building political coalitions to challenge multiple injustices. In the same vein, some have called for a critical race praxis that moves beyond theory to include action in ways that produce social change (Yamamoto, 1997). In *Decolonizing Methodologies: Research and Indigenous Peoples* (2012), Linda Tuhiwai Smith brings into stark relief the embedded nature of imperialism and colonialism in the creation and legitimization of knowledge and research.

Interrogating the Distribution of Power and Resources

Who Gets What, When, How? was the title of Lasswell's (1936) classic political science text—the fundamental question policy analysts have and continue to pursue. CPA pushes further on those questions, asking: *Who benefits from this policy or practice? Who is hurt by this policy or practice? Whose knowledge informs this policy? How are social inequalities not only classed but also raced and gendered?* Eisenstein (2014) argued that capital is intersectional in that it intersects with the raced and gendered bodies that produce labor. Collins and Bilge (2016) argued that "positing that contemporary configurations of global capital that fuel and sustain growing social inequalities are about class exploitation, racism, sexism, and other systems of power fosters a rethinking of the categories used to understand economic inequality" (p. 16). Questions of how power and resources are distributed must be understood in terms of how political actors at global, national, and local levels are linked. This involves attention to many of the new neoliberal policy networks discussed earlier but also a deep historical understanding of how power has become institutionalized particularly around class, race, and gender.

In education, CPA insists on continuing to expose those areas in which power and resources benefit the privileged. For instance, even in the more equitable era of the American welfare state policies, racial segregation was also created and sustained by State policies (Rothstein, 2017), and privileged groups long ago made their suburban enclaves legally or informally off-limits to the poor or people of color. In 1974, the U.S. Supreme Court's *Milliken v. Bradley* decision determined that "parent and school choice" ended where the suburbs began (Green & Gooden, 2016), reproducing a "social justice for the advantaged" (Horsford, 2016) that undermines the struggle for educational equality and opportunity for those with fewer and more limited economic resources and social capital.

Holding Those in Power Accountable for Policy Outcomes

In their 1990 book *Politics, Markets, and America's Schools*, Chubb and Moe argued that the problem with U.S. education was a direct result of democratic institutions and put forth a market-based approach to education reform based on the importance of "holding schools accountable" for their performance, making the case for school choice and competition in ways that would improve student achievement and school performance.

Ironically, however, such neoliberal approaches to school reform, which focused on "holding schools accountable," altogether ignored public accountability, which is central to democratic governance. In fact, public accountability, is defined as

> The obligations of agencies and public enterprises who have been trusted with public resources, to be answerable to the fiscal and the social responsibilities that have been assigned to them. These companies and agencies need to be accountable to the public at large and carry out the duties asked of them responsibly.
> (Black's Law Dictionary, 2017)

Thomas Rogers, former president of the New York State Council of School Superintendents, uses the notion of *reciprocal accountability*. He argues that each level (federal, state, district, school, etc.) should be held accountable for things it can influence. So, for instance, the federal government should be accountable for such things as percent of gross domestic product (GDP) spent on education, spending on research and development, percent of children in poverty, percent without health insurance, percent with poor nutrition, etc. Furthermore, he suggests comparing these percentages with OECD countries that have far better outcomes in these areas than the U.S, and we might add, also have more robust Welfare States. Rogers suggested holding each level accountable through report cards similar to those that many districts are currently using, except that these report cards would contain federal, state, district, and school-level data. So, for instance, under the section of the report card for the federal level, he provides a table that shows the percent of U.S. children in poverty, which is far above that of all European countries and only six percentage points above that of Mexico. These report cards would help to legitimate a concern among school leaders for demanding greater accountability at levels over their heads.

Given the 2017 tax bill that lowered the statutory tax rate on corporations from 35% to 21% on the questionable assumption that they will use the savings to create more jobs, we would add another category to Rogers's report card: Corporate Accountability, or to what extent corporations engage in productive, rather than speculative activities and take seriously their civic responsibility toward their local communities and their collective responsibility to provide jobs that pay a living wage and benefits. Or perhaps those corporations that create jobs get the tax break, but those who don't pay more. But this would be far too rational an analysis. A CPA approach would point out that it was the corporate donors who gave our elected officials an ultimatum to pass the bill or else they would withdraw their dark money (Mayer, 2016a, 2016b).

CONCLUSION

The loss of a sense of the common good has resulted in a growing dissociation between the well-being of one's own and other people's children. It may well be natural that parents should make the welfare of their own children their primary concern. All parents want the best for their children. What we are witnessing, however, is a shift in which parents aren't simply demanding that schools provide a quality education for their children. Instead, they are demanding that schools provide their children with more than what other children are getting (McGrath & Kurillof, 1999; Reeves, 2017). While upper-class parents have always been able to buy a superior education for their children, in an economically squeezed middle class, parents are left to fight each other and poor and working-class parents for privileges and opportunities for their children. Years ago, this was visible as privileged parents left urban centers for racially segregated suburbs with better housing and more amenities. Today, as their children move back, it is visible in gentrifying urban neighborhoods in which poor and working-class parents of color are being displaced from their communities and their schools by largely—but not entirely—White, middle-class newcomers (Cucchiara, 2013; Posey Maddox, 2014).

It also happens inside schools. While academic tracking may be in part due to a belief that students at the same level are best taught together, McGrath and Kurillof (1999) found that many middle-class parents are adamant that their children not be mixed in with other children, unless those children are at similar academic levels. Because academic level tends to correlate so closely with socioeconomic level and race, it is often hard to sort out the real concerns. Regardless of whether middle-class parents are classist, racist, or simply want their child to be competitive in the job market, the result is a society segregated by class and race, even when kids spend the day in the same school. A society, in which individual self-interest becomes a dominant goal, cannot also claim to support goals of social equality.

This chapter has provided only a handful of the critical conceptual tools available for analyzing and challenging education and social policies that have made the U.S. the most unequal and segregated countries in the developed world. Traditional approaches to policy analysis have failed to dig deeply enough into the nuanced ways that social reproduction is maintained. The current obsession with quantification and econometrics has made the field of policy analysis narrower than ever. If done to expose inequalities, quantification can provide us with a broad map of policy problems. Researchers, such as those at the Civil Rights Project at University of California, Los Angeles (UCLA), under the direction of Patricia Gándara and Gary Orfield, have produced critical work of this type. But once we convert complex social categories like race or gender into variables, we have limited our chances for a nuanced analysis. Furthermore, quantitative studies of policy tend to be theoretically agnostic, thus failing to interrogate the assumptions underlying their hypotheses.

CPA requires an explicit standpoint toward social equality at the point of asking research questions or engaging in educational practice, whether as a teacher, counselor, principal, or superintendent. Without this standpoint and the critical reflexivity that must accompany it, it is too easy to be lulled into confusing a manufactured common sense with reality. Much like the way reality TV normalized Donald Trump for millions of Americans, the many myths perpetuated by ideologues in neoliberal think tanks and the corporate-owned media have normalized the isolated individual, separate from society, who makes good or bad choices in a vacuum. Returning "society" to this myth of the individual by re-embedding liberalism in social supports will not be easy, but it can not be done without a more critical approach to policy analysis.

END-OF-CHAPTER QUESTIONS

1. What are the key features of critical policy analysis and how do they differ from traditional policy analysis? What can either approach tell us about the state of American education and the goals of schooling in a pluralist democracy?
2. What is a political ideology and what are the prevailing ideologies reflected in U.S. education research, policy, and reform? How might you describe the relationship between political ideology, education policy, and leadership practice?
3. Consider the economic and humanistic goals of schooling described in this chapter. In what ways are your own beliefs and assumptions concerning the purpose and values of education reflected in these goals? Do you view them as competing or complementary? What other goals of schooling might you add to the two presented here?

REFERENCES

Alexander, M. (2010). *The New Jim Crow: Mass incarceration in the age of colorblindness*. New York, NY: The New Press.

Anderson, G. L. (2009). *Advocacy leadership: Toward a post-reform agenda in education*. New York, NY: Routledge.

Anderson, G. L., & Grinberg, J. (1998). Educational administration as a disciplinary practice: Appropriating Foucault's view of power, discourse, and method. *Educational Administration Quarterly, 34*, 329–353.

Anyon, J. (2005). What "counts" as education policy? Notes toward a new paradigm. *Harvard Educational Review, 75*(1), 65–88.

Anyon, J. (2014). *Radical possibilities: Public policy, urban education, and a new social movement*. New York, NY: Routledge.

Bacchi, C. (1999). *Women, policy and politics: The construction of policy problems*. London, UK: Sage.

Bacchi, C. (2000). Policy as discourse: What does it mean? Where does it get us? *Discourse: Studies in the Cultural Politics of Education, 21*(1), 45–57.

Ball, S. J. (1998). Big policies/small world: An introduction to international perspectives in education policy. *Comparative Education, 34*(2), 119–130.

Ball, S. J. (2007). *Education plc: Understanding private sector participation in public sector education*. London, UK: Routledge.

Ball, S. (2008). *The education debate*. Bristol, UK: The Policy Press.

Ball, S., & Junemann, C. (2012). *Networks, new governance and education*. Chicago, IL: Policy Press.

Baumol, W., Litan, R., & Schramm, C. (2007). *Good capitalism, bad capitalism, and the economics of growth and prosperity*. New Haven, CT: Yale University Press.

Bellei, Cabalin & Orellana, (2014).

Bensimon, E., & Marshall, K. (1997). Policy analysis for postsecondary education: Feminist and critical perspectives. In C. Marshall (Ed.), *Feminist critical policy analysis: A perspective from postsecondary education* (pp. 1–22). London: Falmer Press.

Berliner, D., & Biddle, B. (1995). *The manufactured crisis: Myths, fraud, and the attack on America's public schools.* Reading, MA: Addison-Wesley.

Black's Law Dictionary (2017). Retrieved from

Bourdieu, P., & Passeron, J. C. (1990). *Reproduction in education, society and culture.* Thousand Oaks, CA: Sage Publications.

Braun, A., Ball, S., Maguire, M., & Hoskins, K. (2011). Taking context seriously: Towards explaining policy enactments in the secondary school. *Discourse: Studies in the cultural politics of education, 32*(4), 585–596.

Cherryholmes, C. (1988). *Power and criticism: Poststructural investigations in education.* New York: Teachers College Press.

Chubb, J. E., & Moe, T. M. (1990). *Politics, markets, and America's schools.* Washington, DC: The Brookings Institution.

Collins, J. (2001). *Good to great: Why some companies make the leap and others don't.* New York, NY: Harper Business.

Collins, P. H., & Bilge, S. (2016). *Intersectionality.* Oxford, UK: Policy Press.

Commission on the Skills of the American Workforce. (2007). *Tough choices or tough times.* Washington, DC: National Center on Education and the Economy.

Crenshaw, K. (1988). Race, reform, and retrenchment: Transformation and legitimation in antidiscrimination law. *Harvard Law Review, 101,* 1331.

Crenshaw, K. W. (1995). Mapping the margins: Intersectionality, identity politics, and violence against women of color. In K. Crenshaw, N. Gotanda, G. Peller, & K. Thomas (Eds.), *Critical race theory: The key writings that formed the movement.* New York: The New Press.

Cucchiara, M. (2013). *Marketing schools, marketing cities: Who wins and who loses when schools become urban amenities.* Chicago, IL: University of Chicago Press.

Dahl, R. (1961). *Who governs?: Democracy and power in an American city.* New Haven, CT: Yale University Press.

Davis, A. Y. (1981). *Women, race, & class.* New York: First Vintage Books Edition.

Davis, G. F. (2011). *Managed by the markets: How finance reshaped America.* Oxford: Oxford University Press.

Diem, S., Young, M., Welton, A., Mansfield, K. C., & Lee, P. L. (2014). The intellectual landscape of critical policy analysis. *International Journal of Qualitative Studies in Education, 27*(9), 1068–1090.

Domhoff, G. W. (1999). *Who rules America 2000.* New York, NY: Simon & Schuster.

Easton, D. (1965). *A systems analysis of political life.* New York, NY Wiley.

Edelman, M. (1978). *Political language: Words that succeed and policies that fail.* New York: Academic Press.

Edelman, M. (1988). *Constructing the political spectacle.* Chicago, IL: University of Chicago Press.

Eisenstein, Z. (2014, May 26). An alert: capital is intersectional; radicalizing Piketty's inequality. *The Feminist Wire.*

Fairclough, (2013), Critical discourse analysis and critical policy studies, *Critical Policy Studies,* 7(2), 177–197.

Fisher, M. (2009). *Capitalist realism: Is there no alternative?* The Bothy, UK: Zero Books.

Forgacs, D. (Ed.) (2000). *The Antonio Gramsci reader.* New York: NYU Press.

Foster, J. B. (2016). The opt out revolt: Democracy and Education. *Monthly Review, 67*(10). Retrieved from https://monthlyreview.org/2016/03/01/the-opt-out-revolt/

Foucault, M. (1980). In C. Gordon (Ed.), *Power/knowledge: Selected interviews and other writings, 1972–1977*. New York, NY: Pantheon Books.

Fraser, N. (2013). *Fortunes of feminism: From state-managed capitalism to neoliberal crisis*. New York, NY: Verso.

Friedman, M. (1962). *Capitalism and Freedom*. Chicago, IL: University of Chicago Press.

Fukuyama, F. (1992). *The end of history and the last man*. New York, NY: Free Press.

Galbraith, J. K. (1998). *The affluent society*. Fortieth Anniversary Edition. Boston, MA: Houghton Mifflin Company.

Gee, J. P. (1999). *An introduction to discourse analysis*. New York, NY: Routledge.

Gilborn, D. (2014). Racism as policy: A critical race analysis of education reforms in the United States and England. *The Educational Forum, 78*(1), 26–41.

Green, T., & Gooden, M. (2016). The shaping of policy: Exploring the context, contradictions, and contours of privilege in "Milliken v. Bradley," over 40 years later. *Teacher College Record, 118*(3), 1–30.

Grugel, J., & Riggirozzi, M. P. (2007). The return of the state in Argentina. *International Affairs, 83*(1), 87–101.

Guinier, L. (2004). From racial liberalism to racial literacy: *Brown v. Board of Education* and the interest-divergence dilemma. *The Journal of American History, 91*(1), 92–118.

Guinier, L., & Torres, G. (2002). *The miner's canary: Enlisting race, resisting power, transforming democracy*. Cambridge: Harvard University Press.

Hantzopoulos, M. (2016). *Restoring dignity in public schools: Human rights education in action*. New York, NY: Teachers College Press.

Harvey, D. (2005). *A brief history of neoliberalism*. Oxford, UK: Oxford University Press.

Henze, R., & Arriaza, G. (2006), Language and reforming schools: A case for a critical approach to language in educational leadership, *International Journal of Leadership in Education, 9*(2), 157–177.

hooks, b. (1984). *Feminist theory: From margin to center*. Cambridge, MA: South End Press.

Horsford, S. D. (2010). Mixed feelings about mixed schools: Superintendents on the complex legacy of school desegregation. *Educational Administration Quarterly, 46*(3), 287–321.

Horsford, S. D. (2011). *Learning in a burning house: Educational inequality, ideology, and (dis)integration*. New York, NY: Teachers College Press.

Horsford, S. D. (2016). Social justice for the advantaged: Freedom from racial equality post-Milliken. *Teachers College Record, 118*(3), 1–18.

Kahne, J., & Bowyer, B. (2017). Educating for democracy in a partisan age: Confronting the challenges of motivated reasoning and misinformation. *American Educational Research Journal, 54*(1), 3–34.

Kingdon, J. W. (1984). *Agendas, alternatives, and public policies* (2nd ed.). New York, NY: Harper Collins.

Klein, N. (2007). *The shock doctrine: The rise of disaster capitalism*. New York, NY: Metropolitan Books.

Klein, N. (2015). *This changes everything: Capitalism vs. the climate*. New York, NY: Simon & Shuster.

Labaree, D. (1997). *How to succeed in school without really learning: The credentials race in American education*. London, UK and New Haven, CT: Yale University Press.

Ladson-Billings, G., & Tate, W. (1995). Toward a critical race theory of education, *Teachers College Record, 97*(1), 47–68.

Lakoff, G. (2004). *Don't think of an elephant: Know your values and frame the debate*. New York, NY: Chelsea Green Publications.

Lakoff, G. (2008). *The political mind*. New York, NY: Penguin Books.

Lasswell, H. (1936/1990). *Politics: Who gets what, when, how?* New York, NY: Peter Smith.

Levin, H. (1998). Educational performance standards and the economy. *Educational Researcher, 27*(4), 4–10.

Lock, R., & Spender, J. -C. (2011). *Confronting managerialism: How the business elite and their schools threw our lives out of balance.* New York, NY: Zed Books.

López, G. R. (2003). The (racially neutral) politics of education: A critical race theory perspective. *Educational Administration Quarterly, 39*(1), 68–94.

Lukes, S. (1974). *Power: A radical view.* London, UK: Macmillan Press.

Lukes, S. (2005). *Power: A radical view* (Rev. ed.). London, UK: Macmillan.

Lynch, K. (2012). On the market: Neoliberalism and new managerialism in Irish education. *Social Justice Series, 12*(5). Retrieved from http://hdl.handle.net/10197/4401

Malen, B. (1994). Enacting site-based management: A political utilities analysis. *Educational Evaluation and Policy Analysis, 16*(3), 249–267.

Marx, K., & Engels, F. (1848). *The manifesto of the Communist party.* Marx Engels Archive. Retrieved from https://www.marxists.org/archive/marx/works/download/pdf/Manifesto.pdf

Mautner, G. (2010), *Language and the market society: Critical reflections on discourse and dominance.* London, UK: Routledge.

Mayer, J. (2016a). *Dark money: The hidden history of the billionaires behind the rise of the radical right.* New York, NY: Anchor Books.

Mayer, J. (2016b). *Dark money: The hidden history of the billionaires behind the radical right.* New York, NY: Doubleday.

McGrath, D., & Kurillof, P. (1999). "They're Going to Tear the Doors Off this Place": Upper-middle-class parent school involvement and the educational opportunities of other people's children. *Educational Policy, 13*(5), 603–629.

McLaughlin, M. (1976). Implementation as mutual adaptation: Change in classroom organization. *Teachers College Record, 77*(3), 339–351.

Meyer, J. W., & Rowan, B. (1977). Institutionalized organizations: Formal structure as myth and ceremony. *American Journal of Sociology, 83*(2), 340–363.

Milliken v. Bradley, 418 U.S. 717 (1974).

Mills, C. (2017). *Black rights/white wrongs: The critique of racial liberalism.* New York, NY: Oxford University Press.

Moses, M. (2002). *Embracing race: Why we need race-conscious education policy.* New York, NY: Teachers College Press.

National Commission on Excellence in Education. (1983). *A Nation at risk: The imperative for educational reform.* Washington, DC: Government Publishing Office.

Nguyen (2016), A curriculum of fear: Homeland security in U.S. public schools. Minneapolis: University of Minnesota Press.

Parker, L. & Villalpondo, O. (2007). A race(cialized) perspective on education leadership: Critical race theory in educational administration. *Educational Administration Quarterly, 43*(5), 519–514.

Polanyi, K. (1944). *The great transformation.* New York, NY: Beacon Press.

Pope, D. C. (2001). *Doing school: How we are creating a generation of stressed out, materialistic, and miseducated students.* New Haven, CT: Yale University Press.

Posey-Maddox, L. (2014). *When middle-class parents choose urban schools: Class, race, and the challenge of equity in public education.* Chicago, IL: University of Chicago Press.

Rawls (1971). *A theory of justice.* Cambridge, MA: Harvard University Press.

Reeves, R. (2017). *Dream hoarders: How the American middle class is leaving everyone else in the dust, why that is a problem, and what to do about it.* Washington, DC: Brookings Institution Press.

Rothenberg, R. (1984). *The Neoliberals: Creating the new American politics.* New York, NY: Simon & Shuster.

Rothstein, R. (2017). *The color of law: A forgotten history of how our government segregated America.* New York, NY: Liveright Pub.

Sabatier, P. (Ed.) (1999). *Theories of the policy process.* Boulder, CO: Westview Press.

Saltman, K. (2007). Schooling in disaster capitalism: How the political right is using disaster to privatize public schooling, *Teacher Education Quarterly, 43*(1), 22–41.

Scott, J. T., & Holme J. J. (2017), The political economy of market-based educational policies: Race and reform in urban school districts, 1915 to 2016. Centennial Issue: *Review of Research in Education, 40,* 250–295.

Smith, L. T. (2012). *Decolonizing methodologies.* London: Zed Books.

Smyth, J. (1999). Schooling and enterprise culture: Pause for a critical policy analysis. *Journal of Education Policy, 14*(4), 435–444.

Stiglitz, J. (2010). *Freefall: America, free markets, and the sinking of the world economy.* New York, NY: W.W. Norton & Co.

Taylor, S. (1997). Critical policy analysis: Exploring contexts, texts, and consequences. *Discourse: Studies in the cultural politics of education, 18*(1), 23–35.

Thatcher, M. (1987). *Interview in Women's Own.* Retrieved from https://www.margaretthatcher.org/document/106689

Thomson, P. (2008). Headteacher critique and resistance: a challenge for policy, and for leadership/management scholars. *Journal of Educational Administration and History, 40,* 85–100.

Verger, A. (2012). Framing and selling global education policy: the promotion of public–private partnerships for education in low-income contexts. *Journal of Education Policy, 27*(1), 109–130.

Weatherly, R., & Lipsky, M. (1977). Street-level bureaucrats and institutional innovation: Implementing special education reform. *Harvard Education Review, 47,* 171–197.

Weaver-Hightower, M. (2008). An ecology metaphor for educational policy analysis: A call to complexity. *Educational researcher, 37*(3), 153–167.

Westheimer, J. (Ed.). (2007). *Pledging allegiance: The politics of patriotism in America's schools.* New York, NY: Teachers College Press.

Whitfield, D. (2001). *Public services or corporate welfare.* London, UK: Pluto Press.

Wilson, W.J. (2009). *More than just race.* New York: W.W. Norton.

Yamamoto, E. (1997). Critical race praxis: Race theory and political lawyering practice in post-Civil Rights America, *Michigan Law Review, 95*(4), 821–900.

CHAPTER 3

Public Schools or Private Goods?

The Politics of Choice, Markets, and Competition

In 2017, Secretary of Education Betsy DeVos, a billionaire supporter of school choice policies long before President Trump nominated her to his cabinet, spoke at the National Association of Public Charter Schools annual meeting. She stated that it was time to stop distinguishing schools by their sector, and instead, embrace public, private, and other models in terms of what families decide is most valuable through their selection of schools. Secretary DeVos argued, "I suggest we focus less on what word comes before 'school'—whether it be traditional, charter, virtual, magnet, home, parochial, private or any approach yet to be developed—and focus instead on the individuals they are intended to serve. We need to get away from our orientation around buildings or systems or schools and shift our focus to individual students" (DeVos, 2017).

This focus on individual students and their rights called for by DeVos aligns with neoliberal and libertarian preferences for the allocation of public goods to private sector operators and investors and runs counter to democratic visions of public education and the ideal of the common school. In many ways, DeVos's embrace of market-based educational policies as the primary mechanism for allocating public education in the United States realized an earlier vision imagined by Milton Friedman (1962) in the classic text, *Capitalism and Freedom*. In Friedman's imagination, the role of government in education would be to establish the minimum level of education needed to ensure basic literacy and knowledge, but he would argue that the government need not be the sole or primary provider of schooling. Instead, providing parents with vouchers would allow them to seek schools that aligned with their pedagogical or religious orientation. Friedman suggested that parents could choose from an array of private and public providers. Parents could supplement this money with their own, and Freidman argued that having parents assume the costs of schooling for their children would help ensure that family sizes were commensurate with what families could afford to spend.

The educational services could be rendered by private enterprises operated for profit, or by non-profit institutions. The role of the government would be limited to insuring that the schools met certain minimum standards, such as the inclusion of a minimum content in their programs, much as it now inspects restaurants to ensure that they maintain minimum sanitary standards.

(p. 89)

By the turn of the century, education leaders in urban school systems, many of whom first entered education through Teach For America and identified as Democrats, joined Friedman's libertarian, anti-civil rights philosophy with an ideology that reclaimed market-oriented reforms as being central to emancipatory, equitable education for Black and Latinx children (Rhee & Klein, 2010). This vision included school closures, contracting with private management organizations to operate schools, the use of incentives and competition to drive school, teacher, and system performance, and the embrace of alternative teacher and leadership preparation programs to provide the human capital to work in the new schools these leaders imagined would revitalize public education and maximize the choices of individual parents. Moreover, these education reformers zeroed in on teachers unions as the main organizational obstacle—along with recalcitrant school district leaders—limiting educational freedom and equity.

These efforts saw ideas being taken to scale and implemented in urban school districts such as New Orleans, Los Angeles, Philadelphia, Nashville, New York, and Denver. School and system leaders work in increasingly fragmented and hybridized settings in which the model of the common school as a part of a school district that is overseen by a school board and superintendent is giving way to alternative models for delivering schooling. This institutional diversity includes charter schools, private management of schools, vouchers, and private contracting to deliver online education, school choice infrastructure, teacher and leadership preparation, and the use of vouchers and tuition tax credits to redirect public allocations to private schools at the behest of parents seeking alternatives to public institutions.

In this chapter, we describe the historical antecedents of contemporary school choice policies, their ideological underpinnings, and evidence of their effects on students, school systems, and communities. We consider the unique challenges and opportunities the expansion and implementation of market-based school choice polices pose for school leaders seeking to support diverse, equitable, and excellent public schools and school systems.

SCHOOL CHOICE POLICIES: A LOOK AT THE TERRAIN

The institutional landscape of school choice policies is constantly in flux, making precision about the numbers of particular choice schools, or students within schools difficult to achieve. In 2018, there were charter school laws in forty-four states, with approximately three million children attending them, which amounts to roughly 5% of the U.S. public school population. Charter schools receive support not only from their state legislatures but also from the federal government, beginning with President Bill Clinton. As many observers have noted, charter schools often have bipartisan support. The proposed fiscal year 2017–2018 federal budget would increase charter school funding as well as create a $250 million school voucher program. There are also seventeen school voucher plans and over forty tuition tax credit plans, and approximately two million children are being homeschooled. In addition, there are school choice policies and plans that incorporate goals of racial, linguistic, and socioeconomic desegregation. Many of these plans are voluntary in the sense that policymakers have enacted them without mandates or court orders, and others persist under consent decrees. In addition, as urban districts and surrounding suburbs have grappled with demographic shifts, many policymakers and school leaders are implementing metropolitan school choice plans to encourage greater diversity, access, and equity (Holme & Finnigan, 2013). These inter- and intradistrict choice plans include magnet schools and voluntary transfer programs, and while leaders have had to navigate ongoing racism, resistance, and lack of resources in their design and implementation, these policies remain the only school choice plans that take desegregation, if not integration, and the need for regulation and monitoring of them, seriously (Finnigan & Scarbough, 2013).

Charter Schools

Charter schools are publicly funded schools that are managed by non- or even for-profit groups, usually independent of local districts and free from many state and district regulations in exchange for promises of greater accountability and student learning. They are intended to induce schools to compete for students by adopting more attractive pedagogies and school structures. In fact, despite the enthusiastic, bipartisan endorsement these schools have enjoyed in Washington, D.C. and the strong support they have received from philanthropic organizations such as the Gates Foundation, the Broad Foundation, the Walton Family Foundation, and the Fisher Fund/Pisces Foundation, the record on charter school achievement outcomes is fairly modest, showing great variability within and across states, and even variability within charter school networks (CREDO, 2009, 2013).

Vouchers

Vouchers allow parents to enroll their children in private schools using public funding to partially offset or fully pay for the tuition. While some voucher advocates base their support for them on the grounds of expanding parental freedom and choice, other supporters regard vouchers as a mechanism to incentivize the development of high-performing schools under the assumption that with adequate information, parents will choose schools that are high quality (usually defined as high performing on standardized assessments), leaving underperforming schools to be less likely to be selected, and ultimately, closed if they cannot maintain enrollments. Similarly, the goal of tuition tax credits and education savings accounts, which Welner (2008b) has called "neovouchers" is to use the tax system as a pass-through for parents to subsidize their private school tuition payments. They also serve as a mechanism for corporations to receive tax credits for donations to private schools. Research on vouchers has found mixed results that were highly dependent on the metrics researchers used to determine effectiveness and the controls used to compare students across schools, and much of the research is subject to an "echo chamber" effect (Goldie et al., 2014).

Merit Pay

The goal of merit pay plans for teachers is to incentivize more effective teaching practices, theoretically rewarding teachers who show greater gains in their students' achievement or growth in proficiency levels. There are hundreds of school districts with merit pay plans in place, though the programs differ greatly from one another. Where some plans award cash rewards to individual teachers, other distribute bonuses school wide. This idea, while growing in popularity, is not new, and it has long been controversial. For example, Jabbar (2013) traces the use of incentive payment plans in 19th century England. In the past, and in current contexts, teacher unions and many education researchers have expressed concerns that efforts to evaluate their teaching practice with students by using standardized test scores would conflate possible teacher effects with confounding variables, such as student backgrounds in terms of race, language, and poverty—and the hyper segregation of students by these indicators, motivation), and test-taking ability. The advancement of value-added modeling metrics by researchers leads policymakers who support merit pay plans to believe that they can distinguish teacher effectiveness from these and other factors known to affect student learning and performance on standardized assessments (Glazerman et al., 2010; Kane et al., 2010). Yet critics argue that merit pay plans do not account for the complex nature of teachers' work in schools, which tends to be collaborative and interdependent (Johnson, 1984; see also Murnane & Cohen, 1986), or raise concerns about the suitability of informational mechanisms that will support these programs (Welner, 2008; see also Baker et al., 2010; Goldhaber et al., 2008b; Newton et al., 2010; Schochet & Chiang, 2010). While these plans often hold appeal for reformers, many are short-lived, and their educational benefits, especially in terms of increasing teacher quality or improving student and school performance, are still unclear (Ballou, 2001).

Parent Trigger Laws

The parent trigger is a policy device that provides a mechanism to force the growth of school choice or school reconstitution. The first parent trigger law was passed in 2010 in California, and since then organizations like the Heartland Institute and the American Legislative Exchange Council have become leading supporters of its expansion to other states. To date, seven states have adopted some version of a parent trigger law: California, Connecticut, Indiana, Louisiana, Mississippi, Ohio, and Texas. A majority of parents can trigger transformation of low-performing neighborhood schools by signing petitions indicating their support for such measures. The resulting options vary by state, but they typically include conversion to charter school status. Triggers may also prompt school closure or the removal of a school's administration and leaders and replacement with private, education management organizations.

CHOICE AND COMPETITION

School choice policies can produce a number of forms of competition. These forms can include competition between schools, between charter school networks, between parents, and between systems. There can also be competition for teachers and leaders. Sociological research has demonstrated that students are unequally situated in choice contexts. Schools have an incentive to try to attract students likely to produce higher test scores, and a disincentive to enroll students who have special emotional, physical, or educational needs that require additional resources. For this reason, charter schools have used a wide variety of mechanisms to shape their enrollment. These have included pushing students out with disproportionate discipline practices and the use of marketing and advertising aimed at favored groups (DiMartino & Butler Jessen, 2018).

Two additional arguments undergird contemporary school choice policies. First, theorists posit that when parents are allowed to choose schools for their children that best cohere to their values and desire for quality, the most informed parents who are likely to choose on the basis of academic excellence will drive parents to follow their lead. Therefore, underperforming schools would be forced to compete for their patronage by improving their academic offerings or organizational operations or risk closure. Yet as school choice policies like charter schools have gone to scale, Lafer (2018) found that charters are costing districts millions of dollars in lost funding, thereby destabilizing their ability to compete. Another assumption is that providing parents with choice in their children's schooling is tantamount to fulfilling the promise of the Civil Rights Movement because it devolves power away from school and school district leaders and puts it into the hands of parents (Arons, 1989; Blackwell, 2007; Bolick, 1998). These comparisons with the Civil Rights Movement are complex; given policymaker's use of school choice was to avoid racial integration (Scott, 2018).

"Freedom of Choice" Plans

School desegregation became an important policy goal during the mid-century Civil Rights Movement, led by legal advocates such as the National Association for the Advancement of Colored People, and networks of Black educators throughout the American south (Walker, 2018). These parents, educators, and legal advocates who pushed for school desegregation litigation and laws to dismantle separate and unequal schooling did so because they believed that equal and integrated education was essential for the achievement of civil rights, along with other civil rights protections in labor, housing, and justice policies. As the courts ruled that policymakers had harmed Black children by ensuring separate and unequal schooling, beginning with the landmark *Brown I* and *Brown II* decisions of 1954 and 1955, massive White resistance resulted in the establishment of state-sponsored voucher programs to enable White families to avoid desegregation mandates and, in Virginia, closure of the public schools for several years (Lassiter & Davis, 1998). While African American families had long engaged in alternative institution building due to their exclusion from public education opportunities (Foreman, 2005a), the establishment of vouchers for White children to attend private schools instead of participating in desegregated public schools, one of the first state-sponsored school choice policies, was inextricably tied to racism and racial exclusion (Lassiter & Davis, 1998).

SCHOOL CHOICE AND STUDENT OUTCOMES

The popularity of school choice among urban policymakers has coincided with a larger national education policy context that has shifted from a focus on equity and providing additional support and resources to underserved schools and districts to a focus on excellence and raising standards and test scores (McGuinn, 2006; Wells, 2010). In fact, many charter school advocates claim that the way to achieve greater educational equity is through educational excellence by eliminating test score or graduation disparities between Black and Latinx students and their more advantaged White and Asian peers. Thus, the so-called "achievement gap," rather than broader analyses of social, political, and economic inequalities that result in an "opportunity gap" (Carter & Welner, 2013), or what Ladson-Billings calls the "Education Debt" (Ladson-Billings, 2006), is framed as the major problem of educational equity that choice and competition stand to remedy.

How parents actually choose reveals that school choice logics look very different on the ground, as parent choice—especially the choice of low-income parents of color—is constrained in various ways. First, geographic boundaries, social networks, and familial resources all limit school choice. Given the intractable patterns of inter-school district racial and socioeconomic segregation and court rulings that have curbed interdistrict desegregation policy options, combined with a lack of transportation provisions in many choice plans, low-income parents of color are often limited to choosing schools within district boundaries (Lubienski, 2005; Wells, Warner, & Grzesikowski, 2013).

To have unrestrained school choice, the way that White and affluent parents often do, they would need the resources to move to a suburban district known for its high-quality, well-funded schools though many researchers have noted the tight connections between family socioeconomic status and student performance on standardized assessments, thereby troubling the notions of greater "quality" to be found in wealthy or middle-class suburbs (Schneider, 2017). Another option for families who cannot or don't want to live in these suburbs is to explore private school options. In the case of vouchers, the amount of the voucher is typically not sufficient to cover tuition at the most elite schools, even if parents were to be admitted to these selective institutions Moreover, there is evidence that low-income families and families of color face barriers to equal treatment in pursuing what they believe to be better schools. For example, low-income parents of color who do cross interdistrict lines without the benefit of a voucher (often by falsifying their addresses) are accused of "stealing education" and have been fined and jailed (Applebome, 2011; Spencer, 2015). And middle-class Black and Latinx students in suburban schools often receive unequal treatment in terms of access to college preparatory classes, likelihood of being tracked into low-level courses, and face disproportionate discipline (Lewis, 2003; Lewis-McCoy, 2014).

Moreover, even within urban school-district boundaries, choice for low-income parents of color is constrained by the same factors. Geography is still a factor, as schools have incentives—especially in a competitive educational market where they are judged by test scores—to be located in areas with a smaller high-needs population (Lubienski, Gulosino, & Weitzel, 2009) and parents with limited means struggle to find viable transportation options (Bell, 2009b). Moreover, social networks and access to information—and especially language barriers for parents who are recent immigrants (see Sattin-Bajaj, 2015)—also play a crucial role in which schools parents even know to consider, a process that advantages more educated, well-connected, affluent parents (Ball, 2003; Bell, 2009a; Villavicencio, 2013). Thus, when low-income parents of color choose schools, they do not choose from schools that truly range in quality (Bell, 2009a; Lubienski, 2005).

A second reason that the market logics governing school choice do not align with implementation is that within the collection of schools that low-income parents of color actually choose from, their choices are limited as well. Many "mission-oriented" charter schools (Henig, Holyoke, Brown, & Lacireno-Paquet, 2005) that aim to serve low-income youth locate themselves in urban Black and Latino communities (Lubienski et al., 2009), and are the primary option low-income parents consider besides the traditional public schools in their neighborhood. Charter schools were originally planned to be "factories" of innovation—and indeed, many early urban charter schools were community-based and experimented with a variety of pedagogies and curriculum to serve low-income youth of color.

However, market pressures from the proliferation of large network CMO "No Excuses" charter schools (Miron, Urschel, Aguilar, Mayra, & Dailey, 2012) are causing a significant proportion of urban charter schools to adopt a similar approach (White, 2015)—with an emphasis on high academic standards, tough discipline, and character development (McDermott & Nygreen, 2013). While this pedagogical style might be attractive to some parents, other parents have concerns with the punitive discipline, test score focus, and lack of cultural relevance in these schools (Sondel, 2015; White, 2015). In addition, admittance to these oversubscribed schools generally happens through a lottery, and so rather than simply choosing the school, parents must rely on chance.

Qualitative research demonstrates that even affluent parents in urban districts with school choice feel a great deal of anxiety around the process, as they are overwhelmed with options and concerns that their child will end up in an inferior school (Posey-Maddox, 2014; Roda & Wells, 2013). This is especially true for low-income parents of color where the choices seem to carry even higher stakes, with parents who "win" charter school lotteries feeling blessed and parents who do not feeling dispirited and guilty (Pattillo, Delale-O'Connor, & Butts, 2014). Even though they might exercise agency by doing the hard work of finding the best possible school for their children, they know that White and affluent parents have more political power and are savvy when making their choices in an unequal playing field, and these low-income parents and many parents of color worry whether or not school choice policies will benefit them (Cooper, 2007). Instead of being empowered with the liberty of choice, as the free-market logic would have it, low-income parents of color face barriers that often marginalize them in the process.

CHOICE WITHOUT EQUITY EXACERBATES INEQUALITY: CHOOSING WINNERS AND LOSERS

The anxiety that parents feel around the choice process can be attributed in part to educational inequality in urban school systems (Roda & Wells, 2013). However, rather than choice policies alleviating within district inequality, there is mounting evidence that school choice actually exacerbates inequality and socioeconomic and racial segregation. Modern school choice programs—such as charter schools—provide no regulatory power in terms of traditional equity mechanisms like desegregation or school finance equalization (Frankenberg, Siegel-Hawley, & Wang, 2010). While some school choice policies have promoted racial and socioeconomic integration, such as magnet schools and voluntary district transfer plans (Wells, 1993), the school choice policy context in which parents of color largely choose schools does not currently have strong integrationist provisions, despite the potential of charter schools to do so as a policy tool (Mead & Green, 2012). Indeed, evidence demonstrates that charter schools actually increase racial and socioeconomic segregation (Garcia, 2008; Miron, Urschel, Mathis, & Tornquist, 2010).

Research also demonstrates that charter schools often do not serve proportional numbers of students with special needs (G. Scott, 2012; Winters, 2015) and ELL (English Language Learner) students (Buckley & Sattin-Bajaj, 2011) when compared to traditional public schools in their district. Indeed, parents of special needs children brought a lawsuit against the New Orleans Recovery School District for failing to adequately serve their children (Dreillinger, 2013). While some of this can be attributed to parents of special needs and ELL students not applying to charter schools, due to insufficient information about choice options, within a competitive educational market, charter schools actually have incentives to not serve high-needs students (Jabbar, 2015b; Jennings, 2010). In addition, so-called "No Excuses" charter schools have high attrition rates (Miron, Urschel, & Saxton, 2011; Vasquez Heilig, Williams, McNeil, & Lee, 2011; Woodworth, David, Guha, Wang, & Lopez-Torkos, 2008), suggesting that some of the highest-needs students leave or get pushed out of the schools before they ever graduate. This indicates that parental choice can be curtailed at many points beyond their initial selection of, and admission to a school (Jabbar, 2015b).

Moreover, there is evidence that charter schools' expenditures for students are higher than comparable traditional public schools, given the fact that they attract the support of large philanthropic organizations (Baker, Libby, & Wiley, 2012; Miron et al., 2011; Reckhow & Snyder, 2014). Thus, in many urban districts, there is a stark disparity in the resources and facilities that charter schools offer when compared to public schools, creating a sense of the haves and have-nots. This issue especially comes to a head in the case of charter colocation, a situation where charter schools share space—often rent free—in school district buildings alongside traditional public schools and at times occupy the space that formerly housed schools that are closing due to poor performance. Anger about the disparities in resources and facilities in colocated school buildings has caused a firestorm of controversy in New York City (Otterman, 2011; Pappas, 2012). Critiques charge that this creates an atmosphere of zero-sum competition, pitting the two-school public sectors against each other and causing divisions in the community of color that both types of public schools serve (Fabricant & Fine, 2012; Pappas, 2012). In addition, researchers have found evidence of strategic location of stand-alone schools aimed at attracting desirable students (Henig & MacDonald, 2002).

While some school choice policies can trace their origins to progressive equity policies, others have been shaped by discriminatory impulses to restrict access to public schools on the basis of race, language, poverty, immigration status, or academic performance and ability. Charter schools, vouchers, and other privatization policies challenge the model of the American school district in which a central office oversees and supports the K-12 schools in its jurisdiction. The modern school district emerged in the Progressive era, envisioned and advocated for by reformers seeking to improve the efficiency and quality of public education. These White male reformers believed in centralizing many of the administrative functions of schooling and ridding the nation's schools of fragmentation toward a vision of common schooling (Tyack, 1974). From 1910 to 1960, these efforts resulted in the consolidation of one-room schoolhouses, which were reduced from 200,000 to 20,000.

The resulting bureaucratization of public education did nothing to interrupt the substandard schooling offered to marginalized communities. African Americans, southern European immigrants, Latinos, Asian Americans, and Native Americans engaged in separate and joint struggles to be included in the democratic processes, curricular offerings, and personnel policies that would shape the learning conditions of their children (Donato, 1997; Murtahda & Watts, 2005). Community control movements, efforts to eradicate legal barriers to integration, and fights for bilingual instruction and equal school funding, among other efforts, characterized these struggles (Forman, 2005b; Pedroni, 2007; Tyack, 1974). Among these efforts to realize educational equity, school desegregation has been especially protracted. Through de facto and de jure policies in housing and school district attendance boundaries, federal, state, and local public policymakers institutionalized the separate and unequal schooling that persists throughout the United States (Rothstein, 2015, 2017).

PARENTS AS INDIVIDUAL CONSUMERS

Finally, school choice policies primarily conceive of parents as consumers in an educational market rather than as democratic citizens (Beal & Hendry, 2012; Hill, 2013). The problem with this conception is that even when parents exercise choice and enroll their child in a charter school or school outside of their neighborhood, they still have a stake in the school system (Labaree, 2000). Despite the privatizing effects of choice policies, charter schools are still commonly understood to be public schools and part of urban public school systems (Lubienski, 2001) and expected to fulfill public goods—such as benefits from the increased human capital and political competence that the public school system engenders (Labaree, 2000). Thus, parents not only have a stake in the education of their individual child; they are still citizens and taxpayers, and have a stake in the quality of the overall system.

This holds especially for low-income parents of color. Due to a history of institutional racism that affects all people of color, parents may understand themselves as "linked" to the fate of others in their communities (Dawson, 2003). Even parents of color who do not send their child to neighborhood public schools are still tied to their fate, as they have other family members and friends who attend and work in those schools. These parents have concerns that the larger school system will educate other children that will be a part of their child's life and grow to be citizens in their communities (Pattillo, 2015; Wilson-Cooper, 2005). There is ecology of institutions that make up a neighborhood and parents do not only consider the school that their child attends in isolation from these other dynamics.

School choice policies often are disruptive to communities as demonstrated by the contested nature of charter school expansion in many neighborhoods of color, even as families of color also support, advocate for, and enroll their children in schools of choice (Buras, 2011; Jabbar, 2015a; J. Scott, 2012). Such policies often coincide with school closures, thus eliminating spaces that were once fixtures of neighborhoods (Lipman, 2011). Moreover, given the longer travel time for children to get to school, and the longer school days that children experience in "No Excuses" charter schools, children are spending more time away from their neighborhoods and families.

School choice advocates often frame school choice as choosing to support children over adults, especially in conversations about the self-interest of public school teachers unions. However, this framing obscures the fact that children and teachers of color can be a part of the same communities, and stable employment for adults is of benefit to children. Indeed, public sector employment—in urban institutions, such as education systems—has been crucial in upward mobility for African Americans and building the Black middle class. When school choice policies weaken teachers unions, it disproportionately harms educators of color. An extreme example of this was the mass firing of mostly Black veteran teachers in New Orleans with the restructuring of the school district (Buras, 2011; Jabbar, 2015a). Given the centrality of Black educators in past struggles for racial justice (Walker, 2009), such policies could be stripping communities of color of important political capital.

RACE, GENDER, AND THE ADVOCACY COALITIONS OF SCHOOL CHOICE POLICY ENTREPRENEURS

Historians and sociologists of education have documented the rise of school and school district leadership and management as professions in the early 20th century. As public schools were transformed from small, community-run institutions to large urban systems, administrative progressives, a loosely configured network of business leaders, political elite, and university faculty called for and implemented reforms that would centralize urban school governance in ways that mimicked corporate governance. These reformers realized their goals with increased bureaucratization and specialization of the education profession. Within elite universities, including Harvard, Columbia, and Stanford, schools of education developed programs in "administrative science" and the managers who trained in these programs went on to reshape the governance and management of urban school systems.

The administrative progressives invented school and school district leadership as fields of study and as professional tracks, and largely reserved such positions for White men (Tyack, 1974). The original elite school managers designed the modern urban school systems and experimented with governance structures and loci of control in their search of the "one best system," all the while excluding or limiting the participation of women of all races, poor men, and men of color in leadership positions. Following the Civil Rights and Feminist movements, White women and people of color began making modest inroads into school and district leadership. Indeed, given increased government oversight over equalizing opportunity, the public sphere—including school districts, the military, and federal and state governments—became a somewhat protected space where people of color and women were able to build careers and attain middle-class status (Edsall & Edsall, 1992; Pressman & Wildavsky, 1974).

As people of color and women began running schools and districts in greater numbers, and as the backlash against school desegregation, multiculturalism, and compensatory programs took hold, critiques from elites also emerged about urban systems and schools. Critics asserted that expertise existed not just outside school systems but primarily in the private sector, a space historically dominated and reserved for White men (Chubb, 1997; Osborne & Gaebler, 1992). Moreover, critics alleged that the cause of lackluster school performance was the educators and leaders in public schools. There is general agreement from researchers, practitioners, and policymakers that the conditions under which poor children and children of color are educated are in need of improvement, but the causes attributed to these conditions vary greatly, as do the remedies proposed. In the last thirty years, the policy spotlight has been on market-based solutions to the challenges facing urban schools, including the adoption of charter school laws, voucher programs, management of schools by for-profit and nonprofit private companies, and the school choice provisions of the *No Child Left Behind Act and the Every Student Succeeds Act*. These initiatives have reshaped the demographics of public school leadership in ways that have not been adequately explored in school choice research.

EARLY ARCHITECTS OF AFRICAN AMERICAN EDUCATION: VALUES, PHILOSOPHIES, AND PEDAGOGIES

Political sociologists of education place race, gender, and other social characteristics at the center of their analysis (Watkins, 2001). Watkins examines the early White architects of Black education. He details the political and ideological assumptions of the White architects of Black education in the early 20th century, finding that they valued maintaining the social order, building profits for industry through training Blacks to be manual laborers. Although "Black architects," such as DuBois and Washington, argued for their own political sociology of Black schooling, Watkins argues that they were ultimately minor players who were unable to significantly shape the schooling conditions for African American students in public schools. Writes Watkins, "Political sociology allows the interrogation of human actions and interactions within the context of power. Power is viewed in terms of wealth, property, access, inheritance, and privilege" (p. 4).

Watkins's framing of the historical shapers of Black schooling has modern applications. Whereas the context about which he wrote considered the role of education for newly emancipated Black people, the 21st-century context is one in which a global economy has rendered large segments of the United States labor force redundant, where jobs for high school graduates are increasingly low-status and low-paying, and where access to higher education is shrinking. Black men find themselves more likely to be incarcerated or under the arm of the criminal justice system than in school. It is also a context in which unprecedented advancements into public school leadership, educational professoriate, and the school superintendency has been achieved by women and people of color. At the same time, public schooling is under the scrutiny of the federal and state departments of education, achievements measured by standardized tests have become the benchmark of school quality and hurdles for students to ascend, and there is a pervasive sense from the citizenry that most public schools are failing. School choice through charter schools, alternative small schools, vouchers, and private management is currently the most popular educational reform.

As the new school managers seek to influence schooling from the outside, with emphasis on corporate values—management, efficiency, competition, outcomes, and structured flexibility—many educational researchers emphasize issues of democracy, inclusive/multicultural curricula, social justice, and access to pedagogy that foster critical thinking in their writing and teaching of student teachers and aspiring school leaders (Ball, 2003; Foster, 1997; Ladson-Billings, 1995; Sleeter, 1991). This represents an intriguing shift in education, where experts who have followed the path to professional legitimacy mapped out by early administrative progressives, certification, securing advanced degrees, working in public school systems, find that very legitimacy questioned and challenged by those with little or no public school experience. And leaders and researchers of color in particular, who tend to work in predominantly minority school systems or focus upon multicultural perspectives and social justice, find their work especially critiqued.

Female and Leaders of Color in Public Schooling

Educational privatization can be understood not simply as a shift in the public and private spheres, or a way to improve educational outcomes for children of color, but also as a way for White men to preserve an elite and privileged space in educational leadership and policy (Barlow, 2003; Walsh, 2001). While leadership remains a profession in which the majority are White men, people of color and women have increased their presence in the field. Between 1987 and 1994, the percentage of women principals grew by 11% in elementary schools, and by 5% in secondary schools. Men, however, continued to comprise the majority of school principals at both levels (58.9% in elementary and 85.2% in high school), though salaries between men and women became comparable. In 1994, 10% of principals were Black, and 4.1% were Hispanic, while 84.2% were White. Of those leaders of color, 35% of principals in cities were minority, and they tended to work in large school districts, and 69% of minority principals worked in high minority schools (50% or more students of color) (Fiore, Curtin, & Hammer, 2006; National Center for Education Statistics, 1996). The picture painted by these statistics is one of progress, albeit slow progress. Despite a history of discrimination, people of color and women have made inroads into public school leadership.

They have done so by acquiring educational credentials and rising through the ranks, starting as teachers, then principals, and finally, in school leadership positions (Tillman & Cochran, 2000). For them, the bureaucracies set up by the administrative progressives allowed for somewhat of a predictable (if imperfect) professional trajectory. While Watkins argues that White reformers' actions set up an inferior system of schooling for African Americans, others hold that the leadership of African Americans during this period should not be discounted, and that a commitment to community and social justice distinguished them (Murtadha & Watts, 2005). In addition, researchers have identified the unique strengths that African American women superintendents bring to their work.

> Benefits include opportunities to serve as role models for culturally diverse students, providing a more humanistic and relational style of leadership, and a unique understanding and commitment to ensuring equitable educational opportunities for all students in the present climate of educational reform.
>
> (Tillman & Cochran, 2000)

Still, leadership over school systems for leaders of color often comes when hope for reform has faded. School boards often appoint leaders of color as a last resort to educational turmoil in a district, when resources and political will are scarce, leaving them in precarious positions over struggling school systems (Lewis & Nakagawa, 1995; Murtadha-Watts, 2000). The new school leaders, then, are often unwittingly critiquing the leadership of people of color.

CONCLUSION

Market-based policies change the conception of what a "public" school and public school system are (Lubienski, 2001). Because of the policy mechanisms that govern many school choice policies—characterized by limited regulation and enforcement of civil rights laws—these policies largely attend to private, individualized goals for public education. Parents navigating the terrain laid by policymakers are aware of these shortcomings, and rely on stratified social networks to select and enroll their students in the schools in their communities (Pattillo, 2015). The United States provides a relatively weak social safety net, and schools operate in an environment where low-income students of color often have inadequate housing, lack health care, and live in concentrated poverty and isolated segregation. In lieu of a comprehensive social policy to address these inequities, often the responsibility for solving the manifestation of this inequality in social outcomes falls on the schools (Wells, 2010). Many researchers who have documented the unequal parental access to information and opportunity to enroll their children in "good" schools through school choice policies have concluded that quality schooling shouldn't be left up to choice or chance but rather that educational opportunity should be understood as a right and provided in the broadest ways (Perry, Moses, Cortes, Delpit, & Wynne, 2010).

The evidence on parental choice processes demonstrates that parents utilize a number of considerations when allowed to choose schools for their children. These considerations are often informed by the racial demographics of the school (Schneider & Buckley, 2002). While research demonstrates that parents who are able enroll their children in preferred schools of choice report higher levels of satisfaction, we know comparatively much less about the parents unable to access their preferred schools, or parents whose children enrolled, and left or were pushed out of said schools. Policymakers and school and system leaders wishing to redress the issues with selectivity, segregation, and exclusion that come with parental choice can help to craft choice policies that are race conscious with an eye toward ensuring diverse and equitable access and outcomes, and that anticipate the possibilities of excluding children with special needs.

END-OF-CHAPTER QUESTIONS

1. What are the hallmarks of school choice policies that include provisions for equity and access? How do they differ from school choice polices that do not include such provisions?
2. How does the role of private funding shape the design, implementation, and research evidence on choice policies?

REFERENCES

Applebome, P. (2011, April 27). In a mother's case, reminders of educational inequalities. *New York Times*. Retrieved from: https://www.nytimes.com/2011/04/28/nyregion/some-see-educational-inequality-at-heart-of-connecticut-case.html.

Arons, S. (1989). Educational choice as a civil rights strategy. In N. E. Devins (Ed.), *Public values, private schools* (pp. 63–87). London, UK: The Falmer Press.

Baker, B. D., Libby, K., & Wiley, K. (2012). *Spending by the major charter management organizations: Comparing charter school and local public district financial resources in New York, Ohio, and Texas*. Boulder: The National Education Policy Center. Retrieved from: https://nepc.colorado.edu/publication/spending-major-charter.

Baker, E.L., Barton, P., Darling-Hammond, L., Haertel, E., Ladd, H., Linn, R., Ravitch, D., Rothstein, R., Shavelson, R. & Shephard, L. (2010). *Problems with the use of student test scores to evaluate teachers* (EPI Briefing paper 278). Washington, D.C.: Economic Policy Institute.

Ball, S. J. (2003). *Class strategies and the education market: The middle classes and social advantage.* New York, NY: Routledge.

Ballou, D. (2001). Pay for performance in public and private schools. *Economics of Education Review. 20*(1), 51–61.

Barlow, A. L. (2003). *Between fear and hope: Globalization and race in the United States.* Lanham: Rowman & Littlefield Publishers.

Beal, H. K. O., & Hendry, P. M. (2012). The ironies of school choice: Empowering parents and reconceptualizing public education. *American Journal of Education, 118*(4), 521–550.

Bell, C. (2009a). All choices created equal? The role of choice sets in the selection of schools. *Peabody Journal of Education, 84*(2), 191–208.

Bell, C. (2009b). Geography in parental choice. *American Journal of Education, 115*(4), 493–521.

Blackwell, K. (2007). *School choice and civil rights.* Townhall.com. Retrieved from http://townhall.com/columnists/KenBlackwell/2007/04/06/school_choice_and_civil_rights

Bolick, C. (1998). *Transformation: The promise and politics of empowerment.* Oakland, CA: Institute for Contemporary Studies.

Buckley, J., & Sattin-Bajaj, C. (2011). Are ELL students underrepresented in charter schools? Demographic trends in New York City, 2006–2008. *Journal of School Choice, 5*(1), 40–65.

Buras, K. L. (2011). Race, charter schools, and conscious capitalism: On the spatial politics of whiteness as property (and the unconscionable assault on black New Orleans). *Harvard Educational Review, 81*(2), 296–331.

Carter, P., & Welner, K. (Eds.). (2013). *Closing the opportunity gap: What America must do to give every child an even chance.* New York, NY: Oxford University Press.

Center for Research on Education Outcomes (CREDO). (2009). *Charter school performance in Louisiana.* Palo Alto, CA: Stanford University.

Center for Research on Education Outcomes (CREDO). (2013). *Charter school performance in Louisiana.* Palo Alto, CA: Stanford University.

Chubb, J. (1997). Lessons in school reform from the Edison project. In J. P. Viteretti & D. Ravitch (Eds.), *New schools for a new century: The redesign of urban education* (pp. 86–122). New Haven: Yale University Press.

Cooper, C. W. (2007). School choice as 'motherwork': Valuing African-American women's educational advocacy and resistance. *International Journal of Qualitative Studies in Education, 20*(5), 491–512.

Dawson, M. C. (2003). *Black visions: The roots of contemporary African-American political ideologies.* Chicago, IL: University of Chicago Press.

DeVos, B. (2017, June 13). *Secretary Betsy DeVos prepared remarks national association of public charter schools.* Washington, DC: U.S. Department of Education. Retrieved June 13, 2017 from https://www.ed.gov/news/speeches/secretary-betsy-devos-prepared-remarks-national-association-public-charter-schools

DiMartino, C., & Butler Jessen, S. (2018). *Selling school: The marketing of public education.* New York, NY: Teachers College Press.

Donato, R. (1997). *The other struggle for equal schools: Mexican Americans during the Civil Rights Era.* Albany, NY: SUNY Publishers.

Dreillinger, D. (2013, August 3). Unrelenting New Orleans special education problems alleged in new court filings. *New Orleans Times-Picayune.* Retrieved from: https://www.nola.com/education/index.ssf/2013/08/unrelenting_new_orleans_specia.html.

Edsall, T., & Edsall, M. (1992). *Chain reaction: The impact of race, rights and taxes on American politics*. New York: W. W. Norton.

Fabricant, M., & Fine, M. (2012). *Charter schools and the corporate makeover of public education: What's at stake?* New York, NY: Teachers College Press.

Finnigan, K. S., & Scarbrough, J. B. (2013). Defining (and denying) diversity through interdistrict choice. *Journal of School Choice*, 7, 142–162.

Fiore, T. A., Curtin, T. R., & Hammer, C. H. (2006). Public and private school principals in the United States: A statistical profile, 1987–88 to 1993–94. Retrieved January 30, 2006, from http://nces.ed.gov/pubs/ppsp/94755-2.asp.

Foreman, J. J. (2005). The secret history of school choice: How progressives got there first. *The Georgetown Law Journal, 93,* 1287–1319. p. 1288.

Foreman, J. J. (2005). The secret history of school choice: How progressives got there first. *The Georgetown Law Journal, 93*, 1287–1319.

Foster, M. (1997). *Black teachers on teaching*. New York: The New Press.

Frankenberg, E., Siegel-Hawley, G., & Wang, J. (2010). Choice without equity: Charter school segregation and the need for civil rights standards. Los Angeles: UCLA *Civil Rights Project/Proyecto Derechos Civiles*. Retrieved from: https://www.civilrightsproject.ucla.edu/research/k-12-education/integration-and-diversity/choice-without-equity-2009-report.

Friedman, M. (1962). *Capitalism and freedom*. Chicago: University of Chicago Press.

Garcia, D. R. (2008). Academic and racial segregation in charter schools do parents sort students into specialized charter schools? *Education and Urban Society, 40*(5), 590–612.

Glazerman, S., Isenberg, Dolfin, E., Bleeker, M., Johnson, A., Grider, M. & Jacobus, M. (2010). *Impacts of comprehensive teacher induction: Final results from a randomized controlled study*. Washington, D.C., Mathematica Policy Research.

Goldhaber, D., DeArmond, M., Player, D. & Choi, H. (2008). *Journal of Education Finance. 33*(3), 262–289.

Goldie, D., Linick, M., Jabbar, H., & Lubienski, C. (2014). Using bibliometric and social media analyses to explore the "echo-chamber" hypothesis. *Educational Policy*, 28(2), 281–305.

Henig, J. R. and McDonald, J. 2002. Locational decisions of charter schools: Probing the market metaphor. *Social Science Quarterly*, 83(4), 962–980.

Henig, J., Holyoke, T., Brown, H., & Lacireno-Paquet, N. (2005). The influence of founder type on charter school structures and operations. *American Journal of Education, 111*(4), 487–588.

Hill, K. (2013). *Choice and voice: Parents and political strategies for school improvement*. Paper presented at the American Education Research Association, San Francisco, CA.

Holme, J., & Finnigan, K. (2013). School diversity, school district fragmentation, and metropolitan policy. *Teachers College Record, 115*(11), 1–29.

Jabbar, H. (2013). The case of "payment-by-results": Re-examining an incentive program in 19th-century English schools. *Journal of Educational Administration and History. 45*(3), 220–243.

Jabbar, H. (2015a). 'Drenched in the past:' The evolution of market-oriented reforms in New Orleans. *Journal of Education Policy, 30*(6), 751–772.

Jabbar, H. (2015b). "Every kid is money:" Market-like competition and school leader strategies in New Orleans. *Educational Evaluation and Policy Analysis, 37*(4), pp. 638–659.

Jennings, J. L. (2010). School choice or schools' choice? Managing in an era of accountability. *Sociology of Education, 83*(3), 227–247.

Kane, T., Taylor, E., Tyler, J. & Wooten, A. (2010). Identifying effective classroom practices using student achievement data. *The Journal of Human Resources. 46*(3), 587–613.

Labaree, D. F. (2000). No exit: Public education as an inescapably public good. In L. Cuban & D. Shipps (Eds.), *Reconstructing the Common Good in Education*. Stanford, CA: Stanford University Press.

Ladson-Billings, G. (1995). *The dreamkeepers: Successful teachers of African American children*. San Francisco: Jossey-Bass.

Ladson-Billings, G. (2006). From the achievement gap to the education debt: Understanding achievement in U.S. schools. *Educational Researcher, 35*(7), 3–12.

Lafer, G. (2018). *Breaking point: The cost of charter schools for public school districts*. Oakland, CA: In the Public Interest.

Lassiter, M. D., & Davis, A. B. (1998). Massive resistance revisited: Virginia's white moderates and the Byrd organization. In M. D. Lassiter & A. B. Davis (Eds.), *The moderates' dilemma: Massive resistance to school desegregation*. Charlottesville: University Press of Virginia, pp. 1–21.

Lewis, A. (2003). *Race in the Schoolyard: Negotiating the Color Line in Classrooms and Communities*. Piscataway, NJ: Rutgers University Press.

Lewis, D., & Nakagawa, K. (1995). *Race and educational reform in the American metropolis: A study of school decentralization*. Albany: SUNY Press.

Lewis-McCoy, L. (2014). *Inequality in the Promised Land: Race, Resources, and Suburban Schooling*. Stanford, CA: Stanford University Press.

Lipman, P. (2011). *The new political economy of urban education: Neoliberalism, race, and the right to the city*. New York, NY: Routledge.

Lubienki, C. (2001). Redefining "Public" education: Charter schools, common schools and the rhetoric of reform. *Teachers College Record, 103*(4), 634–666.

Lubienski, C. (2005). School choice as a civil right: District responses to competition and equal educational opportunity. *Equity & Excellence in Education, 38*(4), 331–341.

Lubienski, C., Gulosino, C., & Weitzel, P. (2009). School choice and competitive incentives: Mapping the distribution of educational opportunities across local education markets. *American Journal of Education, 115*(4), 601–647.

McDermott, K. A., & Nygreen, K. (2013). Educational new paternalism: Human capital, cultural capital, and the politics of equal opportunity. *Peabody Journal of Education, 88*(1), 84–97.

McGuinn, P. J. (2006). *No child left behind and the transformation of federal education policy, 1965–2005*. Lawrence: University of Kansas Press.

Mead, J. F., & Green, P. C. (2012). *Chartering equity: Using charter school legislation and policy to advance equal educational opportunity*. Boulder, CO: National Education Policy Center.

Miron, G., Urschel, J. L., Aguilar, Y., Mayra, A., & Dailey, B. (2012). *Profiles of for-profit and nonprofit education management organizations: Thirteenth annual report, 2010–2011*. Boulder: National Education Policy Center. Retrieved from. https://nepc.colorado.edu/publication/EMO-profiles-10-11.

Miron, G., Urschel, J. L., Mathis, W. J., & Tornquist, E. (2010). *Schools without diversity: Education management organizations, charter schools and the demographic stratification of the American school system*. Boulder: National Education Policy Center. Retrieved from: https://nepc.colorado.edu/publication/schools-without-diversity.

Miron, G., Urschel, J., & Saxton, N. (2011). *What makes KIPP work? A study of student characteristics, attrition, and school finance*. New York: National Center for the Study of Privatization in Education, Teachers College, Columbia University. Retrieved from: https://www.edweek.org/media/kippstudy.pdf

Murnane, R. & Cohen, D. (1986) Merit pay and the evaluation problem: Why most merit pay plans fail and a few survive. *Harvard Educational Review*, *56*(1), 1–18.

Murtadha, K., & Watts, D. M. (2005). Linking the struggle of education and social justice: Historical perspectives of African American leadership in schools. *Education Administration Quarterly, 41*(4), 591–608.

Murtadha-Watts, K. (2000). Cleaning up and maintenance in the wake of an urban school administration tempest. *Urban Education, 35*(5), 603–615.

National Center for Education Statistics. (1996). *Issue brief: Where do minority principals work?* (No. IB-2-96). Washington, D.C.: U.S. Department of Education, Office of Educational Improvement.

Newton, X., Darling-Hammond, L., Haertel, E., Thomas, E. (2010). Value-added modeling of teacher effectiveness: An exploration of stability across models and contexts. *Educational Policy Analysis Archives*, *18*(23).

Osborne, D., & Gaebler, T. (1992). *Reinventing government: How the entrepreneurial spirit is transforming the public sector*. New York: Plume.

Otterman, S. (2011). Criticizing School Closings, In a Noisy Annual Ritual. *The New York Times*, p. 18.

Pappas, L. (2012). School closings and parent engagement. *Peace and Conflict: Journal of Peace Psychology, 18*(2), 165–172.

Pattillo, M. (2015). Everyday politics of school choice in the Black community. *DuBois Review, 12*(1), 41–71.

Pattillo, M., Delale-O'Connor, L., & Butts, F. (2014). High stakes choosing: How parents navigate Chicago public schools. In A. Lareau & K. Goyette (Eds.), *Choosing homes, choosing schools* (pp. 237–267). New York, NY: Russell Sage Foundation.

Pedroni, T. C. (2007). *Market movements: African American involvement in school voucher reform*. New York, NY: Routledge.

Perry, T., Moses, R. P., Cortes Jr, E., Delpit, L., & Wynne, J. T. (2010). *Quality education as a constitutional right: Creating a grassroots movement to transform public schools*. Boston, MA: Beacon Press.

Posey-Maddox, L. (2014). *When middle-class parents choose urban schools: Class, race, and the challenge of equity in public education*. Chicago, IL: University of Chicago Press.

Pressman, J., & Wildavsky, A. (1974). *Implementation: How great expectations in Washington are dashed in Oakland*. Berkeley: University of California Press.

Reckhow, S., & Snyder, J. W. (2014). The expanding role of philanthropy in education politics. *Educational Researcher, 43*(4), 186–195.

Rhee, M., & Klein, J. (2010). How to fix our schools: A manifesto by Joel Klein, Michelle Rhee and other education leaders. *The Washington Post*. Retrieved February 23, 2017, from http://www.washingtonpost.com/wpdyn/content/article/2010/10/07/AR2010100705078.html

Roda, A., & Wells, A. S. (2013). School choice policies and racial segregation: Where white parents, good intentions, anxiety, and privilege collide. *American Journal of Education, 119*(2), 261–293.

Rothstein, R. (2015, April). From Ferguson to Baltimore: The fruits of government-sponsored segregation. Retrieved from http://www.epi.org/blog/from-ferguson-to-baltimore-the-fruits-of-government-sponsored-segregation/

Rothstein, R. (2017). *The color of law: A forgotten history of how our government segregated America*. New York, NY: Liveright Publishing Corporation.

Sattin-Bajaj, C. (2015). Unaccompanied minors: How children of Latin American immigrants negotiate high school choice. *American Journal of Education, 121*(3), 381–415.

Schneider, J. (2017). Beyond test scores: A better way to measure school quality. Cambridge: Harvard University Press.

Schneider, M., & Buckley, J. (2002). What do parents want from schools: Evidence from the internet. *Education Evaluation and Policy Analysis, 24*(2), 133–144.

Schochet, Peter Z. and Hanley S. Chiang (2010). *Error Rates in Measuring Teacher and School Performance Based on Student Test Score Gains* (NCEE 2010-4004). Washington, DC: National Center for Education Evaluation and Regional Assistance, Institute of Education Sciences, U.S. Department of Education.

Scott, G. (2012). *Charter schools: Additional federal attention needed to help protect access for students with disabilities: Report to congressional requesters.* Washington, D.C.: US Government Accountability Office. Retrieved from: https://www.gao.gov/assets/600/591435.pdf

Scott, J. (2012). When community control meets privatization: The search for empowerment in African American charter schools. In D. T. Slaughter-Defoe, H. C. Stevenson, E. G. Errington, & D. J. Johnson (Eds.), *Black educational choice: Assessing the private and public alternatives to traditional K-12 public schools.* Santa Barbara, CA: Prageer.

Scott, J. (2018). The problem we all still live with: Neo-Plessyism, and school choice policies in the Post-Obama era. In Rotberg, I. & Glazer, J. (Eds.). *Choosing charters: Better schools, or more segregation?* New York: Teachers College Press.

Sleeter, C. (1991). *Empowerment through multicultural education.* Albany: State University of New York.

Sondel, B. (2015). Raising citizens or raising test scores? Teach For America, "No Excuses" charters, and the development of the neoliberal citizen. *Theory & Research in Social Education, 43*(3), 289–313.

Spencer, K. (2015). Can you steal an education? Wealthy school districts are cracking down on "education thieves." *The Hechhinger Report.* Retrieved from http://hechingerreport.org/can-you-steal-an-education/

Tillman, B. A., & Cochran, L. L. (2000). Desegregating urban school administration: a pursuit of equity for Black women superintendents. *Education and Urban Society, 33*(1), 44–59.

Tyack, D. (1974). *The one best system: A history of American urban education.* Cambridge, MA: Harvard University Press.

Vasquez Heilig, J., Williams, A., McNeil, L. M., & Lee, C. (2011). Is choice a panacea? An analysis of black secondary student attrition from KIPP, other private charters, and urban districts. *Berkeley Review of Education, 2*(2), 153–178.

Villavicencio, A. (2013). "It's Our Best Choice Right Now": Exploring how charter school parents choose. *Education Policy Analysis Archives, 21*(81), 23.

Walker, V. (2018). *The lost education of Horace Tate: Uncovering the hidden heroes who fought for justice in schools.* New York: The New Press.

Walker, V. S. (2009). *Hello professor: A black principal and professional leadership in the segregated south.* Chapel Hill: The University of North Carolina Press.

Walsh, M. (2001, May 2). Hoping to raise profile, school 'industry' forms trade group. *Education Week, 20,* 9.

Watkins, W. (2001). *The white architects of Black education: Ideology and power in America, 1865–1954.* New York: Teachers College Press.

Wells, A. S. (1993). *Time to Choose: America at the crossroads of school choice policy. New frontiers of education.* New York, NY: Hill & Wang Publishers.

Wells, A. S. (2010). Our children's burden: A history of federal education policies that ask (now require) our public schools to solve societal inequality. In M. Rebell & J. Wolff (Eds.), *NCLB at the Crossroads: Reexamining America's Commitment to Closing Our Nation's Achievement Gap.* New York, NY: Teachers College Press.

Wells, A. S., Warner, M., & Grzesikowski, C. (2013). The story of meaningful school choice: Lessons from interdistrict transfer plans. In G. Orfield & E. Frankenberg (Eds.), *Educational delusions? Why choice can deepen inequality and how to make schools fair* (pp. 187–218). Los Angeles: University of California Press.

Welner, K. G. (2008a). The Overselling of Growth Modeling. School Administrator, 65(6), p. 6. Available online at http://www.aasa.org/SchoolAdministratorArticle.aspx?id=5118

Welner, K. G. (2008b). *NeoVouchers: The emergence of tuition tax credits for private schooling.* Lanham: Rowman & Littlefield.

White, T. (2015). Charter schools: Demystifying whiteness in a market of "No Excuses" corporate styled charter schools. In B. Picower & E. Mayorga (Eds.), *What's race got to do with it? How current school reform policy maintains racial and economic inequality.* New York, NY: Peter Lang.

Wilson-Cooper, C. (2005). School choice and the standpoint of African American mothers: Considering the power of positionality. *Journal of Negro Education, 74*(2), 174–189.

Winters, M. A. (2015). Understanding the gap in special education enrollments between charter and traditional public schools evidence from Denver, Colorado. *Educational Researcher, 44*(4), 228–236.

Woodworth, K. R., David, J. L., Guha, R., Wang, H., & Lopez-Torkos, A. (2008). *San Francisco Bay Area KIPP schools: A study of early implementation and achievement. Final report.* Menlo Park: SRI International. Retrieved from: https://www.sri.com/work/publications/kipp-early-implementation-achievement-study.

CHAPTER 4

National or Special Interests?

Federal and State Education Policy and Reform

In 1973, in *San Antonio School District v. Rodriguez,* the U.S. Supreme Court held that "there is no constitutional right to an equal education." Concerned parents from a poor school district in San Antonio challenged the constitutionality of their school funding formula, which was rejected in a 5-to-4 decision. The majority determined that as long as the state provides each child with "an opportunity to acquire" at least "the basic minimal skills necessary," there was no violation of constitutional rights. Thus, variations of spending at the state level, or, in other words, resource inequality, were not the responsibility of the state to address. Despite the highest federal court weighing in on education matters, education is not mentioned in the U.S. Constitution, and unlike countries with centralized ministries of education, the U.S. federal government has historically had a very limited role in what happens in schools.

Rather, education is a state responsibility, and every state constitution includes an "education clause" requiring the establishment and administration of a system of *normal* or *common* schools that provide a basic education to every child. Although these education provisions vary by state, they generally require: (1) the obligation of legislatures to enact laws to govern the public schools, (2) the organization of the public schools as one unit, (3) the ideal that schools are public and governed by the people, (4) the belief that schools are free and common to all, and that (5) tax resources be allocated fairly to equally benefit citizens regardless of wealth, influence, or status (Alexander & Alexander, 2001). Each state also has its own set of statutes, case law, attorney general opinions, and administrative regulations that form the basis for school governance, along with its own judicial system responsible for the review and interpretation of cases to ensure that the actions of state officials are constitutional and just.

Nevertheless, the federal government, despite funding less than 7% of the overall education budget, remains a powerful force in shaping state and local education policymaking and reform. The power struggle between the federal government's vision for an internationally competitive education system that prepares workers for the new global economy, a state's desire to increase its national education rankings, and most recently, the role of education management and reform advocacy organizations to disrupt traditional policymaking processes to advance the political agendas of their leaders and donors, reflects the new education policy arena that ultimately impacts the lives of students, teachers, and school leaders. Given these competing agendas and interests, we ask, who really controls the schools? Furthermore, who truly has the power to "improve" education? What does this improvement look like and who decides?

This chapter explores the perennial tension that exists between federal and state education policy and reform efforts, competing goals of schooling (e.g. economic v. humanistic) and the ideas and ideologies that animate the politics of education policy amid a rapidly shifting policy landscape that includes a growing number of non-state actors and neoliberal policy goals. We begin with an overview of the changing role and influence of the federal government, followed by a discussion of the role that states play in providing education to all students. We then introduce the non-state actors, including for-profit education management organizations (EMOs), charter management organizations (CMOs), education reform advocacy organizations (ERAOs), and philanthropic foundations that in many states have disrupted successful traditional policymaking processes in ways that have diminished the power of traditional state and federal policy actors, while strengthening the role and impact of these new policy networks and shift from government to governance.

FEDERAL ROLE IN EDUCATION POLICY

American school governance reflects a complex web of policymaking and politics across multiple layers and branches of government. Despite the federal government's heightened role in education policy since the authorization of the Elementary and Secondary Education Act (ESEA) in 1965, its reauthorization in 2015 as the Every Student Succeeds Act (ESSA) reflected a pendulum shift from historic levels of federal authority to what became bipartisan support for greater state and local control (Sampson & Horsford, 2017). Nevertheless, "a perennial tension exists between the Tenth Amendment's notion of states' rights and the Fourteenth Amendment's equal protection under the law" (Sampson & Horsford, 2017, p. xx). Those who support federalism and states' rights argue that federal overreach has resulted in an unhealthy balance between the federal government and the states. They advocate for a limited federal role given the U.S. Constitution's silence on providing public education to its citizens and argue, correctly so, that the establishment, governance, and maintenance of a system of public schools are a state responsibility.

The separate and unequal provision of education historically and thus violation of the Fourteenth Amendment's guarantee of equal protection under the law for students based on race, class, language, gender, and ability serve as a rationale for a more active federal role. In fact, the federal government became active in education in 1965, with the passing of the ESEA, a federal statute that provided compensatory funding to low-income schools and other resources. Original areas of funding included those listed below with funding for special and bilingual education added later.

Title I. Financial Assistance to Local Educational Agencies for the Education of Children of Low-Income Families

Title II. School Library Resources, Textbooks, and other Instructional Materials

Title III. Supplementary Educational Centers and Services

Title IV. Educational Research and Training

Title V. Grants to Strengthen State Departments of Education

Title VI. General Provisions

The federal role in education has seen a dramatic increase in influence, attention, and authority since the 2001 passage of the *No Child Left Behind Act*, a reauthorization of the ESEA of 1965. In fact, No Child Left Behind (NCLB) marked a critical turning point in education policy given the significant power granted to the federal government and executive branch, in particular. NCLB also unleashed an increase in private sector contracting through the requirement that schools in need of improvement provide supplementary education services. It was also an opportunity to use the unfunded mandate as a strategy to get states to align policies to federal preferences in exchange for federal revenue.

A Nation at Risk: The Origins of Reform

Our current obsession with test score data and a politics of competition that has sought to reclaim the standing of America's schools as being the best in the world found its origins in the events leading up to and following the publication in 1983 of the *A Nation at Risk* (NAR) report by a bipartisan commission. In 1981, as a member of the Reagan Administration, United States Secretary of Education Terrel H. Bell wanted to study the nation's education problems and marshal public support for change through the creation of a presidential commission on education. The mood of the country was low given a sluggish economy, high interest rates, and widespread unemployment, particularly among youth of color (Bell, 1988; Hunt & Staton, 1996). According to Bell (1988), "There was more soul-searching, wringing of hands, and criticism than confidence in those solutions, and the actions the government did take appeared ineffective. ... I was hearing constant complaints about education and its effectiveness" (p. 114).

Since Reagan did not support the idea of a presidential panel, likely due to his campaign promise to eliminate the Department of Education, Bell exercised his cabinet level authority to create the National Commission on Excellence in Education (NCEE) on August 26, 1981—"to examine the quality of education in the United States and to make a report to the Nation and to him within 18 months of its first meeting" (Bell, 1988; NCEE, 1983, p. 1). More specifically, the commission would be responsible for:

- assessing the quality of teaching and learning in our Nation's public and private schools, colleges, and universities;
- comparing American schools and colleges with those of other advanced nations;
- studying the relationship between college admissions requirements and student achievement in high school;

- identifying educational programs which result in notable student success in college;
- assessing the degree to which major social and educational changes in the last quarter-century have affected student achievement; and
- defining problems which must be faced and overcome if we are successfully to pursue the course of excellence in education (NCEE, pp. 1–2).

These recommendations covered content, standards and expectations, time, teaching, and leadership and fiscal support that, according to the report, "the American people can begin to act on now, that can be implemented over the next several years, and that promise lasting reform" (p. 23). Although the report also acknowledged its proposals were nothing new, its assertion that "The Federal Government has the *primary responsibility* to identify the national interest in education" and "should also help fund and support efforts to protect and promote that interest," (p. 23) reflected a shift concerning the traditional federal role in education.

NAR was likewise ironic in its call to increase the federal government's national interest in education given the cold war politics of the time and the heightened criticism of U.S. schools that resulted from Russia's launch of Sputnik in 1957 and marked Russia making a significant space and science achievement before the U.S. (Bracey, 2008). *NAR* argued "downwardly spiraling pupil performance had rendered the U.S. education system dysfunctional, thereby threatening the nation's technological, military, and economic preeminence" (Guthrie & Springer, 2008, p. 8); at the same time, the Reagan White House planned to abolish the Department of Education. The report's declaration that the federal government "must provide the national leadership to ensure that the Nation's public and private resources are marshaled to address" educational excellence (p. 23) foreshadowed what would become an expanding federal role in education for decades to come, but *NAR* did not provide a clear direction as to the level or kind of resources needed to stem this rising tide of educational mediocrity (Wong & Nicotera, 2004).

FROM EQUITY TO ACCOUNTABILITY

In addition to redefining the federal government's role in education, NAR provided what Wong and Nicotera (2004) posited a "third way" or perspective concerning this newly conceptualized federal role. Unlike the equity and access focus of Johnson's Great Society initiatives during the Civil Rights Era, or even the Emergency School Aid Act of 1972 under the Nixon Administration that sought to support school desegregation efforts, NAR demanded a higher standard for students, parents, and educators. It was also in direct opposition to Reagan's New Federalism, which focused narrowly on efficiency and sought to devolve education to the states and abolish the Department of Education altogether. NAR did not adhere to either of the two prevailing policy paradigms of equity or efficiency but rather to a new paradigm concerned with standards, quality, and excellence.

In fact, the word *efficiency* was mentioned not once in the 36-page document. *Equity* and *equitable* were only stated once each as emphasized in the following passage:

> We do not believe that a public commitment to excellence and educational reform must be made at the expense of a strong public commitment to the *equitable* treatment of our diverse population. The twin goals of *equity* and high-quality schooling have profound and practical meaning for our economy and society, and we cannot permit one to yield to the other in principle or in practice. To do so would deny young people their chance to learn and live according to their aspirations and abilities. It would also lead to a generalized accommodation to mediocrity in our society on the one hand or the creation of an undemocratic elitism on the other.
>
> (NAR, 1983, p. 13)

Reflecting on NAR's impact on the education of poor and minority children in the 21st century, social psychologist Jeff Howard (2003) agreed with much of the report but remained troubled by what he interpreted as "a strong ... rather strange, juxtaposition between the goals of excellence and equity" (p. 85). In reference to the report's sole mention of equity, he concluded that it "seems to turn on the assumption that in a diverse society a commitment to excellence will work at cross purposes to equity, unless the balance is carefully managed" and that "If we put too much emphasis on the drive for equity, we will be left with mediocrity" (p. 85). The policy paradigm shifted from equity in the 1960s, as represented by increased federal aid to disadvantaged schools through the ESEA of 1965 and Title I policy, to excellence in the 1980s. The shift to emphasizing excellence was reflected in the Hawkins-Stafford Amendments of 1988 that required district and state accountability measures for student performance and the evaluation of the Title I program's success in improving student achievement (Wong & Nicotera, 2004). This move from equity to effectiveness and accountability reflected NAR's influence on federal education policy, which became increasingly high-stakes over the next two decades.

President Clinton's *Goals 2000: Educate America Act in 1994* and, of course, the *No Child Left Behind Act of 2001* operationalized this shift by replacing a focus on inputs, funding, and resources with standards, outcomes, and results (Cross, 2004; Darling-Hammond, 2007; Nichols & Berliner, 2007; Welner & Weitzman, 2005). While this change in focus was not inherently bad, a failure to address what President George W. Bush portrayed as the "soft bigotry of low expectations" did exactly that—establish a different set of expectations for students based on demographic and family characteristics, primarily race and class. Rather than be used to identify and remedy educational inequities by race and socioeconomic, the collection and disaggregation of student test scores simply confirmed to the American public that poor minority children were not as smart or high achieving as White children. Not only were these students at risk of school failure; they were the ones responsible for placing the nation at risk.

No Child Left Behind

The start of the 21st century marked an important shift in federal education policy and reform in the United States. In 2001, under President George W. Bush, Congress reauthorized ESEA, which thereafter became known as NCLB (NCLB, 2003). Its expansion of the federal role in education included holding schools accountable for student achievement according to "subgroups" (e.g. racial and ethnic groups, low-income students, students with disabilities, English language learners, etc.) and, perhaps most notably, the disaggregation of test scores by race as a way to measure and address gaps in achievement between different racial groups. As Noguera (2008a) noted, given America's history of associating racial gaps in intellectual ability with genetic differences, "the fact that federal educational policy has made the goal of closing the racial achievement gap a national priority is truly remarkable" (para. 3). Yet subsequent efforts to close the gap and expand educational opportunity have remained largely unsuccessful at addressing racial disparities in U.S. schools (Au, 2009; Carter & Welner, 2013; Darling-Hammond, 2007; Delpit, 2012; Horsford, 2011; Kantor & Lowe, 2006; Ladson-Billings, 2006; Meier & Wood, 2004; Noguera & Wing, 2006; Payne, 2008).

Despite NCLB expiring in 2007, it would take another eight years of political posturing and polarization before new federal education policy would gain the bipartisan support necessary to be reauthorized and signed into law by President Barack Obama as the ESSA (ESSA, 2015). During those eight years, the convergence of top-down, high-stakes accountability reform efforts resulting from NCLB and the systematic collection of student achievement data by race provided evidence of how students were performing by racial group, highlighting the academic success of White and Asian students and persistently low performance of Black and Latino children and youth. In addition, outdated funding formulas, deepening segregation, and decades of achievement gap data have normalized racial disparities at all levels of education, concretizing a narrative of Black academic, intellectual, and cultural inferiorities that has long been critiqued as a pervasive and iniquitous feature of American schooling (Cross, 2007; Delpit, 2012; Du Bois, 1935; Horsford, 2011; Horsford & Grosland, 2013; Noguera, 2008b; Perry, Steele, & Hilliard, 2004; Selden, 1999; Shujaa, 1994; Sizemore, 2008; Watkins, 2001; Yeakey & Henderson, 2003).

The reauthorizations of ESEA in 2001 and 2015 invite reflection in preparation of the implementation of ESSA during the 2017–2018 school year and going forward. Both acts represent substantial policy impacts with implications for schooling at every level. Other federal policy initiatives have been similarly impactful. For example, the Race to the Top (RTTT) program was implemented as part of the American Recovery and Reinvestment Act in response to the worst economic recession in U.S. history. As part of the Obama administration's economic stimulus package, the $4.35 billion allocated for RTTT essentially doubled down on NCLB's focus on high-stakes accountability measures and expanded choice and competition, not only within local school districts but also between states strapped for funding in the postrecession bust. Most of the attention at the federal level, however, has focused on racial achievement gaps and ignored the ways in which the expansion of choice, competition, and a neoliberal focus on global workforce development has reproduced and increased, in many instances, racial inequality and further concretized racial caste in America.

Race to the Top (RTTT)

In 2010, President Obama and U.S. Secretary of Education Arne Duncan announced plans to reform public education through RTTT—a federal grant program whereby states could compete for a share of $4.35 billion in federal education dollars to spur educational innovation. The largest competition of its kind in the nation's history, RTTT sparked the formation of state-level task forces and officials actively collecting school accountability data, revising state policies, and in some instances amending their constitutions to meet the eligibility requirements for funding. These included (a) adopting standards and assessments that contribute to college and career readiness and global competitiveness; (b) building data systems that measure student growth and success and inform teachers and principals about how they can improve instruction; (c) recruiting, developing, rewarding, and retaining effective teachers and principals, especially where they are needed most; and (d) turning around the lowest-achieving schools. This strategy of incentivizing policy through competitive funding emulated the strategies of venture philanthropies, organizations we will discuss in detail in Chapter 6. President Obama (2009) hailed the program as one that would "not be based on politics, ideology, or the preferences of a particular interest group," but rather "whether a state is ready to do what works." He explained,

> By using the best data available to determine whether a state can meet a few key benchmarks for reform—and states that outperform the rest will be rewarded with a grant. Not every state will win and not every school district will be happy with the results. But America's children, America's economy, and America itself will be better for it.

Yet RTTT's emphasis on the politics of markets and competition, as described in Chapter 2, clearly demonstrated a commitment to neoliberal approach to reform and an unabashed attempt to pressure states to align their policies with the administration's federal reform agenda. Its focus on high-stakes testing, teacher and leader accountability, privatization, charter school experimentation, and school turnaround models reflected a neoliberal politics of education and a far cry from Obama's campaign promise to invest in schools (Welner & Burris, 2014). Rather than tempering the damaging effects of NCLB's unprecedented focus on standards and accountability, RTTT became "NCLB's intensifying makeover" (Welner & Burris, 2014, p. 25) and "political cover for state education reformers to innovate and helping states construct the administrative capacity to implement these innovations effectively" (McGuinn, 2015, p. 136).

Yet notably absent from President Obama's campaign promises were policy recommendations related to addressing the growing problem of racial inequality in education—the very space where policymakers are demanding greater results in preparing students academically for college or career and global competitiveness. Pitting states against states, districts against districts, and educators against their peers, RTTT's obsession with competition, including its aim to better prepare U.S. students to compete globally, was especially illogical in its suggestion that state and district competition for funding based on high-stakes accountability in hard economic times would somehow help to lift the nation's most disadvantaged students and schools from the bottom of the metaphorical well. Instead, RTTT's politics of accountability and competition not only failed to acknowledge their current location within the nation's social, economic, and political structures but also did nothing to incentivize collaboration and community or the public good. As such, this era of reform demands new ways of thinking about inequality, particularly for those students "racing to the top" from the bottom rungs of America's economic ladder.

Every Student Succeeds Act (ESSA)

On December 10, 2015, President Obama signed the ESSA into law, making it the eighth reauthorization of the ESEA of 1965. Given the significant gridlock in Washington and accusations of federal overreach in response to its RTTT and ESEA Flexibility programs, ESSA was deemed a "long shot" months before its passage (Hess & Eden, 2017). Nevertheless, it prevailed, marking a major shift in education policy from an era of federal accountability and control to giving power back to the states. This shift reflects the most recent effort to balance the fundamental propositions of the Tenth and Fourteenth Amendments (Hess & Eden, 2017). The perennial tension between the Tenth Amendment's notion that "The powers not delegated to the United States by the Constitution, nor prohibited by it to the States, are reserved to the States respectively, or to the people" and the Fourteenth Amendment's declaration that government shall not "deny to any person within its jurisdiction the equal protection of laws" underscore the complexity associated with the federal role in education, particularly in relation to "the people" or the public.

In the U.S., the violation of these equal protections by states and local school boards has compelled civil rights groups and community advocates to seek support from both the federal government and the courts to advance an ongoing struggle for educational equality, opportunity, and equity (Cross, 2004; Hochschild, 2003; Maeroff, 2010). Whether the question of desegregation (*Brown v. Board of Education, 1954*), funding adequacy and equity (*Serrano v. Priest, 1971*), special education (Education for All Handicapped Children Act, 1975), or the education of English learners (*Lau v. Nichols, 1974*), the role of the federal government has been critical to holding states and local school districts accountable for ensuring educational protections for populations who have been excluded, segregated, and/or discriminated against through local and state-level education policies and practices. While ESSA arguably presents an opportunity for local communities to play a larger role in determining what their local schools and school systems should look like, America's history of elected school boards and state legislators codifying and perpetuating school inequality through policy complicate this ongoing tension between states' rights and equal protection under the law (Sampson & Horsford, 2017).

NEW POLICY ACTORS, REGIMES, AND GOVERNANCE

Historically, federal-, state-, and district-level state actors have been central to the design, approval, and implementation of education policy. There have, of course, always been special interest groups, lobbyists, advocacy organizations, and activists who have attempted to influence policies. However, more recently, there has been a proliferation of policy actors in the political arena that did not exist to any great extent thirty years ago, and these actors are increasingly global. These new global policy actors in education include venture philanthropists, ideological think tanks, private *edu-businesses* and their lobbyists, charter school management organizations, education consultancies, and other policy entrepreneurs (Ball, 2009; Fang, 2017; Scott, 2009). There is also an increase of both grassroots, locally supported organizations and what have been termed *astroturf* or *grasstops* advocacy organizations, groups that employ local advocates, but which are largely funded by corporate money and wealthy individuals, and which cater to the policy preferences of their funders. These new policy entrepreneurs and the global networks that have formed around them have altered the political landscape in education, sometimes gaining greater policy influence than traditional education special interest groups, such as unions and professional associations.

Often referred to as intermediary organizations that mediate between the State, the private sector, and civil society, they increased the political role of new non-State actors leading to what has been referred to as a shift from *government* to *governance* (Ball, 2008; Rhodes, 1997). Because most wealthy philanthropists and corporations use their considerable wealth to promote pro-business and market reforms, their influence has created not only a "new governance" sector outside the State but also a new common sense about how education should be funded and delivered (Friedman, 1962; Salas-Porras, 2005; Scott, 2009).

New policy networks have formed to promote various reforms aimed at privatization of public schools. One of these reforms is the growth of the charter school movement. Since this movement has succeeded in charterizing several urban school districts, the most notable being New Orleans, we will use this movement as an example of how a policy network has grown up around charter schools. While many charter schools were founded to respond to community needs or to present an option that was lacking in the local school district, the larger charter school movement is ideologically anti-union and aims to privatize public schooling. The charter school policy network, which is largely funded by venture philanthropists, includes individual charter schools, management organizations (CMOs and EMOs), charter school real estate development organizations, advocacy groups, alternative leadership and teaching development programs, and research units (Scott, 2015).

EMOs generally operate on a for-profit basis and operate charter and traditional public schools. CMOs generally operate on a nonprofit basis and operate charter schools exclusively. Many of the philanthropies sympathetic to charter schools are also funders of voucher programs and advocacy related to school vouchers (see Chi, 2008; People for the American Way, 1999, 2003).

Education Management Organizations

EMOs and CMOs are organizations that manage one or more schools and receive public funds. They can be for-profit or nonprofit. Founders often are politically connected to state and/or local policymakers, university faculty, and elites from the private sector. These networks enable them to successfully apply for charters, secure community support for their schools, and acquire critical public and private funding. While charter school laws vary from state to state, most forbid for-profit entities from being granted charters. Instead, EMOs will usually form a nonprofit arm or work with an existing nonprofit organization that will then contract with the EMO to run the school. There is evidence that EMOs, in general, are not securing management contracts in a competitive bidding process but rather using political connections and direct outreach to charter schools and school district officials to market their schools. For-profit management of charters has been facilitated by the cooperation of state politicians and corporate and philanthropic actors. More recently, wealthy technology donors and investors like Reed Hastings of Netflix have been active in growing the charter school sector (Garcia, Barber, & Molnar, 2009; Warner, 2016).

Early in the charter school movement in Massachusetts, for example, the conservative think tank the Pioneer Institute actively promoted charter schools. Its then director played a key role in charter legislation, and its executive director served as acting Under Secretary of Education. In addition to raising money for charter schools, "Pioneer also distributed a how-to manual, *The Massachusetts Charter School Handbook*, and sponsors seminars bringing together entrepreneurs selling curriculum packages, management systems, and assessment and evaluation programs in addition to companies, such as A.P.S., that supply these services." (Vine, 1997). In Massachusetts, the lines between the members of the political structure and the members of the for-profit management companies were blurry from the beginning. The ambiguity of charter school legislation provides support for franchises to proliferate.

Similar blurring of public and private characterized the charter school movement in Ohio. John Brennan, a controversial operator of for-profit charter schools, was able to acquire his schools through his political connections (Oplinger & Willard, 1999a). He donated over $1 million to the Republican Party, as well as $89,000 to former Ohio Governor Voinovich's campaign in 1990. In return, he was appointed to chair a commission that would create a voucher program in Ohio. His schools would have directly benefited from the program he created. Brennan, however, turned his attention to charter schools. He had started a private school with his daughter in 1993 that he wanted to convert into a charter in order to get state funding. But the law forbade such conversions for any private schools started before 1997. Brennan got an exception to the law by claiming that he was dissolving his school. The new school, operating in the same building, was approved. He was able to do the same with four other schools. Brennan continued to have access to the new governor, Governor Taft, and was able to get legislation passed that enabled him to accept children from across school boundaries. His company, White Hat Management, operates multiple charter schools in Ohio. By the mid-2000s, his chain of schools is bigger than three-fourths of the school districts in Ohio. Although Brennan may have used his political connections for his own market empowerment, he did not share the wealth. His schools paid teachers just $19,000 a year (Oplinger & Willard, 1999b).

Edison Schools, once the largest for-profit EMO, and formerly a publicly traded company on the NASDQ stock exchange, also benefited from its political connections in Pennsylvania to then Governor Tom Ridge. Over community protest, the state awarded Edison contracts in Chester and Philadelphia to run their troubled schools—in Chester Upland, all of the schools, and in Philadelphia, twenty schools. Although initially then Edison CEO Chris Whittle promised that Edison could run the schools better for less money, the schools contracted out in Philadelphia have been given more money than other schools with mixed results. Still, much of the protest over the contracts was due to the perception that Edison Schools had an inside track to Harrisburg and that the company had become an ally of the Republicans in the state capital.

The path many EMO founders followed in Florida was to first form a non-profit to write and get the charter authorized, and then to contract with itself to run the school. But political connections have also proved important to EMO founders. For example, John Hage, a close advisor to Jeb Bush, former Governor, helped to enact charter schools legislation. He knew nothing of the reform when he began his work, having come from a business and political background, but he saw the opportunity to manage schools, and began a for-profit EMO, Charter Schools USA. "It was a classic business opportunity," he said, "lots of demand and very little supply" (Fischer, 2002). In 2005, one-third of Florida students were attending for-profit charter schools. Some developers have teamed with companies to start schools in new upscale housing tracts. Hage created the nonprofit Polk Charter Foundation and then applied for seven charters, whose applications it copyrighted. The proprietary nature of EMOs in terms of curriculum and charter applications is a hallmark of the new school managers, though, as we discuss in a moment, their curricula tend to be prepackaged programs created by developers who are often connected to the school choice and standard movements.

CMO founders are similarly connected. Two Teach For America (TFA) alumnae, David Levin and Mike Feinberg, founded the KIPP (Knowledge is Power Program) Charter Schools. Their schools have grown from two in the Bronx, New York, and Houston, Texas, in large part due to the financial connections they established through TFA with The Pisces Foundation and the Broad Foundation. Though Levin and Feinberg taught for only a few years, they became executives over a multistate school system, although Feinberg was fired in 2018 over sexual harassment allegations. Now operating 200 schools serving 80,000 children in twenty states, making it the largest charter school network in the country, KIPP is also one of the most popular charter networks that espouses a "no excuses" pedagogy. Their schools are regarded as successful models for teaching low-income children of color, and they have come to be seen as experts on education for minoritized, testifying before Congress, and speaking at the Republican National Convention in 2000.

TFA, an alternative teaching program founded in 1990 by Wendy Kopp, places inexperienced college graduates from prestigious institutions into urban and rural school districts experiencing teacher shortages. Corps members commit to teach for two years, and most leave teaching after their stint is over. TFA alumnae also play a key role in the expansion of school choice and the development of EMOs and CMOs. As mentioned earlier, KIPP founders Levin and Feinberg are alumnae of the program. Many of the teachers in KIPP schools are former TFA corps members. TFA corps members are also in key leadership positions at the Broad Foundation, which is an influential donor to school choice, and holds school choice and market-based competition as the key for school improvement. In addition, TFA maintains a job placement site for its alumnae on its website, on which EMOs and CMOs, as well as technology and financial service corporations and law firms, recruit alumni. Kopp's husband, Richard Barth, has worked for Edison Schools, Inc. and is now the CEO of the KIPP Foundation. Finally, TFA and school choice organizations receive funding from the same donors. Although TFA was initially founded as a stopgap to chronic teacher shortages in urban and rural school districts, many of the teachers it places currently go directly into charter schools operated by CMOs led by former TFA teachers. Thus, there is a direct pipeline between TFA and the education management sector (Trujillo, Scott, & Rivera, 2017).

Venture Philanthropies and Foundations

Central to the expansion of EMOs and CMOs has been the support of particular foundations that support school choice, including the Broad Foundation, The Walton Family Foundation, the Pisces Foundation, and the Bill and Melinda Gates Foundation. These philanthropies regard themselves as distinct from more traditional ones and have come to be known as venture philanthropies. As Minow (2002) observes,

> Growing numbers of entrepreneurs and heirs to accumulated wealth indicate a desire to make their own choices, rather than defer to professionals, and to develop 'their own private visions of the public good.' With the extraordinary opportunities open to millionaires to invest in the public good and with public spending increasingly restricted to nondiscretionary income transfer programs, private philanthropy efforts will play an even larger role in shaping innovative responses to collective needs.
>
> (p. 11)

Historically, the relationship between philanthropy and advocacy in the education for poor and minoritized students has been fraught with racial politics. At the level of representation, most philanthropists and school choice executives are White, while they focus their efforts on schools and school systems that are almost exclusively comprised of minoritized and poor students (Schnaiberg, 1999). Venture philanthropy's arrival has changed and challenged prior philanthropic models by providing funding to for-profit entities and by supporting advocacy-based research. Venture philanthropies include the Walton Family Foundation, the largest funder of K-12 schooling outside of the federal government, and the Broad Foundation.

As we will discuss further in Chapter 6, the Broad Foundation is also a key supporter of school choice reforms. Started in Los Angeles, California, in 1999 by Eli and Edythe Broad, the Foundation's mission is to "improve urban public education through better governance, management, and labor relations" (http://www. broadfoundation.org). While the foundation invests in multiple initiatives related to these three areas, charters and competition are prominent among them. The combination of the funding areas, which recruit business professionals into school and school district leadership, award urban school districts with an annual prize for improved performance and management, and restructure labor unions while also encouraging school choice and competition, perhaps encapsulates the agenda and strategy of the new school managers best. The Broad Center, the gateway for recruiting business executives to work in school districts, has an all-male executive board of which none have experience in public education. While the Broad Foundation does not seek to dismantle public education, it does aim to reshape it according to business practices. The foundation has supported CMOs such as KIPP, Green Dot, and Aspire Public Schools as well as several charter school associations and charter school real estate development organizations. It also funds and operates the Broad Residency for Urban School Leaders, the Broad Academy, and awards the Broad Prize to high-performing charter school networks and school districts.

The Pisces Foundation, which was started by Gap founders Donald and Delores Fisher, is a major donor to KIPP schools. The Fishers donations to KIPP helped to establish the KIPP Foundation and to train and recruit principals. Pisces has also been a supporter of another CMO, Leadership Public Schools, which runs a network of Bay Area, California high schools. As another piece of the network of new school managers, Pisces is the largest private donor to TFA. Anjua Master, managing director, commented, "We don't select charter locations as much as we seek to locate effective leaders. Most important to us is the leader. We invest in people first" (Hartney, 2004).

Another investor in school choice is the NewSchools Venture Fund. One of the founders of this Silicon Valley organization is Kim Smith, who was a founding member of TFA. NewSchools Venture Fund has given Leadership Public Schools $5 million to support its expansion as well as provided deep investments in the growth of several other EMOs and CMOs. NewSchools Venture Fund represents itself as the "new" philanthropy, agnostic about for-profit or nonprofit approaches to education, and regards its funding as investments, some of which provide a monetary return on their investment, and some of which do not. Silicon Valley venture capitalists, as well as the Bill and Melinda Gates Foundation, have financed much of the organizations' efforts to increase new school models, especially charter school management organizations.

The support of these donors is not just financial. The donors also provide legitimacy to the leaders, and access to other social networks in government and business that can further advance the missions of the CMOs and EMOs. Thus, the financiers are the financial backbone helping to restructure, and in many ways, privatize public education leadership and reform. Moreover, private funding drastically alters the ways in which "public" school funding is conceptualized (Scott & Holme, 2002). Evidence indicates that venture philanthropists have the attention of policymakers. A study asking policymakers to rank most influential individuals in educational policy found that Bill Gates was named first, before the Secretary of Education (Swanson & Barlage, 2006).

STATE-LEVEL EDUCATION POLICY AND POLITICS

With the increased role of the federal government and involvement of new policy networks and new non-state political actors, it is easy to forget that Education in the U.S. is actually a decentralized system governed primarily at the state and local levels. Unlike most countries that have national education laws and ministries of education that govern schools, the U.S. constitution does not so much as mention education. Over 90% of K-12 public education in the U.S. is funded at the state and local levels. Most states draw their funding from a combination of income and sales taxes and state lotteries. Most of the rest of the local funding comes from property taxes. Other than the federal laws described earlier, most of the laws and policies that govern education are made in state capitals and some are delegated to district school boards. For instance, each state has different laws governing the authorization of charter schools and the evaluation and certification of teachers and principals. State departments of education also provide information, resources, and technical assistance to schools and school districts.

For this reason, many of the policy entrepreneurs described in the previous section have focused much of their attention on state and local governments. While many of these political actors are actively influencing state and local policies, we will describe in some detail the one that is perhaps most influential, not only in influencing education policy but policies in every sector of society. As we discussed previously, before the 1980s, traditional policy actors in education, like professional associations, teachers' unions, and even individual educators, had greater access to state legislators and had considerable influence on education policy. Prior to the 1980s, business sector organizations like the chambers of commerce and big corporate lobbyists did not see education as a major area of interest, leaving educators to exert considerable influence. But since the 1980s, the business and corporate sectors have become more active, particularly at the state level. A case in point is the American Legislative Exchange Council (ALEC), which we explore next in some detail.

American Legislative Exchange Council (ALEC)

ALEC is composed of state legislators and corporate leaders who collaborate to produce model or template bills that are introduced or promoted by ALEC members within state legislatures. On its website, ALEC states that its mission is "to advance the Jeffersonian principles of free markets, limited government, federalism, and individual liberty, through a nonpartisan public-private partnership of America's state legislators, members of the private sector, the federal government, and general public" (ALEC website, n.d., para 1). ALEC has been actively promoting model legislation for over forty years behind the scenes and largely under the radar of media, the research community, and public sector professionals. But in 2011, The Center for Media and Democracy "leaked" nearly 800 of its model bills to the public making visible the extent to which it has been actively promoting policy initiatives in various sectors, including education, by writing bills that benefit the ideological and financial interests of corporations.

In rapid succession, laws were passed in multiple states that caused national protests. In Wisconsin, the new law was aimed at limiting the rights of public sector unions; in Florida, it was the Stand Your Ground law that made George Zimmerman and Trayvon Martin household names; and in several states, voter ID laws were passed that some claimed were a thinly veiled attempt to take Democratic voters off the roles. Journalists around the country began connecting the dots and identified ALEC as a central culprit in all three cases. What they often didn't say was that ALEC did not act alone but rather was part of a large and proliferating network of new policy actors who have over the last four decades worked largely behind the scenes to accrue significant policy influence at the state and national levels. While not as controversial as other of ALEC's task forces, its education task force continues to quietly sponsor bills in state legislatures that promote a particular set of education policies informed by a free-market, libertarian ideology. The protests and media attention ALEC received primarily as a result of its role in promoting voter ID laws that disproportionally targeted voters of color led many corporations, nonprofits, and legislators to cancel their memberships or support of ALEC. The controversy and the withdrawal of some corporate support led ALEC to close one of its nine task forces—Public Safety and Elections. However, eight task forces, including education, remain that continue to produce model bills.

ALEC receives the vast majority of its funding directly from corporations that pay "membership dues" that are many times the dues paid by legislative members. Membership for legislative members is a largely symbolic $50 a year and represents a mere 2% of ALEC's funding. Corporations can pay up to $25,000 a year or more in membership dues (Graves, 2011). ALEC also takes some money from venture philanthropists, most notably, the Koch brothers, whose father Fred Koch was a founding member of the John Birch Society. David Koch founded *Americans for Prosperity*, which along with the Heartland Institute is part of the inner circle of ALEC's policy network. Other right-wing foundations, such as Castle Rock (Peter Coors), John M. Olin Foundation, the Broad Foundation, and Bradley Foundation, are among ALEC's funders as well as also part of their ideological network.

ALEC has strategically chosen to work at the state level, working closely with the State Policy Network (SPN), which "is made up of free market think tanks—at least one in every state—fighting to limit government and advance market-friendly public policy at the state and local levels" (State Policy Network, 2012, p. 1). SPN, which is heavily funded by the Koch brothers and other venture philanthropists, was set up during the Reagan administration to create smaller versions of the Heritage Foundation in each of the states (Center for Media & Democracy, 2013). These state-level think tanks publish reports, actively place Op-Ed pieces in local newspapers, and help coordinate the promotion of neoliberal and neoconservative bills in state legislatures. SPN itself sits on ALEC's Education Task Force.

The state-level strategy has worked well in the education sector as there has been a relative lack of scrutiny to state-level education policymaking. In education, state-level policy received increased attention in the 1980s during what Mazzoni (1994) called an "eruption" of policy activism at the state level as states mandated "excellence" through standards. States were also a focus of reform in the 1990s as state charter school laws emerged (Mazzoni, 1991) and state-level accountability systems were created (Anderson, 2001). However, as noted earlier, as these state-level accountability systems became federal laws through the passage of NCLB and, later, ESSA, and the subsequent focus on RTTT and Common Core standards, more research and media attention in education has shifted to the federal level (DeBray, 2006; Kaestle & Lodewick, 2007).

Moreover, as news organizations have had to reduce budgets, they are less likely to assign reporters to state houses, leaving lawmakers at the state level with less journalistic scrutiny, and focusing more attention on the contentious issues surrounding NCLB, RTTT, and the Common Core Standards. These developments may have contributed until recently to ALEC receiving little attention from any quarter in spite of the important role it has played at the state policy level. More recently, states are preempting or withholding shared state revenue from municipal governments that adopt ordinances in conflict with state policy, such as minimum wage laws, sanctuary city ordinances, plastic bag bans, LGBT rights, and anti-fracking bans. Many of these cases exemplify how the entangled relationship between race, class, and property maintain a social order and racial hierarchy where communities of color are often at the mercy of a White power structure. For example, a predominantly White state legislature in Alabama preempted the city of Birmingham, a majority Black city, from setting its own minimum wage.

While the political Right has more effectively deployed ALEC style network governance, they have spawned a series of progressive counter-networks, often, themselves, supported by philanthropy. In response to ALEC's promotion of voter ID, Stand Your Ground and anti-labor laws, progressive politicians, think tanks, and advocacy organizations formed counter-networks to challenge ALEC. Color of Change, a new organization, was formed and joined by Common Cause, NAACP, National Urban League, Presente!, People for the American Way, the Congressional Progressive Caucus, and other organizations and politicians. Whether these counter-networks represent a sustainable countervailing force or whether they are merely an ad hoc reaction to ALEC will depend on how effectively they can manage these new forms of network governance (including funding) and the political and discursive strategies that conservative and neoliberal advocacy organizations have so successfully deployed.

A new ALEC-like progressive organization called The State Innovation Exchange (SIX) (formerly, ALICE) has emerged and describes itself as

> a national resource and strategy center that supports legislators who seek to strengthen our democracy, fight for working families, defend civil rights and liberties, and protect the environment. We do this by providing training, emphasizing leadership development, amplifying legislators' voices, and forging strategic alliances between our legislative network and grassroots movements.

While no match for the corporate and philanthropic money pouring into the coffers of right-wing organizations, SIX claims some victories at the state level for progressives. For instance, many states have passed automatic voter registration laws, provisions for paid sick leave and paid medical and family leave, and expansion of earned income tax credit. However, after the 2016 elections, the Republicans controlled the governorship and both legislatures in twenty-six states; the Democrats' controlled only six. The GOP also had numerical majorities in thirty-three legislatures, one shy of the two-thirds required to initiate a convention on constitutional amendments.

CONCLUSION

With the NCLB reauthorization of ESEA in 2001, the federal government was able to leverage the relatively small amount of money—roughly 7% of the education budget—it provided to states to insist on high-stakes accountability systems in all states. But some have argued that while practitioners and researchers shifted their attention to the federal level with NCLB, state legislatures were actively promoting education policies, often led by lobbyists, think tanks, and other organizations like the ALEC, which is part lobbyist, part think tank, and part corporate proxy. While ALEC is just one of many groups that lobby state legislatures, its unique advocacy strategies and its success in promoting legislation, not just in education but across all social sectors, requires greater attention to understanding this new landscape and its implications from a critical policy perspective. For, in the end, perhaps "political influence may be more closely related to a group's ability to build a long-term and sustainable advocacy coalition" (p. 16). As such, questions of *equity* (whether or not state resources are distributed fairly), *adequacy* (the degree to which public education is funded), and *accountability* (whether or not state officials are providing the type of education described in their respective state constitutions) are important not only to the function of governance in public education at the state level but also in relation to interpretation at the federal level and implementation at the district and local levels.

END-OF-CHAPTER QUESTIONS

1. Should American education be the responsibility of the federal government or state governments?
2. What is the best way to ensure a balance of power, if any, between the federal role in education and the state responsibility to provide common or normal schools for all children?
3. What role should nongovernment policy actors play at the federal and state levels of government when it comes to education policy and reform?

REFERENCES

Alexander, K., & Alexander, M. D. (2001). *American public school law* (5th ed.). Belmont, CA: Wadsworth/Thomson Learning.

Anderson, G. L. (2001). Promoting educational equity in a period of growing social inequity: The silent contradictions of Texas reform discourse. *Education and Urban Society, 53*(3), 320–332.

Au, W. (2009). *Unequal by design: High-stakes testing and the standardization of inequality.* New York, NY: Routledge.

Ball, S. (2008). *The education debate.* Bristol, UK: The Policy Press.

Ball, S. (2009) Privatizing education, privatizing education policy, privatising educational research: network governance and the 'competition state,' *Journal of Education Policy, 24*(1), 83–99.

Bell, T. H. (1988). *The thirteenth man: A Reagan cabinet memoir.* New York NY: Free Press.

Bracey G. W. (2008). Disastrous legacy: Aftermath of a nation at risk. *Dissent, 55*(4), 80–83.

Brown v. Board of Education, 347 U.S. 483 (1954).

Carter, P. L., & Welner, K. G. (Eds.). (2013). *Closing the opportunity gap: What America must do to give every child and even chance.* New York, NY: Oxford University Press.

Cross, B. E. (2007). Urban school achievement gap as a metaphor to conceal U.S. apartheid education. *Theory Into Practice, 46*(3), 247–255.

Cross, C. T. (2004). *Political education: National policy comes of age.* New York: Teachers College Press.

Darling-Hammond, L. (2007). Race, inequality and educational accountability: The irony of "No Child Left Behind." *Race Ethnicity and Education, 10*(3), 245–260.

DeBray, E. (2006). *Politics, ideology, and education: Federal policy during the Clinton and Bush administrations.* New York, NY: Teachers College Press.

Delpit, L. (2012). *"Multiplication is for white people": Raising expectations for other people's children.* New York, NY: The New Press.

Du Bois, W. E. B. (1935). Does the Negro need separate schools? *Journal of Negro Education, 4*(3), 328–335.

Education for All Handicapped Children Act of 1975 (Public Law 94–142).

Elementary and Secondary Education Act of 1965 as amended, 20 U.S.C. § 241 (1974).

Eli and Edythe Broad, the Foundation. (1999). http://www.broadfoundation.org.

Every Student Succeeds Act of 2015, Pub. L. No. 114–95, 129 Stat. 1802 (2015).

Fang (2017), Spheres of influence: How American libertarians are remaking Latin American politics. *The Intercept.* Retrieved from https://theintercept.com/2017/08/09/atlas-network-alejandro-chafuen-libertarian-think-tank-latin-america-brazil/

Friedman, M. (1962). *Capitalism and freedom.* Chicago, IL: University of Chicago Press.

Garcia, D. R., Barber, R. T., & Molnar, A. (2009). Profiting from public education: Education management organizations (EMOs) and student achievement. *Teachers College Record, 111*(5), 1352–1379.

Graves, L. (2011, July 13). A CMD special report on ALEC's funding and spending. *Center for Media and Democracy.* Retrieved from http://www.prwatch.org/news/2011/07/10887/cmd-special-report-alecs-funding-and-spending

Guthrie, J. W., & Springer, M. G. (2004). A nation at risk revisited: Did 'wrong' reasoning result in 'right' results? At what cost? *Peabody Journal of Education, 79*(1), 7–35.

Hess, F. M., & Eden, M. (2017). *The Every Student Succeeds Act: What it means for schools, systems, and states.* Cambridge, MA: Harvard Education Press.

Hochschild, A. (2003). *The managed heart: Commercialization of human feeling.* Berkeley: University of California Press.

Horsford, S. D. (2011). *Learning in a burning house: Educational inequality, ideology, and (dis)integration.* New York, NY: Teachers College Press.

Horsford, S. D., & Grosland, T. J. (2013). Badges of inferiority: The racialization of achievement in the U.S. In M. Lynn & A. Dixson (Eds.), *The handbook of critical race theory in education.* New York, NY: Routledge.

Hunt, S. L., & Staton, A. Q. (1996). The communication of educational reform: "a nation at risk." *Communication Education, 45*(4), 271–292.

Kaestle, C., & Lodewick, A. (Eds.). (2007). *To educate a nation: Federal and national strategies of school reform.* Lawrence: University Press of Kansas.

Kantor, H., & Lowe, R. (2006). From new deal to no deal: No child left behind and the devolution of responsibility for equal opportunity. *Harvard Educational Review, 76*(4), 474–502.

Ladson-Billings, G. (2006). From the achievement gap to the education debt: Understanding achievement in U.S. Schools. *Educational Researcher, 35*(7), 3–12.

Lau v. Nichols, 414 U.S. 563 (1974).

Mazzoni, T. L. (1991). Analyzing state school policymaking: An arena model. *Educational Evaluation and Policy Analysis, 31*, 115–138.

Mazzoni, T. L. (1994). State policy-making and school reform: Influences and influentials. *Journal of Educational Policy, 9*(5), 53–73.

McGuinn, P. (2012). Stimulating reform: Race to the top, competitive grants and the Obama education agenda. *Educational Policy, 26*(1), 136–159.

Meier, D., & Wood, G. (Eds.). (2004). *Many children left behind: How the no child left behind act is damaging our children and our schools.* Boston, MA: Beacon Press.

Minow, M. (2002). *Partners, not rivals: Privatization and the public good.* Boston, MA: Beacon Press.

National Commission on Excellence in Education (1983). *A Nation at risk: the imperative for educational reform.* Washington, DC: Government Publishing Office.

Nichols, S. N., & Berliner, D. C. (2007). *Collateral damage: The effects of high-stakes testing on America's schools.* Cambridge, MA: Harvard Education Press.

No Child Left Behind (NCLB) Act of 2001, 20 U.S.C.A. § 6301 *et seq.* (West 2003).

Noguera, P. A. (2008a). Creating schools where race does not matter: The role and significance of race in the racial achievement gap. *In Motion Magazine.* Retrieved from http://www.inmotionmagazine.com/er/pn_creating08.html

Noguera, P. A. (2008b). *The trouble with Black boys … and other reflections on race, equity, and the future of public education.* San Francisco, CA: Jossey-Bass.

Noguera, P. A., & Wing, J. Y. (2006). *Unfinished business: Closing the racial achievement gap in our schools.* San Francisco, CA: Jossey-Bass.

Oplinger, D., & Willard, D. (1999, December 13). David Brennan's white hat management changes the way business, politics and school vouchers mix. *Akron Beacon Journal.*

Payne, C. M. (2008). *So much reform, so little change: The persistence of failure in urban schools.* Cambridge, MA: Harvard Education Press.

People for the American Way Foundation. (1999). *Privatization of public education: a joint venture of charity and power.* Retrieved from http://files.pfaw.org/pfaw_files/file_74.pdf

People for the American Way. (2003). *The voucher veneer: the deeper agenda to privatize public education.* Retrieved from http://www.pfaw.org/press-releases/pfawf-report-exposes-disturbing-agenda-behind-attacks-on-public-education/

Perry, T., Steele, C., & Hilliard, A. G., III. (2004). *Young, gifted, and black: Promoting high achievement among African-American students.* Boston, MA: Beacon Press.

Rhodes, R. A. W. (1997). *Understanding governance: Policy networks, governance, reflexivity and accountability*. Buckingham, UK: Open University Press.

Salas-Porras, A. (2005). Changing the bases of political support in Mexico: Pro-business networks and the market reform agenda. *Review of International Political Economy, 12*(1), 129–154.

Sampson, C., & Horsford, S. D. (2017). Putting the public back in public education. *Journal of School Leadership, 27-N5*, 725.

Serrano v. Priest, 5 Cal.3d 584 (1971).

Schnaiberg, L. (1999, December 1). Entrepreneurs hoping to do good, make money. *Education Week, 19*, 1,14,16.

Scott, J. (2009). The politics of venture philanthropy in charter school policy and advocacy. *Educational Policy, 23*(1), 106–136.

Scott, J. (2015). Foundations and the development of the U.S. charter school policy-planning network: Implications for democratic schooling and civil rights. *National Society for the Study of Education. Teachers College Record, 114*(2), 131–147.

Scott, J., & Holme, J. J. (2002). Public schools, private resources: The role of social networks in California charter school reform. In A. S. Wells (Ed.), *Where charter school policy fails: The problems of accountability and equity* (pp. 102–128), New York, NY: Teachers College Press.

Selden, S. (1999). *Inheriting shame: The story of eugenics and racism in America*. New York, NY: Teachers College Press.

Shujaa, M. J. (Ed.). (1994). *Too much schooling, too little education: A paradox of black life in white societies*. Trenton, NJ: Africa World Press.

Sizemore, B. A. (2008). *Walking in circles: The black struggle for school reform*. Chicago, IL: Third World Press.

State Policy Network Website. Retrieved from http://www.spn.org/.

Swanson, C. B., & Barlage, J. (2006). *Influence: A study of the factors shaping education policy*. Bethesda, MD: Editorial Projects in Education Research Center.

Trujillo, T., Scott, J., & Rivera, M. (2017). Follow the yellow brick road: Teach For America and the making of educational leaders. *American Journal of Education, 123*(3), 353–391.

Vine, P. (1997, September 8–15). To market, to market … The school business sells kids short. *The Nation, 265*, 11–17.

Warner, J. (2016). The battle of Hastings: What's behind the Netflix CEO's fight to charterize public schools? *Capital and Main*. Retrieved from https://capitalandmain.com/the-battle-of-hastings-whats-behind-the-netflix-ceo-fight-to-charterize-public-schools-1012

Watkins, W. H. (2001). *The White architects of black education: Ideology and power in America, 1865–1954*. New York, NY: Teachers College Press.

Welner, K. G., & Burris, C. C. (2014). NCLB's intensifying makeover: Race to the top's troubling changes to rules, incentives, and practice. In C. M. Wilson & S. D. Horsford (Eds.), *Advancing equity and achievement in America's diverse schools: Inclusive theories, policies, and practices* (pp. 25–40). New York, NY: Routledge.

Welner, K. G., & Weitzman, D. Q. (2005). The soft bigotry of low expenditures. *Equity & Excellence in Education, 38*, 242–248.

Wong, K. K., & Nicotera, A. C. (2004). Educational quality and policy redesign: Reconsidering the *NAR* and federal Title I policy. *Peabody Journal of Education, 79*(1), 87–104.

Yeakey, C. C., & Henderson, R. D. (Eds.). (2003). *Surmounting all odds: Education, opportunity, and society in the new millennium*. Charlotte, NC: Information Age.

CHAPTER 5

School District Governance and Education Leadership

A Shifting Landscape

In the U.S., local school boards have given way to a range of new governance structures and policy regimes that constrain the potential for community engagement and democratic practice. These governance alterations have been influenced by a neoliberal education agenda advanced through the unfunded mandates of No Child Left Behind at the federal level, venture philanthropy at the state and local levels, and major policy reforms at the state level in exchange for the hopes of securing competitive funds through Race to the Top. The result of these political alterations is that democratically elected school boards are losing the power they once had.

Granted statutory authority by states, school boards historically have served as key policy actors at the local community level charged with setting district goals, creating district policy, and hiring and supervising their district's superintendent. The democratic potential for participatory engagement through democratically elected school boards has never been fully realized, in that the asymmetries of power have led to the exclusion of many groups made marginal by inequality. The community control movements of the 1960s and 1970s were efforts to make school boards live up to their democratic ideal. The eradication of elected school boards, often replaced with politically appointed governing boards, evinces that opportunities for participatory decision-making are becoming attenuated.

As Usdan (2010) observed, school boards are often "the only entities that provide continuous institutional leadership through times of constant change and administrative churn" (p. 9). Whether elected or appointed, their most important feature, arguably, is representing the concerns and desires of their constituencies, their communities, and the public good. The democratic representation once provided by locally elected schools boards has diminished as multipurpose government actors, such as mayors, governors, and state legislators, have assumed greater authority over education policy generally and urban school district governance in particular (Gold, Henig, & Simon, 2011; Henig, 2013; Wong, 2007). Growing concerns exist over the extent to which local community knowledge, perspectives, and interests are making their way into the education policy arena as nongovernmental actors have shifted education policy priorities while limiting authentic community input and democratic participation (Sampson & Horsford, 2017). This shift has important implications for school leaders at every level but particularly those district- or systems-level leaders who must work to implement the policy goals articulated by their school boards while also yielding considerable power in terms of staffing decisions, curricular decisions, family and community engagement efforts, government and public relations, and resource distribution.

This chapter focuses on education policy and politics at the local school and district levels in response and relation to the new governance structures established at the state level as described in Chapter 3. It also explores the implications for education leaders who work as principals, superintendents, and members of their respective leadership teams on this shifting landscape. We begin with an overview of school governance regimes (Scott et al., 2017; Shipps, 2012), their characteristics, and their respective influence on education policy and reform at the school and district levels. We then explore the impact of such various regimes on the daily professional lives of education professionals amid the restructuring of school districts and the evolution from "government" to "governance" in the education policy process (Scott et al., 2017). This chapter concludes with some discussion of the future (or end) of school districts as we know them and how a return to participatory democracy and shared governance is essential to protecting America's schools and the public good.

NEW GOVERNANCE REGIMES AND THE RESTRUCTURING OF SCHOOL DISTRICTS

Education reformers are restructuring the governance and leadership of urban school systems in profound ways. Beyond the adoption of market-based educational policies we discussed in previous chapters, education reform and advocacy organizations are actively reshaping how school districts and state educational agencies function in a number of school districts throughout the U.S., and lessons from these school districts are being mobilized to shift schooling in other school districts, and in some cases, other countries like Liberia, which used lessons from the governance and school choice reforms in New Orleans to outsource its entire education system to for-profit provider, Bridge Academies.

In 2017, donors to the Los Angeles Unified School District (LAUSD) school board elections made it the most expensive school board race in U.S. history. Donors interested in expanding charter schools included foundations, advocacy organizations, and wealthy individuals like former New York City Mayor Michael Bloomberg. The next biggest source of funding came from teachers unions. The March 2017 school board primary race involved three seats. Together, charter school advocates together spent about $5.4 million to support their favored candidates. The teachers union United Teachers of Los Angeles, in contrast, spent $1.6 million, around $1 million of which supported the candidacy of board president, and charter school skeptic, Steve Zimmer, who ultimately lost his seat (Favot, 2017).

Meanwhile, an intermediary organization founded by the Broad Foundation, Great Public Schools Now, is dedicated to expanding charter schools in LAUSD, with an early goal of converting half of the schools in Los Angeles into charters softened to indicate a goal to increase the number of "quality" schools, traditional public and charter (Great Public Schools Now, 2016). In this case, philanthropy, advocacy, teachers unions, and market-based reforms intersect in ways that stand to alter governance practices but also to shift the schooling contexts, and the nature of teaching and leadership, for millions of children. For example, one of the growing concerns across urban school districts being targeted with so-called "Portfolio Management Model" restructuring efforts is the extent to which districts can sustain themselves fiscally.

In her 2012 study of former New York City Mayor Michael Bloomberg and Chancellor Joel Klein's governing approach to education reform and its impact on city principals, Shipps described four ideal regimes of governance observed in education policy and politics, which serve as a useful typology for framing and reframing the various governance approaches to education reform at the district or systems level. Her typology includes the Administrative Regime, Professional Regime, Market Regime, and Empowerment Regime, which are ideal types only with none existing entirely as described. In reality, a single governance regime is seldom in place in any district, and it is more likely that professional educators experience a mix of the four different regimes described as follows (Table 5.1).

Administrative Regime

Throughout most of the 20th century, the Administrative Regime, which was the dominant governance type for school systems during the Post-WWII years, focused largely on internal operations and accountability through supervision, bureaucratic mandates, established norms, credentialing, and a certain level of social trust and ethos of public service. Although most districts had elected school boards, they were mostly comprised of White and male members, who were typically businessmen. In the 1950s and 1960s, principals and superintendents were also White, male, hierarchical, and authoritarian in their leadership (Shakeshaft, 1989). As such, although there was solidarity among educators, the profession did not reflect racial or gender diversity, much less any desire to include women, people of color, or women of color within its highest leadership ranks.

Nevertheless, as Weick (1976) and Meyer and Rowan (2006) pointed out, education bureaucracies were often "loosely coupled systems" in which teachers were often able to achieve some level of autonomy behind the classroom door. Supervision was not continuous as it is currently under market and testing regimes, and principals were often too busy with management tasks to spend much time with teachers in classrooms. This often provided teachers with a certain level of autonomy for good or ill, allowing dynamic and creative teachers to work wonders with children but also neglecting to help struggling teachers improve.

Table 5.1 School Governance Regimes

Regime	Agenda	Preferred Accountability	Essential Actors	Essential Resources	Essential Relationships
Administrative Regime	Sustain system by buffering it from political interference	Bureaucratic mandates	Teachers, administrators, school board	Technical routines, established norms, legitimate training and credentials, educator cohesion	Solidarity among educators and skepticism about external change agents
Professional Regime	Change the pedagogy and the culture of schools	Professional discretion	Teachers, parents, administrators, elected officials	Educator expertise, parental commitment, intergroup mediation, pedagogical alternatives, increased government funding	Trust between parents and educators across class, race, and ethnic lines
Empowerment Regime	Authorize new decision makers to enable better unprecedented decisions.	Political responsiveness	New decision-makers, education interest groups, elected and appointed officials	New governing institutions. cohesive group representation. uncorrupted leadership, intergroup mediation, legitimate governing alternatives, benefit redistribution	Pacts by interest groups to share decision arenas and decision-making
Market Regimes	Restructure schooling for efficiency and accountability (corporate) or restructure schooling for competition and choice (entrepreneurial)	Performance of market initiatives	System managers, business, elites (corporate) or system managers, private providers, parents (entrepreneurial)	Engaged market sector, revised regulations, public investment in markets, consumer information, legitimate market actors, performance incentives (corporate) or private financing for start-ups (entrepreneurial)	

Professional Regime

The Professional Regime, which shares the Administrative Regime's characteristics in terms of essential actors (i.e. teachers, administrators, school board members, etc.) and buffering the system from political interference and some bureaucratic mandates, assumes a very different agenda, given its focus on changing the pedagogy and culture of schools. This governance type emerged during the 1970s as teachers and principals began to take more control over instruction and their own professional growth and development. By the late 1970s and early 1980s, studies of schools as workplaces portrayed a professional culture in schools where teachers, who were yet overwhelmingly White and female, had little say over their professional development and worked within a culture of isolation in which norms of collegiality were rare (Lieberman & Miller, 1984; Little, 1982). Yet, over time, the Professional Regime would begin to grant educators professional discretion over school-based decisions, such as hiring decisions, creating and sustaining leadership teams and professional learning communities, and leveraging their knowledge and expertise as education professionals. These features, however, would later become co-opted by the Market Regime.

During this time period, a line of education research, known as *effective schools* research, cast effective principals as heroic figures, creating effective schools by providing strong management, instructional leadership, and an orderly climate conducive to learning (Edmonds, 1979). While its portrait of effective principals reinforced a hierarchical view of administration, it was notable that they were expected to be instructional leaders. Previously, male principals taught briefly, moving quickly from the classroom to the principal's office or moving from being an athletic coach to being a principal. As more women began to move into the principalship in the 1980s, they had a deeper understanding of instruction and classroom culture. In some ways, this denoted a return to the original concept of *principal* teacher.

Overall, the effective schools research had a strong and generally positive influence on schools in the 1980s. It is one of the rare cases in which education research had a direct influence on practice. Many practices that we take for granted today were initiated by this research. These included notions like instructional leadership, parent involvement, a clear school mission, high expectations for all students, and frequent monitoring of student progress (Purkey & Smith, 1983). Yet, while it shifted the emphasis for principals from management to instructional leadership, it also reinforced the school hierarchy, as principals were viewed as top-down change agents.

Many reforms of the 1980s and 1990s introduced many reforms that were focused on building shared leadership. Schools introduced professional learning communities and leadership teams that sometimes included community members. Whole school restructuring models showed great promise, including The Coalition of Essential Schools, Accelerated Schools, and Comer Schools, which introduced many innovations that we take for granted today, such as having a teacher teach a math/science or Language arts/social studies block in high school so that they can get to know students better (Meier, 1995). They also were pioneers in creating forms of authentic assessment. While charter schools were originally touted as incubators of teacher-led innovation, they have been disappointing in this regard in comparison with these innovative whole school models, which unfortunately, with the advent of high-stakes accountability systems, have been difficult to sustain.

According to Shipps (2012),

> a Professional Regime relies on classroom educators whose expertise in teaching and learning is at the center of decision-making and governance. Its form of accountability relies primarily on professional discretion, constrained by norms of professional practice and influenced by pedagogical values.
>
> (p. 4)

While never fully realized, the Professional Regime remains a powerful counterpoint to both the Administrative and Market Regimes. Sadly, the cultural conflict and disconnects that exist between a mostly White, middle-class, female teaching force and increasingly nonwhite student population, undermine the possibilities of a Professional Regime that might not recognize, much less value, culturally relevant and responsive pedagogies as a guide for leadership practice.

Market Regime

Market Regimes are committed to "restructuring schooling" through market- and performance-based initiatives that seek to improve efficiency and accountability while expanding choice and competition. The essential actors are not teachers, school leaders, or education professionals but rather "systems managers," private donors, venture philanthropists, and business elites who prioritize performance incentives over pedagogy and private financing over democratic participation. According to Shipps's (2012) typology, Market Regimes consist of three variations: (a) corporate, (b) entrepreneurial, and (c) diverse provider (also referred to as portfolio districts).

The first is the *corporate* variation, which borrows notions of statistical control of product quality from the corporate sector. The premise is that corporate practices of standardized evaluation, curriculum, and services and incentivist policies like pay-for-performance will lead to greater efficiency and accountability. What makes this approach different from the previous Administrative Regime (also a product of corporate influence in the early 20th century) is that control is exercised at a distance through outcomes measures as opposed to an internal supervisory model. Control is also exercised through what some call *concertive* control by shifting "the locus of control from management to the workers themselves, who collaborate to develop the means of their own control" (Barker, 1993, p. 411), typically within narrowly defined limits. The use of outcomes measures also provides indicators consumers can use to choose schools, which brings us to the entrepreneurial variation of the Market Regime.

Entrepreneurialism, which emphasizes competition and client choice, creates conditions in which everyone is either a consumer or a marketer. Schools become autonomous businesses competing for (and selecting or rejecting) clients, which principals competing with each other for students and teachers. The public school system is viewed as a monopoly and the system is privatized as private vendors (many for-profit) compete for public money. Markets are also employed as accountability systems under the assumption that, like businesses, those that fail to attract sufficient clients should be closed.

Most school districts, including New York City, have developed a combination of corporate and entrepreneurial strategies called *Diverse Provider* Regimes, sometimes referred to as "portfolio districts." As Shipps (2012) noted, this regime "combines the standardized outcomes and internal competition of the Corporate Market Regime with an increased supply of schools and client choice adopted from Entrepreneurial Market Regimes" (p. 7). In this way, districts hope to get the benefits of both regimes, but principals often get mixed and sometimes contradictory accountability messages, which ultimately undermine education equality through the misappropriation of precious time, professional talent, and limited financial resources.

In the case of New Orleans, Hurricane Katrina provided the perfect policy window for the Market Regime that sought to take over New Orleans Public Schools after devastation ravaged the city and displaced many of its residents, and thus, the school district's students, teachers, administrators, and support staff. Similarly, albeit due to largely economic forces, cities like Chicago, Philadelphia, Washington, D.C., Detroit, and Denver would follow suit implementing similar regimes despite facing a great deal of resistance from local community organizations, education advocates, teachers unions, and parent organizers and activists.

Empowerment Regime

Finally, the Empowerment Regime is one that is responsive to particular interest groups or organized communities. These might be parent or neighborhood organizations seeking community control or social movement unions, such as the Chicago Teachers Union. There are many interest groups today that present themselves as grassroots advocacy organizations but are actually promoting a Market Regime. Therefore, an Empowerment Regime has to distinguish between grassroots organizations and largely corporate funded and typically anti-union advocacy groups, often referred to as "astroturf" or "grasstops" organizations. This can also be a problem with community organizations and unions as well as it is not always clear who represents the community or, in the case of unions, the rank-and-file membership. There is also increasing evidence of a neoliberal ideological turn in many grassroots organizations who no longer hold faith in the power of government to enact institutional change (Fisher, 2009).

Sometimes, responsiveness within an Empowerment Regime may be to low-income parents in gentrifying communities, or finding ways to engage them in authentic forms of participation in school decision-making. Sometimes, it involves taking an asset rather than deficit view of parents and communities and seeing them as experts on their own children (Gonzalez, Moll, & Amanti, 2005; Green, 2015; Valenzuela, 2016). Empowering regimes are rare, but as we will see in our discussion of democracy in Chapter 7, it remains an ideal that is sometimes partially achieved.

PUTTING THE *PUBLIC* BACK IN PUBLIC SCHOOLS: FROM MARKETS TO COMMUNITY

Although Market Regimes remain dominant in school systems promoting policies like high-stakes accountability, school choice, and pay-for-performance, depending on context, other regimes may emerge or prevail. For instance, in many rural school districts an Administrative Regime may still be dominant, in part because, unlike urban settings in which there are many schooling choices, rural districts often only have a handful of schools. This is also true in many affluent suburbs, where homeowners have chosen to buy a home there, in part because of the political stability and perceived "quality" of the public schools, which is often connected to the percentage of White and Asian children enrolled (Wells & Holme, 2005). Despite their dominance, Market Regimes have been no more effective or successful at improving public schools or school systems. In fact, this governance type in which schools are viewed as business start-ups is a problematic metaphor, given the fact that in the U.S., one out of every five start-up businesses fails in its first year of operation, and half of them do not survive the first five years. From an institutional perspective (Meyer & Rowan, 2006), one might argue that educators have adopted these principals because they enhance the status of educators—better to be called a CEO than a district superintendent.

This does not explain, however, how the status of the public sector has become so degraded. Although advocates for privatization, like U.S. Education Secretary Betsy DeVos, refer deprecatingly to America's public schools as "government schools," those who continue to diminish the role of public institutions and power of public schools fail to understand that in a democracy, government serves as the expression of the public will. The goal for many of those who promote New Public Management is the demise of teachers' unions. Those reformers who are profit-driven have the same endgame. The subtext of much criticism of public education is that unionized adults are looking out for themselves at the expense of our children. They are also viewed as having "gold-plated" pensions that are bankrupting district and state budgets. In some ways, teachers' unions deserve this criticism as they have historically adopted an industrial model with a focus on bread-and-butter issues alone. Many have been slow to oppose New Public Management reforms, and few have built alliances with communities.

The teachers' strike in Chicago during the summer of 2012 demonstrated how a union that views itself as a social movement allied with low-income communities of color can go on strike and have their local communities support them (Uetricht, 2014). Teachers in Chicago transcended bread-and-butter issues to frame themselves as a social movement union, spending years building alliances with community organizations. While they focused on specific reforms, they framed their opposition more broadly as resistance to managerial and neoliberal reforms that were deprofessionalizing teachers and closing public schools in low-income communities of color. Ayers, Laua, and Ayers (2018) provide a point by point response to what they call myths about teachers' unions.

In spite of the social and educational policies that make equitable schooling more difficult, such as increased privatization of public schooling, gentrification and displacement of low-income families, increasing social inequality, and a fraying social safety net for families, school leaders are in a position to make a difference for their students and families and even engage in advocacy for broader policy and social change. The daily work of an elementary school principal in Tucson, Arizona, will look very different from that of an assistant principal of a high school in rural West Virginia or the chancellor of New York City Public Schools, not because of their job descriptions but, rather, because of the unique community knowledge, assets, resources, and power structure that exist within their particular leadership context. Similarly, the demands of a superintendent leading a large, culturally diverse, urban school district in a fast-growing region in the West might vary greatly from that of the CEO of a mayoral-controlled charter district in the South. Regardless of personal, organizational, and occupational contexts (Roegman, 2016), we argue here that democratic participation and shared governance at the local level, while difficult work, are essential to creating high-quality public schools that not only meet the educational and academic needs of students but also serve as pillars of the community—whereby the school is the community, and the community is the school.

DEMOCRATIC PARTICIPATION AND SHARED GOVERNANCE

While most of these early reforms were aimed at increasing organizational communication, building professional capacity, and sometimes just wanting the appearance of inclusion, some did have more democratic intentions. This was particularly true of those that attempted to break down school community barriers by including parents in school decision-making. Studies of these attempts have highlighted the resistance, mostly by principals, to democratic participation even when supported by district leadership. Researchers have documented the many ways participation can be subverted even when diverse groups are brought to the table (Malen & Ogawa, 1988).

In 1988, Betty Malen and Rodney Ogawa studied shared governance arrangements in schools in Salt Lake City that were set up with near-ideal conditions. All relevant stakeholders were included and given broad jurisdiction, policymaking authority, parity protections, and training provisions. Existing literature at the time suggested that such conditions should enable teachers and parents to wield significant influence on significant issues. However, Malen and Ogawa (1988) found the following:

> First, although the site councils are authorized policymakers, they function as ancillary advisors and *pro forma* endorsers. Second, teachers and parents are granted parity, but principals and professionals controlled the partnerships. Third, although teachers and parents have access to decision-making arenas, their inclusion has maintained, not altered, decision-making relationships typically and traditionally found in schools.

(p. 2)

According to their findings, this lack of parent and teacher influence was the result of the following arrangements: principals ultimately controlled knowledge and resources in the school, defended administrative "turf," and viewed the councils as "channels for dispensing information, moderating criticisms, and garnering support, not as arenas for redefining roles, sharing power, and making policy" (Malen and Ogawa, 1988, p. 259). Teachers did not challenge administrative authority because they feared social and professional sanctions, or else, as was the case for many issues, they shared a common professional perspective with the administration.

Parents tended to lack "insider" information and familiarity and were unclear on the parameters of their power. They also shared many characteristics, and thus interests, with the teachers and principals (i.e. middle-class, Caucasian, and well-educated). Furthermore, council agendas were generally controlled by principals (even though the councils were chaired by parents) and confined to safe issues. Institutional norms of propriety and civility kept principals, teachers, and parents on traditional "turf" and cast disagreements as personal affronts, thus restricting discussion, suppressing conflict, and confining discussions to noncontroversial matters. Finally, because district oversight of site council regulations and procedures was minimal, they were often disregarded. Thus, the micropolitics of participation is such that even when participation is carefully orchestrated, most often, power and influence remain in the same hands.

Given that these councils did not seem to shift power relations, researchers wondered what political utility these councils may have had. For instance, there was considerable evidence that principals found the councils useful as a way to present themselves as democratic while essentially retaining decision-making power in their hands (Malen, 1994). As the notion of democratic participation is increasingly linked to choice in an educational marketplace, this need for legitimation through the illusion of participation may be diminishing. As Rowan (2006) suggests, gaining legitimacy in the current institutional environment increasingly requires behaving more like a Chief Executive Officer than a democratic leader.

At the district level, with the popularity of mayoral control, authentic citizen input in many urban districts has diminished, replaced by market-based school choice. School-based decision-making and inquiry are even more circumscribed and co-opted by scripted curricula, high-stakes testing, and test data (Anderson, 2017; Halverson, Grigg, Prichett, & Thomas, 2005). An education industry has grown exponentially, leading to greater commodification and commercialization of professional development (Anderson & Herr, 2011; Burch, 2009). The term "empowerment" is still used to describe teacher and principal autonomy, even while their decisions are driven by testing pressures; they are blamed for school and societal failures; and salaries, benefits, and pensions of public workers are under attack.

Reformers also deploy empowerment to frame choice and privatization policies, but in their framing, power is given to parents to choose schools where the educators and leaders will be forced by market demand to be more responsive to their educational needs and preferences or risk going out of "business" (Scott, 2013). What may be needed is a framework with a stance toward participation and democracy capable of recognizing the difference between authentic and inauthentic forms of participation (Anderson, 1998) as well as whether school choice policies represent a new form of democracy; an example of depoliticization; or, as the title of Carl Boggs's (2000) book exclaims, *The End of Politics*.

THE MICROPOLITICS OF DEMOCRATIC LEADERSHIP

While choice in a marketplace may be replacing the concept of political democracy in many districts, there is another kind of politics that operates at the school level, which is sometimes referred to as micropolitics. Micropolitics can range from which teacher manages to get the biggest classroom to the microaggressions experienced by students, teachers, or administrators of color. In Chapter 2, we critiqued rational approaches to policy and leadership that failed to address the complexities of life in schools. Part of that complexity is that schools are political places in which parents, students, teachers, and administrators struggle constantly over resources, status, and ideological commitments. Ball (1987) and Blase and Anderson (1995) initiated a line of research that focused on school micropolitics or the behind-the-scenes negotiations that occurred within schools. Their goal was to identify approaches to leadership that might result in more democratic school cultures.

Every teacher and every politically savvy parent knows how "political" schools can be. Principals are in a unique position, since they have to mediate policies and politics horizontally (school–community relations) and vertically (from central office to teachers and students and vice versa). In urban schools, located in gentrifying neighborhoods, principals often are caught between pressures to recruit gentry parents and the resources they bring to the school, but in the process, they may be displacing low-income families of color (Posey-Maddox, 2014). Almost every decision a principal makes will privilege someone over someone else, which make these decisions highly political and come with ethical considerations. Based on the findings of research on school micropolitics, Blase and Anderson (1995) developed a leadership matrix based on two continua of leadership (see Figure 5.1). We present this matrix to demonstrate how school politics can be managed in ways that encourage communication, diplomacy, empathy, and collaboration that result in decision-making that includes a broader swath of stakeholders.

The horizontal continuum ranges from open to closed leadership styles. An *open leadership style* is characterized by a willingness to share power. Respondents also reported that open principals were more honest, communicative, participatory, and collegial than closed principals. A *closed leadership style* is characterized by an unwillingness to share power. Respondents reported that closed principals were less accessible, less supportive, more defensive, more egocentric, and seemed more insecure than open leaders. The vertical continuum ranged from a transactional to transformative orientation toward the goals and direction of the organization. These terms were borrowed from James McGregor Burns's (1982) classic book *Leadership*. Transactional leadership is based on exchange relationships among leaders and followers. In return for effort, productivity, and loyalty, leaders offer tangible and intangible rewards to followers. This orientation can be pursued with an

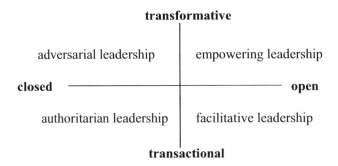

Figure 5.1 Micropolitical Leadership Matrix

open or closed style but tends to create a relatively static environment that seldom disrupts the status quo.

On the other hand, transformative leadership is oriented toward bringing about fundamental change, the object of which is the raising of the consciousness of leader and follower alike around end values of the organization. Transformative leadership tends to be dynamic as it challenges certain aspects of the status quo, and can also be done with an open or closed style.

In his study of school micropolitics, Blase (1991) found that more closed, control-oriented principals created an inauthentic culture in which teachers, students, and parents felt a need to be deceptive and manipulative to get what they needed. Since authentic communication was difficult if not impossible, behind-the-scenes maneuvering became commonplace, and distrust permeated the school. On the other hand, open principals, who were out and about in the school, maintaining constant and authentic communication with teachers, students, and parents, created and fostered a culture of trust and diplomacy. It wasn't that differences, disagreements, and conflict didn't exist but rather that it was handled openly and authentically. This allowed teachers to make their case in open forums rather than behind-the-back maneuvering or face-to-face dissimulation. While teachers reported winning some battles and losing others, they appreciated the sense of trust, fairness, and authenticity that reigned.

Many leaders who fostered authentic, open schools were what Burns referred to as transactional leaders. They maintained a pleasant environment in which authentic communication was possible, but as transactional leaders, they often saw themselves as largely maintaining the status quo. While their schools were more pleasant and productive places to work, this was often bought at the expense of confronting equity issues which are often potentially divisive and messy. Such leaders may prefer to maintain good relations over taking on what they may view as risky and controversial issues. Research on educational leadership is only beginning to understand the importance of risk-taking for effective leadership (Brunner, 1999; Ylimaki, 2005).

On the transformative end of our matrix are leaders who view themselves as advocates. Some advocate from a more closed, go-it-alone, style and others with a more inclusive and open style. The former often engage in advocacy outside the school, being very effective at dealing with the politics of the larger school environment. They are often able to garner resources for the school and they often have charismatic personalities, building a loyal following among a sector of the teaching staff and even of the school community. They are transformative—rather than merely authoritarian—in the sense that they want the school to transcend its current ways of thinking and operating, and often surround themselves with a cadre of talented teachers. While such leaders can be powerful advocates for children, they are often advocates for their own careers as well, and their ambitions and political networks often gain them promotions. When they leave a school, their cadre of loyal followers often leaves with them. Because such leaders tend to create dependent, rather than empowered, followers, those teachers who remain often struggle to defend gains they have made when a new leader takes over.

On the other hand, there were principals who were able to create the caring and authentic culture characteristic of open leadership while also empowering teachers, students, and parents to engage together in participatory and transformative leadership. These leaders called attention to inequities and organized multiple stakeholders to engage together in confronting the conditions leading to such inequities. For instance, if a disproportionate number of Black males were being referred to special education, it is less likely that the transactional leaders—whether open or closed in their leadership style—would confront—or perhaps even notice—the issue. This is because school communities tend to find an equilibrium in which the status quo seems to be more or less working for everyone. There may be constituencies for whom the status quo is not working well, but such constituencies may have little power or access to information.

Transformational leaders—both adversarial ones and empowering ones—are more likely to be willing to upset the status quo to challenge inequities. However, the control-oriented adversarial leader advocates in an authoritarian and paternalistic manner that often fails to garner the support and empowerment of multiple constituencies. Empowering leaders, on the other hand, can more easily achieve goals of social justice while also achieving greater inclusiveness and more authentic and democratic relations. Of course, as with all two-by-two matrices, these quadrants represent ideal types and, as contingency (Fiedler, 1958) and situational leadership (Hersey & Blanchard, 1969) theories have taught us, leaders may need to exhibit different orientations at different stages of one's tenure, for different issues, or for different staffs or schools.

BOX 5.1 GERTRUDE AYERS, PRINCIPAL, HARLEM, NEW YORK

There have always been empowering principals, who have taken risks for the sake of their children and families. We briefly highlight a principal from the 1930s in Harlem, a period of race riots and extreme poverty and joblessness.

Gertrude Ayer battled for years to become a principal in New York City at a time in which African American principals were extremely rare. Finally, in 1935, during the depression, Ayer became the first African American woman principal in the city. Shortly after she was appointed to P.S. 24, Harlem erupted into a riot as a reaction to police brutality, high unemployment, and racial discrimination. According to Johnson (2017),

> In the community-wide hearings about the causes of the riot that followed, Ayer testified about the lack of resources in Harlem schools and her efforts at P.S. 24 to gain the trust of parents and provide additional relief services for unemployed families.
>
> (p. 188)

Previous to becoming a teacher and principal, Ayers was a community organizer and activist for what was then called racial justice and community uplift. She worked on labor issues with the New York City Urban League and did an extensive survey of the working conditions of African American women that documented inequalities experienced by African American women who worked in factories and shops and discriminatory practices in labor unions.

As an educator, she was best known for promoting progressive, project-based curricula and intercultural education. To reduce Black/White racial tensions, she organized intercultural education workshops that were known as "neighborhood home festivals" or "groups conversation method" and were led by Black and White educators together. "When Ayer noted friction between the West Indian and African American students, a social studies unit was planned on life in the Caribbean" (Johnson, 2017, p. 188). She also organized trips for parents and children to local cultural institutions, such as the Schomberg Center for Negro Literature where writers such as Langston Hughes and Richard Wright gave readings.

Like Gertrude Ayers, school leaders today are faced with a complex policy context that pulls them in multiple directions, and this varies from state to state and district to district. For instance, in some districts—especially urban districts—leaders are contending with gentrification, school choice, competition from charter schools, police in schools, colocation, and vendors trying to sell them services. In other districts, especially suburban and rural districts, these issues are not much of a factor. However, issues of inequality and discrimination, whether by race, social class, gender, sexual orientation, or disability, are present in all districts, and school leaders must decide whether they will allow such inequalities to persist or whether they will take on the difficult and stressful task of working to change these conditions (Theoharis, 2007). Even if they decide to do the right thing, re-culturing a school or district is not easy and requires change strategies that are inclusive and the skills and disposition to be successful.

CONCLUSION

Democratic theory would insist in broad inclusion in significant decisions and structures of participation that understand and account for power differentials (Anderson, 1998). But as we have seen, this is often difficult to achieve in practice, given perceived and real conflicts of interest and micropolitical maneuvering. For example, in her 2013 case study of an urban school district in California, Trujillo found that board members and the superintendent "restricted deliberative decision making and failed to provide opportunities for local participation in matters of instruction and personnel" (p. 352). To be sure, a transformative and open leadership style can lead to more democratic and empowering schools but requires great political skill and a strong commitment to democracy and advocacy for children and education.

Although reformers often talk of giving principals and superintendents more autonomy, they have probably never had less, given the recent policy churn at the federal level that has mandated everything from high-stakes testing to teacher evaluation policies. Although, as we noted in the previous chapter, the federal government has no formal policymaking power, it achieves this power through the relatively small but still significant money it holds over states and school districts. Superintendents in some areas have gained autonomy. In districts where there is mayoral control of schools, superintendents or chancellors do not have to answer to school boards. Some districts have given principals more autonomy over budgets and hiring, but they are still highly constrained in the issues that matter most, such as teacher evaluation and curriculum, both being largely driven by high-stakes testing. School choice policies have also turned many principals into entrepreneurs, forced to divert precious time from instructional leadership to marketing their schools.

For school and district leaders, this dramatically shifting policy landscape places increasing demands on both the everyday administration of schools and the negotiation of competing political values, ideologies, and interests. In fact, they will likely find themselves buffeted by macro-level politics such as new policy demands, new market logics, and a for-profit education industry that is relentless in seeking district contracts and other public resources. Although principals and superintendents serve in positions of leadership, contextual factors, institutionalized practices, and external forces often constrain their autonomy and authority.

After more than fifteen years of local school systems responding to and complying with No Child Left Behind's unfunded, top-down accountability mandates, ESSA's devolution of federal authority to states and districts, in theory and perhaps in practice, grants greater decision-making power to the central office administrators, namely the school superintendent. In fact, ESSA's emphasis on local control presents a unique opportunity for superintendents, particularly those leading large urban districts serving large proportions or high-needs students, greater autonomy and flexibility as it relates to defining and measuring school improvement and success. With this increased authority over accountability, however, comes additional pressure associated with the already complicated task of demonstrating improvement across a variety of measures in ways that satisfy a complex and diverse collection of community stakeholders. "Amidst the highly politicized environments of big city school districts, superintendents must serve as collaborators, visionaries, good communicators, and agents of change" (CGSC, p. 1).

School and district leaders must have an understanding of and appreciation for how macro-level social, political, and economic trends shape their environments and the ways in which school local community demographics and histories are critical to their work and its effectiveness. Additionally, microlevel politics at the school and district organization levels presents another set of considerations that must be negotiated by the education leader. Whether urban, suburban, or rural, it is well established that context is important to leadership with evidence suggesting that leaders who are effective in one particular setting might not enjoy that same success in different environments. Nevertheless, the field of education leadership has focused primarily on what school leaders can and must do to improve schools by increasing academic achievement in safe environments. The urgency of meeting the demands of high-stakes testing and accountability standards has, in many ways, left less time for the study and examination of the how context shapes and informs the everyday experiences and actions of education leaders. In Chapter 7, we further examine the politics of shared governance and democratic participation as an opportunity to restore balance to education policy in an era of inequality.

END-OF-CHAPTER QUESTIONS

1. How has the governance and leadership of school districts changed over the last twenty years? What larger social, economic, and/or political forces contributed to this shift?
2. What are the documented challenges associated with democratic participation and shared governance approaches to leadership and reform? How might policymakers and education leaders address such challenges while creating spaces to engage community knowledge and perspectives?
3. In terms of school micropolitics, where would you locate yourself on the micropolitical leadership matrix? Please explain why.
4. Identify and describe the key characteristics or features of each regime that you find to be necessary or essential components for effective governance.
5. Which governing regime do you anticipate will dominate the education policy landscape over the next twenty years and why?

REFERENCES

Anderson, J. D. (1988). *The education of blacks in the south, 1860–1935*. Chapel Hill: The University of North Carolina Press.

Anderson, G. L. (1998). Toward authentic participation: Deconstructing the discourse participatory reforms. *American Educational Research Journal, 35*(4), 571–606.

Anderson, G. L. (2017). Participatory action research as democratic disruption: New public management and educational research in Schools and Universities. *International Journal of Qualitative Studies in Education, 30*(5), 432–449.

Anderson, G., & Herr, K. (2011). Scaling up: "evidence-based" practices for teachers is a profitable but discredited paradigm. *Educational Researcher, 40*, 287–289.

Ayers, W., Laura, C., & Ayers, R. (2018). *"You can't fire the bad ones!": And 18 other myths about teachers, teachers unions, and public education.* Boston, MA: Beacon Press.

Ball, S. (1987). *The micro-politics of the school: Towards a theory of school organization.* London, UK: Methuen.

Barker, J. (1993). Tightening the iron cage: Concertive control in self-managing teams. *Administrative Science Quarterly, 38*(3), 408–437.

Blase, J. (1991). The micropolitical perspective. In J. Blase (Ed.), *The politics if life in schools: Power, conflict, and cooperation* (pp. 1–18). London, UK: Sage.

Blase, J., & Anderson, G. L. (1995). *The micropolitics of educational leadership: From control to empowerment.* New York, NY: Teachers College Press.

Boggs, C. (2000). *The end of politics: Corporate power and the decline of the public sphere.* New York, NY: The Guilford Press.

Brunner, C. (1999). Taking risks: A requirement of the new superintendency. *Journal of School Leadership, 9*(4), 290–310.

Burch, P. (2009). *Hidden markets: The new education privatization.* New York, NY: Routledge.

Burns, J. M. (1982). *Leadership.* New York, NY: Harper.

Edmonds, R. (1979, October). Effective schools for the urban poor. *Educational Leadership, 37*, 15–23.

Favot, S. (2017). UTLA campaign supporting Zimmer now under full investigation; outside spending jumps $1 million in a week to $5.4 million. *LA School Report.* Retrieved from http://laschoolreport.com/utla-campaign-supporting-zimmer-now-under-full-investigation-outside-spending-jumps-1-million-in-a-week-to-5-4-million/

Fiedler, F. E. (1958). *Leader attitudes and group effectiveness.* Urbana: University of Illinois Press.

Fisher, R. (Ed.). (2009). *The people shall rule: ACORN, community organizing, and the struggle for economic justice* (pp. 180–205). Nashville, TN: Vanderbilt University Press.

Gold, E., Henig, J. R., & Simon, E. (2011). Calling the shots in public education: Parents, politicians, and educators clash. *Dissent, 58*(4), 34–39.

Gonzalez, N., Moll, L., & Amanti, C. (2005). *Funds of knowledge: Theorizing practices in households and classrooms.* Mahwah, NJ: Erlbaum.

Great Public Schools Now. (2016). *What is great public schools now?* Retrieved from http://www.greatpublicschoolsnow.org/faq

Green, T. L. (2015). Leading for urban school reform and community development. *Educational Administration Quarterly, 51*(5), 679.

Halverson, R., Grigg, J., Prichett, R., & Thomas, C. (2005). *The new instructional leadership: Creating data-driven instructional systems in schools.* WCER Working Paper 2005–9, Wisconsin Center for Education Research, University of Wisconsin–Madison.

Henig, J. (2013). *The end of exceptionalism in American education: The changing politics of school reform.* Cambridge, MA. Harvard Education Press.

Hersey, P., & Blanchard, K. H. (1969). *Management of organizational behavior: Utilizing human resources.* New York, NY: Prentice Hall.

Johnson, L. (2017). Culturally responsive leadership for community empowerment. In Y. Cha, G. Jagdish, S. Ham and M. Lee (Eds.). *Multicultural education in global perspectives: Policy and institutionalization.* New York, NY: Springer.

Lieberman, A. & Miller (1984). *Teachers, their world, and their work: Implications for school improvement.* Alexandria, VA: ASCD.

Lieberman, A., & Miller, L. (2008). *Teachers in professional communities: Improving teaching and learning.* New York, NY: Teachers College Press.

Little, J. W. (1982). Norms of collegiality and experimentation: Workplace conditions of school success. *American Educational Research Journal, 19*(3), 325–340.

Malen, B. (1994). Enacting site-based management: A political utilities analysis. *Educational Evaluation and Policy Analysis, 16*(3), 249–267.

Malen, B., & Ogawa, R. (1988). Professional-patron influence on site-based governance councils: A confounding case study. *Educational Evaluation and Policy Analysis, 10*(4), 251–270.

Meier, D. (1995). *The power of their ideas.* Boston, MA: Beacon Press.

Meyer, H., & Rowan, B. (2006). Institutional analysis and the study of education. In H. Meyer & B. Rowan (Eds.), *The new institutionalism in education* (pp. 1–14). Albany, NY: SUNY Press.

Posey-Maddox, L. (2014). *When middle-class parents choose urban schools: Class, race, and the challenge of equity in public education.* Chicago, IL: University of Chicago Press.

Purkey S., & Smith. M. (1983). Effective schools: A review. *The Elementary School Journal, 83*(4), 426–452.

Roegman, R. (2016). How contexts matter: A framework for understanding the role of contexts in equity-focused educational leadership. *Journal of School Leadership, 27*, 6–30.

Rowan, B. (2006). The school improvement industry in the United States: Why educational change is both pervasive and ineffectual. In H. D. Meyer & B. Rowan (Eds.), *The new institutionalism in education* (pp. 67–86). Albany, NY: SUNY Press.

Sampson, C., & Horsford, S. D. (2017). Putting the public back in public education. *Journal of School Leadership, 27*, 725.

Scott, J. (2013). School choice and the empowerment imperative. *Peabody Journal of Education, 88*(1), 60–73.

Scott, J., DeBray, E., Lubienski, C., LaLonde, P., Castillo, E., & Owens, S. (2017). Urban regimes, intermediary organization networks, and research use: Patterns across three school districts. *Peabody Journal of Education, 92*, 16–28.

Shakeshaft, C. (1989). *Women in educational administration.* Thousand Oaks, CA: Corwin Press.

Shipps, D. (1997). The invisible hand: Big business and Chicago school reform. *Teachers College Record, 99*, 73–116.

Shipps, D. (2012). Empowered or beleaguered? Principals' accountability under New York City's diverse provider regime. *Education Policy Analysis Archives, 20*(1).

Theoharis, G. (2007). Social justice educational leaders and resistance: Toward a theory of social justice educational leadership. *Educational Administration Quarterly, 43*(2), 221–258.

Trujillo, T. M. (2013). The disproportionate erosion of local control: Urban school boards, high-stakes accountability, and democracy. *Education Policy, 27*(2), 334–359.

Uetricht, M. (2014). *Strike for America: Chicago teachers against austerity.* Brooklyn, NY: Verso.

Usdan, M. D. (2010). School boards: A neglected institution in an era of school reform. *Phi Delta Kappan, 91*(6), 8–10.

Valenzuela, A. (Ed.). (2016). *Growing critically conscious teachers: A social justice curriculum for educators of Latino/a youth.* New York, NY: Teachers College Press.

Weick, K. E. (1976). *Educational organizations as loosely coupled systems. Administrative Science Quarterly, 21*(1), 1–19

Wells, A. S., & Holme, J. J. (2005). No accountability for diversity: Standardized tests and the demise of racially mixed schools. In J. Boger & G. Orfield (Eds.), *Resegregation of the American South* (pp. 187–211). Chapel Hill: University of North Carolina Press.

Wong, K. K. (2007). The education mayor: Improving American's schools. Washington, DC: Georgetown University Press.

Ylimaki, R. (2005). Political risk-taking: Leading literacy education in an era of high-stakes accountability. *The Journal of School Leadership, 15*(1), 1–23.

CHAPTER 6

Philanthropy, Donors, and Private Influence over Public Education

The Case of Charter Schools

Formal public policy actors and agencies shape the politics of education policy though a variety of mechanisms including law, funding, regulations, oversight, sanctions, and rewards. It is common for studies of the politics of education to include examinations of the role of school boards, superintendents, state departments of education, or state legislatures. Yet in an era of rising inequality, a growing body of evidence demonstrates that the role of the private sector, which includes donors, corporations, nongovernmental intermediary organizations, interest groups, foundations, and philanthropies, is in need of scrutiny and greater understanding. Private funding and actors are becoming powerful in shaping state and local education policies, particularly around issues such as school choice, teacher evaluation, and technology in education. Education leaders need to know about the contemporary and historical contexts for these actors.

This chapter considers the emergence of the philanthropic and donor sectors in education policy in an era of growing inequality, and the implications of that influence for equity and democratic participation. We explore the rise and influence of venture philanthropy and wealthy donors as key players in the education policy arena and the implications of their influence on education policy, leadership, and the public good (Blodget, 2006). In order to engage the tensions around philanthropy and its shifting role in shaping educational policy, we draw from critical policy analysis. Of special interest are disparate distributions of power, and stakeholders from all layers of the socioeconomic strata and from different racial/ethnic groups negotiate power arrangements to secure desired policy outcomes. We draw from research on think tanks, advocacy groups, and philanthropies in shaping public policy (Ferrare & Reynolds, 2016; Ferrare & Setari, 2018; Hartney, 2004; Nelson, Drown, Muir, & Meter, 2001; Reckhow, 2013; Rich, 2004; Roelofs, 2003; Smith, 1991; Tompkins-Stange, 2016), and the literatures generated by philanthropic organizations (e.g. mission statements, financial reports, federal tax filings, and evaluation studies of the projects they fund) to map the institutional landscape of these private policy actors and the organizations they fund. We focus especially on the intersection of philanthropy and charter schools, a domain in which policy influence and sector growth are emblematic of the broader trend of private-public policymaking in U.S. education.

PHILANTHROPY IN U.S. EDUCATION: HISTORICAL CONTEXT

Donor and philanthropic influence on education has a history that is entwined with the founding of public schooling. In the U.S., the early 20th century marked the emergence of what we have come to consider traditional foundations a century later. These include the Carnegie Corporation of New York (1911), The Rockefeller Foundation (1913), and the Ford Foundation (1936), funded by wealthy industrialists and their families that sought to contribute to the public good, while also benefiting from tax shelters on their giving. For these wealthy, well-connected elites, foundations served as an effective means for influencing public policy in the areas of health, the arts, education and social welfare, and without the intrusion of government regulation or oversight. They have seeded the development of treasured public institutions, such as universities, libraries, hospitals, and symphonies, as well as a range of services for the poor and underserved. The public tends to view foundations primarily as humanitarian or charitable institutions, and as a result, it dedicates less attention to the political nature of their economic activities, goals, and interests.

Philanthropy has a complex history in U.S. educational policy and race. Wealthy, mostly White male philanthropists funded and helped shape the education of Black children and communities (Anderson, 1988; Tyack, 1974; Watkins, 2001) shortly after Emancipation and the backlash against the Freedman's Bureau's efforts to respond to the needs of formerly enslaved African Americans. Under Reconstruction, or "America's first attempt at interracial democracy", philanthropies played a key role in establishing Black schools in the U.S. South. Whether providing schooling opportunities where they didn't before exist or limiting access to quality education to the privileged, they were also instrumental in the development of normal schools that eventually became Historically Black Colleges and Universities (HBCUs). While these schools gave African Americans access to schooling that public officials were loath to provide, the education many of these schools afforded them often reinforced prevailing views of their social status and future role in American society.

The Julius Rosenwald Fund began supporting Jim Crow institutions but later advocated for racial integration. Inspired by the autobiography of Booker T. Washington, Rosenwald supported Tuskegee University's industrial education program. His funding also helped to construct over 5,000 public schools, shops, and teachers' homes for African Americans. While these institutions provided opportunities for students that otherwise might not have existed, the schools were also organized around specific notions of what African Americans' social status should be, usually aligned with training students for industrial and service work, and acceptance of a permanent second-class citizenship (Anderson, 1988). The schools' pedagogical approaches reflected mainstream, if problematic, thinking about what African Americans needed and their capacity to meet those needs. The tradition of wealthy, mostly White men funding and shaping education for African Americans and others continued into the Progressive Era and persists in the current reform era, where a substantial number of students in foundation-supported charter schools are poor, African American, and Latinx. And within this subset of the sector, many of these schools embrace a "no excuses" pedagogy that involves strict discipline and submissive behavioral norms, expectations for parental involvement, back-to-basics curricula, and longer school days and years (Sanders, Stovall, & White, 2018).

During this period, a network of philanthropists, university researchers, and businessmen worked to restructure schooling systems across the U.S. Wishing to align school administration to business management styles but also to wrest schools from corrupt ward politics that often siphoned schooling resources to curry political favors, these reformers were also informed by notions of what the particular roles and the appropriate social status were for children of different racial and socioeconomic backgrounds (Tyack, 1974). Drawing from the new "science" of intelligence testing, they redesigned curricula to better reflect limited notions of what they thought some students could learn and do, assuming that their visions were the ones that were most appropriate for public policy (Tyack, 1974, p. 130).

Even as these early reformers imagined schooling for African American children, however, Black leaders and educators were articulating and forming schooling imbued with rich thinking about the pedagogical needs and desires of Black children and their communities. Scholars like W.E.B. DuBois and educators like Nannie Helen Burroughs and Anna Julia Cooper (Bair, 2008; Johnson, 2009), for example, advocated for and developed schools for Black children and adolescents based on a belief in those students' inherent intelligence and intellectual potential. The resulting private schools provided a rigorous liberal arts curriculum infused with Black history. These efforts, and the long-standing knowledge base of Black educators teaching in segregated schools, were largely ignored by reformers who ascribed to deficit models of African American children and their communities (Bair, 2008; Walker, 1996, 2009).

While African American leaders and educators articulated distinct and rich visions for schooling, their voices were not included in the imaginings of the elite administrative progressives who remade schooling to map onto principles of scientific efficiency and business management. The work of the philanthropic sector and the administrative progressive education leaders gave birth to the schooling systems that contemporary reformers often wish to dismantle with school choice and privatization reforms. From these Rosenwald-funded, industrial schools in Southern states to the centralized, tracked school systems favored by administrative progressives in the early 20th century, there have been long-standing political tensions between the efforts of elites to provide better schooling and community preferences—with elites usually prevailing over other less powerful stakeholders (Anderson, 1988; Tyack, 1974; Tyack & Cuban, 1995).

Early American foundations were not the staid, ideological-neutral, and risk-averse depictions that often characterize critiques of how they function in contemporary contexts (Hess, 2005). Rather, foundations like the Laura Spelman Rockefeller Memorial set up endowments specifically to advance particular areas of social science research—often dealing with racial issues. In the mid-20th century, the Ford Foundation provided support for organizations pushing for civil rights; later, it was an important funder of Black and Ethnic studies programs at universities around the country. Philanthropic approaches to race have often been complex, revealing seemingly contradictory thinking about racial progress, while also leaving broader social class and racial hierarchies relatively unchallenged.

Yet contradictions and complexities about giving strategies in relation to social and educational equities abound. The Carnegie Corporation funded and commissioned Myrdal's *An American Dilemma,* which questioned the U.S. racial caste system even as it funded programs to maintain South Africa's racial hierarchy through research on the U.S. South's experience managing Blacks (Stanfield, 1985). Stanfield maintains that the giving of these foundations had patrimonial roots that cannot be separated from their effects. In addition, foundation giving reflected the values and beliefs of elites about the need for social change. Moreover, there has been historically an intertwined social network of elites who moved within the philanthropic world. According to Stanfield, this tightly networked sector results in common giving philosophies, norms, and approaches.

As a result of operational abuses, some philanthropists used their foundations for partisan advocacy, tax-avoidance, and self-dealing; for example, the U.S. Congress passed four major pieces of legislation between 1913 and 1969 to regulate them (McIlnay, 1998). Modern philanthropies operate under a federal policy framework established through this legislation: in exchange for tax-exempt status, foundations submit annual federal tax filings, and foundations must spend at least 5% of the past year's assets, which can include reasonable administrative costs. Foundations' investment revenues are also subject to a 1%–2% excise tax (Frumkin, 1998). Tax-exempt organizations cannot be partisan, nor can they engage in self-dealing. Besides these measures, there is little public input into how philanthropies disburse their monies (Roelofs, 2003). Despite federal requirements on annual giving, many foundations still have large endowments that go unspent. In addition, federal requirements do not preclude foundations from participating in advocacy activities, though traditional foundations have not tended to operate as policy advocates in the contemporary era. They have instead funded organizations engaged in advocacy and social change work.

A NEW ERA OF PHILANTHROPY

Critiques of traditional philanthropy range from them being too powerful and immune from public input to being too accessible to organizations seeking to realize social change. For example, many observers have credited foundations with providing resources to a number of social causes, such as being instrumental in advancing the Civil Rights Movement, while some critics have worried about foundations' ability to use private wealth to craft public policy with little or no public debate

(Lagemann, 1992). And critics of traditional philanthropic involvement in public education have argued that foundations have not yielded wide-scale results for all of their investments. Moreover, these critics argue that traditional philanthropies have become too beholden to teachers unions, university schools of education, and other professional associations that lobby public officials to leverage risk-taking in education reform, and as a result, foundations end up supporting the status quo (Hess, 2005). In part, due to this frustration about the slow pace of change, donors and philanthropies have come to see themselves as change agents:

> Growing numbers of entrepreneurs and heirs to accumulated wealth indicate a desire to make their own choices, rather than defer to professionals, and to develop 'their own private visions of the public good.' With the extraordinary opportunities open to millionaires to invest in the public good and with public spending increasingly restricted to nondiscretionary income transfer programs, private philanthropy efforts will play an even larger role in shaping innovative responses to collective needs.
>
> (Minow, 2002, p. 11)

Over the last thirty years, U.S. education has witnessed the rise and influence of a new era of education philanthropy based on the principles of venture capitalism, whereby foundations invest in education reform, management, and advocacy organizations, funding a new network of nongovernment actors who now wield increased power over education policy and reform decisions at every level of government. These relatively recently formed foundations, such as the Broad Foundation (1999), the Bill and Melinda Gates Foundation (2000), and the Walton Family Foundation (1987), have exerted significant policy influence in cities, states, and nationally in Congress and the U.S. Department of Education.

Foundations, while nonpartisan, have ideological bents that map onto their giving strategies. In many ways, the new cadres of foundations that are pursuing more aggressive funding programs than traditional foundations currently engage, and are adopting these approaches from politically conservative foundations that have been employing such strategies for some time (Covington, 1997; Miller, 2003). Moreover, newer philanthropies are similar to traditional philanthropies that often originally began to carry out specific ideological or social policies favored by their namesake donors. The founders and heads of the foundations tend to share similar demographic characteristics: White, male, and wealthy, although the foundation staffs might have more racial and gender diversity (Schnaiberg, 1999).

Two conservative foundations that are exemplars of these strategies are the John M. Olin Foundation, established in 1953 (and shuttered in 2005), and the Lynde and Harry Bradley Foundation, originally established in 1942 and renamed and reorganized in 1985. Olin was responsible for helping to start the several conservative think tanks, including the American Enterprise Institute, the Heritage Foundation, the Manhattan Institute, and the Hoover Institution at Stanford University. The Bradley Foundation has also funded a number of influential researchers, such as Chubb and Moe, whose 1990 publication, *Politics, markets and American schools*, continues to influence school choice scholarship and advocacy. It has also provided millions of dollars

Table 6.1 New Philanthropy, New Language

Traditional Philanthropy	Venture Philanthropy
Grantor	Investor
Grantee	Investee
Gift/Grant	Investment
Deliverables	Social return on investment
Program	Venture
Community impact	Scalable models; proof points
Grant proposal	Theory of change

to legal and advocacy organizations to support the school voucher program in Milwaukee. In addition, under the leadership of Michael Joyce, who also worked at the Olin Foundation, the Bradley Foundation helped establish the Philanthropy Roundtable, which has emerged as a key intellectual network of new philanthropies engaged in school choice funding and advocacy (Miller, 2003).

Despite the similarities between traditional, conservative, and venture philanthropies, there are important differences. Table 6.1 presents the way traditional and new philanthropies differ in their philosophical approaches to funding. Most distinctive is the utilization of market language for social exchanges. Grants become investments, programs are ventures, and measures of impact generally involve the ability to scale up an initiative.

In order to advance charter schools and to grow related market-oriented reforms like teacher merit pay or school closure and reconstitution, venture philanthropies will often seek out promising leaders and organizations to fund. In comparison, traditional philanthropies typically identify broad program areas, and invite applications for funding. Rather than encouraging unsolicited grant proposals, for example, new philanthropies target potential social investments. The emergence of venture philanthropy signals a shift in funding and advocacy paradigms that is reflected in the language the new foundations use to describe their funding interactions.

VENTURE PHILANTHROPY, INEQUALITY, AND CHARTER SCHOOLS

These fiscal challenges confronting many U.S. districts are layered upon racial, linguistic, and socioeconomic segregation in the traditional public schools and charter schools. Schools in the United States are more diverse than at any point in U.S. history in their overall populations, with students of color comprising the majority of public school students in many school districts and some states. Nevertheless, schools are also segregated and stratified by race, poverty, and language. The average Black or Latinx student attends a school where more than 75% of students are minoritized, and in nearly half of these racially homogenous schools, the poverty rates are over 80% (Fiel, 2013; Orfield, Frankenberg, Ee, & Kuscera, 2014; Reardon & Owens, 2014). Because students are learning in segregated learning environments within and across district boundaries, school choice can exacerbate such inequities and increase segregation along other dimensions.

Researchers have also grown concerned over the connection between the educational stratification and the growth of charter schools. Some argue that charter schools are not only deepening racial and linguistic segregation but are also increasingly notable for financial malfeasance. Some estimates indicate that there is evidence of $200 million in charter school fraud in 15 states (Green, Baker, Oluwole, & Meade, 2016). These costs are absorbed by school districts, further challenging their ability to serve their students well.

When considered against the evidence that some charter schools' admissions, expulsion, and discipline policies result in high numbers of students unable to access the promise of charter schools, or unable to stay there once accepted, this financial issue becomes even more important to examine (Jabbar, 2015; Jennings, 2010; Vasquez Heilig, Williams, McNeil, & Lee, 2011). Parents navigate these dynamics in ways that can advantage some children over others within the same community (Pattillo, 2015; Pattillo, Delale-O'Connor, & Butts, 2014). Those children left behind are often in districts under threat of state receivership (Holme, Finnigan, & Diem, 2016). As yet, venture philanthropists giving strategies and organizational missions tend to look favorably on system disruption through the seeding of new leaders and the growth of new charter schools. Analysis of investments reveals a consensus that the expansion of charter school reform, merit pay policies for teachers, or embracing market-oriented approaches to teaching and learning can redress differential performance on standardized assessments, improve graduation rates, and encourage college attendance and persistence.

Meanwhile, educational advocacy groups such as Stand for Children, Democrats for Education Reform (DFER), and Students First have been working to unseat state and local elected officials who do not support school choice and other market reforms and to elect policymakers amenable to this policy agenda. Organizations that are focused on disrupting school systems in order to enact particular market-based reforms have been particularly active and influential over the last decade, and their activity has been heavily supported by foundation funding. For example, representatives from educational advocacy reform organizations share strategies and successes across their school districts, state systems, and policy areas of concern (McGuinn, 2012).

The issue of charter schools and their optimal role in U.S. public education has divided Democrats, as it has nationally. At the national level, DFER, founded by wealthy hedge fund managers in New York, argues that a primary barrier to equity is teachers unions and entrenched school leadership:

We believe that reforming broken public school systems cannot be accomplished by tinkering at the margins, but rather through bold and revolutionary leadership. This requires opening up the traditional top-down monopoly of most school systems and empowering all parents to access great schools for their children.

DFER supports candidates who endorse its educational reform platform, and is agnostic about party affiliation. DFER's core issues emphasize test-based accountability for mayors, teachers, and school leaders, and the ability of parents to choose from a range of schools. These include:

1) Policies which stimulate the creation of new, accountable public schools and which simultaneously close down failing schools; 2) mechanisms that allow parents to select excellent schools for their children, and where education dollars follow each child to their school; 3) governance structures which hold leaders responsible, while giving them the tools to effectuate change and empowering mayors to lead urban school districts; 4) policies that allow school principals and their school communities to select their teams of educators, granting them flexibility while holding them accountable for student performance; and, 5) national standards and expectations for core subject areas, with flexibility for states and local districts to determine how best to meet them.

As we discussed in Chapter 3, this policy platform first emanated from conservative, neoliberal, and libertarian ideals that were hostile to civil rights and state investment in the public sector. The embrace of these ideals by advocates and organizations claiming to be progressive and/or liberal has created political tensions and conflict within and between groups that were historically aligned. The philanthropic sector has invested in constituency building in support of the DFER policy agenda, and dozens of state and local organizations have been seeded from this investment. Teachers unions and some civil rights organizations have found fault with DFER's and philanthropic agendas for education policy given their stance on teacher accountability and comparative silence on civil rights issues like school segregation and disproportionate discipline. In 2012, the Los Angeles County Democrats requested that DFER should cease using "Democrats" in its name because its platform was closely aligned with that of the Republican Party.[1]

A robust policy and planning network has emerged from the hundreds of millions of dollars foundations that have invested. This network is comprised of individual charter schools, management organizations (CMOs), real estate development organizations, research units, social and news media, education reform advocacy organizations (ERAOs), and the alternative teacher and leader preparation programs introduced in Chapter 3 (Ferrare & Setari, 2016; Scott, 2015). The deep and broad financing of this network by philanthropic organizations and foundations cannot be underestimated. For example, many of the same foundations fund charter school networks across several large urban districts with relatively high numbers of charter schools managed by a CMO (Scott & DiMartino, 2008), namely New York, New Orleans, Denver, Nashville, Los Angeles, and Philadelphia, and education technology companies see charter schools as a prime site in which to pilot and scale up online and personal learning platforms. In turn, many of the major donors and philanthropies investing in charter schools and other market-oriented reforms are located in Silicon Valley and are turning their focus to online learning platforms (Burch & Good, 2014; Scott, 2009).

The rise of the donor class in shaping educational policy and creating policy networks also extends beyond the United States, making it important for educational leaders and policy analysts to understand these global education reform and advocacy networks (Ball, 2007; Ball & Junemann, 2011). For example, with support from global foundations and governments, Teach for America's (TFA's) global spin-off, Teach For All, has exported the TFA model to over 40 countries. The emergence of this recent iteration of philanthropy in the U.S. and abroad is accompanied by the growing influence of the donor class, and corporations, on electoral politics, particularly on school board elections, state-level offices, and national representatives. In this regard, the philanthropic and donor influence over public education policy mirrors a national trend, heightened by the Supreme Court's 2010 *Citizens United v. Federal Election Commission* ruling, which allowed unlimited corporate and union independent expenditures on elections and for political action committees (PACs) to proliferate on behalf of candidates or issues.

A number of researchers have investigated venture philanthropy in education (Reckhow, 2013; Tompkins-Stange, 2016). This research has revealed many salient issues, such as the ideological and institutional landscapes of venture philanthropists, their specific areas of focus, and some preliminary effects of venture philanthropy in education (Ball, 2007; Colvin, 2005; Hartney, 2004; Hess, 2005). Other researchers have documented the unequal financial landscape of school choice advocates and opponents, finding that school choice advocates enjoy financial advantages even over well-supported state and national teachers unions (Chi, 2008). In addition, researchers have examined the connection between foundations and evidence production (Scott & Jabbar, 2013, 2014).

Like venture capitalists, venture philanthropies expect aggressive returns on their investments. They measure such returns not necessarily by profit generated, however, but by growth in student achievement; expansion of particular educational sectors, such as educational management organizations or charter schools; and the growth of constituencies who will place political support on public officials to redesign school districts as quasi-public portfolio managers (Bulkley, Henig & Levin, 2010; Greene, 2014; Lake, 2007). While student achievement or growth in learning outcomes is a goal that many educators share, the strategic focus from philanthropists is to remake schools and school governance along corporate models, and issues like democratic participation, civil rights, and selectivity are less of a concern. Venture philanthropists employ similar investment strategies to venture capitalists. In the same way that venture capitalists seek out companies in which to invest and subsequently reap profit, these new philanthropies actively seek out educational reforms, as well as those perceived to be innovators participating in such reforms, for investment (Colby, Smith, & Shelton, 2005).

Through such efforts, philanthropists have provided the financial and advocacy backbone for the expansion and recent resurgence of charter schools. Charter schools have taken hold in key urban "markets," largely due to the coordinated efforts of philanthropists, advocates, researchers, and policymakers (Scott & DiMartino, 2008). As the charter school movement has expanded, a management sector has taken a leadership role in starting and operating charter schools much like franchises or networks. Philanthropists have been attracted to a number of "high-performing" and "no-excuses" charter management organizations whose models suggest that they are capable bringing their operations to scale, as opposed to grassroots charter schools, which tend to be locally grown, stand-alone schools, and by definition, difficult to replicate. A report from the Philanthropy Roundtable on jump-starting the charter school movement argued,

> Clearly, grassroots, "independent" charter schools embody the spirit of the entrepreneurial, accessible charter school movement and will remain an important force in providing a variety of educational options for our children. But it's clear the movement cannot rely entirely on this spontaneous process for the next generation of schools.
>
> (Public Impact, 2004)

Examples of CMOs that venture philanthropists have funded include Green Dot Public Schools (a CMO operating primarily in Los Angeles), the KIPP network (operating across the U.S.), and Uncommon Schools (a CMO operating primarily in the Northeast). These organizations owe much of their recent growth to the support of philanthropists, and as a result, the schools they operate enjoy more total funding than charter schools that function primarily with public funding. Philanthropic support, in addition to charter-friendly federal and state educational policies, has paid off in terms of growth in the number of charter schools; the development of new CMOs; and, as mentioned, the building of capacity in existing ones as well as in the development and support of charter school research and advocacy groups, such as the National Alliance for Public Charter Schools and the Center for Education Reform (CER), the shuttered in 2017 Black Alliance for Educational Options, and the Hispanic Council for Reform and Educational Options (HCREOs). Much of this growth in the charter school network has taken place after a slowing of the movement almost ten years ago.

In 2002, for example, sociologist Amy Stuart Wells argued that there were signs that charter school reform was entering an educational recession since the growth of new schools appeared to be slowing even as the number of states who had adopted charter school legislation had grown (Wells, 2002). In 2001, according to the CER, there were 2,372 charter schools operating, up only 372 schools since 1999. By 2009, charter schools had entered into an educational recovery with laws in 40 states and the District of Columbia, and according to the roughly 6,000 charter schools in operation serving just over two million children. By 2018, that number has grown to laws in 44 states, with over 6% of the total U.S. public schooling population enrolled in charters. In particular cities charter schools make up the majority of the public school system, and the majority of these schools are managed by CMOs.

While charter schools constitute a significant percentage of schools in many cities, including some of the largest school districts in the country and have grown steadily, data indicate that the overall rate of charter school growth has slowed in recent years. According to a report from the pro-charter school Center for Reinventing Public Education, which was funded by the Silicon Schools Fund, until 2013, the sector enjoyed a very steady growth rate, with the total number of charter schools increasing by 6 or 8 percent each year. Since then, the number has fallen steadily, with the growth rate of new charter schools dipping below 2 percent in 2016.

(Lake, Cobb, Sharma, & Opalka, 2018)

CPRE recommended passing state legislation that would require school districts to close and/or consolidate public schools and turn the vacated buildings over to charter school operators in order to meet the demand for facilities that charter school operators see as key to future growth. In this example, we see a state funder contributing to an advocacy-oriented, out-of-state think tank, which, in turn, makes recommendations for state and district level policy changes that could have an impact on schools around the country if implemented. According to researchers at Arizona State University, who have tracked the for-profit educational management sector, as the for-profit MO sector has stagnated, the nonprofit CMO sector has grown (Molnar, Garcia, Miron, & Berry, 2007). While the Center on Reinventing Public Education estimated in 2007 that management organizations operated just 9% of charter schools nationally (National Charter School Research Project, 2007), in several cities targeted by philanthropists for charter school growth, a clear majority of charter schools are managed by CMOs, with districts like Los Angeles and Oakland experiencing fiscal strain as a result of the loss of students to charter schools (Scott & DiMartino, 2008).

Philanthropic support has been instrumental to the growth of CMOs in several important ways. Philanthropies fund the management organizations themselves but also related entities that support and provide a rationale for their existence. This includes nonprofit, nonpartisan, 501(c)(3) organizations that include research centers like the Center for Reinventing Public Education at the University of Washington, mentioned earlier. It also includes charter school real estate development organizations, state charter school associations, and alternative leadership and teacher preparation programs, such as New Leaders for New Schools and TFA, from whose alumni CMOs often draw their leaders, executives, and teachers. It is unlikely that the sector would have grown to its present size without philanthropic support, although federal legislation, such as *No Child Left Behind, Race to the Top, and the Every Child Succeeds Act,* and many states' policy climates also help to create a more favorable policy environment for them to pollinate. It also includes media through sponsored content and social media promotion, and 501(c)(4) organizations that engage in political advocacy.

Figure 6.1 displays the networked connection of giving, with the financial networks as central to the rise of new organizations and leaders, and the stability of existing organizations favorable to charter school growth.

In a guide to funding school choice produced by the pro-school choice Philanthropy Roundtable, Anderson (2004) argued that the most pressing need for donors is to grow the supply of choice schools. "Some of the biggest difficulties that choice schools face are not pedagogical but *operational*: how to find and finance facilities, manage 'back office' administrative tasks efficiently, and develop effective leadership" (p. 39).

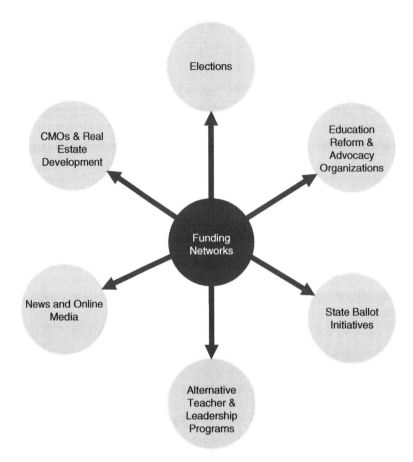

Figure 6.1 The Policy, Planning, and Funding Network of the Charter School Sector

According to Anderson, there are seven imperatives for "reform-minded funders": "fund strategically, be wary of ballot initiatives, help build diverse coalitions, find parent leaders, get political, be prepared to battle in courts, and keep the research and argument coming" (p. 49). In terms of strategic funding, collaboration with established choice groups is encouraged. Also encouraged is the sponsorship of efforts that put parents of color out front instead of "rich, white Republicans" (p. 61).

As mentioned earlier, an important funding strategy of venture philanthropies is to seek out potential investments that align with their organizational giving philosophy and ideological commitments. Many of the new foundations do not accept grant proposals, preferring to seek out their own investments in consultation with their boards of trustees. For example, the Robertson Foundation, a family foundation formed in 1996, is a supporter of school choice and alternative teacher preparation programs like TFA. It does not accept applications for funding but rather identifies the programs that they believe adhere to their tenets. In 2008, its website described this funding philosophy: "The Robertson Foundation takes a targeted, businesslike, results-oriented approach that is modeled more closely on private equity investing than on traditional grantmaking" (http://www.robertsonfoundation.org).

Next, as discussed, venture philanthropies tend to operate as a policy and planning network, often funding the same organizations, pursuing similar funding and advocacy strategies, and pursuing the same educational and policy outcomes. Finally, there appear to be geographic concentrations of venture philanthropic activity, with New York, California, Texas, and Washington, D.C., at the top of the list of foundation spending and schooling systems in Los Angeles, Oakland, Denver, New Orleans, Detroit, Memphis, and Philadelphia also receiving concentrated, cross-philanthropic, and donor investments.

INDEPENDENT EXPENDITURES AND ELECTORAL POLITICS

Another area for investment from philanthropists and donors is in school board and state elections and in ballot propositions through the use of independent expenditures. For example, in the 2016 election in California, two ballot initiatives with significant implications for school funding (Proposition 30, which would levy a tax on wealthy Californians to fund K-16 education, and Proposition 32, which was aimed at stopping the California Teacher Association's ability to use member dues to engage in political advocacy) were presented to California voters. Many donors and organizations supportive of charter schools gave heavily to pass Proposition 32. This measure ultimately failed. At the same time, some prominent donors, such as Eli Broad, whose Broad Foundation has provided significant investments in charter management organizations, publicly supported the passage of Proposition 30 while at the same time invested in its defeat. According to a *Los Angeles Times* exposé, these expenditures were not easy to trace and were aimed at defeating Proposition 30 and passing Proposition 32:

> The donors' money traveled a circuitous path. They contributed to Americans for Job Security, a Virginia trade association. This outfit then passed the money to the Center to Protect Patient Rights in Arizona. The center next sent $11 million to a Phoenix group, Americans for Responsible Leadership, which provided it to the Small Business Action Committee. That committee spent the money on the California campaigns. In another relay, the Center to Protect Patient Rights provided more than $4 million to the America Future Fund in Iowa, which passed the money to the California Future Fund for Free Markets, a campaign committee supporting Proposition 32.
>
> (Blume, Moore, & Smith, 2016)

Independent expenditures through 501(c)(4) advocacy organizations and donors have also shaped local school board elections, which is a growing trend across the United States. According to the Federal Election Commission, independent expenditures are not subject to contribution limits, advocate for a candidate or issue, and are not provided in coordination with a candidate's committee or agents.[2] Large national donors have tended to support pro-reform candidates in Denver, Los Angeles, and Louisiana in order to ensure charter school growth (Reckhow, Henig, Jacobsen, & Alter

Litt, 2017). For example, spending and outside influence on the 2017 Los Angeles Unified School District (LAUSD) Board elections resulted in the most expensive race in history. $6.7 million was spent for three seats prior to the March 7 primary. In total, nearly $15 million was expended on the school board race, which ultimately unseated the School Board President Zimmer. Moreover, there were national endorsements of these local candidates. For example, former Secretary of Education Arne Duncan endorsed charter-friendly candidates Nick Melvoin and Kelly Gonez, and Senator Bernie Sanders endorsed Steve Zimmer and Imelda Padilla. *The Los Angeles Times* reported that charter-affiliated donors spent more than double than teachers unions and other labor groups. Some of these PACs, like the student group LA Students 4 Change (which spent $1 million on the race), had the appearance of being student run but was actually affiliated with the California Charter School Association:

> The group "LA Students 4 Change" is a pro-charter political action committee managed by political consultant John Shallman and working in conjunction with CCSA Advocates. In an interview with Times columnist Steve Lopez, Shallman explained that his team recruited a group of high school students, who appeared in flyers and became involved in the campaign. The students were to be compensated as much as $500 for their help.
>
> (Blume & Poston, 2017)[3]

Figure 6.2 displays the relationship between nonpartisan 501(c)(3) and partisan 501(c)(4) organizations as a tree with different branches, connected by shared financial roots. Increasingly, many nonpartisan organizations have partisan organizational spin-offs, enabling their policy influence to extend further.

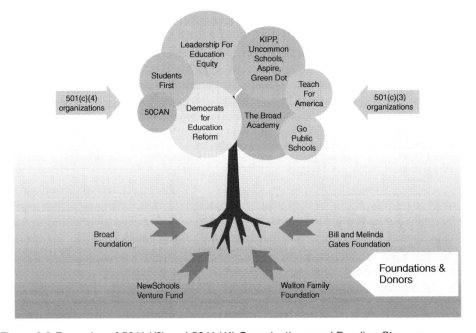

Figure 6.2 Examples of 501(c)(3) and 501(c)(4) Organizations and Funding Streams

Similarly, in the 2016 Oakland, California school board election, top donors to pro-charter school candidates included former New York City Mayor Michael Bloomberg, the TFA PAC Leadership for Education Equity (LEE), Carrie Walton Penner, PACs sponsored by local nonprofit organizations like GO Public Schools, and several leaders of charter school management organizations. Statewide elections in Louisiana, Washington, and Colorado have also received similar donor and philanthropic investments, raising further questions about how such investment shapes democratic participation in a variety of political contexts, and how the issue of charter schools comes to dominate national, state, and local politics. Next, we offer brief descriptions of the following venture philanthropies: The Broad Education Foundation, The Walton Family Foundation, and The NewSchools Venture Fund (NSVF).

BOX 6.1 BRIEF DESCRIPTIONS OF SELECTED VENTURE PHILANTHROPIES

The Broad Education Foundation: Eli Broad made his fortune in finance and real estate. He and his wife Edythe started The Broad Education Foundation in 1999. The Broad Foundation funds governance, management, labor relations, and competition. Since 2001 it has distributed well over $100 million dollars to help start charter schools in a number of cities, though its central focus is CMOs in Los Angeles. At the school district level, the Broad Foundation has been involved with deregulating teacher and leader certification and has produced a tool kit on school closures (https://failingschools.files.wordpress. com/2011/01/ school-closure-guide1.pdf) both to save money and to replace public schools with charter schools. His goal is to have over 50% charter schools in Los Angeles and has heavily financed school board elections there to put pro-charter members in office. The foundation has invested in a number of the fastest-growing CMOs, many of which are located in Los Angeles, including Green Dot Public Schools and the KIPP network. It has also worked with other venture philanthropies to concentrate giving, such as the NSVF. The foundation provided start-up funding for Parent Revolution, the group that developed the "parent trigger" legislation, designed to convert public schools into charters. Broad has also given large sums to Education Reform Now, a pro-charter advocacy organization.

Broad is perhaps best known for his uncertified Broad Foundation Superintendents Academy, which has been producing graduates since 2002. The goal of the academy is to teach prospective superintendents (or in Broad language, Chief Education Officers) free-market, business principals and to recruit urban superintendents from business and the military. Smith (2008) has demonstrated that deregulating educational leadership does not attract more talent to education. While the Broad Academy has been able to place many of its graduates into major urban superintendencies, their effectiveness has been challenged (Howard & Preisman, 2007). However, they generally implement the same neoliberal policies: top-down decision-making, school closings and increase in charter schools, paid outside consultants, sidestepping labor laws and unions, a focus on the "achievement gap" instead of "equal opportunity."

The Walton Family Foundation: Sam and Helen Walton of the Walmart Corporation started the Walton Family Foundation in 1987. Though it funds a range of issues that includes the environment, the Arkansas and Mississippi Delta, and northwest Arkansas, K-12 education reform is a key portion of its funding portfolio. The Foundation has been the largest private funder of K-12 school choice reforms. About its financing of education, the Foundation's website says, "The Walton Family Foundation invests in programs that empower parents to choose the best education for their children" (http://www.walton familyfoundation.org/educationreform/). Funding initiatives include charter schools, school choice, school district improvement (which includes accountability, transparency of student performance and district finance, and merit pay for teachers), and Arkansas education. Within each of these areas, the Foundation targets specific cities, and organizations must serve students within those cities to be eligible for foundation funding.

The NewSchools Venture Fund (NSVF): Kim Smith Brook Byers and John Doerr founded the NSVF in 1998. The NSVF gets its revenue from individual and foundation donors, including the already mentioned Broad Foundation. Located in California, according to its website, the NSVF is a venture philanthropy that "empowers entrepreneurs to transform public education" (http://www.newschools.org). Those interested in funding are encouraged to submit not a grant proposal but a business plan that delineates how the proposed venture will produce measurable outcomes, be scalable, be sustainable, have entrepreneurial leadership, fit with NSVF's investment strategy, and benefit from the NSVF's investment. The NSVF terms its grantee portfolio, "ventures," and it includes both for-profit and nonprofit organizations. Its third fund is focused on funding CMOs, school support organizations, accountability and performance tools, and human capital.

The combined efforts of donors and venture philanthropies have produced significant financial backing for organizations seeking to expand their presence in urban education reform. It is important to consider this combination of funding activity in order to appreciate the scale of policy advocacy being undertaken by the new philanthropy. These data show that it is not just school choice or charter schools that fall under the purview of philanthropic-sponsored educational restructuring but also alternative leadership preparation programs, such as New Leaders for New Schools; choice and charter school advocacy groups, such as The National Alliance for Public Charter Schools; Parent Revolution; the HCREOs; CMOs, such as the KIPP network and Green Dot Public Schools; and organizations geared toward growing CMOs through investments in infrastructure and parental advocacy, such as the Charter School Growth Fund and 50CAN.

SYSTEMIC EFFECTS

Research has demonstrated the positioning of venture philanthropies as "policy patrons" (Tompkins-Stange, 2015) who are contributing to the restructuring of school systems. While charter school research often focuses on the outcomes of schools and CMOs, from the perspective of our critical policy analytic frame, we argue that systemic effects and issues of public sector sustainability must also be considered. Research from Lafer (2018) demonstrated that the growth of charter schools, largely propelled with private funding from foundations and donors, is hurting the ability of school districts to serve the students who remain in their traditional public schools. Lafer estimated that in Oakland, California, the school district loses over $50 million annually, amounting to a decrease of $1,500 per student. Here, we describe the connection between education policies and venture philanthropies in New Orleans, New York, and Los Angeles.

New Orleans

The post-2005 Hurricane Katrina educational landscape in New Orleans has been radically altered. Choice advocates and policymakers saw the disaster as an opportunity to rethink the delivery of public education and moved to a diverse provider model, where the majority of public schools are now charter schools managed by CMOs (Buras, 2011). Post-Katrina (August 2005), the legislature passed Act 35, which allowed for takeover of New Orleans schools. Prior to the Hurricane, the School Performance Score for RSD takeover was 60; the legislature changed this post-Katrina to 87.4 (close to the state average), permitting more schools to enter into the RSD.

New Orleans teachers were fired after the Hurricane, and the teaching force has become far younger and more inexperienced, and there are far fewer Black teachers than before the storm. These policy shifts facilitated the entry and influence of intermediary organizations to enter the New Orleans schooling "market" (DeBray, Scott, Lubienski & Jabbar, 2014) (Nearly 1/3 of all teachers in New Orleans are either TFA or The New Teacher Project-affiliated). Comparatively, the teachers union (United Teachers of New Orleans, a local affiliate of the AFT) has a membership of approximately 1,000 (out of about 3,000 teachers).

CMOs active in New Orleans include KIPP, SABIS, University of New Orleans, Pelican Education Foundation, Broadmoor Charter School Board, New Beginnings School Foundation, Choice Foundation, and the YMCA. The Broad and Fisher Foundations, as well as the NSVF, have provided much of the private support for these reforms. TFA now places record numbers of teachers in New Orleans schools. Also key in the restructuring of New Orleans and other districts, then, has been alternative teaching and leadership programs, whose matriculates staff the new schools. TFA and New Leaders for New Schools, for example, are instrumental in providing the teachers and principals for these new schools, with TFA alumni accounting for 65% of the Fisher Foundation Fellows (a program that prepares leaders to start new KIPP schools) for 2008–2009. In Texas, the Michael and Susan Dell Foundation, as well as several others, have given KIPP millions of dollars to expand the network in Houston.

Los Angeles

The LAUSD, the second-largest school district in the United States, has also seen the number of charter schools within it expand. The LAUSD also has a number of TFA corps members. CMOs operating in LAUSD include Green Dot, KIPP, the Inner City Education Foundation, the Alliance of College Ready Public Schools, Aspire Public Schools, YPI, Bright Star, PUC, Celerity Education Group, Expectations Educational Excellence, Value Schools, and Dialog Foundation. Green Dot Public Schools have been particularly active in the LAUSD, launching public campaigns to take over long struggling district schools. Starting its operation in 2005, it runs 20 schools and describes itself as "the leading public schools operator in Los Angeles, and an important catalyst for education reform, locally and nationally" (http:///www.greendot.org). Philanthropies supporting Green Dot and other CMOs include the Broad Foundation, NSVF, the Fisher Foundation, and the Bill and Melinda Gates Foundation.

During the summer of 2015, a leaked proposal written by the Broad Foundation detailing a $490 million plan to expand charter schools to serve half of LAUSD students emerged to great controversy and concern that such a plan would bankrupt an already financially strained school district (Favot, 2016; Janofsky, 2015). The United Teachers of Los Angeles and the LAUSD Board vociferously opposed the plan (Favot, 2016). The plan to convert a majority of schools into charter schools evolved and resulted in the creation of a new organization called Great Public Schools Now (GPSN), whose donors included the Broad and the Walton Family Foundations. A GSPN mission statement explained,

> This plan is designed to give parents in low-income areas a real choice, real access for their kids, while preserving and augmenting things that are working today.
>
> (GPSN, 2016; Tully, 2016)

New York

Finally, in the New York City Department of Education (NYCDOE), under the leadership of Mayor Bloomberg and Schools Chancellor Joel Klein, charter school reform found a favorable policy environment. Both men worked successfully to have the New York state legislature raise the charter school cap in 2007 to 200 schools. The Walton Family Foundation has been a supporter of a number of New York charter school associations who also lobbied for this increase. Mayor Bill DiBlasio was first elected in 2013 in what many analysts saw as a partial rebuke to the Klein/Bloomberg menu of school reforms. His appointment of a career educator to the Chancellorship of the system, Carmen Farina, was a shift away from the urban system leadership trend of business leaders and people trained by Broad Foundation assuming the helm of urban school districts. The 2017 appointment of Richard Carranza to head the Department of Education furthers this attempt to center educational expertise over business expertise.

Yet New York City leaders face pressure from the state legislature, governor, and a robust charter policy-planning network in New York City and national organizations, particularly those with hubs in New York City. This pro-charter coalition is led by former New York City Council person and Success Academies founder Eva Moskowitz to support the growth and support of charter schools in the city, often through colocation with existing public schools. In 2018 in New York City, there were 227 charter schools serving 114,000 students (New York Charter Schools Center, N.D.). CMOs included KIPP, Success Academies, Uncommon Schools, Achievement First, Beginning with Children, the UFT, and Victory Schools, and most schools were located in Harlem and Brooklyn. TFA and New Leaders for New Schools also place teachers and principals in schools within the NYCDOE. Philanthropies active in funding these organizations include the Broad Foundation, the Fisher Foundation, and the Bill and Melinda Gates Foundation.

There are tens of thousands of students affected by these educational reforms across the three cities discussed earlier and other cities not mentioned. Researchers contest the educational effects of choice, charter, teacher, and leadership programs on students. And while researchers continue to debate the academic effects of charter schools and how to best measure them (Lubienski & Lubienski, 2006; The Charter School Achievement Consensus Panel, 2006), there are also pressing economic, social, and political tensions that require attention.

VENTURE PHILANTHROPY DEMOCRATIC TENSIONS

Venture philanthropy's role in advancing charter school policy and advocacy raises important political, social, and economic tensions. One overarching tension is the issue of sustainability of philanthropic support for charter school reform, especially in an economic downturn. It is unclear how long the network of philanthropies will remain committed to the organizations currently enjoying funding, and without foundation support, many communities where MOs operate the majority of the public schools would be left to figure out how to best proceed. With pressure to show academic results fairly quickly, and with evidence that many charter schools' achievement results are on par with or below those of traditional public schools (Lubienski & Lubienski, 2006), charter schools and CMOs are vulnerable to the judgment of their donors about whether they are effective.

There are broader economic, political, and social tensions that also require discussion. These tensions are heightened in an era of growing inequality where wealth that comes largely from favorable public policies is now directed into mostly tax-exempt foundations, where trustees and philanthropists directly shape public policy for the poor, without the public deliberative process that might have been invoked over school reform policies were that money in the public coffers (Reich, 2005). One estimate holds that in 2006, charitable giving cost the government some $40 billion in tax revenues (Strom, 2007). This is not to romanticize the traditional public policymaking process since numerous examples abound of policymaker neglect of poor communities, wasteful public expenditures, or inefficient and ineffective uses of public resources. Where philanthropy-driven public policy differs, however, it is in the nature of democratic institutions, which incorporate checks and balances through democratic processes that, when working, can attend to these issues.

Because charter school reform operates within a politically charged racial landscape, the concomitant philanthropic support of charter school expansion raises important political and social tensions. For example, while school choice advocates often invoke the expansion of school choice and civil rights as synonymous, traditional civil rights organizations have historically been opponents or neutral on the issue of choice. Venture philanthropy is playing a central role in restructuring public education against the grain of traditional civil rights policy agendas but with the encouragement and support of new rights groups—many of which receive philanthropic funds—and is also a lever for the shift of power within schooling systems that often accompanies school choice reforms (DeBray-Pelot, Lubienski, & Scott, 2007).

Evidence indicates that venture philanthropists' efforts have the attention of policymakers. A 2006 study that asked policymakers to rank most influential individuals in educational policy found that Bill Gates was first, before the-then U.S. Secretary of Education, Margaret Spellings (Swanson & Barlage, 2006). In turn, because of Gates's fiscal and policy influence in education, educational historian Diane Ravitch once opined that he should be regarded as the nation's true schools' superintendent (Ravitch, 2006). A decade later, Ravitch would join those concerned about the effects of philanthropy on public education in her 2016 book, *The Death and Life of the Great American School System: How Testing and Choice Are Undermining Education.*

In addition, reforms and organizations that originate with funding primarily from the philanthropic world can steadily gain public legitimacy and public support. For example, TFA began with philanthropic support. It has received significant federal funding in addition to these donor and philanthropic funds, and is supportive of the charter school movement, with many TFA teachers starting their careers teaching in charter schools that have been founded by TFA alumni (Scott, Trujillo, & Rivera, 2016). Finally, in 2008, inspired by charter schools that posted impressive student achievement gains in California, Governor Arnold Schwarzenegger announced that 29 charter schools would share with selected public schools in $463 million in state money for school construction and modernization projects.

Amidst policy support for the growth of the charter school reform network, political and social tensions regarding equity and democracy also emerge. First, venture philanthropy operates against a historical educational backdrop in which public and private entities have been limited in redressing educational inequalities in K-12 public education by broader social and economic inequalities. Next, the organizations venture philanthropists fund tend to be founded by White men espousing a similar set of ideological and pedagogical approaches to educational reform for primarily children of color, including the need for a return to the educational basics, high academic standards, strict discipline, uniforms, longer school days and academic years, and the use of parental and student contracts to govern expectations (Scott & DiMartino, 2008). Finally, this contemporary philanthropic world is networked, and while school choice reforms are a primary focus of funding and advocacy, a broader set of educational issues, including teacher and principal pay and certification, student testing, and school district management, are often part of their overall reform agenda, which, if systematically adopted, promises to radically restructure schooling for millions of urban students and educational professionals.

Such changes could certainly result in improved schooling for these communities, especially those that have been most disadvantaged by social and educational inequalities, and, indeed, many MOs have posted impressive student achievement on standardized assessment and increased high school graduation rates and entry into four-year colleges by their graduates. And communities of color have often been supportive of many of the charter schools started by CMOs and funded by venture philanthropies, and desperate for the alternatives these schools provide them, resulting in long waiting lists. Yet judged by alternative measures, the expansion of charter school reform can also restrict community or educator preferences for quality schooling that do not align with those of the foundations bankrolling the reform efforts or the school management organization. For example, CMOs limit student access with admissions procedures but also with the implementation of discipline and other school-based policies that result in high numbers of student attrition once students are enrolled. While the extent to which these practices take place is hotly contested by researchers and advocates, there is evidence that some charter schools have disproportionately low enrollments of special education students, English Language Learners, and boys, populations generally known to perform more poorly on standardized assessments. In addition, some CMOs, such as the KIPP network, have high attrition rates, suggesting that struggling students do not find educational havens within those schooling environments (David, Woodworth, Grant, Lopez-Torkos, & Young, 2006; Educational Policy Institute, 2005; Woodworth, David, Guha, Wang, & Lopez-Torkos, 2008). These enrollment patterns have the potential to leave traditional public schools to educate a comparatively high-needs student population that the newly created schools have deemed unsuitable, and to leave them vulnerable to accountability measures that can result in their closure.

To the extent that these enrollment issues are widespread across the charter school sector, judgment of the value of the schools being created requires a broader framing of the issues beyond test scores to an examination of the social and educational processes that the test scores reflect (Scott & Villavicencio, 2009). Much of the philanthropic support for the expansion of CMO-managed charter schools assumes that these schools are defying the odds, making no excuses for their students' racial and socioeconomic backgrounds, and are paragons of educational success (Thernstrom & Thernstrom, 2003; U.S. Department of Education, 2004).

Research on charter schools that partnered with philanthropies or management organizations makes it clear that there are tensions around democratic participation within such schools. External organizations, wanting to show the efficacy of their school design, need to demand of the schools fidelity to their "brand." Donors, having invested in a school or school network, can insist that they have a say in school policy and can withdraw their support if their wishes are not honored (Ascher et al., 2001). Because CMOs are dependent on venture philanthropist's support, they can overpromise achievement results in their quest for financial backing, and foundation reporting requirements can be onerous (National Charter School Research Project, 2007). The need to keep models distinct and intact can preclude local preferences for addressing the particular educational needs of students and communities.

Despite tensions around democratic governance, it is clear that the new philanthropies have the potential to enact positive changes in schooling by infusing much-needed resources into educational innovations other funders or policymakers might deem too risky. Moreover, it is clear that many urban districts are desperate for the kinds of resources and institutional support that philanthropies can provide, given that they strive to serve student populations that are made up overwhelmingly or high-poverty students facing enormous social obstacles.

CONCLUSION

While there has been important racial progress since Reconstruction and the Progressive and Postwar Eras, when early philanthropies emerged, educational inequality persists. A hallmark of this persistence has been the resegregation of previously desegregated school systems, particularly in the south where progress on desegregation was reversed beginning in the 1990s when school districts under court order to desegregate were granted unitary status, and when the courts shift to the right limited the use of race in efforts to desegregate. In addition, one in six U.S. children currently lives in poverty, and in several states, the majority of children enrolled in public school are children of color.

The new philanthropists have amassed wealth though a combination of personal industry, favorable tax policies, and economic expansion. This wealth has afforded them the opportunity to leverage educational policy, a power that similarly interested but less wealthy constituents do not enjoy. Such accumulation of wealth has not been equitably enjoyed across the socioeconomic landscape. Instead, during the 1990s, when many of the new philanthropies were established, the greatest wealth gap in U.S. history emerged (Shapiro, Greenstein, & Primus, 2001). Similarly, the majority of U.S. corporations have paid no federal income taxes for much of the same time period, allowing corporations to amass unprecedented profits, and for executives to enjoy record compensation packages (Shapiro et al., 2001; United States Government Accountability Office, 2008). In the midst of upward wealth concentration, a wealth gap has emerged that has important implications for the educational opportunities of such children, since poverty is associated with significant social impediments to adequate health, safety, nutrition, and early childhood development.

Researchers have also grown concerned over the connection between educational stratification and the growth of charter schools, given hyper-segregation within the sector. Some argue that charter schools are not only deepening racial and linguistic segregation but also increasingly notable for financial malfeasance. Researchers estimate that there is evidence of $200 million in charter school fraud in 15 states (Green et al., 2016). These costs are absorbed by school districts, further challenging their ability to serve their students well. When considered against the evidence that some charter schools' admissions, expulsion, and discipline policies result in high numbers of students unable to access charter schools because of selective admission, or remain due to policies that lead to attrition, this financial issue becomes even more important to examine (Jabbar, 2015; Jennings, 2010; Vasquez Heilig et al., 2011). In addition, the exercise of choice by middle-class parents can advantage their children over less well-off families within the same catchment area (Pattillo, 2015; Pattillo et al., 2014). Those children left behind are often in districts under threat of state receivership, or districts with high rates of school closures in Black and Latinx neighborhoods (Holme et al., 2016; Scott & Holme, 2016).

This historical level of wealth inequality contributes to and intensifies already existing racial and socioeconomic inequalities in schooling and society. For example, many schools engage in individual fundraising through their Parent-Teacher Associations, and the ability to generate significant revenue through these mechanisms is directly related to socioeconomic and racial/ethnic segregation within and across school districts. An analysis of such fundraising processes in the San Francisco Unified School district found that schools with the lowest percentages of students receiving free and reduced priced lunch raised the most funds, with one school raising an additional $1,500 per child (Smith, 2014). Philanthropy and donors have helped to provide resources for new education organizations and to school districts, and funders increasingly link fiscal support to the expansion of school choice policies. Meanwhile, there is growing evidence that the expansion of school choice without strong, enforced equity regulations leads to greater segregation and inequality (Smith, 2015).

The terrain for the politics of education policy has undergone significant transformation in this era of inequality. One hallmark of this transformation is the increased role being occupied by interest groups beyond the traditional educational organizations such as unions and professional associations working as a coalition to shape state policies. Funded by a rise of venture philanthropies, individual donors, and independent expenditures to advocacy organizations, political candidates, and ballot initiatives, this governance context has shifted to one in which education advocacy and reform organizations play much more powerful roles in shaping state, school district, and county educational policy than any time in the state's history (Scott, 2009; Zeichner & Peña-Sandoval, 2015). While advocacy organizations and interest groups work to influence a range of issues related to education policy and practice, a focus on the education reform and advocacy sector in relation to charter school reform and market-based policies offers particular insights into understanding the politics of education (Ferrare & Setari, 2016; Manna & Moffitt, 2014).

Venture philanthropy and its role in school choice advocacy is political because it challenges long-held notions about the allocation of power within school systems, especially the role of parents, teachers, and school and school district leaders. It calls for a rethinking of leaders as managers, and parents as customers and consumers. It also demands a reimagining of the role philanthropies can play in policy formation and in the lives of poor children of color. Finally, it distills the notion of where educational expertise rests, away from schools of education within universities and the teachers and leaders they prepare and toward alternative structures that draw on nontraditional educational reformers, many of whom come from business, law, or advocacy. These shifts in philosophy and practice pose significant changes for the way minoritized and poor students are educated.

There are research, policy, and practical actions that can help ease some of the political tensions that venture philanthropy presents, and that can also help to facilitate democratic and excellent educational reforms. For example, the emergence of venture philanthropy reminds educational policy researchers that they must examine policymaking outside of formal governmental arenas and build theoretical and conceptual models that attend to this dynamic arena. It also suggests that policymakers need to be more aware of philanthropic and advocacy activities in advancing school choice and should develop and enforce existing regulatory procedures to ensure that the public interest is protected. If CMO-run charter schools prove to be more effective, important questions about how they achieve their results must be answered so that traditional public schools can learn and benefit from their educational and management innovations. Finally, educational practitioners and parents must be empowered to make informed decisions about from which organizations they will accept funding or with whom they will collaborate.

Given the policy impact venture philanthropy is having on public education, education leaders must consider the political and philosophical implications of their influence. Much closer scrutiny is also needed in regard to the policy advocacy in which philanthropies engage to assure that private funding does not simply advance private agendas, but, rather, visions for public education are co-constructed with education leaders, teachers, parents, and communities. In addition, leaders should attend to the tensions around democracy, civic engagement, power, and equity when fostering partnerships with philanthropies or organizations funded by them

(Reich, 2005). Especially needed is informed, ethical, and engaged leadership that foregrounds critical understandings of race and inequality and how private interests might further exacerbate such patterns.

QUESTIONS FOR LEADERSHIP, POLICY, AND PRACTICE

This chapter raises questions and implications for education leadership, policy, and practice. Given the current state of deep economic, racial, ethnic, and linguistic inequalities, the relationship between policy influence and wealth needs greater scrutiny as education policy making becomes increasingly privatized (Anderson & Donchik, 2016). There is a strong role for school districts and democratically elected school boards to hold charters and contractors accountable for access and equity. There is an accompanying need to understand that some donor efforts are geared toward radically reshaping governance through the eradication of elected school boards and to contend with the implications of such efforts for democratic participation, which has long been an issue for many poor families and families of color. And donor investments leading to privatization in predominantly Black communities in the United States and internationally must be examined in terms of the racial politics and power asymmetries involved in wealthy investment and policy formation for people of color (Chaney & Myers, 2017).

School boards, school districts, and school leaders can strengthen school district/state agencies' oversight on finance, equity, and enrollments in charter schools. In particular, there is a strong need to invest in transparent research on charter schools that considers issues of equity, democracy, and systemic sustainability. Such research must be accessible and legible for multiple audiences in order to help school board members, parents, and citizens utilize the evidence that is generated. Many foundations that are invested in growing the charter school sector are also investing heavily in research on these efforts. Such funding often shapes the research produced, and more public investment in research and evaluation could serve to mitigate any mistrust that might ensue from advocacy-funded research, whether it is from foundations and donors or labor unions. In democratizing the research evidence, there is a parallel need to better understand the networks propelling these initiatives for parents and community members, to whom funding networks are often opaque.

There are at least four areas where implications and questions are especially abundant.

1. *Sustainability*: While policymakers, especially state legislators, play an important role in legalizing public-private hybrid schooling, the new school managers rely especially heavily upon philanthropy to advance their organizations. It is unclear how long philanthropists will support this sector, and how much money they will be willing to contribute in the future. It is also unclear how the agendas of the philanthropists influence teaching and learning since schools are dependent upon their money for survival. From a broader perspective, the

influx on private money could decrease the pressure on state legislatures to fund schools adequately, which raises concerns for traditional public schools that do not have access to private funding. In other words, the philanthropy could diminish the viability of other public schools—even unwittingly.

2. *Democracy*: A second issue needing closer examination is the relationship between the new school managers and our broader democracy and democratic processes. While the ways in which the public is able to engage in traditional public educational governance are clearly flawed, there exists at least an expectation that public officials respond and involve the public in decision-making. The private sector, from which many of the new school managers come, possesses no such mandate. For example, with virtually no public deliberation and debate, the new school managers and their supporters have drastically expanded school choice policy. The restructuring of the public schools in New Orleans is a key example of this. Ultimately, researchers and theorists must query whether the public sphere expands or constricts in relation to the growth of this new schooling sector.

3. *Community*: An original goal of charter school advocates was to encourage local, grassroots organizations and teachers to start schools that would meet the needs of the students and families within a given community. How does the community-based school survive and flourish amidst market-driven schools and advocates? Another aspect of community that must be further explored is what happens to parental and community voices within schools managed by CMOs.

4. *Equity*: Although the current policy framework tends to define equity in terms of outputs—performance on standardized tests, under the new school managers, we must consider the issue of educational inputs. Do EMO- and CMO-run schools have fewer, similar, or greater resources than traditional public schools? Within the EMO/CMO sector, is there stratification? Another aspect of equity is who has access to the schools and how admissions and discipline policies work on the ground. Are all students accepted, and are disciplinary sanctions meted out fairly? Is there due process for students? These broader equity considerations tend to get lost in the politically charged debates over the meaning of the most recent achievement study.

5. *Diversity*: A final issue requiring further exploration is that of student and community diversity. A key under-examined area is the way in which many CMOs brand and market themselves as service providers to Black and Latino students. Since CMOs are founding the schools, in many ways, they require that the school's racial compositions be homogenous since their marketing and branding present the companies as such. In this regard, the relationship between segregated schools and the new school managers needs examination. In addition, more attention is needed as to how curricula about race, gender, and other multicultural issues are implemented within the schools, if at all needed.

Education leaders do complex work leading schools and systems that require them to be aware of and conversant in federal, state, and local policy directives, regulations, and procedures. Yet the rise of venture philanthropy and its role in shaping public policy presents a new area of terrain for school and system leaders. Education reform and advocacy organizations, funded by philanthropy, are putting pressure on school boards, local schools, and school districts to increase the number of charter schools in their districts, to adopt blended learning platforms using technology from for-profit firms, and to close schools to make way for these approaches to schooling. This chapter helps to make visible the private sector actors working to shape public education policy, and raises important, unanswered questions about equity, transparency, democracy, and inequality that school leaders must navigate.

We close this chapter with an example (See Box 6.2) of a superintendent who challenged his county school board to keep a low-quality virtual charter school out of the district.

BOX 6.2: SUPERINTENDENT MIKE MATSUDA, ANAHEIM UNION HIGH SCHOOL DISTRICT

Mike Matsuda is a superintendent who has gained some notoriety for his stand against a low-quality, for-profit virtual charter school that wanted a contract with his district. Since 2014 he has been superintendent of Anaheim Union High School District in Anaheim, CA, a low-income district with a large immigrant population in the shadow of Disneyland. He is the son of Japanese-American parents who were placed in internment camps during World War II. Because their language and culture were suppressed, Supt. Matsuda has a deep appreciation for bilingualism and encouraging his students to be active and engaged citizens. He was named the 2017 Administrator of the Year by the California Association of Bilingual Education (CABE), and was one of *Education Week's* "Leaders to Learn From" for 2016. (See https://www.youtube.com/watch?v=a_sX2K8ZLlw)

Usually administrators win awards for raising test scores and coloring within the lines. Not only is Superintendent Matsuda an outstanding administrator, he is also a courageous leader who advocates for his students and for public schools. Aware of the research that shows poor results for virtual charter schools, he was upset when the Orange County School Board approved the application of a virtual charter school of questionable quality and ethics.

Epic Charter Schools is an Oklahoma based virtual charter school that applied to the Anaheim City School District to start a virtual charter school there. It is an Education Management Organization (EMO) serviced by a for-profit company, Advanced Academics, which provides the platform and other services. The Anaheim City School District board rejected Epic's proposal but Epic appealed to the Orange County School Board, which conditionally approved Epic's proposal despite a scathing 20-page report from its own charter review team recommending denial.

Many superintendents would not have taken on the powerful county board. Yet Superintendent Matsuda felt it necessary to stand up for his values and confront the board. What's more, his district, along with Anaheim's elementary school district filed a lawsuit against the Orange County Department of Education (OCDE).

This is part of a statement by Superintendent Matsuda to the Orange County School Board.

Thank you for agendizing this discussion on EPIC Charter schools. My name is Michael Matsuda, superintendent of Anaheim Union High School District.

First of all, I would like to make it clear that our Board of Trustees is not opposed to locally authorized charter schools that are transparent and have local control accountability measures so parents and stakeholders can be heard.

As we have learned, Epic Charter Schools, a large, online charter network based in Oklahoma, is currently under investigation for fraud in Oklahoma. I have reviewed your approval of the EPIC charter school's appeal from Anaheim Elementary School District's denial of the charter application. We have serious concerns and agree with your staff's original recommendation to deny their appeal.

We understand the Charter was conditionally approved yet we find no evidence that those conditions have been satisfied. We have seen a list of vendors for epic all of whom are from Oklahoma. Does this Board have no concern about the transfer of taxpayer funds from California to Oklahoma? Does this board understand the impact on the education of the students of our districts when 10% of the monies are guaranteed to go to a private entity with virtually no transparency in place? Does this board understand that the students of this charter are only guaranteed one time a month face to face meetings with "teachers"? Can this board guarantee both the high school and elementary districts that the special education and English learner needs of all students will be fulfilled as required by law?

Especially in the case of online charter schools, the public needs to question how, without proper oversight, students are being supported, not only academically but also socially and emotionally. National reports on online charter schools say that they have dramatically lower test scores than traditional public schools, and that students are not getting adequate social emotional support.

I urge you to rely upon your excellent staff and their fine work presented to you that has underscored the false promises that Epic has suggested. By even the lowest standard no one could suggest Epic is providing an education that leads to successful college and careers. If Epic is allowed to grow without any transparency, accountability and oversight, the futures of students, families and the greater community will be at stake.

One of the Orange County board members defended Epic, calling Matsuda's statement a rant that was "insult inflicting, filled with malice, misinformation and pure fiction" (Palmer, Oct. 4, 2016). These are the kinds of attacks that democratic leaders who advocate for the welfare of their students can anticipate as they work for social justice for their students. But we have seen the unethical exploitation that has occurred with some for-profit universities preying on the public's money (Wong, February 23, 2015). Disreputable companies are selling their wares in K-12 education with very little oversight as well, and superintendent are in a position to protect the public's interest.

END-OF-CHAPTER QUESTIONS

1. In what ways are venture philanthropies and traditional philanthropies similar? In what ways are they distinct?
2. How do race, power, and inequality matter in the context of philanthropic support for public education?
3. What are the democratic possibilities and pitfalls of philanthropic involvement?
4. Why does the context of rising inequality matter for the study of philanthropic involvement in education policy?
5. What are the possibilities and dilemmas for education leaders: principals, teacher leaders, and system leaders in a context of deepening inequality, reduced state support, and growing philanthropic involvement in schooling?

NOTES

1   http://www.lacdp.org/wp-content/uploads/2012/05/LACDP-2012-DFER-Cease-Desist-Final.pdf.
2   https://www.fec.gov/help-candidates-and-committees/making-disbursements-pac/independent-expenditures-nonconnected-pac/.
3   https://www.latimes.com/local/la-me-edu-school-election-money-20170521-htmlstory.html.

REFERENCES

Anderson, J. D. (1988). *The education of blacks in the south, 1860–1935*. Chapel Hill: The University of North Carolina Press.

Anderson, B. (2004). *A donors guide to school choice* Washington, D.C.: The Philanthropy Roundtable.

Anderson, G., & Donchik, L. M. (2016). Privatizing schooling and policymaking: The American Legislative Exchange Council and new political and discursive strategies of education governance. *Educational Policy, 30*, 322–364.

Ascher, C., Echazarreta, J., Jacobowitz, R., McBride, Y., Troy, T., & Wamba, N. (2001). *Going charter: New models of support*. New York: Institute for Education and Social Policy New York University.

Bair, S. D. (2008). Educating black girls in the early 20th century: The pioneering work of Nannie Helen Burroughs (1879–1961). *Theory & Research in Social Education, 36*(1), 9–35.

Ball, S. J. (2007). *Education plc: Understanding private sector participation in public sector education*. London, UK: Routledge.

Ball, S., & Junemann, C. (2011). Education policy and philanthropy: The changing landscape of English educational governance. *International Journal of Public Administration, 34*, 646–661.

Blodget, H. (2006). Grant away: Why venture philanthropy is important, even if it sounds ridiculous [Electronic Version]. *Slate*. Retrieved from http://www.slate.com/id/2153457/

Blume, H. (2016, November 22). Two L.A. schools get grants to clone their success. The amount is small, but the symbolism is huge. *Los Angeles Times*. Retrieved from http://www.latimes.com/local/education/la-me-edu-gpsn-planning-grants-lausd-20161122-story.html

Blume, H. & Poston, B. (2017, May 21). How L.A.'s school board election became the most expensive in U.S. history. *Los Angeles Times*. Retrieved from http://www.latimes.com/local/la-me-edu-school-election-money-20170521-htmlstory.html

Bulkley, K., Henig, J., & Levin, H. (Eds.). (2010). *Politics, governance, and the new portfolio models for urban school reform* (pp. 277–304). Cambridge, MA: Harvard Education Press.

Buras, K. (2011). Race, charter schools, and conscious capitalism: On the spatial politics of Whiteness as property (and the unconscionable assault on Black New Orleans). *Harvard Educational Review, 81*(2), 296–330.

Burch, P., & Good, A. (2014). *Equal scrutiny: Privatization and accountability in digital education*. Cambridge, MA: Harvard Education Press.

Chaney, M., & Myers, M. (2017). Privatizing public education in New Orleans and Liberia: A tale of two colonies. Paper prepared for presentation at the Annual Meeting of the American Education Research Association. San Antonio, TX.

Chi, W. C. (2008). *The impact of advocacy funding on the school choice debate*. Boulder, CO: Education Policy Research Unit.

Colby, S., Smith, K., & Shelton, J. (2005). *Expanding the supply of high-quality schools*. Boston, MA: The Bridgespan Group, Inc.

Colvin, R. L. (2005). A new generation of philanthropists and their great ambitions. In F. M. Hess (Ed.), *With the best of intentions: How philanthropy is reshaping K-12 education* (pp. 21–48). Cambridge, MA: Harvard Education Press.

Covington, S. (1997). *Moving a public policy agenda: The strategic philanthropy of conservative foundations*. Washington, DC: The National Committee for Responsive Philanthropy.

David, J., Woodworth, K., Grant, E., Lopez-Torkos, A., & Young, V. (2006). *Bay Area KIPP Schools: A study of early implementation, First Year Report 2004–2005*. Menlo Park, CA: SRI International.

DeBray, E., Scott, J., Lubienski, C., & Jabbar, H. (2014). Intermediary organizations in charter school policy coalitions: Evidence from New Orleans. *Educational Policy, 28*(2), 175–206.

DeBray-Pelot, E., Lubienski, C., & Scott, J. (2007). The institutional landscape of interest-group politics and school choice. *Peabody Journal of Education, 82*(2–3), 204–230.

Educational Policy Institute. (2005). *Focus on results: An academic impact analysis of the Knowledge is Power Program (KIPP)*. Virginia Beach, VA: Educational Policy Institute.

Favot, S. (2016, June 21). Internal document shows LA Unified disputes some findings of UTLA-funded study on charter schools. *LA School Report*. Retrieved from http://laschoolreport.com/

internal-document-shows-la-unified-disputes-some-findings-of-utla-funded-study-on-charter-schools/

Ferrare, J. J., & Reynolds, K. (2016). Has the Elite Foundation Agenda Spread Beyond the Gates? An Organizational Network Analysis of Nonmajor Philanthropic Giving in K–12 Education. *American Journal of Education, 123*(1), 137–169.

Ferrare, J. & Setari, R. (2018). Converging on choice: The interstate flow of foundation dollars to charter school organizations. *Educational Researcher, 47*(1), 34–45.

Fiel, J. E. (2013, October). Decomposing school resegregation: Social closure, racial imbalance, and racial isolation. *American Sociological Review, 78*(5), 828–848.

Frumkin, P. (1998). The long recoil from regulation: Private philanthropic foundations and The Tax Reform Act of 1969. *American Review of Public Administration, 28*(3), 266–286.

Great Public Schools Now. (2016). *High-quality public schools for Los Angeles students.* Retrieved from Great Public Schools Now website: http://www.greatpublicschoolsnow.org/

Green, P., Baker, B., Oluwole, J., & Mead, J. (2016). Are we heading toward a charter school bubble? Lessons from the subprime mortgage crisis. *University of Richmond Law Review, 50,* 783. Retrieved from https://papers.ssrn.com/sol3/papers.cfm?abstract_id=2704305

Greene, J. (2014, November 14). How is a portfolio district different from a school district? *Education Next.* Retrieved from http://educationnext.org/portfolio-district-different-school-district/

Hartney, M. T. (2004). A powerhouse charter-funder aims for the next level. Retrieved January 11, 2005, from http://www.philanthropyroundatable.org/magazines/2004/SeptOct/Powerhouse.htm

Hess, F. (Ed.). (2005). *With the best of intentions: How philanthropy is reshaping K-12 education.* Cambridge, MA: Harvard Education Press.

Holme, J. J., Finnigan, K. S., & Diem, S. L. (2016). Challenging boundaries, changing fate? Metropolitan inequality and the legacy of Milliken. *Teachers College Record, 118*(3), 1–40.

Howard, R. & Preisman, J. (2007). The bankrupt "revolution": Running schools like businesses fails the test. *Education and Urban Society, 39*(2), 255–263.

Jabbar, H. (2015). "Every kid is money": Market-like competition and school leader strategies in New Orleans. *Educational Evaluation and Policy Analysis, 37*(4), 638–659.

Janofsky, M. (2015, September 22). Zimmer accuses Broad charter plan of strategy to 'bring down' LAUSD. *LA School Report.* Retrieved from http://laschoolreport.com/zimmer-accuses-broad-charter-plan-of-strategy-to-bring-down-lausd/

Jennings, J. L. (2010). School choice or schools' choice? Managing in an era of accountability. *Sociology of Education, 83*(3), 227–247.

Johnson, K. (2009). Gender and race: Exploring Anna Julia Cooper's thoughts for socially just educational opportunities. *Philosophia Africana, 12*(1), 67–82.

Lafer, G. (2018). *Breaking point: The cost of charter schools for public school districts.* Oakland, CA: In the Public Interest.

Lagemann, E. C. (1992). *The politics of knowledge: The Carnegie Corporation, philanthropy, and public policy.* Chicago, IL: University of Chicago Press.

Lake, R. (2007). *Identifying and replicating the "DNA" of successful charter schools.* Seattle: University of Washington, National Charter School Research Project, Center on Reinventing Public Education.

Lake, R., Cobb, T., Sharma, R., & Opalka, A. (2018). *The slowdown in Bay Area charter school growth: Causes and solutions.* Retrieved from https://www.crpe.org/sites/default/files/crpe-slowdown-bay-area-charter-school-growth.pdf

Lubienski, C., & Lubienski, S. T. (2006). Charter, private, public schools and academic achievement: New evidence from NAEP mathematics data. Retrieved February 1, 2006, from http://www.ncspe.org

Manna, P., & Moffitt, S. (2014). *New education advocacy organizations in the U.S. states: National snapshot and a case study of Advance Illinois*. Retrieved from The Wallace Foundation: www.wallacefoundation.org/knowledge-center/pages/new-education-advocacy-organizations-in-the-u.s.-states-national-snapshot-and-a-case-study-of-advance-illinois.aspx

McGuinn, P. (2012). Fight club: Are advocacy organizations changing the politics of education? *Education Next, 12,* 25–31.

McIlnay, D. (1998). Philanthropy at 50: Four moments in time [Electronic Version]. *Foundation News and Commentary*. Retrieved June 16, 2008, from http://www.foundationnews.org/CME/article.cfm?ID=1053

Miller, J. J. (2003). *Strategic investment in ideas: How two foundations changed America*. Washington, DC: The Philanthropy Roundtable.

Minow, M. (2002). *Partners, not rivals: Privatization and the public good*. Boston: Beacon Press.

Molnar, A., Garcia, D. R., Miron, G., & Berry, S. (2007). *Profiles of for-profit management organizations: Ninth annual report 2006–2007*. Tempe: Commercialism in Education Research Unit, Education Policy Studies Laboratory, Arizona State University.

National Charter School Research Project. (2007). *Quantity counts: The growth of charter school management organizations*. Seattle: Center on Reinventing Public Education, University of Washington.

Nelson, F. H., Drown, R., Muir, E., & Meter, N. V. (2001). Public money and privatization in k-12 education. In S. Chaikind & W. Fowler (Eds.), *Education finance in the new millennium: AEFA 2001 yearbook* (pp. 173–190). Larchmont, NY: Eye on Education, Inc.

Orfield, G., Frankenberg, E., Ee, J., & Kuscera, J. (2014). *Brown at 60: Great progress, a long retreat and an uncertain future*. Los Angeles, CA: Civil Rights Project.

Pattillo, M. (2015). Everyday politics of school choice in the black community. *DuBois Review, 12*(1), 41–71.

Pattillo, M., Delale-O'Connor, L., & Butts, F. (2014). High stakes choosing: How parents navigate Chicago Public Schools. In A. Lareau & K. Goyette (Eds.), *Choosing homes, choosing schools* (pp. 237–267). New York, NY: Russell Sage Foundation.

Philanthropy Magazine. (2005). Mass-producing excellence [Electronic Version]. Retrieved October 1, 2007, from http://prt.timberlakepublishing.com/article.asp?article=747&paper=0&cat=150

Public Impact. (2004). *Jump-starting the charter school movement: A guide for donors* Washington, DC: The Philanthropy Roundtable.

Ravitch, D. (2006). Bill Gates, the nation's superintendent of schools. *The Los Angeles Times*. Retrieved from: http://articles.latimes.com/2006/jul/30/opinion/op-ravitch30.

Reardon, S., & Owens, A. (2014). 60 years after *Brown*: Trends and consequences of school segregation. *Annual Review of Sociology, 40,* 199–218.

Reckhow, S., Henig, J. R., Jacobsen, R., & Litt, J. A. (2017). "Outsiders with deep pockets": The nationalization of local school board elections. *Urban Affairs Review*, 1–29.

Reckhow, S. (2013). *Follow the money: How foundation dollars change public school politics*. New York, NY: Oxford University Press.

Reich, R. (2005). A failure of philanthropy. *Stanford Social Innovation Review,* Retrieved from: https://ssir.org/articles/entry/a_failure_of_philanthropy

Rich, A. (2004). *Think tanks, public policy, and the politics of expertise*. Cambridge, UK: Cambridge University Press.

Roelofs, J. (2003). *Foundations and public policy: The mask of pluralism*. Albany: State University of New York Press.

Sabatier, P., & Jenkins-Smith, H. (1999). The advocacy coalition framework: An assessment. In P. Sabatier (Ed.), *Theories of the policy process* (pp. 117–166). Boulder, CO: Westview Press.

Sanders, R., Stovall, D., & White, T. (2018). *Twenty-First-Century Jim Crow schools: The impact of charters and vouchers on public education*. Boston, MA: Beacon Press.

Schnaiberg, L. (1999, December 1). Entrepreneurs hoping to do good, make money. *Education Week, 19,* 1,14,16.

Scott, J. (2015). Foundations and the development of the U.S. charter school policy-planning network: Implications for democratic schooling and civil rights. *National Society for the Study of Education, Teachers College Record, 114*(2), 131–147.

Scott, J. (2009). The politics of venture philanthropy in charter school policy and advocacy. *Educational Policy, 23*(1), 106–136.

Scott, J., & Villavicencio, A. (2009). School context and charter school achievement: A framework for understanding the performance "black box." *Peabody Journal of Education, 84*(2), 227–243.

Scott, J. T., & DiMartino, C. C. (2008). Hybridized, franchised, duplicated, and replicated: Charter schools and management organizations [Electronic Version]. *Forum on the future of public education.* Retrieved from http://theforum.ed.uiuc.edu/choice

Scott, J., & Holme, J. (2016). The political economy of market-based educational policies: Race and reform in urban school districts, 1915 to 2016. *Review of Research in Education, 40,* 250–295.

Scott, J., & Jabbar, H. (2013). Money and measures: Foundations as knowledge brokers. In D. Anagnostopoulos, S. Rutledge, & R. Jacobsen (Eds.), *The infrastructure of accountability: Mapping data use and its consequences across the American education system* (pp. 75–92). Cambridge, MA: Harvard Education Press.

Scott, J., & Jabbar, H. (2014). The hub and the spokes: Foundations, intermediary organizations, incentivist reforms, and the politics of research evidence. *Educational Policy, 28*(2), 233–257.

Shapiro, I., Greenstein, R., & Primus, W. (2001). *Pathbreaking CBO study shows dramatic increases in income disparities in 1980s and 1990s: An analysis of the CBO data.* Washington, DC: Center on Budget and Policy Priorities.

Smith, J. A. (1991). *The idea brokers: Think tanks and the rise of the new policy elite.* New York, NY: The Free Press.

Smith, B. A. (2008). Deregulation and the New Leader Agenda: Outcomes and Lessons from Michigan. *Educational Administration Quarterly, 44*(1), 30–65.

Smith, J. A. (2014, January 22). Public schools, private money. *San Francisco Public Press,* pp. A3–A5.

Smith, J. A. (2015, January 21). San Francisco faces a challenge: Promoting educational options without undermining classroom diversity. *San Francisco Public Press,* pp. B1, B5, B7.

Stanfield, J. H. (1985). *Philanthropy and Jim Crow in American social science.* Westport, CT: Greenwood Press.

Strom, S. (2007). Big gifts, tax breaks and a debate about charity [Electronic Version]. *The New York Times.* Retrieved September 6, 2007, from http://www.nytimes.com/2007/09/06/business/06giving.html

Swanson, C. B., & Barlage, J. (2006). *Influence: A study of the factors shaping education policy.* Bethesda, MD: Editorial Projects in Education Research Center.

The Charter School Achievement Consensus Panel. (2006). *Key issues in studying charter schools and achievement: A review and suggestions for national guidelines* (No. NCSRP White Paper Series, Number 2). Seattle, WA: The National Charter School Research Project, The Center on Reinventing Public Education.

Thernstrom, A., & Thernstrom, S. (2003). *No excuses: Closing the racial achievement gap in learning.* New York, NY: Simon and Schuster.

Tompkins-Stange, M. (2016). Policy patrons: Philanthropy, education reform, and the politics of influence. Cambridge, MA: Harvard Education Press.

Tully, S. (2016, June 16). New plan in L.A. would support all types of public schools, not just charters. *Education Week.* Retrieved from http://blogs.edweek.org/edweek/parentsandthe public/2016/06/plan_to_expand_la_charter_schools_altered_to_support_all_types_of_public_ schools.html

Tyack, D. (1974). *The one best system: A history of American urban education.* Cambridge, MA: Harvard University Press.

Tyack, D., & Cuban, L. (1995). *Tinkering toward utopia: A century of public school reform.* Cambridge, MA: Harvard University Press.

U.S. Department of Education. (2004). *Successful charter schools.* Washington, DC: Office of Innovation and Improvement.

United States Government Accountability Office. (2008). *Comparison of the reported tax liabilities of foreign- and U.S.-controlled corporations, 1998–2005.* Washington, DC.

Vasquez Heilig, J., Williams, A., McNeil, L. M., & Lee, C. (2011). Is choice a panacea? An analysis of black secondary student attrition from KIPP, other private charters, and urban districts. *Berkeley Review of Education, 2*(2), 153–178.

Walker, V. S. (1996). *Their highest potential: An African American school community in the segregated south.* Chapel Hill: The University of North Carolina Press.

Walker, V. S. (2009). Second-Class integration: A historical perspective for a contemporary agenda. *Harvard Educational Review, 79*(2), 269–284.

Watkins, W. H. (2001). *The White architects of Black education.* New York, NY: Teachers College Press.

Wells, A. S. (Ed.). (2002). *Where charter school policy fails: The problems of accountability and equity.* New York, NY: Teachers College Press.

Woodworth, K., David, J. L., Guha, R., Wang, H., & Lopez-Torkos, A. (2008). *San Francisco Bay Area KIPP Schools: A study of early implementation and achievement.* Menlo Park, CA: SRI International.

Zeichner, K., & Peña-Sandoval, C. (2015). Venture philanthropy and teacher education policy in the U.S: The role of the New Schools Venture Fund. *Teachers College Record.* Retrieved from http://www.tcrecord.org/PrintContent.asp?ContentID=17539

CHAPTER 7

The "New Professional"

Teaching and Leading under New Public Management

In 2008, the New York City Department of Education mandated that every school have an inquiry group (Robinson, 2010). In theory, anyone who believes that teachers should engage in collaborative inquiry and be provided with lots of student data should support this policy, although some might object to its being mandated. However, when the focus is almost exclusively on testing data or other quantitative outcomes, such policies can have problematic consequences. An account by a teacher in New York City is typical of anecdotes widely shared by teachers who are frustrated at how tightly scaffolded (Talbert, 2012) and protocoled (McDonald, 2007) these inquiry groups tend to be. In too many cases, while claiming to empower teachers and principals with data, they may be, in reality, deprofessionalizing them.

The teacher reported that the inquiry group in her school observed that their most pressing problem was that an alarming number of their students were dropping out between ninth and tenth grade. They decided to select fifteen ninth graders and do interviews and focus groups with them. Their goal was to better understand the issues they were facing and to see if some of them might be school- or classroom-related and therefore amenable to intervention by the school. When the data coach from the central office attended their next inquiry group meeting, they were told that they didn't seem to understand how the inquiry group was supposed to work. They were to use testing data to identify deficits in their students' achievement and to provide remediation. This meant using spreadsheets of student test scores to identify which skills needed reteaching. The teachers felt that their own approach to school inquiry was not valued and began to feel that the inquiry groups were not meant to be about authentic inquiry at all. Rather, they suspected that they were put in place, at least in part, as a way to get teachers to use the quantitative data that the district was generating through their contracts with data gathering, warehousing, and management firms. They felt that these "inquiry groups" were, in fact, more about data—and a certain type of data—than any kind of authentic inquiry.

A typical data-driven approach was that of SAM (Scaffolded Apprenticeship Model) which "engages a team of teachers in systematically using evidence of struggling students' skill gaps to both design instructional responses and re-design systems that inhibit their skill development" (Talbert, 2012, p. 5). Of course, "skill gaps," in too many cases, refer to spreadsheets of test data, not teacher-generated formative assessments. Some have argued that this sole attention to individual student data encourages a meritocratic view of schooling and undercuts a more complex understanding of sociocultural, socioemotional, and out-of-school factors that impact children (Berliner, 2009). On a more pragmatic level, teachers complain that there is too much lag time between the test and when they get the data—data that, they argue, is often unreliable. Perhaps most importantly, it reduces teaching and learning to a process of test-remediate, test-remediate, test-remediate which impoverishes teaching and provides little professional development or judgment for teachers.

In fairness, some forethought and structure do need to be in place for successful collaborative inquiry to occur in schools, and good data and evidence should trump the mere intuition, prejudice, and urban myths that can dominate discussions among teachers. Moreover, some principals were able to use the mandated spaces the inquiry groups provided to promote and support authentic inquiry, and many data coaches had a more expansive notion of inquiry and teaching. And we may be slowly beginning to recognize how high stakes testing's neglect of the affective and socioemotional dimension of students' lives leads to low achievement and dropping out of school (see Lynch, Baker, & Lyons, 2009). Nevertheless, the issue from the district's perspective was one of getting a "buy in" from teachers to use the eighty-million-dollar Achievement Reporting and Innovation System (ARIS) database that the New York City Department of Education had purchased (and which is now defunct). While the new district superintendent brings a somewhat different philosophy regarding the use of data, the damage to the teaching profession and the creation of a narrow culture of data utilization will be hard to reverse.

We could provide many more examples of how teachers and principals feel that they are not involved in decisions that affect their professional lives and how their professional judgment is disrespected in a narrow accountability culture. There is a growing body of research that documents a major shift over the last three decades in what it means to be a professional. Our example in Chapter 1 of the impact of the creation of education markets on school administrators is another example of how market-based reforms shift professionalism from a public service to an entrepreneurial ethos. This shift is occurring in both the private and public sectors, and across the various public sectors. In the rest of this chapter, we will describe NPM and discuss how it has created a "new professional," and how shifts in the political economy and the policy context have led to a tendency toward deprofessionalization.

NEW PUBLIC MANAGEMENT AND THE NEW PROFESSIONAL

Throughout this book, we have argued that public sector professionals, including teachers and school leaders, are being reshaped by new modalities of governance that incentivize new practices and conceptions of teaching and leading and how they think about themselves as professionals. As we have noted elsewhere in this book, researchers refer to these new modalities with a variety of terms, including *NPM, new managerialism, portfolio management models, neo-Taylorism,* or simply the latest iterations of privatization and neoliberalism (Au, 2011; Bulkley, Henig & Levin, 2010; Evetts, 2009; Exworthy & Halford, 1999; Trujillo, 2014).

How the governance of organizations in the public sector has been transformed by networks of "reformers" is the subject of *New Public Management,* a term that emerged first in Europe in the 1990s. Of course, public organizations have always been *managed,* but in the last four decades, there has been a shift from a rule-governed, administrative, bureaucratic management regime to a market- and outcomes-based, corporate management regime borrowed from the business world.[1] The following are the most common ideas and practices transferred from the corporate sector (Bottery, 1996; Hood, 1991; Ward, 2011):

- The introduction of markets and quasi-markets within and between public organizations (e.g. schools).
- Closing low-performing organizations and creating "start-ups" that are often outside of local democratic control (e.g. charter schools).
- An emphasis on explicit standards and measures of performance.
- Greater emphasis on outcomes and their measurement using quantitative data.
- Greater use of standardization and "scaling up" of practices.
- Contracting out public services to vendors in the private sector and the increased use of consulting companies.
- The public sector as an emerging profit center.
- A trend toward temporary and short-term workers and against unionization.
- Administrative decentralization and bounded autonomy.
- Greater discipline and parsimony in resource use in a context of austerity and disinvestment in the public sector.

Most educators have experienced these practices in their daily professional lives. More veteran educators may remember a time before these practices were dominant. Moreover, not all states or school districts have adopted all of these policies, although NCLB and Race to the Top forced most states to adopt most of them.

A new generation of new public managers influenced by NPM is reminiscent of the elite, mostly White male reformers of the early 20th century. Under the influence of Frederick Taylor and bureaucratic theories popular at the time, they "professionalized" public school leadership and worked to standardize *and* differentiate instruction according to scientific and business principles (Tyack, 1974). Meanwhile, this new iteration of public management also comes from outside of the education profession, and questions the qualifications and expertise of educational professionals who have largely followed the trajectory set by the early reformers. Namely, traditional school leaders tend to attain certification from higher education institutions and acquire experience as classroom teachers and school principals before assuming positions in school district leadership.

The new policy entrepreneurs and their networks described in previous chapters have promoted NPM. Coming largely from the private and corporate sectors, these reformers have promoted school choice, privatization, alternative pathways to certification, anti-unionism, test-based accountability, and small schools for urban school reform. Given that NPM is less prevalent in well-financed suburban districts, and that the student demographics of most urban school districts tend to be majority African American and Latino children from low-income families, this means that race and social class are central to these reforms.

In the rest of this section, we will draw on our discussion of *critical policy analysis* in Chapter 2 to provide an analysis of the ways teaching and leading are being reengineered by neoliberal policies and NPM practices that have created what sociologists of the professions call a "new professional" within the public sector. In order to critically analyze these changes in policy and practice, we will work across social sectors (education, business, public health, criminal justice, etc.) and compare policies internationally. Unfortunately, most scholarship in education is produced within narrow disciplinary and sectorial "silos," and is country specific in its research focus, even though neoliberal school reforms are not a global phenomena. And this is not only true in the field of education. Researchers across fields are so specialized they can't possibly understand the proverbial elephant but only the trunk, a leg, or the tail. And yet, what is happening to educators today is also happening to nurses, social workers, doctors, and police officers.

A "new professionalism" (Evetts, 2009, 2011) is being constructed in all professions and in most countries. While it is enacted differently depending on local contexts, the struggles and dilemmas of the British, Chilean, Australian, Indian, and U.S. teachers, principals, and professors are strikingly similar, as are the neoliberal policies these countries have implemented since the 1980s. A few countries have taken a different route. Finland is probably the best known, and there, the government invests heavily in education, teachers are still highly professionalized, they see teaching as a long-term career, and their professional judgment is respected (Adamson, Astrand, & Darling-Hammond, 2016; Salhberg, 2015). In Finland, there are no standardized tests, charter schools, vouchers, or any of the other market policies that some countries use instead of following a public investment strategy. And yet, Finland scores among the very top nations in the world in educational achievement. Some school districts in the U.S. have also eschewed NPM reforms with good results (Kirp, 2013).

Returning to Max Weber's classic distinction between instrumental and substantive rationalities might help us frame this neoliberal shift, at least at the organizational level. Max Weber focused heavily on the threat that the instrumental rationality of bureaucracies represented for society. In such organizations, he argued that people tended to be means to ends, rather than ends in themselves. Human relations theories were instrumental in their call for treating people well and including them in decisions, not so much because this is the way people should be treated but, rather, because they tended to be more productive and less likely to unionize (Carey, 1995).

Weber sought more substantive forms of rationality in which people were ends in themselves and in which social ends took precedent over individual goals. So-called post-bureaucratic organizations have changed in form, but, as we will see, they continue to operate on the basis of instrumental rationality, a tendency exacerbated in public organizations as they increasingly operate in a marketized environment. In other words, as some scholars have noted, the new forms of market managerialism that have replaced the old forms have merely created a new "iron cage" which may turn out to be more restrictive than the old bureaucratic one (Au, 2011; Barker, 1993; Bourke, Lidstone, & Ryan, 2015; Locke & Spender, 2011; Samier, 2017).

In "flattened hierarchies," sometimes referred to as network organizations, pyramidal hierarchy is replaced by a horizontal elite core and a mass periphery with minimal mediation and communication between the two. While new business models attempt to manage through these more flexible, network organizations, rather than through bureaucratic hierarchies, there is some evidence that this has intensified instrumental rationality, not reduced it. These new flexible organizations are part of a growing neoliberal business model to which some social theorists attribute a growing inauthenticity in organizations (Sennett, 1998). They have developed greater flexibility to respond to markets, not to meet the human needs of those who work in them. Fitzgerald and Gunter (2017) call this new flexibility "Uberization," which presents itself as part of a sharing economy but is more focused on centralization and cost reduction, and which results not in sharing but in shifting the risk of doing business to the worker and the customer (Nurvala, 2015).

Moreover, as market relations become dominant in all aspects of our lives, it becomes increasingly difficult to think beyond individual competition toward any sense of a common good. While most people think of neoliberalism as a purely economic model, it has important social and cultural consequences that we are only beginning to understand. Richard Sennett (2006) provides perhaps the most eloquent account of the ways that shifts in political economy have resulted in cultural shifts in our workplaces and in the ways we live our lives. Since the corporate workplace is increasingly the model for schools, Sennett's work has important implications for 21st-century school leaders. In his qualitative study of several corporations, Sennett has identified characteristics of work in what he calls the *new capitalism*. We will provide a condensed version of his argument here.

Sennett (2006) traces the recent phenomenon of globalization back to the breakdown in 1973 of the Bretton Woods controls over the global circulation of money. A 1944 conference held in Bretton Woods, New Hampshire, established the rules for global commercial and financial relations in the post-World War II years, including tying national currencies to the gold standard.

In the decades following Bretton Woods, there were large amounts of new capital seeking short-term investments. By the 1990s, stock prices began to replace profit as a goal for many businesses, inaugurating what many called the "new economy."

Money was made not by owning and producing but by trading and later speculation, better known as financialization. This new speculative and flexible approach to capital has changed work life and institutional structures, particularly in sectors of capitalism such as finance, insurance, real estate, media, communications, and high technology, where short-term exchange replaces long-term relationships. To fit into this new "fast" capitalism, workers had to give up notions of stability of employment and become flexible, mobile, workers in a constantly changing global economy.

Furthermore, workers became disposable as capital continuously sought to cut labor costs though automation and outsourcing. Neoliberal management books of the 1990s, like the best seller *Who Moved My Cheese?*, use a childlike allegory about mice who embrace change to prepare the ideological terrain for the new entrepreneurial worker. The lesson is that it is better to see losing one's job as an opportunity for some better entrepreneurial opportunity that surely lies around the corner. The new entrepreneurial culture that is promoted in all sectors of society prepares employees for this new world of unstable employment in the new "risk" society (Beck, 1992). Along with this new instability of work comes intensification of work leading to longer work hours and greater levels of stress and anxiety. As unions were decimated (down from 35% unionized workers in the private sector to under 7% by 2018), wages also stagnated.

However, Sennett (1998) argues that such trends are actually counterproductive for business, since the cost to business of the resulting short-term employment is that it reduces employee loyalty and organizational memory. Moreover, with shorter contracts, project work in teams, and a highly competitive internal work environment, authentic relationships are less likely to form because of short timelines. This continuous employee turnover and the tendency to use temporary workers and outside consultants weaken institutional knowledge. He argues that these new tendencies are good for the bottom line and stock prices but are not good for the long-term health of businesses, national productivity, or the building of relationships and personal character. In fact, he titled one book in his trilogy, *The Corrosion of Character: The Personal Consequences of Work in the New Capitalism* (Sennett, 1998). The creation of authentic human ties cannot easily occur in transient workplaces and communities.

As principals in schools are moved from school to school, and teacher turnover, especially in urban districts, grows, a similar phenomenon occurs in education (Ronfeldt, Loeb, & Wyckoff, 2013). Flexible organizations in a choice environment mean that teachers, administrators, and students will be more mobile, leading to less stability and a weakening of professional expertise and organizational capacity. New, younger teachers may tolerate increased intensification and standardization of work, but many experienced teachers with families and a strong professional culture are tending to change careers or retire early (Stone-Johnson, 2014). This phenomenon seems even more prevalent in charter schools and with the advent of Teach for America (Darling-Hammond, 1994: Thomas & Mockler, 2018). The very notion of teaching or administration as a lifelong career is becoming a thing of the past. In the long run, this may have devastating effects on the quality of schooling.

Sennett (2006) also identifies other personal deficits associated with this new neoliberal culture. The first is the demise of the work ethic. Only a fool would delay gratification in the new flexible workplace. Employees report feeling a sense of personal betrayal as companies trade loyalty to workers for short-term profits. While some "boot camp" charter schools may harness the idealism of elite twenty-somethings for a time, eventually, they burn out and move on to more lucrative careers. Second, this loss of long-term employment, with its associated benefits and pensions, makes it more difficult for newer generations of employees to create life narratives. While much Welfare State employment was not exciting, it provided people with a life narrative in which they could pay a mortgage over thirty years, look forward to a pension and social security, and plan for vacations. In today's neo-liberal, risk society (Beck, 1992), there is an absence of any way to think strategically about one's life, one's sense of purpose, future goals, and economic security.

Flattened hierarchies or network organizations present themselves as more democratic, but they represent a new concentration of power without centralization of authority. According to Sennett (1998),

> this absence of authority frees those in control to shift, adapt, reorganize without having to justify themselves or their acts. In other words, it permits the freedom of the moment, a focus just on the present. Change is the responsible agent; change is not a person.
>
> (p. 115)

Internal units are created to compete with each other for contracts. Outside consultants are brought in to do the dirty work that management used to do. Senior management can claim they are taking their cue from the expert consultants who come in and leave quickly. In this impersonal environment, no relationships are built, as no one has to take responsibility for decisions. Upper management with its stronger networks moves more often as new opportunities arise. Personnel records take the place of humans who are being standardized, so "performance" can be compared (just as high-stakes testing in education allows students, teachers, and schools to be compared as a prerequisite for a marketized system). Flexibility to adjust to changes in the market is gained. This is perhaps good news for stockholders seeking short-term profits, upper-level executives, and consultancy firms, but it isn't clear who else benefits, or what it contributes to the common good. It also, according to Sennett, makes long-term, authentic relationships less likely.

This new model is being intentionally implemented in school districts across the country. In New York City, under Mayor Bloomberg, a corporate model was implemented. Upper-level public administrators contracted out to private companies or took private sector positions in the burgeoning education services industry. As districts disappeared, principals had a "choice" of vendors and networks. Public-private partnerships were the vehicle and discourse for this shift in work culture (Robertson, Verger, Mundy, & Menashy, 2014). This restructuring of the institutional environment dramatically changed the work culture of schools. While it is true that some professionals thrive in such environments, most principals in New York City reported being more beleaguered than empowered (Shipps, 2012). If Sennett's analysis of the new corporate culture is any indication, in education, we can expect to see less employee loyalty, more work stress, and a performance culture. Table 7.1 provides a brief overview of periods of professionalization.

Table 7.1 Periods of Professionalization

	Occupational Professionalism (from within) 1950s to 1980s	Organizational Professionalism (from above) 1990s to present	Democratic Professionalism Emerging
Principal role	Principal as hierarchical and patriarchal, leader	Principal modeled on CEO but lacking executive power (chooses vendors, more control over hiring, etc.)	Principal facilitator and advocate in alliance with community
Teacher professionalism	Teacher professionalization within a public bureaucracy	Emergence of parallel systems of professionalization and deskilling	Professionalization of culturally responsive, democratic teachers
Pedagogy	Deficit-based, subtractive pedagogy for the poor. Some innovation.	Deficit-based, subtractive and test driven pedagogy. Little innovation.	Asset-based, additive, innovative and culturally responsive pedagogy
Political-economic context	Commitment to distributive justice	Commitment to unregulated markets and competition as creating greater prosperity	Recommitment to distributive justice as well as racial, gender, and environmental justice.
View of individual	Individual and social welfare	Competitive individualism	Individual and social empowerment and human rights
Pedagogy and race	Race neutral, color-blind approaches	Race neutral, color-blind approaches	Culturally responsive pedagogy
Form of government and governance	*Government* through bureaucratic control (as opposed to *governance* through steering, influencing, and partnering)	Minimal *government* (deregulation); *governance* through steering, incentivizing, and partnering	*Government* provides needed regulation and hybrid *governance* that emphasizes professional and community control
Approach to accountability/ teacher assessment	Public school accountability, primarily through mix of local control (school boards), professional supervision, testing, and bureaucratic control	Public school accountability, primarily through federal government regulation (NCLB). High-stakes testing/outcomes-based, school choice.	Public school accountability through greater public, reciprocal, and internal accountability. Peer assistance and review (PAR).

Public/Private relationship	Public-private sectors as separate realms with different aims and interests. Separation of church and state.	Public-private partnerships with nonprofit and for-profit sectors. Outsourcing to private sector. Breakdown of separation of church and state.	Some public–nonprofit collaboration (civil society). Separation of church and state.
Local school governance	District superintendents, school boards	Mayoral control; district superintendents as CEOs	District superintendents, school boards, community organizing
Role of unions	Bread-and-butter issues, industrial/business model	Bread-and-butter issues, industrial/business model	Social movement unionism, alliances with communities
Definition of equity	Equity defined as "equal educational opportunity" with emphasis on inputs	Equity defined as "closing the achievement gap" with focus on outcomes	Equity defined as equality of inputs (resources) and outcomes, measured authentically
School governance	Hierarchical	"Distributed leadership" limited to school professionals, largely advisory	Shared governance with community engagement
Student assessment	Student assessment mainly teacher centered	Student assessment through high-stakes testing	Student assessment through multiple data sources including quality performance-based testing and teacher designed evaluations
Curriculum	Curriculum based on textbook publishers	Scripted, "evidence-based" curriculum based on standards, increasingly delivered through technology	Rich, rigorous, culturally relevant curriculum based on standards developed with teacher and community input
Student discipline	Zero tolerance	Zero tolerance	Positive, restorative discipline

THE EMERGENCE OF NEW PROFESSIONALISM

Evetts (2011) conceptualizes the shift in professionalism as one from emphasizing "notions of partnership, collegiality, discretion and trust to increasing levels of managerialism, bureaucracy, standardization, assessment and performance review" (p. 407). Scholars of new professionalism argue that while there are some continuities from the "old" professionalism, a shift has occurred as professionals are increasingly managed and controlled, a tendency that Evetts (2011) refers to as *organizational* professionalism or professionalism "from above" (p. 407). She contrasts this with *occupational* professionalism or professionalism "from within" and documents a shift from professional to managerialist values.

This shift suggests a decrease in professional autonomy and in control over one's profession through the exercise of professional judgment and through professional associations, and an increase in control by managers in work organizations. This control is characterized by rational-legal control, standardized work procedures and practices, and external forms of regulation and accountability measures, or what some have called governing or steering from a distance (Kickert, 1995; Rose, 1993). Although a discourse of "autonomy" and "empowerment" is sometimes used to promote current education reforms, such autonomy is exceedingly constrained and often part of a strategy of tightening up "loosely coupled systems" (Honig & Rainey, 2012; Meyer & Rowan, 2006). In other words, as we will discuss in more detail later, while in older public bureaucracies, teachers could create autonomy (for good or ill) by shutting the classroom door, the "post-bureaucratic" organizations of today are more tightly coupled as high-stakes testing can breach the door and enter the classroom, in many cases, standardizing how and what teachers teach.

This shift from occupational to organizational professionalism may seem more dramatic for some professions, such as physicians, who are increasingly leaving private practice for large hospitals and health organizations. Teachers, on the other hand, have always worked largely within public or private bureaucracies, but the loosely coupled nature of educational systems buffered teachers from more direct forms of control, depending chiefly on internal forms of accountability (Carnoy, Elmore, & Siskin, 2003; DiPaola & Tschannen-Moran, 2005; Weick, 1976). This meant that while the bureaucracy and principals exerted a certain level of hierarchical control, teachers exercised a great deal of autonomy in their classrooms. They were only under direct control when they were being observed by principals or supervisors. Welch (1998) documents parallels between today's reforms and business-led reforms of the 19th and early 20th centuries, when forms of efficiency were imposed on schooling through the imposition of a business ethos. In his analysis of the British Revised Code of 1860 whose centerpiece was "payment by results," he documents the audit culture of the time, which, like today, resulted in creative compliance. According to Welch,

> teachers 'stuffed and almost roasted' their pupils on test items once the teachers knew that the visit of the inspector was imminent. Other teachers secretly

trained their pupils so that when they were asked questions they raised their right hands if they knew the correct answer but their left if they did not, thus creating a more favorable impression upon the visiting inspector.

(p. 161)

Nearly 150 years later, such pressures are having a similar effect. The following is from the Columbus dispatch in Columbus, Ohio, but newspapers across the country are full of similar stories.

Answer sheets and test booklets arrive at districts in securely taped boxes, shipped by FedEx or UPS. Packets are shrink-wrapped and are supposed to be stored in a locked room until test time. But in some districts, teachers got access last school year. Some made copies. Others shared the questions with students ahead of time, or gave answers during the test. And a few devised nonverbal signals to cue children that their answers were incomplete. For all the lock-and-key procedures and explicit rules, more teachers cheated on Ohio standardized tests than ever before.

(Smith Richards, 2006, p. 4)

The difference between these two examples is that in the second one, teachers are controlled from a distance and by a faceless inspector that comes shrink-wrapped and delivered by UPS or, today, more likely, through a computer screen.[2] These forms of control not only bypass the principal and superintendent, and flow directly into the classroom but also decrease the amount of autonomy teachers and principals have over curriculum and instruction.

Some have argued that principals appear to have benefited by receiving greater autonomy over such things as budgets and hiring, and appear to be re-professionalizing (Jarl, Fredrikson, & Persson, 2011). But they are encouraged to professionalize around the principles of NPM and do so independent of teachers, which reinforces a management-worker split. Furthermore, alternative pathways to the principalship—and teaching as well—have weakened attempts at professionalization through the usual channels of certification and professional associations. As we will discuss later, these channels are deserving of extensive critique (see Labaree, 2004; Freidrich, 2014; Zeichner, 2014); however, they represent an important public investment in public education, view teaching and administration as careers, and provide some assurance that those who teach our children have had some professional training.

NEW ENTREPRENEURIAL PROFESSIONALS WITHIN AN AUDIT CULTURE

From policing to teaching to practicing medicine, the shift to NPM elaborated earlier has reconstituted most occupations and professions. In education, a new generation of teachers and administrators is being socialized into a very different workplace with a different conception of teaching and leading. While teachers increasingly teach to the test, leaders are expected to lead to the test. Since control is now exercised through market discipline and high-stakes tests that increasingly drive what goes on in classrooms, principals are being given more and more "autonomy," oftentimes to exercise leadership over less and less (Shipps, 2012). Nearly 25% of teachers are no longer prepared in universities though coursework and student teaching but rather through alternative pathways, such as Teach for America. These teachers develop very different professional identities, are more scripted in their teaching methods, tend to be more anti-union, and most do not see teaching as a career (Thomas & Mockler, 2018). Increasingly, school administrators are also being developed similarly through alternative pathways, such as New Leaders for New Schools, Relay Graduate School, and many are from the TFA pipeline (Mungal, 2016).

Some see promise in the notion of distributed leadership as a way to build greater professional capacity. But while workplaces are being redesigned to intensify *work* and distribute it horizontally, *power* is being distributed *upward* by centralizing policy over curriculum and instruction through high-stakes testing and mayoral control. According to Evetts (2011), these developments are shifting the locus of control from a previous focus on professional judgment to control through policies that increase top-down forms of organizational professionalism and reduce occupational professionalism in which judgment comes from within the profession. The new teacher and administrator are put in a position in which they must look to market- and test-based forms of accountability for direction rather than their professional instincts, training, associations, or unions.

The ability of new digital technologies to integrate management information systems and standardize the labor process promises to intensify this tendency (Burch, 2014; Selwyn, 2011). In fact, Courtney (2017) argues that as privatization has turned more technological with cyber charter schools and predictive analytics using big data, "the conceptual opacity underpinning educational leadership now renders that very leadership obsolete by enabling a corporate agenda where the locus, goals and mechanisms of decision-making are globalised, privatized and consequently, are moving out of schools completely" (p. 24). Increasingly, core decisions about hiring, budgeting, curriculum, instruction, etc., are being made in boardrooms far from the school, perhaps even in another country.

As we move more and more toward external forms of accountability, we lose many of the advantages of internal accountability. According to Carnoy et al. (2003), internal forms of accountability include

> Individual teachers' and administrators' beliefs about teaching and learning, their shared understanding of who their students are, the routines they develop for getting their work done, and the external expectations from parents, communities, and administrative agencies under which they work.
>
> (p. 3)

Ironically, this shift in accountability has narrowed their professional discretion while also expanding and intensifying their role expectations. Summarizing research in changing teacher roles in the U.S., Valli and Buese (2007) discuss a widening scope of teacher responsibilities, including heightened expectations of collaboration outside the classroom, strict adherence to new curricular and instructional requirements, and the collection and analysis of assessment data.

While these additional role expectations could expand—and, under certain circumstances, have expanded—educators' professionalism (Stillman, 2011), it has more often tended to reduce it to working within an audit culture of external metrics that requires being accountable to standards and criteria that they had no part in developing (Apple, 2004; Strathern, 2000). As noted at the beginning of this chapter, even where professional learning communities are in place, the data teachers are encouraged to analyze and the tasks they rehearse are typically not their own. In most cases, conception and execution have been successfully separated (Apple & Jungck, 1992). This separation mimics proletarianization in which craft labor was fragmented and replaced by factory wage labor.

The shift to greater external accountability has exposed educators not only to new forms of control through an audit culture and curbs on their professional judgment but also, as we illustrated in Chapter 1, to a marketized environment that forces them to compete both internally with each other and externally with other organizations. So, professionals, adept at coexisting with bureaucratic forms of control, find themselves in new territory. Freidson (2001) viewed professionalism as a mechanism for organizing some aspects of social life based on expertise and social trust. Professionals depend on this social trust with the public for their legitimacy. In this sense, professionalism both competed with and provided some protection from both market and bureaucratic forms of organization. As professionalism is eroded as a countervailing force to both bureaucracy and markets, social trust and public capacity-building are eroded as well.

EDUCATING THE NEW EDUCATION PROFESSIONAL

The idea of preparing teachers and administrators in universities is fairly recent and it is only during the decades from 1960 to 1990 that universities trained the vast majority of teachers and administrators. Previously, teachers were trained in secondary schools, normal schools, teachers institutes, teachers colleges, or even school districts, and administrators prior to the 1960s were often merely handed the keys to the building with the well wishes of the superintendent. Since the 1990s, there has been an explosion of alternative pathways to teacher and administrator preparations outside of universities and increasing numbers of for-profit and online programs. Smith and Pandolfo (2011) report that since 2007, the leading producers of teachers in Texas are two for-profit online programs: "A+ Texas Teachers" and "iteach Texas."

As noted in previous chapters, new policy networks have laid the ground for this shift, heavily funded by venture philanthropy. Philanthropists such as the Carnegie, Rockefeller, and Ford Foundations have for decades funded initiatives to improve the preparation of teachers and administrators in colleges and universities. However, in the last two decades, venture philanthropy has shifted toward supporting alternative pathways outside of universities for the preparation of teachers and administrators (Mungal, 2016; Reckhow, 2013). This support has ultimately resulted in legislation that opens up teacher education to a free market of nonprofit and for-profit operators, and in some states hardly any regulations at all.

Known as the "warm body" law, Arizona Senate Bill 1042, signed into law in May 2017 by Republican Governor Doug Ducey, permits "persons" with a college degree to bypass Arizona's regular teacher certification process to obtain grades six to twelve teaching certificates (Straus, 2017). They should have five years of relevant experience, but "relevant experience" was not defined. In Arizona, charter school "teachers" were already exempt from state certification requirements. Since 2009, the Arizona Legislature has cut school district capital funding by 85%, while it has increased charter school funds for capital purchases and facilities by 15% (Straus, 2017).

Furthermore, Section 2002(4) of Title II of the 2015 Every Student Succeeds Act (ESSA) encourages states to support independent "teacher preparation academies." The previous version of the law encouraged alternative certification programs within education schools, and in most states, alternative teacher education programs were required to partner with a certification-granting institution. The new law also requires states to recognize certificates from these stand-alone academies, "as at least the equivalent of a masters degree in education for the purpose of hiring, retention, compensation, and promotion in the state."

This legislation was strongly supported by, among others, the New Schools Venture Fund (NSVF), founded by social entrepreneur Kim Smith and funded by venture philanthropists John Doerr and Brook Byers (Horn & Libby, 2011). NSVF is a single node of a dense network of venture philanthropists promoting the privatization of teacher and administrator preparations.

Zeichner (2014), while calling for significant reform of university-based teacher education, defends it on the following grounds:

1. With over 3.6 million teachers, and with between 70% and 80% prepared in university programs, it is doubtful whether a free market of private programs could meet the capacity needs of such a large system. The emphasis of alternative pathways, such as Teach for America or The New Teacher Project, on attracting the "best and brightest" ignores the content of teacher preparation and the fact that we can't recruit all of the teachers we need from the ranks of elite colleges.

2. Shifting the preparation of teachers and administrators to a more school-based, clinical model runs the risk of merely reproducing the status quo. Nor do districts have the capacity to take over the preparation of teachers and administrators without a significant infusion of resources.

3. Countries that lead the world in educational performance have done so in part because of public investment in the preparation of teachers in colleges and universities.

Zeichner (2014) concludes that "the solution to the problems of college and university-based teacher education is to redesign and strengthen the system, not to abandon it" (p. 561). The new public sector professional is in part a product of the kind of professional preparation they have received, but, as we have documented here, they are also formed by new neoliberal policies and the ways these policies have transformed organizational management culture.

WORKING TOWARD DEMOCRATIC PROFESSIONALISM

Teaching and school administration as professions have been under attack for a long time and some of the criticisms have merit (Friedrich, 2014; Levine, 2006). Traditional bureaucracies and the older model of professionalism were notorious for resisting change and failing to meet the needs of many children in urban districts (Meier, 1995; Payne, 2008; Rogers, 2006). Furthermore, claims to professionalism by school personnel have often marginalized the voices of low-income parents and communities (Driscoll, 1998; Green, 2015). The task ahead is not to merely reassert "traditional" professionalism wholesale but rather to better understand how to resist the most egregious assaults on professionals, while acknowledging the weaknesses of traditional models of professional training and professional accountability.[3] Such resistance would insist on a professional ethos with democratic participation and the public good at its center.

Table 7.1 compares various aspects of *occupational* (1950s–1980s) and *organizational* professionalism (1990s to present) and suggests what democratic professionalism might look like. While largely aspirational, there are many examples of *democratic* professionalism already in existence. Occupational professionalism in teaching was characterized by some attempts to provide a more child-centered approach that honored the multiple intelligences that children brought to school (Gardner, 1993) and even low-income students had access to instruction in art, music, and physical education. While the typical classroom was traditional and teacher led, there was considerable innovation around the edges, such as open classrooms, schools without walls, and other Deweyian approaches that were popular though not numerous (Goodlad, 1984).

By the 1990s, state-level accountability systems based on business models were promoted that aligned instruction, curriculum, and standardized tests. The passage of NCLB in 2001 intensified this tendency nationally and increased the stakes by comparing schools and punishing those with lower test scores. Many schools that served poor children did not teach untested subjects; encouraged more teacher-led and standardized instruction; diminished art, music, physical education, and recess; and ignored students' multiple intelligences. Charter schools, which were supposed to encourage innovations that would be transferred to public schools, instead too often embraced paternalistic approaches based on old-fashioned Catholic School models: strict discipline, uniforms, single-sex education, and rote learning (McDermott & Nygreen, 2013).

While it is clear that low-income children will likely need greater levels of scaffolding to make up for the out-of-school factors that favor more affluent, mostly White students (Berliner, 2009, Delpit, 1995), they should not receive a fundamentally different education. Since Anyon's (1980) early studies of how social reproduction involved a fundamentally different classroom experience for the poor and working class, we have known that all children deserve an asset-based, innovative, loving, culturally responsive pedagogy with a well-trained, certified teacher and a principal who empowers parents and the school community. This should be the goal of the new *democratic professional* (see Anderson, 2009; Dzur, 2008; Keith, 2015; Sachs, 2003; Woods, 2005).

The good news is that this new democratic professionalism and the policies and practices that might support it are already in place in many districts and schools. More recently, community schools and wraparound services are making schools more responsive to low-income communities (Keith, 2015). Restorative justice programs are replacing zero tolerance discipline policies in many schools (Lustick, 2017). Some districts are using peer assistance and review (PAR) to evaluate teachers. In this approach, teachers do peer evaluations and the district partners with the teachers' union to make tenure and promotion decisions (Goldstein, 2010). There are also districts that are waiving high-stakes testing requirements for schools that experiment with authentic assessment (n.a. 2017). Culturally responsive teaching has made inroads in many schools, replacing a "boot camp" approach that blames students and families for low achievement (Gay, 2010). Some teachers' unions are making alliances with communities and building solidarity to not only protect their conditions of work but also to resist NPM reforms (Nunez, Michie, & Konkol, 2015). Participatory Action Research, especially with youth, represents an alternative pedagogy and can open more democratic spaces in schools and communities (Anderson, 2017; Cammarota & Fine, 2008). All of these practices and policies are laying the groundwork for challenging the "new professional" that NPM is shaping and replacing it, not with the "old professional" but rather with a new democratic professional capable of restoring social trust.

Luckily, there are alternative ways of conceptualizing professionalism that do not involve deprofessionalization and the elimination of academic training and certification but rather involve building greater professional and social trust and greater inclusion of those we serve, whether they are patients, students, soldiers, or inmates. Democratic professionals do not yearn for a reassertion of what many view as their lost sense of status and authority. Instead, they seek to democratize their practices and their organizations. Movements in bioethics, public journalism, and restorative justice are examples of professionals seeking to regain public trust. Dzur (2008) believes that

> Far from a deprofessionalization or anti-institution movement, these democratic reformers still value the specific, specialized knowledge of the seasoned journalist and editor, well-studied and practiced physician, and well-trained

and experienced judge and attorney. As they try to be more democratic and help laypeople gain useful civic skills, they also seek to transform ossified conceptions of professionalism, but they are in no way anti-professional.

(p. 3)

Most current reforms that attempt to improve education have been imported from business, but there are other sectors that are far more appropriate for seeking ideas. For instance, the concept of restorative justice has been imported into education from criminal justice. Community schools and wraparound services are influenced by social work. The importance of mindfulness comes from religious spirituality, and the importance of caring and wellness, from nursing. Our obsession with the efficiency principles of NPM has blinded us to the very kind of conceptual borrowing that we need to successfully care for and teach our most vulnerable students.

CONCLUSION

Fenwick (2016) makes a distinction between professional *responsibility* and *accountability*. Professional responsibility refers to "the expectation for professionals to respond to social needs in particular ways. Accountability is about how professionals are expected to justify or account for the ways they perform those responsibilities" (p. 9). While professional responsibility is centered on the professional's own judgment and ethics, professional accountability is centered on professionals' compliance with externally imposed indicators of performance. As we can see, the accountability systems we have in place often pressure the "new" professional to behave "irresponsibly."

The example that opened this chapter illustrates how teachers who opted for a more humanizing approach toward the ninth graders that they wanted to retain were encouraged to use spreadsheets of test scores instead. While this may seem like an extreme case, it resonates with most teachers who see their responsibility as serving the whole child. Our example in Chapter 1 of the entrepreneurial principal illustrates the extent to which market-based, incentivist policies drive principals to ignore social needs in favor of *their* school, *their* students, and *their* careers. Like the police officer who needs to arrest one more kid to make his Comstat numbers, professionals are increasingly being pushed into socially irresponsible behavior by narrow systems of accountability. Solbrekke and Sugrue (2014) argue that the notion of professional *responsibility* leads to more proactive activity, while professional *accountability* results in more reactive behavior.

This raises the question of professional resistance to accountability measures that pressure professionals to behave "irresponsibly." How might professionals "responsibly" resist "irresponsible" accountability schemes? And how much risk are professionals willing to tolerate as they feel ethically compelled to engage in principled resistance to irresponsible policies? Effective resistance would have to consider how education professionals make sense of, and negotiate, a complex ecosystem of federal and state policies, district mandates, venture philanthropy, policy networks, local advocacy groups, and market competition (Koyama, 2014). It would have to be clear about not only what and whom is being resisted but also toward what end. It is also more effective and less risky to resist collectively than individually. The 2018 statewide teacher strike in West Virginia and the 2012 Chicago Teachers strike (Nunez et al., 2015) are reminders of the power of solidarity.

Teachers and school leaders who seek to engage in what Achinstein and Ogawa (2006) call "principled resistance" to market-driven and prescriptive education policies need resistance strategies, each of which must be tailored to the circumstances at hand (see Anderson & Cohen, 2015, for example). Strategies of resistance that enable educators merely to work *around* NPM, however, will have a very limited and short-term impact. Resistance needs to be more than a refusal; it must be productive—that is, it must generate an understanding of public education that transcends market ideology and the audit culture. The resistance we have in mind would generate a *democratic professionalism*.

But *democracy* can be understood in many ways and is often appropriated in ways that are not authentic; as we saw in our discussion of micropolitics in Chapter 4, it can be used merely to legitimate nondemocratic practices. The following chapter takes up the issue of what democracy means for education and the role that teachers and leaders play in defending it.

END-OF-CHAPTER QUESTIONS

1. Reflect on your own initial and ongoing professional development. To what extent were you trained as a "new professional"?
2. How does your current work environment reflect the tenets of New Public Management?
3. To what extent do you feel that you work within an "audit culture"? How much does high-stakes testing affect you? How does school choice affect your decisions as a teacher or principal?

NOTES

1   The previous bureaucratic form of organizing and managing schools was also borrowed from industrial business leaders who propagated organizing efficient schools around the factory model. However, as professional organizations, they contained—in theory, at least—a strong professional and public ethos.

2   According to a marketing report from the Educational Technology Industry Network (ETIN), the testing industry grew 57% in the last three years with an annual income of $2,500,000,000 in 2013 (Richards & Stebbins, 2014). The testing industry is the leading edge in the conversion from print to digital education.

3   By "traditional," we mean relatively recent university-based professional preparation as opposed to previous apprenticeship models.

REFERENCES

Achinstein, B., & Ogawa, R. (2006). (In) fidelity: What the resistance of new teachers reveals about professional principles and prescriptive educational policies. *Harvard educational review, 76*(1), 30–63.

Adamson, F., Astrad, B., & Darling-Hammond, L. (2016). *Global educational reform: How privatization and public investment influence education outcomes.* New York, NY: Routledge.

Anderson, G. L. (2009). *Advocacy leadership: Toward a post-reform agenda in education.* New York, NY: Routledge.

Anderson, G. L. (2017). Participatory action research as democratic disruption: New public management and educational research in Schools and Universities. *International Journal of Qualitative Studies in Education, 30*(5), 432–449.

Anderson, G., & Cohen, M. (2018). *The new democratic professional: Confronting markets, metrics, and managerialism.* New York, NY: Teachers College Press.

Anderson, G. L., & Montoro Donchik, L. (2015). The Privatization of education and policy-making: The American Legislative Exchange Council (ALEC) and network governance in the United States. *Educational Policy.* Online First.

Anyon, J. (1980). Social class and the hidden curriculum of work. *The Journal of Education, 162*(1), 67–92.

Apple. M. (2004). Schooling, markets, and an audit culture, *Educational policy, 18*(4), 614–621.

Apple, M. W., & Jungck, S. (1992). You don't have to be a teacher to teach this unit: Teaching, technology and control in the classroom. In A. Hargreaves & M. Fullan (Eds.), *Understanding teacher development* (pp. 20–42). New York, NY: Teachers College Press.

Au, W. (2011). Teaching under the new Taylorism: High-stakes testing and the standardization of the 21st century curriculum. *Journal of Curriculum Studies, 43*(1), 25–45.

Baker, B. (2017, September 9). Reality check: Trends in school finance. *School Finance 101.* Retrieved from https://schoolfinance101.wordpress.com/2017/09/09/realty-check-trends-in-school-finance/

Ball, S. (2001). Performativities and fabrications in the education economy: Towards the performative society. In D. Gleason & C. Husbands (Eds.), *The performing school: Managing, teaching and learning in a performance culture* (pp. 210–226). London, UK: Routledge/Falmer.

Ball, S., & Junemann, C. (2012). *Networks, new governance and education.* Chicago, IL: Policy Press.

Barker, J. (1993). Tightening the iron cage: Concertive control in self-managing teams. *Administrative Science Quarterly, 38*(3), 408–437.

Barton, P. E., & Coley, R. J. (2010). *The Black-White Achievement Gap: When Progress Stopped.* Policy Information Report. *Educational Testing Service.*

Beck, U. (1992). *Risk Society: Towards a New Modernity.* New Delhi: Sage.

Berliner, D. (2009). Poverty and potential: Out-of-school factors and school success. Boulder and Tempe: Education and the Public Interest Center & Education Policy Research Unit. Retrieved from http://epicpolicy.org/publication/poverty-and-potential

Biesta, G. (2007). Why "what works" won't work: Evidence-based practice and the democratic deficit in educational research. *Educational Theory, 57*(1), 1–22.

Boggs, C. (2001). *The End of Politics.* New York, NY: Guilford Press.

Bottery, M. (1996). The challenge to professionals from the New Public Management: Implications for the teaching profession. *Oxford Review of Education, 22*(2), 179–197.

Bourke, T., Lidsone, J. Ryan, M. (2015) Schooling Teachers: Professionalism or disciplinary power? *Educational Philosophy and Theory, 47*(1), 84–100.

Brown, E., & Makris, M. V. (2017). A different type of charter school: In prestige charters, a rise in cachet equals a decline in access. *Journal of Education Policy, 33*, 85–117.

Bulkley, K., Henig, J., & Levin, H. (2010). *Between public and private: Politics, governance, and the new portfolio models for urban school reform.* Cambridge, MA: Harvard Education Press.

Burch, P. (2009). *Hidden markets: The new education privatization.* New York, NY: Routledge.

Burch, P. (2014). *Equal Scrutiny: Privatization and accountability in digital education.* Cambridge, MA: Harvard Education Press.

Burris, V. (2008). The interlock structure of the policy-planning network and the right turn in U.S. state policy. *Research in Political Sociology, 17*, 1–35.

Cammarota, J., & Fine, M. (Eds.). (2008). *Revolutionizing education: Youth participatory action research in motion.* New York, NY: Routledge.

Carey, A. (1995). *Taking the risk out of democracy: Corporate propaganda versus freedom and liberty.* Urbana: University of Illinois Press.

Carnoy, M., Elmore, R. and Siskin, L. (2003). *The new accountability: High schools and high stakes testing.* New York: RoutledgeFalmer.

Coleman, J., Campbell, E., Hobson, C., & McPartland, J. (1966). *Equality of educational opportunity.* Washington, DC: U.S. Government Printing Office.

Convertina, C. (2017). State disinvestment, technologies of choice and 'fitting in': Neoliberal transformations in U.S. public education. *Journal of Education Policy, 32*(6), 832–854.

Cohen, M. (2013). In the back of our minds always': Reflexivity as resistance for the performing principal. *International Journal of Leadership in Education, 17*, 1–22.

Courtney, S. (2017). Privatizing educational leadership through technology in the Trumpian era. *Journal of Educational Administration and History. 50*(1), 23–31.

Crawford, J. (2007, June 6). A diminished vision of Civil Rights: No Child Left Behind and the growing divide in how educational equity is understood. *Education Week, 26*(39), 31, 40.

Darling-Hammond, L. (1994). Who will speak for the children; How "teach for America" hurts urban schools and students. *Phi Delta Kappan, 76*(1), 21–27.

Delpit, L. (1995). *Other people's children: Cultural conflict in the classroom.* New York, NY: The New Press.

Denhardt, J., & Denhardt, R. (2011). *The new public service: Serving, nor steering.* Armonk, NY: M.E. Sharpe.

DiPaola, M., & Tschannen-Moran, M. (2005). Bridging or buffering? The impact of schools' adaptive strategies on student achievement. *The Journal of Educational Administration, 43*(1), 60–71.

Driscoll, M. E. (1998). Professionalism versus community: Is the conflict between school and community about to be resolved? *Peabody Journal of Education, 73*(1), 89–127.

Dzur, A. (2008). *Democratic professionalism: Citizen participation and the reconstruction of professional ethics, identity and practice.* University Park, PA: The Pennsylvania State University Press.

Evetts, J. (2009). New professionalism and New Public Management: Changes, continuities, and consequences. *Comparative Sociology, 8*, 247–266.

Evetts, J. (2011). A new professionalism? Challenges and opportunities. *Current Sociology, 59*(4), 406–422.

Exworthy, M., & Halford, S. (1999). *Professionals and the new managerialism in the public sector.* Buckingham, UK: Open University Press.

Fang, L. (2017, August 9). Sphere of influence: How American libertarians are remaking Latin American politics. *The Intercept.* Retrieved from https://theintercept.com/2017/08/09/atlas-network-alejandro-chafuen-libertarian-think-tank-latin-america-brazil/

Fenwick, T. (2016). *Professional responsibility and professionalism: A sociomaterial examination.* New York, NY: Routledge.

Fisher, M. (2009). *Capitalist realism: Is there no alternative?* Hants, UK: Zero Books.

Fitzgerald, T. & Gunter, H. (2017). Debating the agenda: The incremental uberization of the field. *Journal of Educational Administration and History. 49*(4), 257–263.

Foster, W. (1986). *Paradigms and promises: New approaches to educational administration.* Buffalo, NY: Prometheus Books.

Foucault, M. (1991) [1978, February 1]. "Governmentality," Lecture at the College de France. In G. Burchell, C. Gorden, & P. Miller (Eds.), *The Foucault effect: Studies in governmentality.* Chicago, IL: University of Chicago Press.

Frankenberg, E., Siegel-Hawley, G., & Wang, J. (2011). Choice without equity: Charter school segregation. *Education Policy Analysis Archives, 19*(1). Retrieved from http://epaa.asu.edu/ojs/article/view/779

Freidson, E. (2001). *Professionalism: The third logic.* Cambridge, UK: Polity.

Friedman, M. (1962). *Capitalism and Freedom.* Chicago, IL: University of Chicago Press.

Friedrich, D. (2014). "We brought it on ourselves": University-based teacher education and the emergence of boot-camp-style routes to teacher certification. *Education Policy Analysis Archives, 22*(2), 21.

Gardner, H. (1993). *Multiple intelligences.* New York, NY: Basic Books.

Gates, B. (2011, February 28). How teacher development could revolutionize our schools. *Washington Post.* Retrieved from http://www.washingtonpost.com/wp-dyn/content/article/2011/02/27/ AR2011022702876.html

Gay, G. (2010). *Culturally responsive teaching: Theory, research, and practice* (2nd ed.). New York: Teachers College Press.

Goldstein, J. (2010). *Peer review and teacher leadership: Linking professionalism and accountability.* New York: Teachers College Press.

Gonzalez, N., Moll, L, & Amanti, C. (2005). *Funds of knowledge: Theorizing practices in households and classrooms.* Mahwah, NJ: Lawrence Erlbaum.

Goodlad, J. (1984). *A place called school.* New York, NY: McGraw-Hill.

Green, T. (2015). Leading for urban school reform and community development. *Educational Administration Quarterly, 51*(5), 679–711.

Harvey, D. (2005). *A brief history of neoliberalism.* Oxford, UK: Oxford University Press.

Honig, M., & Rainey, L. (2012). Autonomy and school improvement: What do we know and where do we go from here? *Educational Policy, 26*(2), 465–495.

Hood, C. (1991). A public management for all seasons? *Public Administration, 69*, 3–19.

Horn, J., & Libby, K. (2011). The giving business: Venture philanthropy and the New Schools Venture Fund. In P. Kovacs (Ed.), *The Gates Foundation and the future of U.S. public education* (pp. 168–185). New York, NY: Routledge.

Hrabowski, F., & Sanders, M. (2015, Spring). Increasing racial diversity in the teacher workforce: One university's approach. *Thought & Action*, 101–116.

Jarl, M., Fredrikson, A., & Persson, S. (2011). New public management in public education: A catalyst for the professionalization of Swedish school principals. *Public Administration. 90*(2), 429–444.

Keil, R. (2009). The urban politics of roll-with-it neoliberalization, *City, 13*(2–3), 231–245.

Keith, N. (2015). *Engaging in social partnerships: Democratic practices for campus-community partnerships.* New York: Routledge.

Kickert, W. (1995). Steering at a distance: A new paradigm of public governance in Dutch higher education. *Governance, 8*(1), 135–157.

Kirp, D. (2013). *Improbable scholars.* Oxford, UK: Oxford University Press.

Koyama, J. (2014). Principals as bricoleurs: Making sense and making do in an era of accountability. *Educational Administration Quarterly, 50*(2), 279–304.

Labaree, D. (2004). *The trouble with ed schools.* New Haven, CT: Yale University Press.

Lakoff, G. (2008). *The political mind: Why you can't understand 21st-century politics with an 18th-century brain.* New York, NY: Viking.

Levine, A. (2006). *Educating school teachers.* Princeton, NJ: The Education Schools Project.

Locke, R., & Spender, J-C. (2011). *Confronting managerialism: How the business elite and their schools threw our lives out of balance.* New York, NY: Zed Books.

Lustick, H. (2017). Making discipline relevant: Toward a theory of culturally responsive schoolwide discipline. *Race, Ethnicity, and Education, 20,* 681–695.

Lynch, K., Baker, J., & Lyons, M. (2009). *Affective equality: Love, care, and injustice.* New York, NY: Palgrave Macmillan.

McDermott, K., & Nygreen, K. (2013). Educational new paternalism: Human capital, cultural capital, and the politics of equal opportunity. *Peabody Journal of Education, 88*(1), 84–97.

McDonald, J. (2007). *The power of protocols.* New York: Teachers College Press.

Meier, D. (1995). *The power of their ideas.* Boston, MA: Beacon Press.

Meyer, H., & Rowan, B. (2006). Institutional analysis and the study of education. In H. Meyer & B. Rowan (Eds.), *The new institutionalism in education* (pp. 1–14). Albany: SUNY Press.

Milstein, M. (1990). Plateauing as an occupational phenomenon among teachers and administrators. *Journal of Personnel Evaluation in Education, 3*(4), 325–336.

Mungal, A. S. (2016). Teach for America, Relay Graduate School, and the charter school networks: The making of a parallel education structure. *Education Policy Analysis Archives, 24*(17).

New Teachers' Roundtable. (2015). Retrieved from http://www.tejno.org/

Nunez, I., Michie, G. & Konkol, P. (2015). *Worth striking for: Why education policy is every teacher's concern.* New York: Teachers College Press.

Nurvala, J. (2015). "Uberization" is the future of the digitalized labor market. *European View, 14*(2), 231–239.

Payne, C. (2008). *So much reform. So little change.* Cambridge, MA: Harvard.

Putnam, R. D., Frederick, C. B., & Snellman, K. (2012). *Growing class gaps in social connectedness among American youth.* Cambridge, MA: Harvard Kennedy School of Government. Retrieved from https://sites.hks.harvard.edu/saguaro/research/SaguaroReport_Diverging SocialConnectedness_20120808.pdf

Reardon, S. (2013, May). The widening income achievement gap. *Educational Leadership, 70*(8), 10–16.

Reckhow, S. (2013). *Follow the money: How foundation dollars change public school politics.* New York, NY: Oxford University Press.

Richards, J., & Stebbins, L. (2014). Behind The Data: Testing and Assessment-A PreK-12 U.S. Education Technology Market Report. Retrieved from Washington, DC:

Robertson, S., Verger, A., Mundy, K., & Menashy, F. (Eds.). (2014). *Public private partnerships in education: New actors and modes of governance in a globalizing world.* Cheltonham, UK: Edward Edgar Pub.

Robinson, M. (2010). *School perspectives on collaborative inquiry: Lessons learned from New York City, 2009–2010.* New York: Consortium for Policy Research in Education.

Rogers, D. (2006). *110 Livingston Street: Politics and bureaucracy in New York City school system.* Clinton Corners, NY: Eliot Werner Pub.

Ronfeldt, M., Loeb, S., & Wyckoff, J. (2013). How teacher turnover harms student achievement. *American Educational Research Journal, 50*(1), 4–36.

Rose, N. (1993). Government, authority, and expertise in advanced liberalism. *Economy and Society, 22*(3), 283–300.

Sachs, J. (2003). *The activist teaching profession.* London: Open University Press.

Sahlberg, P. (2015). *Finnish lessons, 2.0: What can the world learn from educational change in Finland?* New York, NY: Teachers College Press.

Samier, E. A. (2013). Where have the disruptions gone? Educational administration's theoretical capacity for analysing or fomenting disruption. *International Journal of Leadership in Education, 16*(2), 234–244.

Scott, J. (2009). The politics of venture philanthropy in charter school policy and advocacy. *Educational Policy, 23*(1), 106–136.

Scott, J. (2011). Market-driven education reform and the racial politics of advocacy. *Peabody Journal of Education, 86*, 580–599.

Selwyn, N. (2011). 'It's all about standardization'–Exploring the digital (re)configuration of school management and administration. *Cambridge Journal of Education, 41*(4), 473–488.

Sennett, R. (1998). *The corrosion of character: The personal consequences of work in the new capitalism.* New York, NY: Norton.

Sennett, R. (2006). *The culture of the new capitalism.* New Haven, CT: Yale University Press.

Shipps, D. (2012). Empowered or beleaguered? Principals' accountability under New York City's diverse provider regime. *Education Policy Analysis Archives, 20*(1).

Shipps, D., & White, M. (2009). A new politics of the principalship? Accountability-driven change in New York City. *Peabody Journal of Education, 84*(3), 350–373.

Smith Richards, J. (2006, October 22). Cheating is up—Among teachers Pressure for state-test success driving some to break the rules *The Columbus Dispatch*, p. 4.

Smith, M., and N. Pandolfo. 2011. "For-Profit Certification for Teachers is Booming." *New York Times.* November, 27th National Edition, p. A33A.

Solbrekke, T., & Sugrue, C. (2014). Professional accreditation of initial teacher education programs: Teacher educators' strategies –between 'accountability' and 'responsibility'. *Teaching and teacher education, 37*, 11–20.

Sondel, B. (2017). The new teachers' roundtable: A case study of collective resistance. *Critical Education, 8*(4), 1–22.

Stillman, J. (2011). Teacher learning in an era of high-stakes accountability: Productive tension and critical professional practice. *Teachers College Record, 113*(1), 133–180.

Stone-Johnson, C. (2014). Parallel professionalism in an era of standardization. Teachers and teaching: *Theory and practice. 20*(1), 74–91.

Strathern, M. (Ed.). (2000). *Audit cultures: Anthropological studies in accountability, ethics, and the academy.* London, UK: Routledge.

Strauss, V. (May 14, 2017). In Arizona, teachers can now be hired with absolutely no training in how to teacher. *The Washington Post.* www.washingtonpost.com/news/answer-sheet/wp/2017/05/14/in-arizona-teachers-can-now-be-hired-with-absolutely-no-training-in-how-to-teach/?utm_term=.f46abd240b97

Talbert, J. (2012). *Inquiry-based school reform: Lessons from SAM in NYC.* Stanford University, Center for Research on the Context of Teaching.

Taylor, M. (2006). *From Pinochet to the 'third way': Neoliberalism and social transformation in Chile.* London, UK: Pluto Press.

Thomas, M. & Mockler, N. (2018). Alternative routes to teacher professional identity: Exploring the conflated sub-identities of Teach for America Corp Members. *Education Policy Analysis Archives, 26*(6).

Trujillo, T. (2014). The modern cult of efficiency: Intermediary organizations and the new scientific management. *Educational Policy, 28*(2), 207–232.

Tyack, D. B. (1974). *The one best system: A history of American urban education*. Cambridge, MA: Harvard University Press.

Valli, L., & Buese, D. (2007). The changing roles of teachers in an era of high-stakes accountability. *American Educational Research Journal, 44*(3), 519–558.

Verger, A., Lubienski, C., & Steiner-Khamsi, G. (Eds.). (2016). *World yearbook of education, 2016: The global education industry*. London, UK: Routledge.

Ward, S. (2011). The machinations of managerialism: New public management and the diminishing power of professionals. *Journal of Cultural Economy, 4*(2), 205–215.

Weick, K. (1976). Organizations as loosely-coupled systems. *Administrative Science Quarterly, 21*(1), 1–19.

Welch, A. R. (1998). The cult of efficiency in education: Comparative reflections on the reality and the rhetoric. *Comparative Education, 34*(2), 157–175.

Woods, P. (2005). *Democratic leadership in education*. London: Sage.

Zeichner, K. (2014). The struggle for the soul of teaching and teacher education in the USA, *Journal of Education for Teaching: International research and pedagogy, 40*(5), 551–568.

CHAPTER 8

In Pursuit of Democratic Education

Putting the Public Back in Public Schools

Americans generally agree that the U.S. is a democracy. We know that "dark money" has distorted elections (Mayer, 2016); corporate lobbyists have too much influence over our politicians (Drutman, 2015); and, with the election of Donald Trump as president, many Americans are reading books like George Orwell's *1984,* Aldous Huxley's *Brave New World,* and Sinclair Lewis's *It Can't Happen Here*, which are about how antidemocratic forces can take over societies. And yet, we are still a republic with a constitution and three more or less functioning branches of government. But the structures of democracy, which includes public schools, can weaken greatly over time, and our democratic skills and habits can atrophy from disuse. Many Americans profess to support the *concept* of public schooling but send *their* children to private schools. In this chapter, we explore the many meanings of democracy and how, with the current laser-like focus on producing human capital for international competition, schools are largely abdicating their responsibility to educate a new generation to defend democratic principles (Labaree, 1997; Westheimer, 2007).

While we have addressed concerns in previous chapters about confusing consumer choice with political democracy and what it means for a school to be "public," in this chapter, we will explore these issues in greater detail. The writing on democracy is vast and we can only scratch the surface, but John Dewey's many books set the standard for its implications for education. In 1927, a period much like our own, and two years before the stock market crashed, Dewey wrote about the alarming growth of forces that made democratic deliberation more difficult. In *The Public and its Problems* (1927), he elaborated on the forces that stood in the public's way. His list was a familiar one: special interests, the inordinate power of corporations, mind-numbing entertainment, selfishness and a focus on the individual, and a lack of interest in political affairs. His book was a response to Walter Lippman's *The Phantom Public* (1925), in which he argued that the public had little capacity to engage in rational deliberation on public issues and challenged the very existence of "public" in the U.S. Dewey, while cognizant of the obstacles, was confident that improvements in communications and education could restore to the public its political voice.

A decade earlier, Dewey had written *Democracy and Education* (1916), a classic in the Education field. In it, Dewey argued that democracy should be a daily lived experience, not limited to voting for political candidates. He supported school boards and elections in general but felt that this form of political democracy was fragile and only a fraction of what it meant to be a democratic citizen. For Dewey, democracy had to be lived in the classroom, in the school, and in everyday life. Dewey would have objected to viewing choice in a marketplace as a form of democracy. He would have pointed out that without participating in collective decision-making through democratic organizations, citizen's political skills would atrophy and they would be unlikely to defend larger democratic principles of a liberal democracy.

While it is impossible to discuss notions of democracy, education, and the "public" without reference to Dewey, views on democracy and education have become even more contentious in recent decades. In this chapter, we will discuss democracy and public education by presenting different ways in which democracy is viewed in current policy debates. The first, following Dewey, is how we model democracy in school and district governance. Who should be included in decision-making, and in which areas? How do we structure spaces for open deliberation? How wide should inclusion be? Should it extend beyond the school, to parents and community members? What mechanisms should be used to achieve broad inclusion in democratic decision-making?

The second sense of democracy goes beyond inclusion in decision-making to inclusion in the benefits of society—a quality education being one of those benefits. This sense of democracy links it to human and civil rights and *equal educational opportunity*, and requires us to do a kind of equity audit of our schools (Capper & Young, 2015; Johnson & Avelar Lasalle, 2010) and our society. While in previous chapters, we have critiqued the "audit culture" that high-stakes testing has produced, here, we refer to how principals and teachers can use data and inquiry to monitor how equitable their school is. To what extent are our schools racially and socioeconomically segregated or tracked internally? How equitably are schools being funded? Who is in special education? Who is in programs for the gifted and talented? Who is being suspended at high rates? Who is being bullied? Who is being pushed out by gentrification? How might economic, social, and cultural capital be more evenly distributed in schools and in society?

The third sense of democracy is the question of what it means for a school to be "public." A school is not "public" merely because it receives public funds but rather because it is transparent and accountable to the public and works to foster a democratic public sphere and a common good. If we are part of the "public," then we relate to public schools as citizens, not as consumers. This confusion is endemic in our society as markets and choice are being presented as replacements for political democracy (Chubb & Moe, 1990). It is only through the fostering of democratic citizenship and a democratic, public sphere that we, as citizens, can hold both the State and the Market accountable. It is also the job of the State to hold the market accountable through regulation, a job the neoliberal State has failed to do, in part because of corporate lobbying and contributions to politicians (Drutman, 2015). In the following three sections, we will develop these three meanings of democracy—inclusion in democratic governance, inclusion in society's benefits, and the meaning of "public"—in more detail.

DEMOCRACY AS DEMOCRATIC PARTICIPATION IN DECISION-MAKING

In Chapter 5, we discussed how hierarchical forms of governance in schools gave way in the 1980s to experiments with shared governance. We described in some detail Malen and Ogawa's (1988) study of site-based management and the obstacles encountered in early attempts to be more participatory in school-level decision-making. Unfortunately, the record on successful attempts at participatory decision-making in schools is still spotty. While many schools have leadership teams and "PLCs" (professional learning communities), they are too often democratic in name only. In the previous chapter, we described a teacher inquiry group in which teachers were supposed to be able to make decisions based on their own school-based inquiry or action research. Yet the so-called inquiry group was largely an attempt to get teachers to use an expensive database the district had purchased. While having a lot of data available can enhance a teacher's decision-making, in too many cases, "inquiry" is defined merely as "data use," typically test data on spreadsheets. In such cases, the goal is to use this data to reteach topics based on test items that students did poorly on. In this way, inquiry is connected to high-stakes testing and other quantitative outcomes data, and reduces teaching to a process of test, remediate, test, remediate, test, remediate. This is an impoverished notion of teaching but is dominant in many schools as teachers "teach to the test" and leaders "lead to the test."

But what would it take to achieve more authentic forms of inquiry and participation in decision-making? Anderson (1998) developed a framework for thinking about what authentic forms of participation might take. Table 8.1 presents a series of interrelated questions through which to interrogate the authenticity of current approaches to participation. This framework consists of five central questions: (1) Participation toward what end? (2) Who participates? (3) What are relevant spheres of participation? (4) What conditions and processes must be present locally to make participation authentic? (i.e. the micropolitics of participation), (5) What conditions and processes must be present at broader institutional and societal levels to make participation authentic? (i.e. the macropolitics of participation).

Table 8.1 A Framework for Moving Toward Authentic Participation

Authenticity as…	Key questions
Micropolitical considerations	
Broad inclusion	Who participates?
Relevant participation	Participation in which spheres?
Authentic local conditions and processes	What conditions and processes should be present locally?
Macropolitical considerations	
Coherence between means and ends of participation	Participation toward what end?
Focus on broader structural inequities.	What conditions and processes should be present at broader institutional and societal levels?

Some of these questions are self-explanatory. For instance, the first question about the *ends of participation* relates to the example of the inquiry group in which the ends for the teachers were to engage in authentic and collaborative inquiry and to explore how they might identify practices that were leading to students dropping out of school. But the ends for the district were to get teachers to use their new database and engage in data-driven decision-making limited to quantitative outcomes data. When things like inquiry groups or leadership teams are mandated, as they often are in school districts, it makes sense to question whose ends they serve. Authentic participation can seldom be mandated, but that doesn't mean leaders can't appropriate mandates to generate authentic and collaborative spaces in schools.

The question of *who participates* has been a contentious issue in schools. It is often assumed that shared governance in schools is limited to teachers and administrators. Including parents, students, or community members in school decisions is more complicated. Many teachers see professional decisions as their prerogative, while parents may feel that teachers are insufficiently culturally responsive or have low expectations for their children. Furthermore, as we discussed in Malen and Ogawa's (1988) study in Chapter 5, simply having everyone around the table does not mean that they are equally invited to participate. Power relations, access to information, and norms of civility often determine levels of participation by different constituencies. Authentic dialogue about these issues is difficult but not impossible if a school can create a welcoming atmosphere for parents.

For parents, and particularly low-income parents, authentic participation would have to move beyond merely volunteering in the school to (1) governance and decision-making, (2) organizing for equity and quality, (3) input toward a culturally responsive curriculum, and (4) home educational support. Much current literature also questions whether parent and community participation can be effective without understanding how particular parents or communities view their schools and how they define involvement (Gold, Simon, & Brown, 2004; Green, 2015; Ishimaru, 2014).

Teachers want *relevant participation.* They do not want to have to divert time and energy into decision-making domains that they view as nonrelevant or frivolous. Presenting empirical data on teacher participation, Bacharach, Bamberger, Conley, and Bauer (1990) argued that school reformers needed to progress beyond the "monolithic myth" of teacher participation in decision-making and determine which specific decision domains teachers wished to participate in. While there is still some disagreement on specifics, most researchers of teacher participation agree that core areas of participation which are central to both the core technology of the school and the core areas of interest for teachers are the areas of budget, personnel, instruction, and curriculum (Reitzug & Capper, 1996). Although most of a school's budget goes to teacher salaries, there are often considerable discretionary funds for site-based budgetary decisions. Besides budget, teachers also want input into personnel issues, particularly hiring, an area in which principals and teachers currently have greater participation. On the other hand, high-stakes testing and, increasingly, technology (Burch & Good, 2014) drive curriculum and instruction often over the heads of teachers and administrators.

As for *what conditions and processes should be present locally*, reformers tend to borrow models of participation from the corporate closet. "Quality circles" of workers making decisions may work in Germany, where workers benefit from shared governance even at the top of their corporations (see Addison, 2009). However, in the U.S., they are more likely a way for management to increase production and speed up the work routines.

It might make more sense to look to mission-driven, nonprofit organizations for a more appropriate model. Based on a national study of Social Change Organizations (SCOs), Ospina and Foldy (2005, 2010) suggest that SCOs are a neglected source from which to enhance our understanding of leadership. SCOs are generally located within a growing civil society sector of advocacy organizations within both the public and the nonprofit sectors. They include "community-based and alternative organizations and groups connected to social movements, as well as networks of organizations engaged in civic reform" (p. 6). For these grassroots organizations, leadership is directly focused on goals of advocacy and social change. The democratic goals of these organizations lead, according to Bryson and Crosby (1992), to problems of sharing power within the organization as well as through interorganizational coordination. They suggest that this creates the need for a form of public leadership that is essentially different from leaders pursuing more restricted organizational goals.

As school and district leaders begin to view themselves as advocates for children and communities, models of leadership developed from SCOs might be more instructive than those developed from corporate organizations (Ishimaru, 2014). The leadership framework that Ospina and Foldy (2005) developed

> poses that the consistent use of a set of leadership **drivers**, anchored in a set of **assumptions** and **core values** of social justice, helps members of these organizations engage in **practices and activities** that **build collective power,** which is then **leveraged** to produce **long-term outcomes** for social change. Together, the drivers, assumptions and core values act as an integrated philosophy or worldview that becomes a powerful source of meaning to help frame and to ground the practices, activities and tools used to engage in action and accomplish the work effectively (bold in original).
>
> (p. 12)

The emphasis on shared assumptions and core values focused on social justice and the ongoing dialogue required to reach sufficient consensus to act together is central to SCOs but largely neglected in schools because it is too often viewed as conflict producing. Like other organizations, SCOs struggle with conflict, but there is an acknowledgment that underlying assumptions and core values are central to the organization's very existence. Schools that serve low-income children and children of color are often operating on a set of underlying assumptions that hold unjust practices in place. Johnson (2002) calls this stage of school change "killing the myth and building dissatisfaction," meaning that teachers must reject the school's status quo and take an authentic look at the ways they may be perpetuating inequality in their schools and refuse to tolerate practices that are not equitable. This calls for deep dialogue about teachers' assumptions about their students and commitment to social justice before proceeding with school change.

This mission-driven approach to social justice might address some of the problems that Malen and Ogawa (1988), and subsequent researchers found with attempts at shared decision-making. It makes collective power, not the individual power of the principal or teacher the primary goal. This might make it more likely that local conditions might involve more sharing of information, as well as power. It might make it more likely that marginalized stakeholders like students, low-income parents, and community organizers might be seen less as threats to the status quo and more as allies in struggle.

Ospina and Foldy's (2005) framework calls for a series of ongoing practices that include cultivating collaborative capacity, using collective identity narratives to build solidarity, engaging in dialogue across difference, organizing, public policy advocacy, community building, direct service provision, grassroots leadership development, developing interorganizational capacity, and network building. While these activities are not all foreign to school leaders, they are far from central to leadership models that are currently available.

What Conditions and Processes Should Be Present at Broader Institutional and Societal Levels?

Much of this book is an attempt to better understand why we have abandoned attempts to create a more equitable society and how this affects what it means to be a teacher or leader today. Inequalities in the U.S. have reached the levels of the 1920s Gilded Age of the robber barons. And yet, the 2017 tax bill promises to increase levels of inequality even more. *The New York Times* reports that those who will most benefit from the Republicans' tax bill are big corporations, multimillionaires, private equity managers, private schools, liquor stores, lawyers, tax accountants, and President Trump and his family (Drucker & Rappeport, 2017, December 16). It cuts the corporate tax rates and raised the exception on the estate tax to $22 million, giving a massive tax cut to the very wealthy. On the other hand, the *Times* reports that those who will be most hurt by the tax plan are the elderly; low-income families; immigrants; people buying health insurance; and homeowners in the states of New York, New Jersey, and California. The tax bill repealed the individual health insurance mandate, which will cause insurance premiums to rise. The Congressional Budget Office estimates that 13 million Americans are projected to lose their health insurance under the plan.

In Chapter 2, we argued for finding ways to hold the powerful accountable for policy outcomes, and described Thomas Rogers, former president of the New York State Council of School Superintendents, notion of *reciprocal accountability*. This essentially means that not just schools would have a report card, but each level of government (federal, state, and district) as well as the corporate sector and Wall Street bankers should be held accountable for things they can influence. Such a report card might be a way to reframe who is "making excuses" for tolerating the levels of social inequality we are experiencing and the social policies that have produced them. Our crisis of social inequality has been passed discursively from the neoliberal State onto our public schools.

DEMOCRACY AS INCLUSION AND EQUAL EDUCATIONAL OPPORTUNITY

Throughout this book, we stress the need to defend public schools against attempts to privatize them. But the public schools we need are not the public schools we've historically had. Leaders who want to provide equal educational opportunity should have a clear-eyed understanding of how our public schools have been organized to privilege those who are already privileged. We can't interrupt privilege, whether by race, class, gender, language, sexual orientation/gender identity, disability, and their intersections, if we do not understand how it operates at the levels of *structure* and *culture*, and how the two levels reinforce each other. There are many frameworks that can help us understand how privilege is socially reproduced. There are a variety of critical theories that do the job, each highlighting different issues: critical race theories, critical feminist theories, queer theories, critical disability theories, neo-Marxist theories, some post-structural theories, socio-material theories, and we could go on. Some of these we discussed in Chapter 2. We use theories in the plural, since under each of these categories of theories, there are many different theorists.

To discuss democracy in terms of social inclusion, we've chosen to use French sociologist, Pierre Bourdieu's theory of social reproduction (Bourdieu & Passeron, 1970/1990), which was originally based on the reproduction of social class, though he also studied the reproduction of gender roles as well (Bourdieu, 2001). Although, other than viewing it as a form of cultural capital, he did not address race to any great extent. Others, however, have appropriated his work with a focus on race (Carter, 2007; Delpit, 1995; Lewis, 2003; Stanton-Salazar, 2011; Wallace, 2017; Yosso, 2006). Bourdieu defines the privileged as those whose *economic, cultural, and social capital* have greater exchange value within social fields (Bourdieu & Passeron, 1970/1990). In our case, we focus on the education field.

The possession of *economic* capital means that some can leave the public school system altogether by purchasing a more privileged education and sending their children to elite, nonpublic, independent private schools, some of which charge upward of $50,000 a year per child. Or they can afford to buy a home in a school district with well-funded, elite schools and claim to be strong supporters of "public schools." It is important to acknowledge that while 90% of K–12 students attend public schools (including charter schools as "public"), our public schools have traditionally been highly stratified because of the ways we fund them. Suburbs with high property values tend to have better resourced schools and draw on a middle- to upper-middle-class student population that is also disproportionately White.

This is where economic and social capital converge. Parents are not only choosing private and suburban schools because the additional resources provide an enriched curriculum, better facilities, and guidance counselors with links to Ivy League universities. They are also purchasing the social networks their children will enter and the lifelong social capital they will acquire as their friendship groups take their places near the top of the social hierarchy. Throughout their lives, they will be socializing with similarly privileged children and parents. Academically, this means accelerated classes that prepare youth for prestigious universities that lead to privileged careers. It also means that when it comes time to choose a life partner and possibly form a family, that partner is also likely to be a member of this privileged class. Bourdieu called this *social reproduction*, or the passing down of class, gender, and race privilege from one generation to the next, and, at least in the France of the postwar years, he saw schools and universities as central mechanisms of social reproduction. Other sociologists refer to this tendency by the upper classes to maximize opportunity for their own children as *opportunity or dream hoarding* (Reeves, 2017; Wright, 2009).

But only the elite can afford elite private schools and suburban school districts that provide an equivalent elite public school experience. While middle-class parents can buy homes in non-elite, middle-class suburbs and neighborhoods, most have to rely more on their social and cultural capital than on their economic capital. So, they may have to use their social and cultural capital to more aggressively work the system to get the best teachers and other resources from their local public schools and make sure that their children are in the honors and gifted programs.

In urban areas, many middle-class professionals are gentrifying low-income neighborhoods. They may bring resources to the parent-teacher organization and hypothetically integrate schools by class and race, but there is much evidence that they are also displacing many local residents and selecting public or charter schools that have reached a "tipping point" of White middle-class children (Cucchiara, 2013; Posey Maddox, 2014) or a new breed of "prestige" charter schools (Brown & Makris, 2017; Hankins, 2007).

Principals are in the awkward position of feeling that they need to recruit these parents and the potential resources they bring to the school, even as they realize that they are displacing local families (McGhee & Anderson, in press). Washington, D.C., formerly known as the Chocolate City because of its large African American population, now has more charter schools than public schools, and there is compelling evidence that the charter schools are being used by gentrifying parents to escape the public schools that are mostly populated by low-income children of color (Mann & Bennett, 2016).

Once elites and the middle class (which probably includes most of us who are writing or reading this) have deployed their considerable resources of economic, cultural, and social capital, the working class and poor, who are disproportionately Black and Latino, are left with the schooling options that remain. Some of the more savvy parents, who can afford it, may rent an apartment in a "good" school district or use a relative's address who lives there. A few might take advantage of "choice" policies to find a charter or public school they like better than their zoned school. A handful of talented students get plucked out by gifted programs or college access programs like Goldman Sachs funded, Prep for Prep. These students' journey from public housing to the Ivy Leagues is trumpeted in the media and lends support to the American myth of meritocracy (McNamee & Miller, 2009).

But these opportunities, while welcome, are anomalies. For the most part, given the relatively low exchange value of their capital, low-income parents simply cannot compete with elite and middle-class parents, which is why choice and voucher policies are so problematic. The choices low-income parents are left with are extremely limited, and the value of a voucher is unlikely to be enough to buy their way into elite schools.

A key concept developed by Bourdieu is the notion of a *cultural arbitrary*. This means that there is nothing *inherently* better or worse about anyone's cultural capital. The same cultural capital that low-income youth use to effectively navigate their own community is often not going to have a high exchange value in a school classroom and vice versa (Delpit, 1995). This speaks to the need to help students develop the ability to shift registers (deploy different forms of cultural capital) in different settings. But unlike many paternalistic charter schools, this must be done with a deep respect for the *habitus* (the cultural capital acquired though child-rearing) of the student (McDermott & Nygreen, 2013). This habitus is strongly linked to one's identity and, if devalued, whether intentionally or not, can have disastrous effects on a student's sense of self.

It is now common, in this age of a rhetoric of high expectations for low-income children, for principals to assign Ivy League colleges to children in the early grades and grace the walls of classrooms with Ivy League university banners. This is clearly better than the dreadful warning some teachers are rumored to give children in New York City: "There is a cell at Riker's Island with your name on it." And yet, it almost seems cruel to raise Ivy League expectations for low-income children, unless we are willing as educators and as a society to create the structural scaffolding it would take to make that a more likely reality than the jail cell.

We live in an age in which claims that "the system is rigged" are finding increased resonance on both sides of the political divide. The pipeline to prison metaphor has replaced the original pipeline to college metaphor. This is born out in fact. In 2016, the U.S. Department of Education released a report that documents how state and local spending on prisons and jails has increased at triple the rate of funding for public education for preschool through grade twelve education in the last three decades (Stullich, Morgan, & Schak, 2016). Increasingly, these jails and prisons are owned and operated by for-profit corporations with an incentive to increase their number of "customers" (Brickner & Diaz, 2011).

The time may be ripe for exposing, as Bourdieu attempted to do, how those of us with a certain kind of economic, cultural, and social capital maintain and pass on our privilege. But it wasn't always this way to the same extent. The U.S. used to have greater social upward mobility than European countries like France, where Bourdieu developed his class-based theory. Now, France and all of Europe have more upward social mobility than the U.S. (Wilkinson & Pickett, 2009). In addition to greater class inequality, our schools and our society are becoming more racially segregated (Orfield & Frankenberg, 2014). Educators, particularly those who work in low-income communities, are in many ways the canary in the mine. They are the ones who see these inequalities up close, even though most do not themselves live in low-income communities. But there is a tendency to want to fix the students and their families rather than the social policies that have caused the problem.

The generation called the Millennials, who enter the education field, often does so with a mission to work for social justice. At nearly every high school and university graduation ceremony, principals, university Deans, and Presidents exhort their graduates to go forth and change the world. Programs like Teach for America and the KIPP charter franchise attract thousands of idealistic middle-class young adults looking for an opportunity to change the world and work for social justice. The same is true for university-based programs that prepare teachers and administrators. And yet, too many of these programs aim at giving poor children of color cultural makeovers, as if a test-driven education and learning middle-class cultural capital will alone lift them into the middle class. Few programs address the structural and policy changes that are needed if social justice is to be sought with any kind of empirical realism (Anyon, 2014).

BOURDIEU AND SYMBOLIC VIOLENCE

A major tenet of Bourdieu and Passeron's (1970/1990) *Reproduction in Education, Society and Culture* was the idea that the social reproduction of privilege from generation to generation could partly be understood in economic terms (tax codes, inheritance laws, the appropriation by capitalists of the surplus value of workers' and women's labor, etc.) but that the rarity of social class upward mobility during most historical periods had to be understood also in cultural terms. The authors lay out the subtle and usually unconscious mechanisms through which dominant groups in society make their own particular form of cultural capital appear to be the natural way of being in the world. Thus, taking arbitrary cultural capital (e.g. white skin, a particular way of pronouncing words, a manner of dress, etc.) which has no inherent superiority and succeeding in imposing it as a dominant social norm through social institutions, particularly through formal schooling, represents what Bourdeau called *symbolic violence*.

Skin color is part of one's cultural capital, although it is sometimes hard to disentangle from social class (Leonardo, 2012). In the U.S., white skin typically has a higher social exchange value than black or brown skin, which leads to forms of symbolic violence that are seldom viewed as such. Decades ago, Rist (1977) described how children were often placed in reading groups by skin color or social class markers (clothing, hair style, dialect, etc.). Today, studies of school suspensions and referrals to special education show the same tendencies to privilege the class and race-based cultural capital of privileged students over those with cultural capital that has a lower exchange value in classroom contexts (Ahram, Fergus, & Noguera, 2011).

Key to Bourdieu's theory of *social/economic* reproduction is how *cultural* reproduction occurs and, for subordinate groups, the disconnect between the cultural capital they obtain through child-rearing (*habitus*) and the cultural capital implicitly valued in formal schooling. Some scholars have used the term "culturally responsive pedagogy" to describe a pedagogy that is effective with children from low-income and culturally diverse families (Gay, 2010; Ladson Billings, 1995). However, implicit in their work is a recognition that most dominant teaching and schooling practices have traditionally been culturally responsive in the sense that they have tended to be congruent with the primary habitus of White, middle-class families.

Deborah Meier (2002) explains how this symbolic violence occurs in schools,

> ...what the most successful students had going for them was that even in kindergarten, with their hands eagerly raised, they were ready to show off their school smarts. Starting on day one, certain forms of knowledge and skill – the stuff they've eagerly brought with them from home – was confirmed and honored, thus increasing their self-confidence to take still more risks...But many other students never found a replacement for a school and teacher who didn't recognize their genius, who responded with a shrug or a look of incomprehension as they offered their equally eager home truths. They too soon learned that in school all they could show off was their ignorance. Better to be bad, or uninterested, or to just silently withdraw.

(p. 15)

Two important Bourdieuan concepts are alluded to in this passage. First, Meier's allusion to the reaction of students who are victims of symbolic violence represents strategies that run the gamut from the relatively passive internalization of their lack of worth to "being bad" or engaging in other forms of resistance. Fine (1991) documented how in some low-income urban high schools, the youth who dropped out showed higher rates of mental health on psychological tests than those who remained and were subjected to daily forms of symbolic violence. Cummins (1986) showed how the older children in immigrant families did better academically than their younger siblings because they were not exposed to as many years of symbolic violence.

Second, the shrug or the "look of incomprehension" captures the spirit of symbolic violence, which is inflicted on students often by well-meaning, capable, caring teachers. These teachers are often simply incapable of recognizing, much less valuing, the cultural capital the student brings to the classroom. This child's cultural capital, which has a high exchange value at home, has little exchange value in a classroom led by a teacher unfamiliar or unappreciative of the child's cultural capital. This is more than a problem of cross-cultural misunderstanding or ignorance, since one's cultural capital is part of one's habitus and is viewed as simply the natural order of things. It is more closely related to Bourdieu's notion of "misrecognition." Teachers take their habitus for granted "precisely because [they are] caught up in it, bound up with it; [they] inhabit it like a garment. [They] feel at home in the world because the world is also in [them], in the form of the habitus" (Bourdieu, 2000).

In fact, according to Bourdieu and Passeron (1970/1990), it is the very invisibility of the operation of symbolic power that makes it so effective.

> Every power to exert symbolic violence, i.e. every power which manages to impose meanings and to impose them as legitimate by concealing the power relations which are the basis of its force, adds its own specifically symbolic force to those power relations.

(p. 4)

In this way, inequitable social relations are likely maintained not simply through bad teaching as current school reform efforts assume but also through the everyday pedagogy of dedicated and caring teachers, who are often unaware that they are contributing to the social reproduction of inequality.

Issues of power and inclusion are also important at the level of staffing. Harry Walcott's (1973) classic ethnography, *The Man in the Principal's Office,* captures how schools were run somewhat like families during most of the 20th century. The male principal was in charge, and the female teachers' job was to care for the children. As late as the 1950s, only 18% of school principals were women, and those were mostly in elementary schools. Less than 1% of superintendents were women (Grogen & Shakeshaft, 2010). Teachers and principals of color were extremely rare. While those numbers have improved considerably, we still have a long way to go, and in some areas, such as attracting and promoting teachers and leaders of color, we seem to be going backward (Teachers Unite!, 2014).

On a more positive note, Bourdieu has developed the concepts of cultural *reproduction* and cultural *production.* Subordinated groups also *produce* culture under difficult circumstances, and these subcultures often sustain these groups against forms of physical and symbolic violence (Scott, 1990). Afrocentric education and hip-hop culture are examples of this cultural resiliency and are used by many culturally responsive teachers for healing the damage done through symbolic forms of violence (Ginwright, 2004). Many school leaders are also trying to fight against forms of symbolic violence by focusing on the whole child and her multiple intelligences. We provide in Box 8.1 the example of Jamaal Bowman, a Bronx, New York middle school principal, whose school is exemplary in this regard.

BOX 8.1 JAMAAL BOWMAN, PRINCIPAL, BRONX, NEW YORK

Jamaal Bowman, principal of Cornerstone Academy for Social Action (CASA) middle school in the Bronx is committed above all to educating the whole child. This central belief has placed him at odds with many current school reforms, including high-stakes testing. It's not that CASA's test scores haven't been high. It had the highest combined reading and math growth score average in New York City in 2015. It has also ranked in the top 10% in the city in middle school attendance since it opened. These high rankings buy him some autonomy and political protection for speaking out, but he is proudest of CASA's productivity in the arts. Being the principal of a school in the Bronx where hip-hop originated, Principal Bowman is himself an advocate of using cultural forms that are relevant to his students' experiences.

CASA students have produced expository, argumentative, and narrative writing as well as poetry, and students have written and produced over ten social justice music videos that have been featured on local news outlets. CASA takes citizenship education seriously as well. When the Grand Jury in

Ferguson, Missouri, failed to indict a police officer in the fatal shooting of an unarmed teenager, Michael Brown, CASA's 270 students marched in their Eastchester neighborhood, chanting, "No Justice, No Peace" and "We Will Not Be Silent," the name of a song they wrote themselves. The march ended with a rally in which Principal Bowman gave a talk to the students about the Ferguson tragedy.

He credits hip-hop for helping him through some rough times growing up in New York City, and has made hip-hop a generative theme at the school to bring students into the arts and political education. He and his school are currently the focus of a documentary, *CASA: An Education Revolution*, which will serve as a counter-story to documentaries like *Waiting for Superman* and other corporate-funded celebrations of charter schools and vouchers. Besides helping to produce the documentary, his other forms of advocacy include a blog https://jamaalabowman.wordpress.com/ and his work with the New York State Allies for Public Education (NYSAPE), which helped to spearhead the opt out movement across America. The opt out process involves parents engaging in an act of civil disobedience by signing forms that opt their students out of taking high-stakes exams. According to Jamaal, "All kids are brilliant and adults have to create the environment that nurtures their brilliance. Education is more than just a test score."

DEMOCRACY AS DEFENDING THE PUBLIC

In the Soviet Union and Eastern Europe, we have seen what happens to democracy when the State colonizes the private sector and civil society. Citizens are unable to exercise their rights as citizens, and the State is unable to supply the economic dynamism that regulated markets provide. But democracy is also threatened at the other extreme. If the market and private sector take over the role of the State or powerful corporations have inordinate power over the State, then citizens can no longer participate in a robust political democracy but rather become resigned and passive consumers. Each form of extremism, too much State or too much market, creates a deficit of democracy.

Ironically, it was conservative economist, Milton Freidman, who warned that if government grew too big, it could be taken over by corporations. But what Freidman didn't say was that corporations had been amassing power since the 19th century. Few Americans are aware that the King of England chartered the first corporations in America. The notion widely held today that corporations are private enterprises would have appeared nonsensical to any American up to the end of the 19th century. Corporations under the British monarchy were formed to promote the interests of the monarchy, and they were held on a short leash. Many of the original American colonies, such as the Massachusetts Bay Company, were in fact British corporations chartered to stake claims in the New World. After the American Revolution, corporations were chartered by the American states in the interests of their citizenry, which at the time was limited to White, propertied males.

At least legally, then, corporations were public institutions created by special charters of incorporation granted by state legislatures to serve the common good. Although many corporations chartered to build such things as canals or colleges also created wealth for individuals, the primary function of the corporation was to serve the public interest. People, through their legislature, retained sovereignty over corporations, and legislatures dictated rules for "issuing stock, for shareholder voting, for obtaining corporate information, for paying dividends and keeping records. They limited capitalization, debts, landholdings, and sometimes profits" (Grossman & Adams, 1995, cited in Derber, 1998, p. 124).

However, popular sovereignty and legislative control over corporations began to unravel during the late 19th century. The Fourteenth Amendment of the U.S. Constitution, created to protect the equal rights of freed slaves, was used as a legal tool to provide corporations with the legal rights of a person. Much like today, conservative judges during the Gilded Age of the early 20th century were cynically allied with powerful corporate friends. These judges and corporate leaders colluded to turn public control over corporations into a violation of the Fourteenth Amendment, which holds that no state "shall deprive any person of life, liberty, or property, without due process of law." Thus, the courts of the Gilded Age broke with the state grant theory of public accountability over corporations and supported instead a conception of corporations as a voluntary contract among private people. In this way, a public institution, created and controlled by a sovereign people, became a private institution or "enterprise" whose existence was independent of the state *and largely immune from public accountability.*

More recently, under the court case, *Citizens United,* courts have used the First Amendment to the Constitution to view massive corporate contributions to political campaigns as an expression of free speech, thus supporting the notion that a corporation is the equivalent of a human being under the law. Also, corporations are amassing power globally, and in many cases, they can sue countries that put laws in place that they don't like. This occurs through Investor-state dispute settlement provisions that are featured in many trade agreements, including the North American Free Trade Agreement (NAFTA), nine U.S.-E.U. bilateral investment treaties, and the ill-fated Trans-Pacific Partnership (TPP) (Perez-Rocha, 2014, December 3).

What is perhaps even more remarkable is that this history of the shift of corporations from publicly accountable, chartered enterprises to private enterprises is virtually unknown among the general public in the United States. Such accounts do not appear in high school history texts, nor are they taught in colleges of education, in spite of the current attempts to privatize public schools.

Why should we care whether a corporation is state-controlled or not? This question goes to the heart of the debate about public school privatization. What are public institutions, and what makes them different from private ones? Increasingly, corporations are taking over many public functions and heavily impacting public policy. For instance, corporations affect political outcomes with their campaign contributions and lobbyists. Today, out of the 100 organizations that spend the most on lobbying, ninety-five represent businesses. The largest companies have upward of 100 lobbyists representing them (Drutman, 2015). These lobbyists were largely responsible for the 2017 tax law that reduced corporate taxes from 35% to 21% (down from 52% in the 1960s). They claimed that the 35% statutory tax rate on U.S. corporations was the highest in the world, and that cutting corporate taxes would create new jobs, but neither of these claims is actually supported by evidence.

While the corporate statutory tax rate is 35%, the *effective* tax rate, once loopholes and other diversions are accounted for, is only half that amount, which is in line with what corporations pay in other comparable countries. Bevins and Blair (2017, May 9) further argue that

> economic theory and data do not support the idea that cutting these rates would encourage further investment in the U.S. or benefit Americans in general; we find that such cuts would primarily benefit a small number of high-income capital owners while increasing the regressivity of the tax system overall.
>
> (Paragraph 2)

But it gets worse. Through the American Legislative Exchange Council (ALEC), which we described in Chapter 3, corporate leaders and legislators virtually cowrite model bills for legislators to introduce pro-corporate laws in State legislatures (Anderson & Donchik, 2016). Many see the growing economic influence of corporations and their control of legislatures and major media as a direct threat to American democracy.

The issue of whether we insist on being citizens instead of consumers goes to the heart of why public schools—with all of their many imperfections—must be defended if we want to claim to be citizens in a democracy. Public schooling and teachers in the U.S. have been successfully undermined by corporate leaders and the think tanks they fund, and in the process, they have diminished our trust in public institutions. There is much evidence that countries with a strong public ethos and social trust in public institutions are also successful in other areas including levels of prosperity, equality, and happiness (Wilkinson & Pickett, 2010). Using Finland as an example, Pasi Sahlberg (2007) discusses good governance and why it makes sense to cultivate professional trust instead of putting in place policies like high-stakes testing that send a message to teachers that they are not trusted professionally.

> The culture of trust can only flourish in an environment that is built upon good governance and close-to-zero corruption. Tellingly, Finland also performs well in international good-governance rankings. Public institutions generally enjoy high public trust and regard in Finland. Trusting schools and teachers is therefore a natural consequence of a generally well-functioning civil society. Honesty and trust, as Lewis (2005) observes, are often seen as among the most basic values and the building blocks of Finnish society (p. 157). Finland has many successful private corporations, but it demonstrates the extent to which a strong private sector and public sector can co-exist.

It has taken the U.S. system of governance many decades to overcome political corruption and the nepotism that reigned in education when principalships were political appointments (Teachout, 2014). By the post-WWII years, however, our public institutions were highly trusted and regarded by most Americans. People reported liking their public schools; post offices were trusted to deliver the mail and packages; NASA put rockets into outer space; public sector professionals were respected as public servants; National parks were heavily visited and well run, as were V.A. hospitals (Goodsell, 2004).

It is also true that in a country that was founded by propertied White men who disenfranchised women, nonwhites, and the poor, we have sometimes given our public institutions far more trust than they deserve (see Rothstein, 2017). And yet, over time and through democratic social movements, we have struggled to expand social justice. While our public schools are segregated by race and class, they are also the spaces in which, at least at the discursive level, children are exposed to ideals of gender and racial equality, discourses they may be less likely to encounter at home, in the media or in many religious institutions.

Today, the public sector is being degraded and diminished. Public sector professionals do not feel respected and NPM's teacher-proof reforms show little respect for their judgment. These reforms, including high-stakes testing and the deregulation of charter schools, have led to an increase in cheating, corruption, and scandal (Calefati, 2016; Center for Popular Democracy, 2017, May). Even those democratic, public spaces, like school boards have become victims of corporate control. Not only is their adherence to political democracy attacked ideologically as less efficient than school choice and vouchers (Chubb & Moe, 1990), they are seen as an obstacle to education profit-seeking. Elected school boards have been a thorn in the side of corporations trying to get lucrative contracts. According to Lafer (2014),

> With charter schools, tech companies can cut a deal with a single executive covering hundreds of schools, and the product choice may reflect financial rather than pedagogical criteria. By contrast, public-school curricula are set by officials who are accountable to a locally elected board prohibited from any financial relationship with vendors. As Hastings explains, "school districts [are hard] to sell to because [they] are really reacting to voter forces more than to market forces."
>
> (Paragraph 18)

The corporate solution is to take over the school boards. Increasingly, money from wealthy individuals and corporations is outspending beleaguered teachers' unions and winning school board elections. Los Angeles's 2017 school board election was the most expensive on record. Pro-charter organizations spent $9,695,351 million compared to $5,221,273 of union money, resulting in a majority of board members who are pro-charter and anti-union (Blume & Poston, 2017, May 21). This influx of hedge fund and corporate money into school board elections is occurring across the country.

A CAMPAIGN TO DEGRADE THE PUBLIC

While public schools do indeed have many imperfections, they are not "broken"; rather, they have steadily improved over that last 100 years. As Berliner and Biddle (1995) argued, the crisis of our public schools' system is not its quality, it is its inequality. Low-poverty and unionized states, like Massachusetts, compare favorably with top-ranked countries globally. Our education system compares poorly in general because our levels of inequality and our rates of poverty are higher than countries in Europe and Asia that outperform us. Calls to "nuke" the system, tear it down, disrupt it, and start from scratch are irresponsibly repeated by those who want to privatize the education system. This mantra has been repeated so often that it has passed into "common sense," even though Americans consistently report high marks for their own public schools.

According to the Gallup Poll, 75% of Americans are happy with their children's public school, and that percent has never fallen below 68% since 1999. Yet 53% of Americans are dissatisfied with the quality of education children receive in the U.S. overall (Huffington Post, 2012). Gallup speculates that this may be the case because of media reports that the U.S. does not measure up in international comparisons of education achievement scores. And yet, a recently released United Nations International Children's Emergency Fund (UNICEF) Report Card (Hudson & Kuhner, 2016) suggests that the problem is less our public schools than our levels of inequality. The report card ranks developed countries on the size of their relative income gap. "This measure of bottom-end inequality captures how far the poorest children are being allowed to fall behind the 'average' child in each country" (p. 4). The U.S. ranks in the bottom third of developed countries, behind Turkey and Estonia.

Since Ronald Reagan declared "government is not the solution, it's the problem," there has been a decades-old onslaught, led by the corporate sector in alliance with both Republican and Democratic administrations. The Clinton administration deregulated the banks, contributing to the 2008 economic crisis, and the Obama administration bailed them out and failed to hold any of them accountable (Elsinger, 2017). Whereas accountability seems in short supply on Wall Street, a moral panic has been constructed around the lack of accountability of our teachers and principals. A decades-long campaign has promoted the general common sense that the private sector can do no wrong and the public sector can do no good.

Yet defending public schools means acknowledging the system's accomplishments while at the same time acknowledging that our public schools have been complicit in reproducing inequalities by financing schools through property taxes and devaluing certain forms of social and cultural capital. These are the areas that need reform. Yet privatization and choice have only exacerbated these tendencies since choice will always favor those with the economic, social, and cultural capital to exercise it. In fact, today, schools are often more segregated than the neighborhoods they are located in (Hemphill & Mader, 2015). This suggests that if parents are dissatisfied with their neighborhood schools, they can vote with their feet and send their children to public gifted programs, schools of choice, charter schools, or private schools. This is particularly the case in gentrifying neighborhoods. While we are conditioned to think that choice is always an unmitigated good, it has also contributed to schools highly segregated by class and race (Orfield & Frankenberg, 2014; Reardon, 2013).

CONCLUSION

All three of the issues addressed in this chapter have long been intractable problems for public schools in the U.S. We have not figured out how to effectively create mechanisms for widespread participation by multiple constituencies. As Malen and Ogawa (1988) and subsequent studies have shown, school-based participation is difficult to achieve and sustain. School boards represent a democratic space but have tended historically to be controlled by elites, a trend that continues with heavy corporate funding of school board elections (Blume & Poston, 2017, May 21).

While progress has been made over the years in public schools through inclusionary polices for disabled students and bilingual education, schools still reflect the class and racial segregation we tolerate in the U.S. In addition, well-funded campaigns to degrade public schools, teachers, and their unions have led to diminished public trust in our democratic institutions. As educators, our role is to educate the public about the trade-offs involved in privatizing our schools and our policy process. As our skewed economy produces more and more millionaires and billionaires who can flood our political system with money, educators will have to take their role as advocates for public education more seriously. But to be credible, the advocacy will need to be for more democratic schools, more democratic teachers' unions, and more community engagement.

The reformed teachers' union in Chicago provides an example. Rather than merely fight for bread-and-butter issues for teachers, they reached out to community organizations to build alliances. When they had to go on strike, the community supported them and their struggle against corporate reforms that closed their schools and provided a test-driven education for their children. Ultimately, the goal must be to win back an authentic democracy that is threatened by corporate agendas and a neoconservative backlash that wants to take education and the country back to a pre-civil rights time few want to revisit.

END-OF-CHAPTER QUESTIONS

1. How democratic is the organization you work in? Use Table 8.1 to analyze how authentic participation is in your organization. If you don't work in an organization, you can use any other organization you are familiar with.
2. Analyze your own educational history and be prepared to discuss the exchange value of the cultural, social, and economic capital of you and your family. Were you able to "cash in" on it educationally, or did it have a low-exchange value?

3. Think of examples in which you think the private sector has outperformed the public sector. Think of examples in which you think the public sector has out-performed the private sector. Why is it important that our military, our prisons, our schools, our social services, and our government remain public?

REFERENCES

Addison, J. (2009). *The economics of codetermination: Lessons from the German experience.* New York: Palgrave MacMillan.

Ahram, R., Fergus, E., & Noguera, P. (2011). Addressing racial/ethnic disproportionality in special education: Case studies of Suburban School Districts. *Teachers College Record, 113*(10), 2233–2266.

Anderson, G. L. (1998). Toward authentic participation: Deconstructing the discourse of participatory reforms. *American Educational Research Journal, 35*(4), 571–606.

Anderson, G. L. (2017). Participatory action research as democratic disruption: New public management and educational research in schools and universities. *International Journal of Qualitative Studies in Education, 30*(5), 432–449.

Anderson, G. L., & Bernabei Middleton, E. (2014). LeaderPAR: A participatory action research framework for school and community leadership. In I. Bogatch & C. Shields (Eds.), *Handbook of social justice and educational leadership* (pp. 275–289). New York, NY: Springer.

Anderson, G. L., & Montoro Donchik, L. (2016) The Privatization of education and policy-making: The American Legislative Exchange Council (ALEC) and network governance in the United States. *Educational Policy, 30*(2), 322–364.

Anderson, G., & Herr, K. (2011). Scaling up: "evidence-based" practices for teachers is a profitable but discredited paradigm. *Educational Researcher, 40,* 287–289.

Anyon, J. (2014). *Radical possibilities: Public policy, urban education, and a new social movement.* New York, NY: Routledge.

Arellano-Gault, D. (2010). Economic NPM and the need to bring justice and equity back to the debate on pubic organizations. *Administration and Society, 42*(5), 591–612.

Argyris, C., & Schon, D. (1978). *Organizational learning: A theory of action perspective.* Reading, MA: Addison Wesley.

Bacharach, S., Bamberger, P. Conley, S. & Bauer, S. (1990). The dimensionality of decision participation in education organizations. *Educational Administration Quarterly, 26*(2), 126–167.

Barber, B. (2004). *Strong democracy: Participatory politics for a new age.* Berkeley: The University of California Press.

Berliner, D. (2009). *Poverty and potential: Out-of-school factors and school success.* Boulder and Tempe: Education and the Public Interest Center & Education Policy Research Unit. Retrieved from http://epicpolicy.org/publication/poverty-and-potential

Berliner, D., & Biddle, B. (1995). *The manufactured crisis: Myths, fraud, and the attack on America's public schools.* Reading, MA: Addison-Wesley.

Bevins, J., & Blair, H. (2017, May 9). *Competitive distractions: Cutting corporate tax rates will not create jobs of boost incomes for the vast majority of American families.* Economic Policy Institute. Retrieved from http://www.epi.org/publication/competitive-distractions-cutting-corporate-tax-rates-will-not-create-jobs-or-boost-incomes-for-the-vast-majority-of-american-families/

Black, W. (2008). The contradictions of high stakes accountability 'success': A case study of focused leadership and performance agency. *International Journal of Leadership in Education, 11*(1), 1–22.

Blase, J. (1991). The micropolitical perspective. In J. Blase (Ed.), *The politics if life in schools: Power, conflict, and cooperation* (pp. 1–18). London, UK: Sage.

Blase, J., & Anderson, G. L. (1995). *The micropolitics of educational leadership: From control to empowerment.* New York, NY: Teachers College Press.

Blume, H., & Poston, B. (2017, May 21). How L.A.'s school board election became the most expensive in U.S. history. *The Los Angeles Times.* Retrieved from http://www.latimes.com/local/la-me-edu-school-election-money-20170521-htmlstory.html

Boggs, C. (2000). *The end of politics: Corporate power and the decline of the public sphere.* New York, NY: The Guilford Press.

Bourdieu, P. (2000). *Pascalian meditations.* Stanford, CA: Stanford University Press.

Bourdieu, P. (2001). *Masculine domination.* Stanford, CA: Stanford University Press.

Bourdieu, P., & Passeron, J. (1970/1990). *Reproduction in education, society and culture* (2nd ed.). London, UK: Sage Publications.

Brickner, M., & Diaz, S. (2011). Prisons for profit: Incarceration for sale. *Human Rights, 38*(3), 13–16.

Brown, E., & Makris, M. V. (2017). A different type of charter school: In prestige charters, a rise in cachet equals a decline in access. *Journal of Education Policy, 33*, 85–117.

Bryson, J., & Crosby, B. (1992). *Leadership for the common good: Tackling public problems in a shared-power world.* San Francisco, CA: Jossey-Bass.

Burch, P. (2009). *Hidden markets: The new education privatization.* New York, NY: Routledge.

Burch, P. & Good, A. (2014). *Equal scrutiny: Privatization and accountability in digital education.* Cambridge, MA: Harvard Education Press.

Calefati, J. (2016, April). California virtual academies: Is online charter school network cashing in on failure? *The Mercury News.* Retrieved from http://www.mercurynews.com/2016/04/16/california-virtual-academies-is-online-charter-school-network-cashing-in-on-failure/

Cammarota, J., & Fine, M. (Eds.). (2008). *Revolutionizing education: Youth participatory action research in motion.* New York, NY: Routledge.

Capper, C. A., & Young, M. D. (2015). The equity audit as the core of leading increasingly diverse schools and districts. In G. Theoharis & M. Scanlan (Eds.), Leadership for increasingly diverse schools (pp. 186–197). New York, NY: Routledge.

Carey, A. (1995). *Taking the risk out of democracy: Corporate propaganda versus freedom and liberty.* Urbana: University of Illinois Press.

Carpenter, S. (2015). The "local" fetish as reproductive praxis in democratic learning. *Discourse: Studies in the Cultural Politics of Education, 36*(1), 133–143.

Carter, P. (2007). *Keepin' it real: School success beyond Black and White.* Oxford, UK: Oxford University Press.

Center for Popular Democracy. (2017, May). *Charter school vulnerabilities to waste, fraud, and abuse.* Retrieved from https://populardemocracy.org/sites/default/files/Charter-School-Fraud_Report_2017_web%20%281%29.pdf

Chubb, J., & Moe, T. (1990). *Politics, Markets, and America's schools.* Washington, DC: The Brookings Institute.

Cochran-Smith, M., & Lytle, S. (2009). *Inquiry as stance: Practitioner research for the next generation.* New York, NY: Teachers College Press.

Cuban, L. (2004). *The Blackboard and the bottom line: Why schools can't be businesses.* Cambridge, MA: Harvard University Press.

Cucchiara, M. (2013). *Marketing schools, marketing cities: Who wins and who loses when schools become urban amenities.* Chicago, IL: University of Chicago Press.

Cummins, J. (1986). Empowering minority students: A framework for intervention. *Harvard Educational Review, 56*(4), 649–657.

Delpit, L. (1995). *Other people's children: Cultural conflict in the classroom.* New York, NY: The New Press.

Deming, W. E. (1986). *Out of the Crisis.* Boston, MA: MIT Press.

Deming, W. E. (1993). *The new economics for industry, government, and education.* Boston, MA: MIT Press.

Derber, C. (1998). *Corporation nation.* New York: St. Martin's.

Dewey, J. (1916). *Democracy and education.* New York, NY: Free Press.

Dewey, J. (1927). *The public and its problems.* New York: Holt.

Driscoll, M. E. (1998). Professionalism versus community: Is the conflict school and community about to be resolved? *Peabody Journal of Education, 73*(1), 89–127.

Drucker, J. & Rapaport, A. (Dec. 16, 2017). The tax bill's winners and losers. *The New York Times.*

Drutman, L. (2015). *The business of America is lobbying: How corporations became politicized and politics became more corporate.* Oxford, UK: Oxford University Press.

Edmonds, R. (1979). Some schools work and more can. *Social Policy, 9,* 28–32.

Elsinger, J. (2017). *The chickenshit club: Why the justice department fails to prosecute executives.* New York, NY: Simon & Shuster.

Fiedler, F. E. (1958). *Leader Attitudes and Group Effectiveness.* Urbana: University of Illinois Press.

Fine, M. (1991). *Framing dropouts: Notes on the politics of an urban public high school.* Albany: SUNY Press.

Freire, P. (1970). *The pedagogy of the oppressed.* New York, NY: Continuum.

Gay, G. (2010). *Culturally responsive teaching: Theory, research, and practice* (2nd ed.). New York: Teachers College Press.

Ginwright, S. (2004). *Black in school: Afrocentric reform, urban youth & the promise of hip-hop culture.* New York, NY: Teachers College Press.

Gold, E., Simon, E., & Brown, C. (2004). A new conception of parent engagement: Community organizing for school reform. In F. English (Ed.), *Handbook of educational leadership: New dimensions and realities.* Thousand Oaks, CA: Sage Pub.

Gonzalez, N., Moll, L., & Amanti, C. (Eds.). (2005). *Funds of knowledge: Theorizing practices in households and classrooms.* Mahwah, NJ: Lawrence Erlbaum.

Goodsell, C.T. (2004). *The case for bureaucracy: A Public administration polemic.* Washington, DC: Congressional Quarterly Press.

Green, T. (2015). Leading for urban school reform and community development. *Educational Administration Quarterly, 51*(5), 679–711.

Grogen, M., & Shakeshaft, C. (2010). *Women and educational leadership.* San Francisco, CA: Jossey-Bass.

Gronn, P. (2000). Distributed properties: A new architecture for leadership. *Educational Management and Administration, 28*(3), 317–338.

Grossman, R., & Adams, R. (1995). *Taking care of business: Citizenship and the charter of incorporation.* Cambridge, MA: Charter, Ink.

Habermas, J. (1987). *The theory of communicative action: Vol. 2: Lifeworld and system: A critique of functional reason* (T. McCarthy, Trans.). Boston, MA: Beacon Press.

Halverson, R., Grigg, J., Prichett, R., & Thomas, C. (2005). *The new instructional leadership: Creating data-driven instructional systems in schools.* WCER Working Paper 2005–2009, Wisconsin Center for Education Research, University of Wisconsin, Madison.

Hankins, K. (2007) The Final Frontier: Charter Schools as New Community Institutions of Gentrification, *Urban Geography, 28*(2), 113–128.

Hatcher, R. (2005). The distribution of leadership and power in schools. *British Journal of Sociology of Education, 26*(2), 253–267.

Hemphill, C., & Mader, N. (2015). Report: Schools are more segregated than neighborhoods. *Inside Schools.* Retrieved from https://insideschools.org/news-&-views/report-schools-are-more-segregated-than-neighborhoods

Herr, K., & Anderson, G. (2008). Teacher research and learning communities: A failure to theorize power relations? *Language Arts, 85*(5), 382–391.

Hersey, P., & Blanchard, K. H. (1969). *Management of organizational behavior: Utilizing human resources.* New York, NY: Prentice Hall.

Hudson, J., & Kuhner, S. (2016). *Fairness for Children: A league table of inequality in child well-being in rich countries.* Report Card 13. Innocenti, Italy: UNICEF Office of Research.

Huffington Post. (2012). *American Public Education: Gallup poll results show majority of Americans dissatisfied.* Retrieved from http://www.huffingtonpost.com/2012/08/31/gallup-poll-results-show-_n_1844774.html

Ishimaru, A. M. (2014). When new relationships meet old narratives: The journey towards improving parent-school relations in a district-community organizing collaboration. *Teachers College Record, 116*(2), 29–40.

Johanek, M., & Puckett, J. (2006). *Leonard Covello and the making of Benjamin Franklin High School.* Philadelphia, PA: Temple University Press.

Johnson, R. (2002). *Using data to close the achievement gap.* Thousand Oaks, CA: Corwin Press.

Johnson, R., & Avelar La Salle, R. (2010). *The wallpaper effect: Data strategies to uncover and eliminate hidden inequalities.* Thousand Oaks, CA: Corwin Press.

Keith, N. (1999). Whose community schools? New discourses, old patterns. *Theory into Practice, 38*(4), 225–234.

Kerr, K., Dyson, A., & Gallannuagh, F. (2016). Conceptualizing school-community relations in disadvantaged neighbourhoods: Mapping the literature. *Educational Research, 58*(3), 265–282.

Khalifa, M. (2012). A re-new-ed paradigm in successful urban school leadership: Principal as community leader. *Educational Administration Quarterly, 48*(3), 424–467.

Klein, N. (2017). *No is not enough: Resisting Trump's shock politics and winning the world we need.* Chicago, IL: Haymarket Books.

Labaree, D. (1997). *How to succeed in school without really learning: The credentials race in American education.* London, UK and New Haven, CT: Yale University Press.

Ladson-Billings, G. (1995). Toward a theory of culturally relevant pedagogy. *American Educational Research Journal, 32*(3), 465–481.

Lafer, G. (2014, October 13). What happens when your teacher is a video game? *The Nation.* Retrieved from www.thenation.com/article/what-happens-when-your-teacher-robot/

Lave, J. (1988). Situating learning in communities of practice. In L. Resnick, S. Levine, & L. Teasley (Eds.), *Perspectives of socially shared cognition* (pp. 63–82). Washington, DC: American Psychological Association.

Lave, J., & Wenger, E. (1991). *Situated learning: Legitimate peripheral participation.* Cambridge, UK: Cambridge University Press.

Leonardo, Z. (2012). The race for class: Reflections on a critical raceclass theory of education. *Educational Studies, 48*(5), 427–449.

Lewis, A. E. (2003). *Race in the schoolyard.* New Brunswick, NJ: Rutgers University Press.

Lewis, R. (2005) *Finland, cultural lone wolf.* Yarmouth, ME: Intercultural Press).

Lieberman, A., & Miller, L. (2008). *Teachers in professional communities: Improving teaching and learning.* New York, NY: Teachers College Press.

Little, J. W. (1982). Norms of collegiality and experimentation: Workplace conditions of school success. *American Educational Research Journal, 19*(3), 325–340.

Little, J. W. (1990). The persistence of privacy: Autonomy and initiative in teachers' professional relations. *Teachers College Record, 91*(4), 509–536.

Lippman, W. (1925). *The phantom public.* New York: Transaction pub.

Malen, B. (1994). Enacting site-based management: A political utilities analysis. *Educational Evaluation and Policy Analysis, 16*(3), 249–267.

Malen, B., & Ogawa, R. (1988). Professional-patron influence on site-based governance councils: A confounding case study. *Educational Evaluation and Policy Analysis, 10*(4), 251–270.

Mann, B., & Bennett, H. (2016). *Integration without integrating: How gentrification and community socioeconomic trends relate to differences in charter and traditional schooling options in Washington DC.* Paper presented at the Annual meeting of UCEA, Detroit.

Mayer, J. (2016). *Dark money: The hidden history of the billionaires behind the rise of the radical right.* New York, NY: Anchor Books.

Mayrowetz, D., Murphy, J., Louis, K. S., & Smylie, M. (2007). Distributed leadership as work redesign: Retrofitting the job characteristics model. *Leadership and policy in schools, 6*(1), 69–101.

McDermott, K., & Nygreen, K. (2013). Educational new paternalism: Human capital, cultural capital, and the politics of equality. *Peabody Journal of Education, 88*(1), 84–97.

McGhee, C. & Anderson, G.L. (in press). Market Regimes, Gentrification and the Entrepreneurial Principal: Enacting Integration or Displacement? *Journal of Policy and Leadership.*

McLaughlin, M. (1976). Implementation as mutual adaptation: Change in classroom organization. *Teachers College Record, 77*(3), 339–351.

McLaughlin, M. W., & Talbert, J. E. (2006). *Building school-based teacher-learning communities: Professional strategies to improve student achievement.* New York, NY: Teachers College Press.

McNamee, S., & Miller, R. (2009). *The meritocracy myth.* Lanham, MD: Rowman & Littlefield.

Meier, D. (2002). *In schools we trust: Creating communities of learning in an era of testing and standardization.* Boston: Beacon Press.

Orfield, G., & Frankenberg, E. (2014, May 15). *Brown at 60: Great progress, a long retreat, and an uncertain future.* The Civil Rights Project, UCLA.

Ospina, S., & Foldy, E. (2005, September). *Toward a framework for social change leadership.* Paper presented at the Annual Meeting of the Public Management Research Association, Los Angeles, CA.

Ospina, S., & Foldy, E. (2010). Building bridges from the margins: The work of leadership in social change organizations. *The Leadership Quarterly, 21*(1), 292–307.

Payne, C. (2007). *I've got the light of freedom: The organizing tradition and the Mississippi freedom struggle.* Berkeley: University of California Press.

Perez-Rocha, M. (2014, December 3). When corporations sue governments. *The New York Times.* Retrieved from https://www.nytimes.com/2014/12/04/opinion/when-corporations-sue-governments.html

Peters, T., & Waterman, R. (1982). *In search of excellence: Lessons from America's best-run companies.* New York, NY: Collins.

Posey Maddox, L. (2014). *When middle-class parents choose urban schools: Class, race, and the challenge of equity in public education.* Chicago, IL: University of Chicago Press.

Purkey, S., & Smith, M. (1983). Effective schools: A review. *The Elementary School Journal, 83*(4), 426–452.

Ravitch, D. (2013). Geoffrey Canada's charter schools get mixed, unimpressive results on common core tests. Retrieved from https://dianeravitch.net/2013/08/22/geoffrey-canadas-charter-schools-get-mixed-unimpressive-results-on-common-core-tests/

Reardon, S. (2013). The widening income achievement gap. *Educational Leadership, 70*(8), 10–16.

Reeves, R. V. (2017). *Dream hoarders: How the American upper middle class is leaving everyone else in the dust, why that is a problem, and what do about it.* Washington, DC: Brookings Institute Press.

Reitzug, U. & Capper, C. (1996). Deconstructing site-based management: Possibilities for emancipation and alternatives means of control. *International Journal of Educational Reform, 5*(1), 56–59.

Rist, R. (1977). *The urban school: Factory for failure: A study of education in American society.* Cambridge: MIT Press.

Rogers, J., & Terriquez, V. (2009). "More Justice": The role of organized labor in educational reform. *Educational Policy, 23*(1), 216–241.

Rothstein, R. (2017). *The color of law: A forgotten history of how our government segregated America.* New York, NY: Liveright Pub.

Sahlberg, P. (2007). Education policies for raising student learning: The Finnish approach. *The Journal of Education Policy, 22*(2), 147–171.

Saltman, K. (2009). The rise of venture philanthropy and the ongoing neoliberal assault on public education: The case of the Eli and Edythe Broad Foundation. *Workplace, 16*, 53–72.

Sappington, N., Baker, P. J., Gardner, D., & Pacha, J. (2010). A signature pedagogy for leadership education: Preparing principals through participatory action research. *Planning and Changing, 41*(3/4), 249–273.

Scherer, M. (December 2008/January 2009). Driven dumb by data? *Educational Leadership, 66*(4), 5.

Schon, D. (1984). *The reflective practitioner: How professionals think in action.* New York, NY: Basic Books.

Scott, J. C. (1990). *Domination and the arts of resistance: Hidden transcripts.* New Haven, CT: Yale University Press.

Sergiovanni, T. (1999). *The life world of leadership: Creating culture, community, and personal meaning in our schools.* San Francisco, CA: Jossey-Bass.

Shakeshaft, C. (1989). *Women in educational administration.* Thousand Oaks, CA: Corwin Press.

Shipps, D. (1997). The invisible hand: Big business and Chicago school reform. *Teachers College Record, 99*, 73–116.

Shirley, D. (1997). *Community organizing for urban school reform.* Austin: University of Texas Press.

Shutz, A. (2006). Home is a prison in the global city. The tragic failure of school-based community engagement strategies. *Review of educational Research, 76*(4), 691–743.

Spillane, J. P., Halverson, R., & Diamond, J. B. (2001). Investigating school leadership practice: A distributed perspective. *Educational Researcher, 30*(3), 23–28.

Stanton-Salazar, R. D. (2011). A social capital framework for the study of institutional agents and their role in the empowerment of low-status students and youth. *Youth and Society, 43*(3), 1066–1109.

Stullich, S., Morgan, I., & Schak, O. (2016, July). *State and local expenditures on corrections and education.* Washington, DC: U.S. Department of Education.

Teachers Unite! (2014). The disappearance of Black and Latino teachers in New York City. https://teachersunite.org/wp-content/uploads/2017/10/Disappearance-report-October-17-2014-1.pdf

Teachout, Z. (2014). *Corruption in America: From Benjamin Franklin's snuff box to Citizens United.* Cambridge, MA: Harvard University Press.

Valli, L., Stefanski, A., & Jacobson, R. (2006). Typologizing school-community partnerships: A framework for analysis and action. *Urban Education, 5*(7), 719–747.

Walcott, H. (1973). *The man in the principal's office.* New York: Altamira Press.

Wallace, D. (2017). Reading 'Race' in Bourdieu? Examining black cultural capital among black Caribbean Youth in South London. *Sociology, 51*(5), 907–923.

Westheimer, J. (Ed.). (2007). *Pledging allegiance: The politics of patriotism in America's schools.* New York, NY: Teachers College Press.

Wilkinson, R. & Pickett, K. (2009). *The spirit level: Why greater equality makes societies stronger.* New York: Bloomsbury.

Whyte, W. F. (1990). *Participatory action research.* Thousand Oaks, CA: Sage.

Wilkinson, R., & Pickett, K. (2010). *The spirit level.* New York, NY: Bloomsbury Press.

Wolcott, H. (1973). *The man in the principal's office.* Lanham, MD: Altamira Press.

Woods, P. (2004). Democratic leadership: Drawing distinctions with distributed leadership. *International Journal of Leadership in Education, 7(1)*, 3–26.

Wright, E. O. (2009). Understanding class. Towards an integrated analytical approach. *New Left Review, 60*, 101–116.

Yosso, T. (2006). Whose culture has capital? A critical race theory discussion of community cultural wealth. *Race, Ethnicity and Education, 8*(1), 69–91.

CHAPTER 9

Building Power

Community Organizing, Student Empowerment, and Public Accountability

Our critical policy analysis of corporate-funded policy networks and their success at imposing neoliberal policies at the state, local, and federal levels may have the unintended consequence of producing an overwhelming sense of despair or cynicism. Also, some may feel that we have been overly critical of such reforms as high-stakes accountability or charter schools. These are fair questions to raise and there is room for disagreement on all of these issues as long as the disagreements are based on evidence. But depressing or not, educators need to know what they are up against if they are to lead a social movement to reappropriate public schooling that is equitable and democratic. It is true that powerful interests with corporate money have amassed great power in the policy arena, but these "Astroturf" or "grasstops" organizations are no match for powerful grassroots social movements composed of educators, parents, citizens, and students. In this chapter, we will focus not only on critical policy *analysis*, as we have in previous chapters, but also on critical policy *praxis,* that is, how policy activism from the ground up helps to both create change and inform policy analysis.

There is good news in this regard. While corporations and often well-intended, but misinformed billionaires can outspend educators, there are numerous examples of communities coming together to defend a democratic vision of public schooling. To take just one relatively recent example, in 2017, after sixteen years of state control, the Philadelphia schools took back control and will be governed by a local school board. While teachers and the teachers' union were central figures in the struggle, a much broader coalition formed to elect a progressive mayor of Philadelphia and governor of Pennsylvania. They also elected civil rights lawyer, Larry Krasner, as the district attorney for Philadelphia. Helen Gym, longtime community activist and now a Philadelphia Council Member, describes how the movement in Philadelphia evolved.

You know, one of the best things about the pushback around public education, you know, the state takeover of public education, the privatization of public education, is that eventually, over a period of time, because so many of us were coming together from different places—we were unifying around a broad-based movement around our public schools—we were really talking about our children, our neighborhoods, our families and the city. So, it became much bigger than an education fight. It actually became very much a unifying force that pulled together grassroots activists that were involved with youth justice work, that had been involved with the criminal justice system, that were looking at questions about politics and integrity, that were educators, of course, but were fundamentally engaged with a lot of deep-seated, deep-rooted issues in our city, including immigrants, sanctuary cities, the fight for—you know, the pushback against cutting efforts at anti-poverty programs. So, all of these forces came together and became this really broad-based movement.

In particular, the education movement and the criminal justice movement so closely align together, because so many of our young people are involved in dysfunctional systems. So, we've got one out of five high school students who are either involved in the criminal justice or DHS, our Department of Human Services, and that requires us to think very differently. So when we're talking about our public schools, and if people come in and give us solutions that only talk about increasing test scores or cutting away extraneous services, like counselors and nurses or after-school programs or support services, because they're not focused in on the basics that would allow them to better pass, you know, a test score that's crafted out of Princeton Review or out of K12 or one of these other types of multinational companies, then parents are going to push back. We're going to talk about the realities of what our young people live with, are living with today. We're going to talk about the reality of access to services and support services in our city that make a huge difference in changing young people's lives. So this, fundamentally, became much bigger than an education movement.

(Democracy Now, 2017, December 13)

While we have documented setbacks, including corporate money influencing school board elections, there are also plenty of examples of victories when people are organized to defend their schools and communities.

CPA AS CRITICAL POLICY *PRAXIS*

In her book *Radical Possibilities*, the late Jean Anyon (2014) suggested that educators might potentially represent the center of a social movement that insists on addressing not just the educational policies that lead to educational underachievement but also the broader social policies that create the larger social conditions that lead to underachievement. Her prediction of a social movement with education at its core is being born out in city after city, as community organizers, activist unions, and grassroots advocacy organizations form coalitions across sectors to push back against the influence of corporations and wealthy individuals attempting to privatize education.

Anyon's call for action emphasized the following tenets: (1) *Education researchers and activists could not merely study or advocate around education alone.* As we have emphasized throughout this book, education policies are intimately linked to social policies and cannot be disentangled. Furthermore, within the public sector, teachers, nurses, doctors, social workers, and police officers are all working under neoliberal and New Public Management regimes (Anderson & Cohen, 2018). They have a common interest but are too often isolated into academic and activist silos. (2) *We need academics to help us understand underlying causes and policy actors behind the symptoms that we experience on a daily basis, but we also need alliances between academics and activists, many of whom are education practitioners* (Collins & Bilge, 2016). This does not always mean that academics or school practitioners have to become activists themselves, though some might, but rather that they work together with activist-led organizations to develop the kind of policy knowledge and language that are needed by social movements attempting to bring about change (Dumas & Anderson, 2014).

While *critical policy analysis* provides tools to reframe, study, and analyze policies, teachers, counselors, leaders, or academics today inhabit workplaces that are being rapidly restructured around them by neoliberal policies. This means that *analysis* and *actions* to counter neoliberal policies have to be engaged at the same time and inform each other. This requires greater attention to *critical policy praxis.* Collins and Bilge (2016) put it this way:

> A praxis perspective does not merely apply scholarly knowledge to a social problem or set of experiences but rather uses the knowledge learned within everyday life to reflect on those experiences as well as on scholarly knowledge. This praxis perspective does not separate scholarship from practice, with scholarship providing theories and frameworks, and practice relegated to people who apply those ideas to real-life settings or to real-life problems. Instead, this set of concerns sees both scholarship and practice as intimately linked and mutually informing each other, rejecting views that see theory as superior to practice.
>
> (p. 42)

Increasingly, educational practitioners themselves are demanding that they be included at all stages of policy development. The notion of participatory policymaking and participatory action research is gaining some traction, especially in fields like public health (Minkler & Wallerstein, 2003), international development (Jordan & Kapoor, 2009), and youth development (Ginwright, Noguera, & Cammarota, 2006). For instance, we are seeing teachers organizing their own critiques of policy though organizations such as *Teachers Unite, NYC* (http://www.teachersunite.net/), and *Teachers for social justice, Chicago* (http://www.teachersforjustice.org/). Other grassroots organizations led by community activists, teachers, and academics include *Network for Public Education* (NPE), *Badass Teachers Association, Fair test* (The National Center for Fair and Open Testing), *Save our Schools, United Opt Out* (The Movement to End Corporate Education Reform), *Rethinking Schools*, and *Alliance for Quality Education* (New York).

In an attempt to provide this practitioner perspective, we have provided throughout the book portraits of educational practitioner/activists who have engaged in critical policy praxis as well as on the ground examples of what this looks like in schools. Here, we present an example of Marcus Foster, an educator who, as a teacher, principal, and superintendent, engaged in critical policy praxis throughout his career.

Marcus Foster was an African American school leader in the 1960s and early 1970s, best known as principal of Simon Gratz High School in Philadelphia and superintendent of Oakland, California. Foster illustrates the raw courage required of leaders who choose to promote democracy and social justice and the risk-taking this role requires. While, in reality, few educational leaders will risk death, Foster's tragic story highlights the importance of the work of school leaders and the impact they can have when they harness the power of their communities. In the political turmoil of that period, Marcus Foster was viewed as too radical by some but not radical enough by some others. The story of this courageous school leader did not have a happy ending. He was murdered in Oakland by members of the extremist Symbionese Liberation Army, better known for their abduction of heiress Patty Hearst. John Spencer has written a history of Foster's professional life in: *In the Crossfire: Marcus Foster and the Troubled History of American School Reform.*

Foster's leadership provides a counterpoint to the contemporary managerial principal. Based on the micropolitical matrix in Chapter 5, he would be considered an empowering principal—both transformative and democratic in his approach. Back in 1971, he advocated for something he called "new leadership." Unlike the "new professional" we described in Chapter 7, he saw principals as catalysts to empower those around them to engage in not just leadership but also advocacy for children and families. Rather than turn to business leaders as models, Foster viewed African American clergy as providing a more appropriate model.

> Ours is a time that requires leadership, not just administration. New ground will be broken by teachers, parents, community people, as well as by principals and others up the line. Fortunately, we can find some excellent examples of this "new leadership" in other realms of endeavor. I am thinking particularly of the clergymen (sic.) who, in the last two decades [1950s and 1960s] have transformed their roles by extending the power of their faith beyond the church walls. Martin Luther King, Jr. preached love and hope as he marched through Southern towns. Father Groppi led his congregation in Midwest urban centers. These men came to believe that a meaningful ministry required them to bring religion to the places it was needed. It went beyond praying. When political action was needed to move the spirit, they engaged in politics. When it was economics, as in the case of Rev. Leon Sullivan, who founded the Opportunities Industrialization Centers, the preaching led to jobs.

The kind of flexibility that characterized these leader-ministers has got to be built into our roles as leader-educators. In my own career, I have sometimes played the salesman, the community organizer, the economist, the fund-raiser, and the speechmaker. One incident reported in the next chapter describes my role as producer of a guerrilla-theater play. I am not saying that everyone involved in education has to be a one-man band. What is important is that one comes to accept the diversity of tasks needed to make education work. One has to be open to working with people doing these unexpected things. This obviously is a very different attitude from sitting back while waiting for outsiders to get the job done.

(Foster, 1971, 17–18)

There is a long tradition among African American teachers and leaders of viewing their work as educators as part of a larger civil rights movement (Dillard, 1995; Johnson, 2017; Tillman, 2004; Walker, 2005) African American principals like Marcus Foster often found themselves promoted to under resourced urban schools and districts that served low-income, children of color. This was often done as a symbolic gesture to the community in lieu of addressing serious resource inequalities between Black and White communities. For instance, at Gratz High School, Foster was brought in to replace a White principal who was under attack from community activists.

While Marcus Foster understood and fought structural forms of oppression, he had no patience for teachers and principals who removed the onus on them to improve education by merely pointing a finger at unjust laws or poverty. But he didn't think the answer was to pressure them with punishments and humiliation or testing regimes. On the contrary, he saw teachers beaten down by bureaucracy and a "Don't rock the boat" mentality. His solution was not to gut the system of democratic participation, retool school leaders into entrepreneurs, and introduce market forces. In his initial speech as the new Oakland superintendent, he tried to set up a new incentive system based not on fear of being punished for failure but on encouraging risk-taking and mobilizing communities to demand more from their schools.

Another thing we want to do in Oakland is to send out a different signal about the reward system. In most bureaucracies, those who can keep their departments cool and running smoothly usually win the praise. Such systems work for those who get along with their immediate superiors. The watchword is: don't let anything exciting happen, don't do anything that might lead to negative publicity.

We are going to do it another way in Oakland. The reward system will work for those who dare to take risks. There may be failures, but if everything we do meets with success, we may not be reaching far enough beyond our grasp. We need to take risks even if turmoil is sometimes the result—as may happen when some of you try to establish meaningful relationships with your community. But given the insipidness of so many institutions, perhaps a little turmoil is not a bad thing … Dare to be fluid, dare to be potent, dare to be powerful in bringing about the changes we need.

(pp. 156–157)

Although Foster was himself an extraordinary and charismatic leader, his goal was to make leaders of others: teachers, students, and communities. His vision was a daring one, not limited to the kinds of platitudes one often finds in school mission statements. He had his pulse on the day-to-day operation of his school or district but always with his eye on another horizon. He was not interested so much in keeping control of his constituencies, as in empowering them. What would Marcus Foster say were he to return today to see our segregated, low-income urban high schools? What would he make of their metal detectors, their security cameras, and their roving police officers and military recruiters? He would likely not be totally surprised, but he would also likely ferret out those signs of hope in a growing community organizing and student activist movement. See Box 9.1 for a more contemporary example of courageous leadership by superintendent John Kuhn who wrote a protest letter to Texas legislators.

BOX 9.1 JOHN KUHN LETTER, SUPERINTENDENT OF MINERAL WELLS INDEPENDENT SCHOOL DISTRICT, TEXAS

This is an open letter issued by John Kuhn, Who at the time was superintendent of the Perrin-Whitt Consolidated Independent School District in Texas. Addressed to Texas legislators, this plea for help is modeled on the famous letter that William Barret Travis sent from the Alamo right before it fell in 1836. Kuhn refers to plans by Texas Gov. Rick Perry to cut billions of dollars from public school funding.

From: John Kuhn, Superintendent, Perrin-Whitt CISD

To: Senator Estes, Representative Hardcastle, Representative Keffer, and Representative King during these grave times:

Gentlemen,

I am besieged, by a hundred or more of the legislators under Rick Perry. I have sustained a continual bombardment of increased high-stakes testing and accountability-related bureaucracy and a cannonade of gross underfunding for 10 years at least and have lost several good men and women. The ruling party has demanded another round of pay cuts and furloughs, while the schoolhouse be put to the sword and our children's lunch money be taken in order to keep taxes low for big business. I am answering the demand with a (figurative) cannon shot, and the Texas flag still waves proudly from our flagpole. I shall never surrender the fight for the children of Perrin.

Then, I call on you my legislators in the name of Liberty, of patriotism & everything dear to the American character, to come to our aid, with all dispatch. The enemy of public schools is declaring that spending on a shiny new high-stakes testing system is "non-negotiable"; that, in essence, we must save the test but not the teachers. The enemy of public schools is saying that Texas lawmakers won't raise 1 penny in taxes in order to save our schools.

If this call is neglected, I am determined to sustain myself as long as possible and fight for the kids in these classrooms like an educator who never forgets what is due to his own honor & that of his community. Make education a priority!

With all due respect and urgency,

John Kuhn
Superintendent
Perrin-Whitt CISD

See John Kuhn on You Tube: https://www.youtube.com/watch?v=64B5kv JDcrY

BUILDING POWER: FROM DATA-DRIVEN TO DEMOCRACY-DRIVEN DECISION-MAKING

Distributing leadership beyond the school may seem impractical given that the principal's role expectation has traditionally been to buffer teachers from parents and keep the community at arm's length (Driscoll, 1998). Distributing any significant leadership to students also tends to come up against norms of hierarchy and control. However, if we look at the progress that has been made in shifting teacher culture from one of isolation to one of visiting each other's classrooms and engaging in learning communities, it seems probable that we might shift a school culture that keeps parents and communities at arm's length to one of school-community collaboration. There is a growing recognition that in order to have successful schools, we need to build professional capacity within the schools, but we also need to build greater capacity in communities—however this is defined—so that children come to school ready to learn and so that communities can hold their schools accountable in ways that do not distort the education of their children the way high-stakes testing does (Gold, Simon, & Brown, 2004; Green, 2015; Ishimaru, 2014; Khalifa, 2012).

A community-based approach to accountability requires a shift from school-centric notions of accountability to community-centric ones (Shutz, 2006). Community-centric accountability raises questions such as: How well is the school meeting the needs of this community? Does the school engage in culturally responsive practices? Does the school scaffold onto the home learning styles and "funds of knowledge" (Gonzalez, Moll, & Amanti, 2005) that students bring to the school? To what extent are school professionals seeing assets in a community, not just deficits (Valenzuela, 1999)? This would mean that school leaders should not solely rely on top-down, vertical accountability but should also cultivate internal accountability as well as horizontal accountability from the community—a kind of *democracy-driven decision-making*. This horizontal or "public" accountability can also become a power base for the principal to defend community priorities.

While some see parent choice of schools as a community-centric approach to accountability, we have argued that consumerism represents a retreat from political democracy. Within a community-centric framework, leaders recognize that relationships, power-sharing, social trust, and active engagement are the substance of accountability. Understanding schools as embedded in community means that building professional capacity within schools also requires building community capacity and relationships beyond the school. Of course, this is easier said than done, but it has been done by some school and district leaders such as Leonard Covello (Johanek & Puckett, 2006), Marcus Foster (Spencer, 2014), Tamara Contreras (see page 27), Jamaal Bowman (see page 176), and many others.

One reason our thinking about both building professional capacity and democratic participation gets muddled is that we tend to conflate several different traditions of shared decision-making. Table 9.1 provides a summary of three traditions, which would perhaps be better represented as a Venn diagram, since they do overlap in some areas, and ultimately each has some aspect to contribute to school improvement. Currently, those approaches influenced by business, what we call here *data-driven decision-making,* have gained dominance, co-opting the others and introducing what some call new forms of managerialism into the public sector.

The first tradition in Table 9.1 comes from cognitive and social psychology and promotes the notions of communities of practice and professional learning communities (PLCs). The PLC tradition attempts to distribute leadership and

Table 9.1 Traditions of School-Based Management

Tradition	Goals of Inquiry	Theoretical Foundations
Professional learning communities	Capacity-building Professional development Organizational development	Distributed cognition Communities of practice Organizational learning
Data-driven decision-making ("Quality Circles")	Raise productivity Work redesign Continuous improvement Profit for vendors	Market/rational choice theory Total quality management; New public management; Neo-classical economics (Freidman)
Participatory action research	Social justice advocacy Community schools Critical consciousness Problem-posing	Participatory research (Freire) Community organizing Democratic and critical Theories Critical pedagogies

learning across roles within schools. Theories of situated learning, distributed cognition, activity theory, and other sociocultural approaches to cognition showed great potential to help us understand how learning occurs among professionals (Lave, 1988; Rogoff, 1990) and between schools and communities (Gonzalez et al., 2005)[1]. These theoretical approaches were aimed at professional capacity building, collaborative reflection and inquiry, and professional and organizational development. The PLC tradition was popular during the 1980s and 1990s as school reform focused on teacher professionalization and the life world of schools (Habermas, 1987; Sergiovanni, 1999). The PLC approach also overlapped with the teacher-as-researcher movement, which tended to see teachers as ethnographers of their classrooms and as reflective practitioners engaging in systematic and intentional cycles of data gathering and reflection (Cochran-Smith & Lytle, 2009; Schon, 1984). While schools still use the language of PLCs, they have largely become more like the second tradition in Table 9.1, *data-driven decision-making*, in which data and spreadsheets too often stand in for genuine dialogue and inquiry (Cochran-Smith & Lytle, 2009).

The second tradition in Table 9.1 comes from business, specifically the work of Deming (1986) and what his followers call total quality management, which became popular in education in the 1980s. The tradition is largely driving school-based management and inquiry today. It is informed by theoretical frameworks from business and management studies focusing on the use of decision-making teams, data utilization, work redesign (Mayrowetz, Murphy, Louis, & Smylie, 2007), and local autonomy to increase production (Shipps, 2012). Popular business notions like statistical control of product quality, continuous improvement, quality circles, and teaming helped to legitimate inquiry teams and data warehousing in schools and other technologies that many would claim were inappropriate to the purposes of education (Cuban, 2004). The notion that captured the attention of some educators was the idea of "quality circles" and the inquiry cycles of plan, act, observe, and reflect, which looked superficially like action research. At its best, it promoted a form of organizational learning and data analysis that improved business productivity (Argyris & Schon, 1978; Whyte, 1990). But its use in education has largely created a culture of quantification and contrived collegiality (Hargreaves, 1994).

A third tradition is informed by participatory action research, direct democracy, critical dialogue, and community organizing (Barber, 2004; Cammarota & Fine, 2008; Freire, 1970; Ishimaru, 2014; Shirley, 1997). Shutz (2006) argues that school-centric attempts at community involvement have largely failed and that more community-centric approaches are needed. *Participatory action research* includes the central idea of *praxis* but insists on a participatory stance in which inquiry is done *with* and not *on* or *for* participants (e.g. students, teachers, parents, communities, etc.). The notion of participatory policymaking and participatory policy research is gaining some traction, especially in fields like public health (Minkler & Wallerstein, 2003), international development (Kapoor & Jordan, 2009), and youth development (Ginwright et al., 2006). Some education researchers are also building participatory projects with communities and practitioners in order to engage in *critical policy praxis*. As noted earlier, the notion of praxis creates a dialogical relationship between theory and practice and creates conditions for combining theory and research with the experiences of those who enact policies in schools and communities (Drame & Irby, 2015; Gonzalez et al., 2007; Shdaimah et al., 2009).

There are historical examples of this approach from Leonard Cavello's community-based approach (Johanek & Puckett, 2006) to the Freedom Schools and their role in the Civil Rights Movement (Payne, 1995/2007). Building community capacity and power is a goal of community organizing and it has been successfully used to leverage approaches of school reform that respond to community needs (Rogers & Terriquez, 2009; Shirley, 1997; Warren & Mapp, 2011). Gold et al. (2004) view building community capacity and power through grassroots leadership development as creating a form of public accountability for schools and districts. Again, the point is not that principals should be trained as community organizers but that principals can make links to organizers and their communities to promote a balanced approach to improving the education of their students in ways communities feel are important (Green, 2015; Ishimaru, 2014; Khalifa, 2012).

Clearly, the three traditions described earlier have a family resemblance and overlap in significant ways. The point is not to pit these approaches against each other but rather to help educators be more explicit about the traditions they are working out of. Technical problems need to be solved, and sometimes quantification and spreadsheets are the best way forward. This can be true in helping to track and document unequal graduation rates, referrals to special education, and suspension data. Schools also need to build professional capacity. PLCs have challenged teacher isolation and promoted an important shift in school cultures in many schools. However, there is also a long history of conflict between schools and communities—especially low-income communities that neither spreadsheets nor PLCs have effectively addressed (Carpenter, 2015; Driscoll, 1998; Podair, 2002). While a community-based, participatory stance is better positioned to address these issues of power, quantification and spreadsheets may be needed as principals work with communities to expose inequities (Johnson & Avelar La Salle, 2010). Meanwhile, professional capacity needs to be nurtured through PLCs to build the necessary skills to address the inequities that are exposed.

The division between schools and communities has a long history (Podair, 2004) but has become more pronounced in many paternalistic "no excuses" approaches to schooling—particularly many urban charter schools that equate communities with street culture and attempt to "make over" students with "middle class values" and a "Protestant ethic" (Whitman, 2008). Such schools, mostly franchise charter schools, like Uncommon Schools, KIPP, Achievement First, etc., keep parents and the community at arm's length and eschew the language of culturally responsive or multicultural education. From the perspective of some urban residents, this may be appealing since many poor communities, divested of jobs and infrastructure, are living at a survival level in which basic issues of strictness, discipline, and safety are viewed as paramount (Wilson, 2009). McDermott and Nygreen (2013) argue that "new paternalism appeals to a wide range of diverse political constituencies; however, idealized media accounts of these schools likely overestimate their power to close achievement gaps and produce mobility for urban youth" (p. 84).

Empowering Students: Creating Third Spaces in Education

We began this chapter with a community victory as Philadelphians organized to regain democratic control over their school district. Another victory of student and community organizing occurred in Arizona, as a 2010 ban on a Mexican-American Studies (MAS) program in the district of Tucson was overturned. In response to a lawsuit brought by students and parents, Judge A. Wallace Tashima said that the ban was motivated by racial discrimination and violated students' constitutional rights.

The MAS program in Tucson had carefully documented its students' academic success and was featured in the documentary film *Precious Knowledge*. The program began in 1998 with a few courses and grew to 43 classes, serving 1,500 students in elementary, middle, and high school in Tucson. The purpose of the program was to create a student community centered around culturally relevant learning with Mexican-American history as a central theme. Another goal was to develop critical consciousness and critical thinking to empower students by helping them develop positive identities leading to growing self-confidence and better academic results.

This program represents a form of student empowerment that does not rely on paternalistic, boot camp models that teach students obedience and provide a test-driven education. While this humanistic space was created within a public school district, the conservative Arizona context and its focus on Mexican-American or Chicana/o history ultimately led to its being closed down.

Dominant institutions have self-protective responses that organizational theorists call "dynamic conservatism" (Ansell, Boin, & Farjoun, 2015). Alternative spaces can be opened up, but if those spaces are not congruent with the dominant culture of the organization or its institutional environment, they are often eventually closed up. It is sometimes easier to open up these spaces in elite private schools where a critical approach to education is seen as less threatening, although even there, they may be closed down if they become controversial (Herr, 1999).

Public schools have never been ideal spaces for humanistic education, in part because of the ways they evolved, first through what Callahan (1962) describes as the "cult of efficiency" promoted by early 20th-century business leaders and more recently by NPM, in which the efficient factory model has evolved into test-driven reforms emphasizing efficiency, accountability, and choice. This focus has eliminated all goals of schooling except economic ones, as discussed in Chapter 2. But most alternatives to public schools are either progressive private schools that are restricted to those who can afford them or charter schools, which have not lived up to their original claims of incubating innovation (Lubienski, 2003; Preston, Goldring, Berends, & Cannata, 2011). While some charter schools are innovative, most are too often even more traditional and test-driven than the public schools. While private schools may have more humanistic, progressive pedagogies, their hidden curriculum is one of privilege and exclusion (Kenway & McCarthy, 2016).

The most interesting spaces in education today may be what some theorists call "third spaces." These spaces can appear for a time in public or charter schools, but they tend to become a threat to the dominant reform model or the dynamic conservatism of the organization. Third spaces have traditionally emerged in "informal education" settings that are either nonprofits or voluntary organizations, which are typically mission-driven (Rodriguez, 2015). Some examples of these spaces might be after-school programs like Global Kids, Afro-centric Saturday schools, alternative schools within public school districts, freedom schools during the civil rights movement (Jackson & Howard, 2014), spaces created to support girl's identities, such as in a Ciudad Juarez high school described by Cervantes-Soon (2017), and "popular" high schools in taken-over factories in Argentina (Mendez, 2015). The MAS program in Tucson, described earlier, is an example of the creation of a third space.

Some third spaces are created for nondominant groups to explore their identities vis-à-vis the dominant culture, while others can be "contact zones" in which youth who normally would not interact socially are brought together to build trust (Torre & Fine, 2008). Gutierrez (2008) describes a summer program for low-income and immigrant youth at UCLA that she calls a "collective third space, in which students begin to reconceive who they are and what they might be able to accomplish academically and beyond" (p. 148).

More specifically, Gutierrez (2008) describes what she terms "socio-critical literacy" as

> a historicizing literacy that privileges and is contingent upon students' soci-ohistorical lives, both proximally and distally. Thus, my work with youth from nondominant communities has necessarily emphasized the development of literacies in which everyday and institutional literacies are reframed into powerful literacies (Hamilton, 1997) oriented toward critical social thought. A distinguishing feature of sociocritical literacy is its attention to contradictions in and between texts lived and studied, institutions (e.g., the classroom, the academy), and sociocultural practices, locally experienced and historically influenced.
>
> (p. 149)

In a cultural sense, third spaces represent hybrid spaces in which students are developing identities relating to their sociohistorical location in society. From a postcolonial perspective, *first* space represents the original culture of home and community (Bhabha, 2004). However, students from nondominant cultures must interact with *second* space, which is the space of the dominant culture, which includes schools. Many anthropologists and sociologists of education have documented over several decades the dilemmas of identity this presents for students. Some succeed in developing healthy dual identities, but too many have internalized the negative messages of "second space" dominant culture (Delpit, 1995; Mehan, Hubbard, & Villanueva, 1994; Nasir, McLaughlin, & Jones, 2009).

Third space, then, as Gutierrez (2008) elaborates, is a hybrid space in which students can explore their identity negotiations from a sociohistorical perspective that provides them with the tools to develop dual identities and to develop a critical consciousness that empowers them to not only survive individually within the dominant culture but also become advocates for change (Stanton-Salazar, 2011). Programs such as the one in Tucson or the one Gutierrez describes have documented their academic successes. It is their success in empowering youth through helping them forge powerful identities that leads to their academic success.

This is a very different approach to educating low-income children of color than the obedience, "boot camp" approach promoted by mostly White venture philanthropists and entrepreneurial charter school leaders.

A Third Space for Teachers

We end this chapter with a description of a third space for teachers, the New Orleans New Teachers' Roundtable (NTRT), as an illustration of what democratic professionals might do in order to educate themselves about the communities they work in. Our nation's teaching force is 84% White, while the percent of nonwhite students has risen above 50% (Hrabowski & Sanders, 2015, Spring). In many urban areas, the percent of nonwhite students is far higher. This has created a massive demographic gap in our teaching force. The percentage of males in general and especially males of color also lags far behind. Given these demographics, White teachers are often teaching almost exclusively students of color. This makes the ongoing work of this teachers' collective not only a form of resistance but also an ongoing attempt by mostly White teachers to interrogate their motivations and how they might develop more culturally responsive pedagogies.

BOX 9.2 NEW TEACHERS' ROUNDTABLE (NTRT)

Between 2005 and 2015 in post-Katrina New Orleans, charter schools replaced the public school system staffed heavily with Teach for America (TFA) graduates who were hired on at-will contracts with no job security and no union. These teachers were largely White and idealistic believing that by teaching in low-income New Orleans schools, they were promoting social justice. The aftermath of Hurricane Katrina made New Orleans a particularly sympathetic location for young idealists. As these new TFAers flooded into New Orleans, they were displacing Black teachers. Between 2005 and 2015, the number of Black teachers went from 71% to 49% and certified teachers from 79% to 56%.

The Teachers' Roundtable of New Orleans was founded by largely White, TFA corps members who were beginning to question to what extent they were, in fact, "doing good" in spite of their best intentions. They were "increasingly wary of TFA, 'no excuses' charter schools, and the educational landscape of New Orleans" (Sondel, 2017, p. 6). One of their goals was to interrogate their own racism and challenge White supremacy in New Orleans. The NTRT is a teacher-founded and teacher-driven organization that provides new teachers the option of participating in a "supportive community where educators engage in personal reflection and critical dialogue about racial, cultural, and economic justice in New Orleans public schools and are inspired to take action with their students' communities to build a more liberatory education system" (New Teachers' Roundtable, 2015). According to Sondel (2017),

While NTRT has had multiple iterations, it currently functions as a democrat-ically run collective of educators. Each of these collective members pays annual dues; meets monthly to organize logistics; and gathers biannually for a weekend retreat to reflect on their practices, discuss their long-term vision, read and discuss critical scholarship, and plan for upcoming events. To reach out to other novice teachers, the collective organizes monthly potlucks, dur-ing which they build community and explore the historical and socio-political context of New Orleans through exposure to; critical scholarship, guest speakers from the community, and/or film screenings. Collective members also plan several larger events and workshops throughout the year for new teachers in partnership with other community-based organizations. At nearly every event, meeting, potluck, or retreat I observed, NTRT protected time for participants to share a meal and a piece of their personal story.

(p. 7)

As the NTRT members would surely acknowledge, the collective is a work in progress, but their taking the initiative to educate themselves about those things they need to know to become more effective teachers in the context in which they are working is exemplary of democratic professionalism. Teachers can't wait around for democratic leaders. We will end this chapter with a few quotes from members of the NTRT.

I went to a [NTRT] teach-in where they showed a video about the 5,000 teachers who were fired. My mind was blown. I had no idea. Because the rhetoric I heard from my principal and from other people was like, 'all these black lazy teachers were a drain on the system.

(NTRT member)

Having had the analysis, I'm able to empathize more … [But] there are teachers out there who I have conversations with who are great teachers, but truly and honestly believe that some kids are just bad, and their fami-lies are to blame and the city is to blame … Now I find myself saying stop. Parents generally want the best for their kids, no parent wants bad things for their children.

(NTRT member)

The work with the collective sustains me to do the work at school. Part of it is selfish, but if I wasn't doing activism work I would just feel like I was a part of a hopeless system. And I would literally be hopeless. I don't know if we'll see the effects of our work, even in my lifetime, but I can't sit still on a moving train. It's going somewhere. I just can't sit back.

(NTRT member)

END-OF-CHAPTER QUESTIONS

1. What do you see as possible risks, obstacles, or pushback on teachers and principals who attempt to build coalitions with students, parents, and community leaders?
2. Have you participated in a professional Learning Community (PLC)? How authentic was it? What did you accomplish there that you couldn't have accomplished on your own?
3. Have you ever experienced being part of a "third space"? What was it like? What are the advantages of working in third spaces? What are disadvantages?

NOTE

1   In practice, these three traditions might all be present in a PAR project and some scholars see a theoretical overlap between theories associated with PLCs and those associated with PAR (Cammarota, 2009–2010).

REFERENCES

Anderson, G., & Cohen, M. (2018). *Forging the new democratic professional: Beyond corporate management and entrepreneurialism in education*. New York, NY: Teachers College Press.

Ansell, C., Boin, A., & Farjoun, M. (2015). Dynamic conservatism: How institutions change to remain the same. *Research in the Sociology of Organizations, 44*, 89–119.

Anyon, J. (2014). *Radical possibilities: Public policy, urban education, and a new social movement*. New York, NY: Routledge.

Argyris, C., & Schon, D. (1978). *Organizational learning: A theory of action perspective*. Reading, MA: Addison Wesley.

Barber, B. (2004). *Strong democracy: Participatory politics for a new age*. Berkeley, CA: The University of California Press.

Bhabha, H. (2004). *The location of culture*. London, UK: Routledge.

Callahan, R. (1962). *Education and the cult of efficiency*. Chicago, IL: The University of Chicago Press.

Cammarota, J., & Fine, M. (Eds.). (2008). *Revolutionizing education: Youth participatory action research in motion*. New York, NY: Routledge.

Carpenter, S. (2015). The "local" fetish as reproductive praxis in democratic learning. *Discourse: Studies in the Cultural Politics of Education, 36*(1), 133–143.

Cervantes-Soon, C. (2017). *Juarez girls rising: Transformative education in times of dystopia*. Minneapolis: University of Minnesota Press.

Cochran-Smith, M., & Lytle, S. (2009). *Inquiry as stance: Practitioner research for the next generation*. New York, NY: Teachers College Press.

Collins, P. H., & Bilge, S. (2016). *Intersectionality*. Oxford, UK: Policy Press.

Cuban, L. (2004). *The blackboard and the bottom line: Why schools can't be businesses*. Cambridge, MA: Harvard University Press.

Delpit, L. (1995). *Other people's children: Cultural conflict in the classroom*. New York, NY: The New Press.

Deming, W. E. (1986). *Out of the Crisis*. Cambridge, MA: MIT Press.

Democracy Now. (2017, December 13). *Major education victory in Philadelphia as parents, teachers & activists reclaim control of schools.* Retrieved from https://www.democracynow.org /2017/12/13/ major_education_victory_in_philadelphia_as

Dillard, C. B. (1995). Leading with her life: An African American feminist (re)interpretation of leadership for an urban high school principal. *Educational Administration Quarterly, 31*(4), 539–563.

Drame, E., & Irby, D. (2015). Positionality and racialization in a PAR Project: Reflections and insights from a school reform collaboration. *The Qualitative Report, 20*(8), 1164–1181. Retrieved from http://nsuworks.nova.edu/tqr/vol20/iss8/2

Driscoll, M. E. (1998). Professionalism versus community: Is the conflict between school and community about to be resolved? *Peabody Journal of Education, 73*(1), 89–127.

Dumas, M. J., & Anderson, G. (2014). Qualitative research as policy knowledge: Framing policy problems and transforming education from the ground up. *Education Policy Analysis Archives, 22* (11). Retrieved from http://epaa.asu.edu/ojs/article/view/1483

Foster, M. (1971). *Making schools work: Strategies for changing education.* Philadelphia, PA: The Westminster Press.

Freire, P. (1970). *The pedagogy of the oppressed.* New York, NY: Continuum.

Ginwright, S., Noguera, P., & Cammarota, J. (Eds.). (2006). *Beyond resistance! Youth activism and community change: New democratic possibilities for practice and policy for America's youth.* New York, NY: Routledge.

Gold, E., Simon, E., & Brown, C. (2004). A new conception of parent engagement: Community organizing for school reform. In F. English (Ed.), *Handbook of educational leadership: New dimensions and realities.* Thousand Oaks, CA: Sage Pub.

Gonzalez, E. R., Lejano, R., Vidales, G., Conner, R., Kidokoro, Y., Fazeli, B., & Cabrales, R. (2007). Participatory action research for environmental health: Encountering Freire in the urban barrio. *Journal of Urban Affairs, 25*(1), 77–100.

Gonzalez, N., Moll, L., & Amanti, C. (2005). *Funds of knowledge: Theorizing practices in households and classrooms.* Mahwah, NJ: Lawrence Erlbaum.

Green, T. L. (2015). Leading for urban school reform and community development. *Educational Administration Quarterly, 51*(5), 679.

Gutierrez, K. (2008). Developing a sociocritical literacy in the third space. *Reading Research Quarterly, 43*(2), 148–164.

Habermas, J. (1987). *The theory of communicative action: Vol. 2: Lifeworld and system: A critique of functional reason* (T. McCarthy, Trans.). Boston, MA: Beacon Press.

Hamilton, M. (1997). Keeping alive alternative visions. In J. -P. Hautecoeur (Ed.), *Alpha 97: Basic education and institutional environments* (P. Sutton, Trans.). Hamburg, Germany: UNESCO Institute for Education.

Hargreaves, A. (1994). *Changing teachers, changing times: Teachers' work and culture in the postmodern age.* New York, NY: Teachers College Press.

Herr, K. (1999). Private power and privileged education: De/constructing institutionalized racism. *Journal of Inclusive Education, 3*(2), 111–129.

Hrabowski, F., & Sanders, M. (2015, Spring). Increasing racial diversity in the teacher workforce: One university's approach. *Thought & Action, 14*, 101–116.

Ishimaru, A. M. (2014). When new relationships meet old narratives: The journey towards improving parent-school relations in a district-community organizing collaboration. *Teachers College Record, 116*(2).

Jackson, T., & Howard, T. (2014). The continuing legacy of freedom schools as sites of possibility for equity and social justice for Black Students. *Western Journal of Black Studies, 38*(3), 155–162.

Johanek, M., & Puckett, J. (2006). *Leonard Covello and the making of Benjamin Franklin high school.* Philadelphia, PA: Temple University Press.

Johnson, L. (2017). Culturally responsive leadership for community empowerment. In Y. Cha, G. Jagdish, S. Ham, & M. Lee (Eds.), *Multicultural education in global perspectives: Policy and institutionalization.* New York, NY: Springer.

Johnson, R., & Avelar La Salle, R. (2010). *The wallpaper effect: Data strategies to uncover and eliminate hidden inequalities.* Thousand Oaks, CA: Corwin Press.

Jordan, S., & Kapoor, D. (2016). Re-politicizing participatory action research: Unmasking neoliberalism and the illusions of participation. *Educational Action Research, 24,* 134–149.

Kenway, J., & McCarthy, C. (Eds.). (2016). *Elite schools in globalizing circumstances: New conceptual directions and connections.* New York, NY: Routledge.

Khalifa, M. (2012). A re-new-ed paradigm in successful urban school leadership: Principal as community leader. *Educational Administration Quarterly, 48*(3), 424–467.

Lave, J. (1988). Situating learning in communities of practice. In L. Resnick, S. Levine, & L. Teasley (Eds.), *Perspectives of socially shared cognition* (pp. 63–82). Washington, DC: American Psychological Association.

Lubienski, C. (2003). Innovation in education markets: Theory and evidence on the impact of competition and choice in charter schools. *American Educational Research Journal, 40*(2), 395–443.

Mayrowetz, D., Murphy, J., Louis, K. S., & Smylie, M. (2007). Distributed leadership as work redesign: Retrofitting the job characteristics model. *Leadership and policy in schools, 6*(1), 69–101.

McDermott, K. A., & Nygreen, K. (2013). Educational new paternalism: Human capital, cultural capital, and the politics of equal opportunity. *Peabody Journal of Education, 88*(1), 84–97.

Mehan, H., Hubbard, L., & Villanueva, I. (1994). Forming academic identities: Accommodation without assimilation among involuntary minorities. *Anthropology & Education Quarterly, 25*(2), 91–117.

Mendez, G. (2015). Bachillerato IMPA: Middle school education for adults at a recovered factory. In E. Rodriguez (Ed.), *Pedagogies and curriculums to (re)imagine public education: Transnational tales of hope and resistance.* New York, NY: Springer.

Minkler, M., & Wallerstein, N. (Eds.). (2003). *Community-based participatory research for health.* San Francisco, CA: Jossey-Bass.

Nasir, N. S., McLaughlin, M., & Jones, A. (2009). What does it mean to be African-American? Constructions of race and academic identity in an urban public high school. *American Educational Research Journal, 46*(1), 73–114.

Payne, C. (1995/2007). *I've got the light of freedom: The organizing tradition and the Mississippi freedom struggle, with a new preface.* Berkeley: The University of California Press.

Podair, J. (2002). *The strike that changed New York: Blacks, whites and the ocean hill-Brownsville crisis.* New Haven, CT: Yale University Press.

Preston, C., Goldring, E., Berends, M., & Cannata, M. (2011). *School innovation in district context: Comparing traditional public schools and charter schools.* Nashville, TN: National Center on School Choice.

Rodriguez, E. (Ed.). (2015). *Pedagogies and curriculums to (re)imagine public education: Transnational tales of hope and resistance.* New York, NY: Springer.

Rogers, J., & Terriquez, V. (2009). "More justice": The role of organized labor in educational reform. *Educational Policy, 23*(1), 216–241.

Rogoff, B. (1990). *Apprenticeship in thinking: Cognitive development in social context.* Cambridge, UK: Cambridge University Press.

Sergiovanni, T. (1999). *The life world of leadership: Creating culture, community, and personal meaning in our schools*. San Francisco, CA: Jossey-Bass.

Schon, D. (1984). *The reflective practitioner: How professionals think in action*. New York, NY: Basic Books.

Shdaimah, C., Stahl, R., & Schram, S. (2009). When you can see the sky through your roof: Policy analysis from the bottom up. In E. Schatz (Ed.), *Political ethnography: What immersion contributes to the study of power* (pp. 255–274). Chicago, IL: University of Chicago Press.

Shipps, D. (2012). Empowered or beleaguered? Principals' accountability under New York City's diverse provider regime. *Education Policy Analysis Archives, 20*(1), 1–32.

Shirley, D. (1997). *Community organizing for urban school reform*. Austin: University of Texas Press.

Shutz, A. (2006). Home is a prison in the global city. The tragic failure of school-based community engagement strategies. *Review of Educational Research, 76*(4), 691–743.

Sondel, B. (2017). The new teachers' roundtable: A case study of collective resistance. *Critical Education, 8*(4), 1–22.

Spencer, J. (2014). *In the crossfire: Marcus Foster and the troubled history of American school reform*. Philadelphia: University of Pennsylvania Press.

Stanton-Salazar, R. D. (2011). A social capital framework for the study of institutional agents and their role in the empowerment of low-status students and youth. *Youth and Society, 43*(3), 1066–1109.

Tillman, L. (2004). African American principals and the legacy of brown. *Review of Research in Education, 28,* 101–146.

Torre, M., & Fine, M. (2008). Participatory action research in the contact Zone. In J. Cammarota & M. Fine (Eds.), *Revolutionizing education youth participatory action research in motion* (pp. 23–44) New York, NY: Routledge.

Valenzuela, A. (1999). *Subtractive schooling: U.S.-Mexican youth and the politics of caring*. New York: SUNY Press.

Walker, V. (2005). Organized resistance and black educators' quest for school equality, 1878–1938. *Teachers College Record, 107*(3), 355–388.

Warren, M., & Mapp, K. (2011). *A match on dry grass: Community organizing as a catalyst for school reform*. Oxford, UK: Oxford University Press.

Whitman, D. (2008). *Sweating the small stuff: Inner-city schools and the new paternalism*. Washington, DC: Thomas B. Fordham Institute.

Whyte, W. F. (1990). *Participatory action research*. Thousand Oaks, CA: Sage.

Wilson, W. J. (2009). *More than just race: Being black and poor in the inner city*. New York, NY: W.W. Norton.

CHAPTER 10

Reclaiming the Power of Education

Possibilities for Democratic Schooling

> Democracy cannot succeed unless those who express their choice are prepared to choose wisely. The real safeguard of democracy, therefore, is education.
> —Franklin D. Roosevelt

We opened this book reflecting on the activism and leadership of elementary school students and their parents, civil rights attorneys, and advocates across five local communities, who, together, comprised the plaintiffs in the historic *Brown v. Board of Education* case. Despite their efforts to use the courts to demand educational equality for Black students under a "separate-but-equal" system, racial inequality remains a predictable feature of American education, reflecting the nation's larger problem of racial caste and economic inequality—two problems the schools are expected, ironically, to help solve. Although a good number of critical legal, policy, and education scholars have characterized the *Brown* decision as an empty promise that failed to hold school district and officials accountable for preventing Black students access to White schools, the case yet serves as a symbol to many of America's commitment to equal education and pathway to the proverbial American dream.

Or, as we asked in the introduction to this book, is America dreaming? Perhaps this is just one of the countless symptoms of what Labaree (2012) diagnosed as "school syndrome"—Americans' long-held "magical belief" that with schooling, we can somehow have it both ways, achieving the contradictory goals of promoting access and equality while preserving advantage and privilege (Labaree, 2012; Reeves, 2014). Policy declarations and institutional commitments to educational equity, diversity, and social justice have resulted in "so much reform, but so little change" (Payne, 2008) *but for* the intentional, coordinated, and strategic actions of students, parents, teachers, leaders, community coalitions, and advocates driven by a belief in the democratic possibilities and power of education.

We are seeing signs of coalitions forming. For instance, teacher wildcat strikes of 2018 in West Virginia, Oklahoma, Kentucky, Arizona, and North Carolina were in part inspired by their students mobilizing nationally around gun control and a route to citizenship for dreamers. They also learned lessons from the success of the 2012 Chicago teachers' strike (Nunez, Michie, & Konkol, 2015). Movements like Occupy Wall Street, Black Lives Matter, #Me Too, and the Standing Rock pipeline protesters have generated momentum and new discourses: *the 99%, Water is life, me too,* and *Black lives matter.* What is significant about the 2018 statewide teachers' strikes is that they were striking not just because of austerity policies, low wages and an assault on their pensions but also because of their opposition to reforms imposed by non-educators that are having a deprofessionalizing effect on their work (Anderson & Cohen, 2018). These may be states that vote conservatively, but neoliberal education reforms have been promoted by conservatives *and* liberals, and the teachers are standing up to politicians from both parties as well as to mainstream teachers' unions that have too often gone along with NPM reforms.

In this final chapter, we use critical policy analysis to summarize and organize our concluding thoughts, followed by recommendations for recasting contemporary education policy discourses and moving from inquiry to praxis through leadership, reflection, and action. We close with a call for activist leadership through the following actions: (1) resisting efforts to dismantle education as a public good; (2) reclaiming a vision for education grounded in participatory democracy, equality, and justice; and (3) revolutionizing how education leadership is conceptualized, practiced, and sustained.

CRITICAL POLICY ANALYSIS: IMPLICATIONS FOR PRAXIS

> The paradox of education is precisely this - that as one begins to become conscious one begins to examine the society in which he is being educated.
> —James Baldwin

How might we both oppose the worst excesses of NPM, while using those democratic practices and policies that currently exist to build not a new education reform movement but rather a broader paradigm shift and social movement led by educators? It will take more than tweaking to humanize our public schools; yet we needn't start from scratch either. While we don't want to return to the past, we can revive some older ideas and practices that worked well, and we can draw on some current innovative practices that, like flowers growing through the cement, have shown resiliency and great promise.

We discuss both opportunities for opposition and advocacy, and current practices that show promise for building more equitable, rigorous, and humane public schools. *First,* as educators, we should give up the notion that business models and the private sector are more innovative or appropriate for managing and improving educational systems (Abrams, 2016; Cuban, 2004; Lock & Spender, 2011; Mazzacuto, 2015). *Second,* we need to take seriously the need for educators to be advocates for low-income families and children and to do so in concrete ways both inside and outside schools (Anderson, 2009). This often means teaching and leading against the grain and taking risks. *Third,* and related to being an advocate, is to mobilize policymakers to return to a policy of public investment in our social infrastructure, including our public schools. Especially since 2008, we have seen a shift toward austerity and privatization of the public sector instead of public investment. Countries that have rejected NPM and heavily and smartly invest in schools and teachers outperform those that don't (Adamson, Astrand, & Darling-Hammond, 2016). The teachers that are striking and walking out across America are calling for greater public investment in education. Where are the educational leaders? *Fourth,* unless we change our current epistemology of research and practice, nothing will change; we will continue to think in top-down, outside-in, scaling up approaches to educational change (Anderson, 2017). Why not explore bottom-up and inside-out approaches to change and scaling down to humanize education? *Finally,* and related to this, there is a need to shift power relations and hold those in power accountable. This will be the most difficult as we face massive amounts of what Jane Mayer (2014) calls "dark money" flowing into our political and educational systems from corporations and venture philanthropists, and donors like the Koch brothers. We believe that educators, along with other professionals who are suffering from NPMs' reliance on markets, metrics, and managerialism, can be the core of a movement to regenerate a moribund sense of a public sphere, a common good, and greater social equality (Anyon, 2014).

Nearly five decades ago, in his book *Pedagogy of the Oppressed,* Paulo Freire (1970) lamented, "We are surrounded by a pragmatic discourse that would have us adapt to the facts of reality. *Dream and utopia,* are called not only useless, but positively impeding" (p. 1). What we hope to provide in this chapter is a vision for the future of public schooling that encourages us to dream about what may seem like a utopia yet is grounded in some existing practices and policies, though these practices may not be dominant currently. Marcus Foster, whose leadership we highlighted in the previous chapter, rejected using rigid accountability models that sought to punish teachers and leaders. He felt teachers and leaders were already too restrained by custom, bureaucracy, and low expectations. His way of thinking about accountability was to incentivize teachers and leaders to take risks and to look to the community for accountability—a kind of public accountability to one's community, not accountability through markets and school choice.

This way of thinking about professionalism requires a commitment to not just implementing educational practices but engaging in educational praxis. Freire (1970) insisted that literacy meant reading the *word* and the *world.* Any education worth the name teaches us to read the world, not just the word. It teaches us to decode systems of power, and this is best done with others. Some tenets of praxis include:

- Understanding the individual and school-level processes as contextualized by macro-level social processes and structures.
- These social processes and structures are understood within a historical context.

- Theory and practice are integrated. Practice informs theory and theory informs practice.
- The subject-object relationship is transformed into a subject-subject relationship through dialogue.
- The community and the professional together produce critical knowledge aimed at social transformation.

More on this below, but these tenets apply to good teaching as well as good professional practice. It is in this spirit that we provide the following critical policy analysis.

#1: EXHIBIT AN ETHOS OF PUBLIC SERVICE AND A COMMON GOOD: IMPORTING BUSINESS MODELS WON'T IMPROVE EDUCATION NOR MAKE IT MORE EQUITABLE

During the last century of education history, we've seen the imposition of two business models: the first, business model 1.0, emerged in the early 20th century and gave us the "efficient," factory model school, and the second, business model 2.0, gave us a system based on privatization, market choice, and high-stakes accountability. What both business models have in common is that they are undergirded by assumptions of hyper-efficiency, meritocracy, bureaucracy, standardization, and quantification. These assumptions are deeply embedded in our culture, but for some time now, we have been on the cusp of a general recognition that these business models have never served the vast majority of children, teachers, leaders, or communities well (Anderson & Cohen, 2018; Cuban, 2004, 2007).

Some have argued that educators who followed the democratic and progressive, child-centered approach of John Dewey were overshadowed by the administrative progressives who gave us the industrial business model of the early 20th century (Cremin, 1964). They bequeathed us factories and bureaucracies that were possibly more efficient in the private sector but transferred to education resulted in the "factory model" school (the ultimate "scaling up") and the standardization of learning (Taubman, 2009). Too many reformers today forget that the public bureaucracies they now criticize were at one time the business model du jour.

To be fair, business model 1.0, which promoted bureaucratic meritocracy, did replace patronage and corrupt political nepotism with civil service exams and professional certification requirements. Politicians could no longer appoint the guy who helped them get elected or their hapless brother-in-law to a principalship. Moreover, those public bureaucracies were largely run by public servants, most of whom had an ethos of service to a common good, unlike our current era of entrepreneurial leaders who work under market pressures, just like the private sector. Yet, while cults of efficiency, standardization, and bureaucracy may have been appropriate for manufacturing and franchising businesses, educators have been digging ourselves out of the hole of first-wave business models since the dawn of the 20th century (Anderson & Cohen, 2018; Callahan, 1962; Gelberg, 1997).

In previous chapters, we've described business model 2.0 (New Public Management), the late 20th and early 21st-century transfers of business principals into the public sector, so we won't repeat it here. But the second failure of business models in a century (see Lock & Spender, 2011) leaves us asking what would our dream public school be if we could see students not only as human capital but also as complex; multidimensional; diverse; and, in many cases, wounded human beings who need healing (Ginwright, 2015). To return to Paulo Freire (1970), what would a humanizing and equitable education look like, and what kind of society do we need to foster it? All great theorists of education, from John Dewey and Anna Julia Cooper to Carter G. Woodson and Paulo Freire, recognized that schools and society had a synergistic relationship. Children needed to be nurtured in a caring and democratic school and society.

If we return to all of the goals of schooling described in Chapter 2, it would mean bringing the multiple goals of schooling into greater balance. The economic, human capital goal has colonized previous goals such as promoting democratic citizenship, fostering a common good or cultivating students' physical, affective, and aesthetic development. As we caution throughout this book, decolonizing our schools shouldn't mean a return to some golden age of public schooling. While public schools in the postwar years were probably not as bad as Hollywood movies and right-wing think tanks have depicted them, they did have serious shortcomings related to business model 1.0's bureaucratic factory model and a meritocratic ideology that justified discrimination by class, race, and gender (McNamee & Miller, 2009).

But they have improved over time, although not for all children. Compare Frederick Wiseman's documentary, *High School I* (1960), which depicts long boring days of what Freire called "banking" or unidirectional, knowledge transmission education, with *High School II* (1994), in which Wiseman visits Central Park East, a member of the Coalition of Essential Schools. The differences are dramatic and demonstrate what is possible when factory model high schools are "scaled down," detracked, and humanized (see Meier, 1995). On the other hand, small schools require time and patience, and cannot be "brought to scale" quickly as they have in some urban districts.

Until business model 2.0 nearly wiped them out, there were some promising coalitions of school models that attempted to improve public schools rather than marketize and privatize them. Some examples were the Coalition of Essential Schools, Comer schools, and Accelerated Schools. While reformers impatiently declared these public school innovations too little, too late, it would be interesting to speculate where we would be today had we continued these innovations and reformed the broader systems they were nested in. Such schools generally had their own approach to dissemination of their innovations and they did not include replication and standardization. The replication and standardization of charter franchises ensure that little innovation will occur, just as today's McDonald's hamburger is not essentially different from the one mass-produced in the 1950s.

It is ironic that with evidence showing that the public sector may actually be more innovative and entrepreneurial than the private sector, we continue to look to the private sector for solutions in education. Mazzucato's (2015) *The Entrepreneurial State* documents how virtually every innovation in the development of computers, smartphones, and tablets was funded almost exclusively by government agencies, mostly defense-related agencies, such as Defense Advanced Research Projects Agency (DARPA). This includes the internet, microprocessors, the multi-touch screen, SIRI, GPS, liquid-crystal display, lithium ion batteries, and many more. The vaunted entrepreneurialism of Silicon Valley is largely limited to creating apps and commercializing innovations produced by the federal government.

And this is not just the case with the information technology (IT) industry: almost every major technology has been the result of large-scale and long-term investment by the State, something venture capitalists seldom have the patience for. The growth of the biopharmaceutical industry was not, as is often argued, the result of venture capital or other business finance promoting innovation in the private sector but rather was the result of government investment and ongoing support. "Seventy-five percent of the NMEs [new molecular entities] trace their research not to private companies but to publically funded National Institute of Health (NIH) labs in the US" (Mazzacuto, 2015, p. 73). In Mazzacuto's (2018) subsequent book, she analyzes how we think about value (or wealth) creation and extraction, and challenges the current notion that the wealthy and the private sector are the "makers" and the welfare state and the poor are the "takers". She demonstrates the many ways the state creates wealth and the private sector extracts wealth.

Within the public schools there are still some remnants of progressive public sector reforms left that could form the building blocks of a new paradigm of schooling:

1. Although the Coalition of Essential schools has been dissolved, New York City has a consortium of thirty-six schools, the *New York Performance Standards Consortium,* that have a waiver to do alternative assessment for Regents exams. Instead of taking the exams, students must demonstrate mastery of skills in all subjects by designing experiments, making presentations, writing reports, and defending their work to outside experts (Robinson, 2015). Consortium schools report much higher college attendance rates than regular high schools.
2. The community schools movement shows promise in many cities as well. In 2013, the Association for Supervision and Curriculum Development (ASCD) and the US Centers for Disease Control and Prevention (CDC) developed the Whole School, Whole Child, Whole Community approach, which combines a whole child philosophy, community engagement, and health services (Lewallen, Hunt, Potts-Datema, Zaza, & Giles, 2015; See also, Maier, Daniel, & Oakes, 2017).
3. The replacement of zero tolerance discipline approaches with culturally responsive approaches to restorative justice are humanizing schools and reducing suspensions, when enacted authentically (Lustick, 2017).
4. In several U.S. cities, districts have used a more democratic way of holding teachers accountable, called Peer Assistance and Review (PAR). This approach involves teachers evaluating one another with union and administrative input. Goldstein (2010) describes how the approach works:

With PAR, designated "consulting teachers" provide support to new teachers and struggling veteran teachers (collectively called "participating teachers"), and also conduct the summative personnel evaluations of the teachers they support. The consulting teachers report to an oversight panel composed of teachers and administrators from across the district, co-chaired by the teacher union president and a high-ranking district office administrator. The panel holds hearings several times a year, at which consulting teachers provide reports about participating teacher progress and ultimately make recommendations about the continued employment of each participating teacher.

(p. 54)

While such a model requires a high level of trust among teachers that the union won't be co-opted, it provides a peer-review process and is far better than using test scores to evaluate teachers.

5. While the notion of culturally responsive teaching has been around for a while (Gay, 2010; Ladson-Billings, 1994), the standardized testing emphasis of NPM has forced many teachers to eliminate non-tested topics and adopt a more test-oriented instruction. In addition, the new breed of franchise charter schools and many public schools have chosen to de-emphasize these approaches in favor of a depoliticized, paternalistic, "boot camp" and scripted approach to instruction. However, culturally responsive teaching is making a revival in some stand-alone charters and many public schools (Milner IV, 2015; Nieto, 2014). See Box 10.1 for a description of culturally responsive teaching.

BOX 10.1 COALITION FOR EDUCATIONAL JUSTICE: CULTURALLY RESPONSIVE EDUCATION 101

Culturally responsive education...

- Connects curriculum and teaching to students' experiences, perspectives, histories, and cultures.
- Advances student's academic achievement and sense of themselves as agents for change.
- Helps students sustain their connection to their own language.

Our public schools are full of biases and inequities—both conscious and unconscious—which impact students' lives every day.

- In 2015, only 15% of children's books were by or about African Americans or Latinos (1).
- In 2015, a McGraw-Hill high school history textbook in Texas said that African Americans were brought to the United States as "workers" (2).
- Studies have shown that White teachers have lower expectations for

students of color; they are significantly less likely to expect Black students to finish high school and college (3).

- Studies show that Black boys are seen as threatening and dangerous for the same behavior that is seen as innocent when White kids do it. White kids will be tolerated or even admired as leaders for the same behaviors that get kids of color suspended (4).
- A recent study showed that preschool teachers watch Black boys in the classroom more than other children, increasing the chances that they catch "bad" behavior (5).
- Many research studies have shown that culturally responsive education works (6).
  - Increases student engagement, participation, and curiosity in the classroom.
  - Teaches students to value their perspectives and think of themselves as good students.
  - Advances students' political awareness and empowerment.
- Students in K-12 who participated in Tucson's Mexican-American Studies program were (7):
  - Significantly more likely to pass state standardized tests and graduate high school.
  - More engaged in literature and history lessons.
  - More likely to have positive perception of their ability to succeed in math and science.
- Ninth-grade students who participated in San Francisco's Ethnic Studies Program showed (8):
  - Increased student achievement and graduation rates.
  - Increased attendance, grade point average, and credits earned.

1. http://ccbc.education.wisc.edu/books/pcstats.asp
2. http://www.nytimes.com/2015/10/06/us/publisher-promises-revisions-after-textbook-refers-to-african-slaves-as-workers.html?_r=0
3. http://research.upjohn.org/cgi/viewcontent.cgi?article=1248&context=up_workingpapers
4. http://www.apa.org/news/press/releases/2014/03/black-boys-older.aspx
5. http://news.yale.edu/2016/09/27/implicit-bias-may-help-explain-high-preschool-expulsion-rates-black-children
6. http://www.nea.org/assets/docs/NBI-2010-3-value-of-ethnic-studies.pdf
7. http://www.huffingtonpost.com/2014/12/01/mexican-american-studies-student-achievement_n_6249592.html?1421108833
8. http://news.stanford.edu/2016/01/12/ethnic-studies-benefits-011216/

This is only a handful of ideas and practices that currently exist. We don't have to invent new practices to work to transform public education, just promote more humanizing practices and oppose those policies that make them less likely to be successful. While these building blocks can form the basis for necessary changes in policies and approaches to schooling, there are also broad assumptions and paradigms that underlie our current reforms that will need to be confronted as well.

#2 ADVOCATE FOR LOW-INCOME CHILDREN AND FAMILIES AND CHALLENGE POLICIES THAT FAIL TO ADDRESS RACED, CLASSED, AND GENDERED INEQUALITIES

Today's education leaders must understand power and the ways in which power, politics, and policy governance shape not only their role in their respective classrooms, schools, or districts but also the policies and politics that govern their profession. Despite narratives around equity, inclusion, and integration, the reality is that America's school system is segregated by race and class and will stay that way until we confront the reality of racial caste in American society. The ongoing struggle for educational equality for poor children of color, particularly Black, Latino/a, immigrant, and refugee children, a growing share of which are also Muslim and/or speak a language other than English at home, has been characterized by some as "apartheid schools" although history would tell us that these schools are as American as apple pie.

Closing "achievement gaps," closing "failing" schools, or firing ineffective teachers doesn't confront the realities of America's classed and raced caste systems, which continue to maintain Black people at the "bottom of society's well" (Bell, 1992), while other communities of color negotiate their location on the spectrum of political Blackness in relation to Whiteness or, rather, a racial continuum from non-Whiteness to Whiteness. A critical policy approach to pursuing the possibilities of democratic education requires familiarity with the policy landscape, political climate, and various sources of power in terms of funding, policymaking, and accountability, both private and public. Transformative leaders, such as those we have featured throughout this book, tend to have a deep understanding of their policy environment and classed, raced, and gendered power relations. Here are some of the things they do:

Implications for Praxis

- Participate in professional associations meetings, convenings, conferences, and other opportunities to learn about the latest in education policy at the local, regional, and national levels.
- Subscribe to education newsletters, blogs, journals, and other legitimate sources of education news and current events to stay engaged with the education and larger policy and political issues being debated in the public sphere. A good

place to start is: *Education Week, Rethinking Schools, NEAToday* (NEA), *Phi Delta Kappan, American Educator* (AFT), Educational Leadership (ASCD), Education Policy Analysis Archives (open access), Journal for Critical Education Policy Studies (open access), and School Administrator (AASA). Read books about education and social policy. Many can be found in this book's reference list.

- Become familiar with your elected and appointed representatives at the local, state, and federal levels and their positions on education issues, and if you live in a community other than where you work, be sure to know who represents your students, families, and local school community members.
- Conduct background research on those who are funding education initiatives and/or related community development efforts to better understand the values and ideology supporting their investment in this work. Who serves on the board of directors? Which foundation is funding the initiative? What political campaigns or other causes has this philanthropic organization funded, and to what end?

#3 SUPPORT POLICIES OF PUBLIC INVESTMENT IN EDUCATION, NOT A STRATEGY OF MARKETS AND MEASURING OUTCOMES

Part of the neoliberal NPM agenda has been a shift from an emphasis on "inputs" of the system (resources and public investment) to one of markets and high-stakes "outputs" (measuring outcomes). Especially since the 2008 recession, investment in public education has diminished, leading to lower teachers' salaries, benefits, and pensions. Low salaries in combination with a sense that they are being disrespected and deprofessionalized by NPM led to the wildcat strikes in 2018 by teachers in West Virginia, Oklahoma, Kentucky, Arizona, and Colorado (Weiner, 2018). Teachers in these politically conservative states have educated themselves about the ways in which their gendered profession is being degraded, and they have drawn a line in the sand.

Global comparisons of countries that have adopted a public investment strategy in education with those that have chosen markets and metrics demonstrate that a public investment strategy achieves higher overall achievement and greater equity of outcomes. Finland, which chose public investment, saw its achievement rates soar, while just next door, Sweden, which chose a voucher system and high-stakes testing, saw its rates plummet (Astrand, 2016). Canada (especially Ontario), which chose public investment over markets, has outperformed the U.S. (Fullan & Rincon-Gallardo, 2016), and socialist Cuba's academic achievement leaves the rest of Latin America in the dust (Carnoy, 2016).

But one needn't look to other countries for comparisons. U.S. states that have followed a public investment strategy consistently outperform states that have not. Several high-performing states in the northeast, such as Massachusetts, Vermont, Connecticut, New Hampshire, and New Jersey, have increased and attempted to equalize funding; invested in high-quality standards, assessments, and professional development; and supported early childhood education and child health and welfare. These are also states with high levels of unionized teachers.

The pro-charter Center for Education Reform (CER) and the corporate-funded, neoliberal American Legislative Exchange Council (ALEC) both give these states Ds and Cs on their annual report cards. ALEC's highest rankings go to states that are largely nonunion and deregulated, allowing for-profit charter schools and vouchers. States like Arizona, Florida, Indiana, and Betsy DeVos's Michigan, along with Washington, D.C., received the highest ratings. None of these states outperform states that have followed a public investment and teacher professionalization strategy.

We can also look to the U.S. past for an example of public investment. Although marred by racist housing policies (Rothstein, 2017) and a state finance system based on property taxes, the U.S. had a strategy of public investment during the years of the Great Society in the 1960s when the Elementary and Secondary Education Act was passed. The Civil Rights movement had also removed some barriers to education for African Americans. The labor movement had produced well-paid, blue-collar jobs, and opportunities were expanding in higher education through state investment that produced low state tuition, increased financial aid, and affirmative action programs. During this period, the CUNY system in New York City had free tuition and open admissions. It should not be surprising that the achievement gap between Black and White students and between income levels saw the largest reductions during the 1960s and 1970s. The gap in higher education enrollments was nearly eliminated during this period. City College (often referred to as the working class's Harvard) and other CUNY campuses, for instance, between the 1950s and the 1970s went from being overwhelmingly White to among the most racially diverse campuses in the nation.

And yet, these policies of public investment were eroded by a well-funded campaign to dismantle the welfare state and replace it with an ideology of disinvestment from the public sector (Phillips-Fein, 2009). This was accompanied by the idea, promoted by Nobel Prize-winning economists like James Buchanan and Milton Freidman, that redistributive economic policies that addressed the opportunity gap were a kind of Robin Hood mentality that stole from the more deserving affluent members of society to give to the undeserving poor (McLean, 2017). The fact that the poor in the U.S. were disproportionally made up of racial minorities was seldom acknowledged openly, but a kind of "dog whistle" politics made it clear to those who were listening in a racist frequency that it meant taking money from White people and giving it to people of color (Lopez, 2015). In the current climate created by President Donald Trump, the dog whistle has been replaced by some with a racist and xenophobic megaphone.

Implications for Praxis

- Identify ways to demonstrate, articulate, and even quantify to the public the tangible and intangible benefits of public education to society.
- Become familiar with the role of media in the policy process and more specifically how education issues are presented in the media and perceived by the public, and develop relationships with local and national education reporters.

- Utilize organizing efforts and strategies (e.g. press conferences, sit-ins, marches, protests, boycotts, strikes, etc.) that draw media interest and public attention to a particular issue.
- Connect an agenda that supports public education with other progressive agendas that require and rely on high-quality schools and systems of education (e.g. environmental justice, restorative justice practices, early learning education, worker rights and apprenticeships, gender equity, etc.).

#4 CHANGE YOUR EPISTEMOLOGY OF PRACTICE (AND RESEARCH): CENTERING EMANCIPATORY KNOWLEDGE AND MARGINALIZED PERSPECTIVES

Researchers, policymakers, educators, nonprofit organizations, and local service providers who seek authentic community perspectives and input must locate and center local and community knowledge and the marginalized whose forgotten perspectives are seldom included in mainstream narratives. Also know that this work requires an investment of time and commitment, so ensure that you incorporate an adequate amount of time for outreach and related activities, and ensure that you have identified the major stakeholders, policy actors, and influential organizations, who will be able to ensure that the perspectives you collect from a particular community are actually representative of that community.

From an education policy and leadership perspective, emergent work in the areas of bilingual education leadership, impact of homelessness on educational outcomes (Pavlakis, Goff, & Miller, 2017), implications of federal education policy on Indigenous education (Mackey, 2017), complexities of leading schools in gentrifying neighborhoods (McGhee & Anderson, 2018), and additional work documenting the voices and experiences of students and parents of color (Ginwright, 2015) have contributed richly to the education research literature.

An increase in the number of scholars utilizing critical race theory and nontraditional methodologies that are more critical, participatory, and action-oriented has increased our knowledge as a field in important ways that a White, Western, male perspective could not and did not capture over the last century (Collins & Bilge, 2016). Fortunately, a growing number of scholars who are of color, women, and LGBT persons in the field of education have begun to transform the nature of what constitutes research, for whom, and to what end. The group that is missing in the academy though, as well as in the ranks of teachers and administrators, is the poor. This means that we must have our ears to the ground as we represent communities who are struggling with economic stressors we may not be intimately familiar with.

And yet, educational research has not had the kind of impact on practice and policy that scholars would like (Dumas & Anderson, 2014). In part, this may be because few have seriously challenged the *technocratic knowledge framework* that sees knowledge in applied fields as created in universities; disseminated through journals (usually behind pay walls), conferences, consultants, and workshops; and utilized by practitioners in schools (see Box 10.2).

BOX 10.2 TECHNOCRATIC KNOWLEDGE FRAMEWORK

A linear, chronological process:

Knowledge **creation** (in universities, policy think tanks, and r&d centers)

Knowledge **dissemination** (unidirectional: publication, conferences, workshops, consultancies, vendors)

Knowledge **utilization** (practice, policy)

This traditional framework has been ineffective for decades and pathologizes school practitioners as "resistant" to reforms they had no role in creating. A democratic approach to knowledge requires an *emancipatory knowledge framework* that problematizes a linear, top-down research "delivery" system. It also promotes a more simultaneous, dialogical process in which the creation of knowledge is done in multiple sites and with a participatory stance with diverse participants (see Box 10.3). This might include a broad continuum of possibilities from traditional academic research to community or site-based research led by community or student organizers or school practitioners. To the extent that students, teachers, or community organizations are seeking knowledge to solve problems relevant to their lives, they will seek knowledge from other sites, including academic research. Ironically, in an emancipatory knowledge framework, schools and communities are more likely, not less, to seek out academic research.

BOX 10.3 EMANCIPATORY KNOWLEDGE FRAMEWORK

A simultaneous, dialogical process:

Knowledge **creation** (in multiple sites, with diverse participants)

Knowledge **circulation** (multidirectional: knowledge/power)

Knowledge **enactment** (agentic subjects at all levels)

An emancipatory knowledge framework challenges the idea that school practitioners should be mere implementers or utilizers of knowledge rather than creators of knowledge. Teachers' tendency to resist, modify, or reappropriate reforms is viewed by NPM reformers not as a necessary adaptation of policy to practice but rather as distorting the "fidelity" of implementation (Achinstein & Ogawa, 2006). And yet, decades of research have shown that the agency that practitioners exercise has a positive effect on policy as it recontextualizes the policy, adapting it to the local reality (McLaughlin, 1976). An emancipatory knowledge framework would include a more explicit form of participatory policymaking and knowledge production in which those at different levels of the system collaborate to produce policy knowledge (Dumas & Anderson, 2014). In an emancipatory framework, knowledge isn't disseminated "downward," but rather circulates and is multidirectional.

Some researchers have characterized the gap between scholars and practitioners as reflecting separate cultures (Ginsberg & Gorostiaga, 2001) and universities are being supplanted as knowledge brokers by think tanks and other organizations that more effectively straddle social fields (Anderson, De La Cruz, & Lopez, 2017). Unless the technocratic knowledge framework changes to reflect changing times, academics and their research—qualitative or quantitative—will continue to be viewed as largely irrelevant to schools, practitioners, and progressive policymakers.

Implications for Praxis

- Push deeper into more horizontal forms of teacher professional development that are inclusive of student and community perspectives and teachers' unions. Understand that principals don't lose power by sharing it. They gain greater power to achieve objectives.
- A promising horizontal practice is PAR or teachers evaluating each other with union and administrative inputs, as we discussed earlier.
- Promote authentic performance-based assessments over paper and pencil tests and remove the high stakes from testing.
- Support social movement unionism, allied with communities that fight for equitable social and educational reforms. Most teachers unions are industrial union models that focus mainly on bread-and-butter issues. These bread-and-butter issues are important, especially given how underpaid teachers are and how vulnerable their pensions are. But unless we build broad coalitions to fight for social justice for all children, unions will continue to be vulnerable to anti-union attacks led by corporate-funded political organizations like ALEC (Anderson & Donchik, 2016).

#5 INTERROGATE THE DISTRIBUTION OF POWER AND RESOURCES AND HOLD THOSE IN POWER ACCOUNTABLE

States and school systems across the country have relinquished significant control over education to the private sector, buying into the business model of education that has used high-stakes standardized testing, market competition, and charter school franchising as a form of scaling up and standardizing "innovations." Reformers can be applauded for their sense of urgency about improving teaching and learning so that all students can be college ready, but urgency must be balanced with an understanding of the complexity of schools and systems and the longer timelines often needed to create deep change (Payne, 2008). Like many countries that invest in the professional development of teachers and then look to them to lead change with community input, we need to find more organic forms of professional responsibility and the dissemination of innovation across schools and districts.

But educators are in a difficult position. Both major political parties have bought into NPM reforms, and they are being promoted by powerful organizations with massive amounts of money. In addition, a relatively new actor has appeared on the scene. For-profit companies see public education as a profit center. These "edu-businesses" have powerful lobbies in Washington, network with ALEC and similar organizations, and have gone global, nearly taking over entire public school systems in countries like Liberia and Haiti, and threatening to profit from Puerto Rico's economy ravaged first by vulture capitalists and then by hurricanes (Klein, 2018).

For-profit companies have produced textbooks for public schools for a long time, and many new products and technologies may be worth purchasing. However, district and building administrators are often the only line of defense against the massive push to exploit public money. It is becoming increasingly apparent, for instance, that virtual schools in many states are a scam to profit off public money by receiving the same allocation as brick-and-mortar schools. Thanks in part to ALEC's education task force, chaired by K-12, Inc. (Anderson & Donchik, 2016), "between 2008 and 2014, 175 bills that expanded online schooling options passed in 39 states and territories (including the district of Columbia)" (Rook, 2017, p. 145).

K-12, Inc. was founded Ronald Packard, with heavy investment from Michael Milkin, the symbol of Wall Street Greed, Gordon Gekko, portrayed by Michael Douglas in the movie *Wall Street*. Milkin did two years in prison for securities fraud. Meanwhile, his new company, K-12, Inc., settled a federal lawsuit for $6.8 million for allegedly inflating "stock prices by misleading investors with false student performance claims" (Rook, 2017 p. 149). In addition to improprieties, virtual schools have proved to be so ineffective that many states are canceling their contracts (Miron & Gulosino, 2016, April). While some companies are reputable, the technology industry, including testing, data warehousing, and management, has grown massively and spends millions lobbying Washington and statehouses for policies that favor their industries (Burch & Good, 2014). District and building administrators need to educate themselves about this growing education industry and be good stewards of public funds.

As we have noted throughout this book, we see this tendency of the State's dis-investment from education along with the growth of a for-profit industry that sees schools and districts as profit centers as an existential threat to the very concept of public education. As austerity policies are imposed around the world, public invest-ment shrinks, creating a bigger opening for these companies. What might resistance look like for educators in the face of such formidable and well-funded forces?

At a professional level, the task ahead is not to reassert "traditional" profession-alism but rather to better understand how to engage in what Achinstein and Ogawa (2006) call "principled resistance" to the most egregious assaults on professionals, while acknowledging the weaknesses of the old professionalism and constructing a vision of a new democratic professionalism (Anderson & Cohen, 2018; Zeichner & Pena-Sandoval, 2015). At a minimum, such a vision would insist on a professional ethos with the public good at its center.

At the collective level, there is a growing grassroots resistance to all of these ten-dencies and many public sector professionals and low-income communities of color are engaged in these struggles. The current neoliberal reform model in education is encountering increasing resistance. The mainstreams of both political parties were rejected in the 2016 U.S. elections, suggesting that the American public is seeking profound change. The wildcat teachers' strikes in the American heartland may be a harbinger of things to come. But we can't sit back and wait for it to happen. Educators are on the front lines of a growing social movement—of a plethora of social movements that are beginning to find their voices and to build alliances across race, gender, class, and ideology. We have to turn off the mainstream corporate-funded media and begin listening to alternative sources of information, other educators, other public sector employees, and our students and their communities. Fox News, CNN, and MSNBC are merely seeking ratings. The mainstream corporate media may not be fake news, as Donald Trump claims, but it is less news than infotainment, following the latest shiny object and bereft of any investigative reporting of important issues.

Implications for Praxis

- Demand a return to a strategy of public investment in education and discontinue the cheaper but ineffective market-based, high-stakes accountability approach.
- Support school desegregation through controlled choice programs like those in Cambridge, MA and Wake County, NC.
- Replace quasi-markets and charter schools with community schools that provide wraparound services but also redefine school-community relationships.
- Challenge private requests for public funding absent a public accountability plan.
- Organize resistance to the privatization of public schooling, especially the growth of the for-profit sector in the public sphere. Early notions of public-private partnerships were viable approaches to address intractable social problems (Minow, 2002), but we are increasingly seeing the colonization of the public sector by the private sector through a discourse of "partnership."
- Require annual public accountability reporting comparable to what is required of traditional public schools from any education providers using public dollars or resources.

  - Seek data on the extent to which schools replaced punitive, zero tolerance approaches to discipline with positive discipline approaches, such as restorative justice.
  - Seek data on the types and quality of educational services made available to English learners and their families and the expansion of bilingual and dual language programs for students and families representing a diversity of racial, ethnic, cultural, and socioeconomic backgrounds.

THE TRANSFORMATIVE POWER OF EDUCATION AND LEADERSHIP

The history of education leadership in America is filled with many impressive and courageous figures who engaged in acts of resistance, reimagining, and revolutionary thinking in order to disrupt and/or transform systems of schooling in powerful and important ways. Whether the parents who risked their safety and the safety of their children as plaintiffs in the *Brown v. Board of Education* case to resist government-sanctioned racially segregated schools or present-day school leaders resisting Trump's policies to deport undocumented students to countries they've never lived in, there is great need for activist leadership that builds on the work of community organizers and progressive social movements, and leads "against the grain" (Ishimaru, 2014).

Indeed, revolutionary thinking is critical to this project as America's schools, much like the nation itself, were never great to begin with for those who were not part of the dominant classes. If nothing more, Trump's presidency has compelled us to challenge our historical amnesia or perhaps intentional ignorance, around issues of White supremacy, patriarchy, and dangers of religious zeal and domestic terrorism in ways that hold important implications for the future of American education. Education leaders committed to the ideals of equality, democracy, and justice must engage an activist leadership approach that is not simply reactionary but seeks to build a system of schools greater than how we found them.

As Robert Greenleaf, who coined the term *servant leadership*, explained, "Revolutionary ideas do not change institutions. People change them by taking risks to serve and lead, and by the sustained painstaking care that institution building requires." In that same spirit, we offer the following ways in which education leaders might take advantage of this current political moment to (1) resist efforts to dismantle education as a public good; (2) reclaim a vision for education grounded in equality, liberation, and justice; and (3) revolutionize how education leadership is conceptualized, practiced, and sustained.

1. **Resist efforts to dismantle education as a public good.** Today's education leaders must serve as the leading voices and advocates for high-quality public schools. This requires defending public education as a pillar of democratic society and resisting efforts to weaken or altogether dismantle the notion that education is a public good. To be fair, education has its problems, and educational institutions, like other organizations in both the private and public sectors, are far from perfect. Educational leaders should not allow critics of education as a public good to control a narrative claiming that public schools are "broken" and need to be "fixed" or, better yet, replaced with charter schools or incentivized to improve through competition and privatization. Instead, they should resist what has now become a mainstream discourse in education and replace it with one that reminds the public of the important role and contributions that education can and must play in an open, free, and democratic society. This includes actively resisting education policies, programs, and practices that claim to promote equity but really only exist to enrich those who benefit from the exploitation of disenfranchised communities.

2. **Reclaim a vision of education grounded in equality, liberation, and justice.** For the last two decades, American education has focused narrowly on standardization, high-stakes testing and accountability, and superficial attempts to close an "achievement gap" that remains nothing more than a reflection of racial caste in America. We cannot normalize such structures through

the collection and dissemination of data that focuses on "winners" and "losers" rather than creating conditions that foster and support the growth, learning, and development of children and youth. By reclaiming a vision of education that is grounded in the ideals of equality, liberty, and justice, education leaders can accomplish two important things: (1) restore a much-needed commitment to understanding the history of American education from multiple perspectives, and the role that schools and school leaders have played in either undermining or advancing these ideals and (2) creating conditions and intellectual spaces that invite, foster, and facilitate civil discourse, dialogue, and mutual understanding.

3. **Revolutionize how education leadership is conceptualized, practiced, and sustained.** The field of education leadership is being left behind when it comes to its ability to be nimble and responsive to the needs of today's students, families, and communities. Surely, the Trump Administration's policies and the uncertainty that they have created pose many challenges to school leaders who have a professional duty to ensure the safety and education of their students and the families they serve. In fact, while instructional leadership is important and has become the preeminent frame upon which to measure and assess the effectiveness of school leaders, the current moment demands a distinct priority shift as we process not only the short-term impact of Trump's policies but the medium- and long-term impacts they will have on America's schools and, even more importantly, democracy.

The two surely go together and it will take bold and courageous leadership to not simply improve test scores and work to remove persistently low-performing schools from a state watch list but to seriously reflect on the purpose and values we hold for education and why we as education leaders entered the profession in the first place. The times require that we take an active leadership role to mobilize school communities to convince policymakers to prioritize education and build bridges and coalitions that demand a system of schools that supports a racially and culturally pluralist society that is strongest when united in vision and purpose.

CONCLUSION

We are nearing a consensus in the U.S. that NPM and business models have never served the vast majority of children, teachers, leaders, or communities well (Anderson, 2009; Cuban, 2004, 2007; Gelberg, 1997). Moving forward, it is critical to seize this moment in which we can determine the role that schools must play in a democratic society. If we miss this moment, we will not be able to galvanize the groups and individuals who are currently engaged in the resistance to the authoritarian regime that is currently in the White House and what it represents in terms of its dismantling of democratic practices and investments and support for high-quality public schools.

Exhibit A is billionaire Betsy DeVos, the woman who leads the Department of Education, and contributed $9.5 million to President Trump's campaign. She has no education degree, has never taught in or led a public school or sent her children to one, and supports the funding of for-profit Christian schools with public funds. Only by building alliances and coalitions across a range of progressive causes like women's rights, LBGTQ rights, immigration rights, environmental justice, and criminal justice reform can public education find its rightful place among the nation's priorities.

If America's schools are to recognize their collective power as sites of possibility and transformation through teaching and learning, knowledge production, and the critical and original thinking essential to a vibrant, inclusive, and representative democracy, we must restore the democratic ideal and seek greater balance between public and private sectors and interests. This is not to suggest that economic goals are not important; they are. They should be supplemented by goals such as developing the skills of democratic citizenship; personal enhancement through music, the arts, and the joy of learning for its own sake; and in ways that model meaningful cultural diversity, inclusion, and integration based on true social equality, mutual respect, and a shared commitment to the public good.

REFERENCES

Abrams, S. (2016). *Education and the commercial mindset.* Cambridge, MA: Harvard University Press.

Achinstein, B., & Ogawa, R. (2006). (In)fidelity: What the resistance of new teachers reveals about professional principles and prescriptive educational policies. *Harvard Educational Review, 76*(1), 30–63.

Adamson, F., Astrad, B. Darling-Hammond, L. (Eds.) (2016). *Global educational reform: How privatization and public investment influence education outcomes.* New York: Routledge.

Anderson, G. L. (2009). *Advocacy leadership: Toward a post-reform agenda in education.* New York, NY: Routledge.

Anderson, G. L. (2017). Participatory Action Research as Democratic Disruption: New Public Management and Educational research in Schools and Universities. *International Journal of Qualitative Studies in Education.*

Anderson, G. & Cohen, M. (2018). *The new democratic professional: Confronting Markets, Metrics, and Managerialism.* New York: Teachers College Press.

Anderson, G.L., De La Cruz, P., Lopez, A. (2017). New Governance and New Knowledge Brokers: Think Tanks and Universities as boundary organizations. *Peabody Journal of Education, 92,* 4–15.

Anderson, G. L., & Montoro Donchik, L. (2016) The Privatization of education and policymaking: The American Legislative Exchange Council (ALEC) and network governance in the United States. *Educational Policy, 30*(2), 322–364.

Anyon, J. (2014). *Radical possibilities: Public policy, urban education, and a new social movement.* New York, NY: Routledge.

Astrand, B. (2016). From citizens into consumers: The transformation of democratic ideals into school markets in Sweden. In F. Adamson, B. Astrand, & L. Darling-Hammond (Eds.), *Global education reform: How privatization and public investment influence education outcomes* (pp. 73–109) New York, NY: Routledge.

Bell, D. (1992). *Faces at the bottom of the well: The permanence of racism.* New York: Basic Books.

Burch, P. & Good, A. (2014). *Equal scrutiny: Privatization and accountability in digital education.* Cambridge, MA: Harvard Education Press.

Callahan, R. (1962). *Education and the cult of efficiency.* Chicago, IL: The University of Chicago Press.

Carnoy, M. (2016). Four keys to Cuba's provision of high quality public education. In F. Adamson, B. Astrand, & L. Darling-Hammond (Eds.), *Global education reform: How privatization and public investment influence education outcomes* (pp. 50–72). New York, NY: Routledge.

Collins, P. H., & Bilge, S. (2016). *Intersectionality.* Oxford, UK: Policy Press.

Cremin, L. (1964). *The transformation of the school: Progressivism in American education, 1876–1957.* New York, NY: Vintage.

Cuban, L. (2004). *The blackboard and the bottom line: Why schools can't be businesses.* Cambridge, MA: Harvard University Press.

Cuban, L. (2007). Hugging the middle: Teaching in an era of testing and accountability. *Education Policy Analysis Archives, 15*(1). Retrieved May 26, 2008 from http://epaa.asu.edu/epaa/v15n1/

Dumas, M. J., & Anderson, G. (2014). Qualitative research as policy knowledge: Framing policy problems and transforming education from the ground up. *Education Policy Analysis Archives, 22*(11). Retrieved from http://epaa.asu.edu/ojs/article/view/1483

Freire, P. (1970). *The pedagogy of the oppressed.* New York, NY: Continuum.

Fullan, M., & Rincon-Gallardo, S. (2016). Developing high-quality public education in Canada: The case of Ontario. In F. Adamson, B. Astrand, & L. Darling-Hammond (Eds.), *Global education reform: How privatization and public investment influence education outcomes* (pp. 169–193). New York, NY: Routledge.

Gay, G. (2010). *Culturally responsive teaching: Theory, research, and practice* (2nd ed.). New York: Teachers College Press.

Gelberg, D. (1997). *The "business" of reforming American schools.* New York: SUNY Press.

Ginsberg, M. & Gorostiaga, J. (2001). Relationships between theorists/researchers and policy makers/practitioners: Rethinking the two cultures thesis and the possibility of dialogue. *Comparative Education Review, 45*(2), 173–189.

Ginwright, S. (2015). *Hope and healing in urban education: How urban activists and teachers are reclaiming matters of the heart.* New York, NY: Routledge.

Goldstein, J. (2010). *Peer review and teacher leadership: Linking professionalism and accountability.* New York, NY: Teachers College Press.

Hernandez, J. (2013, August 13). Mayoral candidates see Cincinnati as a model for New York schools. *The New York Times.* Retrieved from http://www.nytimes.com/2013/08/12/nyregion/candidates-see-cincinnati-as-model-for-new-york-schools.html?pagewanted=all&_r=0

Ishimaru, A. M. (2014). When new relationships meet old narratives: The journey towards improving parent-school relations in a district-community organizing collaboration. *Teachers College Record, 116*(2), 23–40.

Johnson, L. (2017). Culturally responsive leadership for community empowerment. In Y. Cha, Gundara, J., S. Ham, and & M. Lee (Eds.). *Multicultural education in global perspectives: Policy and institutionalization.* Singapore: Springer.

Keith, N. (1999). Whose community schools? New discourses, old patterns. *Theory into Practice., 38*(4). 225–234.

Kerr, K., Dyson, A., & Gallannuagh F. (2016). Conceptualizing school-community relations in disadvantaged neighbourhoods: Mapping the literature. *Educational Research., 58*(3), 265–282.

Labaree, D. (2012). *Someone has to fail: The zero-sum game of public schooling.* Cambridge, MA: Harvard University Press.

Klein, N. (2018). *The battle for paradise: Puerto Rico takes on the disaster capitalists.* Chicago, Haymarket Books.

Ladson-Billings, G. (1995). Toward a theory of culturally relevant pedagogy. *American Educational Research Journal, 32*(3), 465–481.

Lewallen, T., Hunt, H., Potts-Datema, W., Zaza, S., & Giles, W. (2015). The whole school, whole community, whole child model: A new approach for improving educational attainment and healthy development for students. *Journal of School Health, 85*(11), 729–739.

Lock, R., & Spender, J. -C. (2011). *Confronting managerialism: How the business elite and their schools threw our lives out of balance.* New York, NY: Zed Books.

Lopez, I. H. (2015). *Dog whistle politics: How coded racial appeals have reinvented racism and wrecked the middle class.* Oxford, UK: Oxford University Press.

Lustick, H. (2017). Making discipline relevant: Toward a theory of culturally responsive schoolwide discipline. *Race, Ethnicity, and Education, 20*, 681–695.

Maier, A., Daniel, J., Oakes, J., & Lam, L. (2017). *Community schools as an effective school improvement strategy: A review of the evidence.* Palo Alto, CA: Learning Policy Institute.

Mayer, J. (2016). *Dark money: The hidden history of the billionaires behind the rise of the radical right.* New York, NY: Anchor Books.

Mazzucato, M. (2015). *The entrepreneurial state: Debunking public vs. private sector myths.* New York: Perseus Books.

Mazzacuto, M. (2018). *The value of everything: Making and taking in the global economy.* London: Allen Lane.

McGhee, C. & Anderson, G.L. (in press). Market Regimes, Gentrification and the Entrepreneurial Principal: Enacting Integration or Displacement? *Journal of Policy and Leadership.*

Mackey, H. J. (2017). The ESSA in Indian Country: Problematizing self-determination through the relationships between federal, state, and tribal governments. *Educational Administration Quarterly, 53*(5), 782–808.

McLaughlin, M. (1976). Implementation as mutual adaptation: Change in classroom organization. *Teachers College Record, 77*(3), 339–351.

McLean, N. (2017). *Democracy in chains: The deep history of the radical right's stealth plan for America.* New York, NY: Viking.

McNamee, S., & Miller, R. (2009). *The meritocracy myth.* Lanham, MD: Rowman & Littlefield.

Meier, D. (1995). *The power of their ideas: Lessons from a small school in Harlem.* Boston: Beacon Press.

Milner, IV, R. (2015). *Rac(e)ing to class: Confronting poverty and race in schools and classrooms* Cambridge, MA: Harvard Education Press

Minow, M. (2002). *Partners, not rivals: Privatization and the public good.* Boston, MA: Beacon Press.

Miron, G. & Gulosino, C. (April 2016). *Virtual schools report 2016.* Boulder, CO: National Education Policy Center.

Nieto, S. (Ed.) (2014). *Why do we teach now?* New York: Teachers College Press.

Nunez, I., Michie, G. & Konkol, P. (2015). *Worth striking for: Why education policy is every teacher's concern.* New York: Teachers College Press.

Pavlakis, A. E., Goff, P., Miller, P. M. (2017). Contextualizing the impacts of homelessness on academic growth. *Teachers College Record, 119*(10),

Payne, C. M. (2008). *So much reform, so little change: The persistence of failure in urban schools.* Cambridge, MA: Harvard Education Press.

Phillips-Fein, K. (2009). *Invisible hands: The making of the conservative movement from the New Deal to Reagan.* New York, NY: W.W. Norton.

Reeves, R. V. (2017). *Dream hoarders: How the American upper middle class is leaving everyone else in the dust, why that is a problem, and what do about it.* Washington, DC: Brookings Institute Press.

Robinson, G. (2015). NYC schools that skip standardized tests have higher graduation rates. The Hechinger Report. Retrieved from hechingerreport.org/nyc-schools-that-skip-standardized-tests-have-higher-graduation-rate.

Rook, N. (2017). *Cutting school: Privatization, Segregation, & the End of Public Education.* New York: The New Press.

Rothstein, R. (2017). *The color of law: A forgotten history of how our government segregated America.* New York, NY: Liveright Pub.

Taubman, P. (2009). *Teaching by numbers: Deconstructing the discourse of standards and accountability in education.* New York, NY: Routledge.

Weiner, L. (2018). Walkouts teach U.S. labor a new grammar for struggle. *New Politics, 17*(1), 1–18.

Zeichner, K. & Pena-Sandoval, C. (2015). Venture philanthropy and teacher education policy in the U.S.: The role of the New Schools Venture Fund. *Teachers College Record, 117*(6), 67–85.

Index